REVITALIZING A NATION

REVITALIZING A NATION

Competition and Innovation in the US Transportation System

BY CLIFFORD WINSTON, JIA YAN,
AND ASSOCIATES

BROOKINGS INSTITUTION PRESS
Washington, D.C.

Copyright © 2024 by The Brookings Institution

PUBLISHED BY BROOKINGS INSTITUTION PRESS
1775 Massachusetts Avenue, NW
Washington, DC, 20036
www.brookings.edu/bipress

CO-PUBLISHED BY ROWMAN & LITTLEFIELD
An imprint of The Rowman & Littlefield Publishing Group, Inc.
4501 Forbes Boulevard, Suite 200, Lanham, Maryland 20706
www.rowman.com

86-90 Paul Street, London EC2A 4NE

British Library Cataloguing in Publication Information Available

Library of Congress Cataloging-in-Publication Data Available

ISBN 978-0-8157-4040-7 (cloth : alk. paper)
ISBN 978-0-8157-4041-4 (pbk. : alk. paper)
ISBN 978-0-8157-4042-1 (ebook)

♾™ The paper used in this publication meets the minimum requirements of American
National Standard for Information Sciences—Permanence of Paper for Printed Library
Materials, ANSI/NISO Z39.48-1992.

Contents

1

Introduction

CLIFFORD WINSTON AND JIA YAN

An efficient transportation system supports the functioning of a modern economy in several ways. First, firms can sell their products to consumers in many markets and doing so enables them to produce at greater scale, which reduces their costs. Second, multiple firms can compete in a market, which prevents monopoly pricing and poor service. Third, consumers can choose among a variety of products produced locally, in other cities, and abroad. Fourth, employers are better able to match their job requirements with specific workers' skills. Fifth, firms and people are better able to locate near one another in cities and industrial clusters and by doing so become more productive through agglomeration economies. At the same time, more frequent and widespread interactions among individuals and firms increase the likelihood of innovations and technological advances that widely benefit the public and spur macroeconomic growth. Finally, transportation systems can expand households' leisure time options with affordable domestic and international travel opportunities.

Because transportation provides significant and extensive benefits to a nation, and because a transportation system is constantly evolving, policymakers can substantially increase a nation's welfare by implementing policies that improve the system's performance. In this book, we argue that greater *competition* and *innovation* are the primary sources of transportation improvements and that policymakers can promote competition and innovation more effectively by reforming many of their transportation policies.

Transportation improvements can directly increase the welfare of users of the transportation system, such as travelers and shippers, and indirectly increase the welfare of participants in other sectors affected by transportation, such as labor, industry, and trade. Through those direct and indirect welfare gains, transportation can improve the performance of an entire economy.

Postwar Evolution of the US Transportation System

The evolution of the transportation system as the United States emerged from World War II is a useful starting point for understanding how greater competition and innovation improved the system's performance. The US federal government funded major investments in transportation infrastructure that enabled the major modes to operate more efficiently. Construction of the Interstate Highway System, which began in 1956, and the construction of new airports to accommodate the longer takeoff distances of jets, which began in 1962 with the opening of Washington Dulles International Airport, significantly contributed to the nation's welfare (Allen and Arkolakis 2014; Morrison and Winston 1985). Investments in large metropolitan areas to build new suburban rail transit systems, funded by all levels of government, followed the huge federal investments in highway and airport infrastructure. The introduction of commercial jet service in 1958 was a major innovation in transportation technology and service that occurred during the initial postwar period.

At first blush, it appeared that the United States was on its way to building the best transportation system money could buy. However, inefficiencies created by pervasive public sector involvement in transportation, which Adam Smith (1776) had remarkably predicted long ago, had steadily worked their way into the system, including but not limited to:

— *excess capacity* as the road and rail networks were not designed in accordance with what commerce could pay but were overbuilt to serve low-density areas of the country with little freight or passenger traffic;

— *growing deficits* as spending on public infrastructure and services could not be financed solely by users and required growing support from general tax revenues; and

— *misallocation of transportation revenues* as repairs were often conducted in a poor manner (and sometimes not at all), leading to premature deterioration of infrastructure. This situation was not easy to remedy because of the difficulty of raising new revenues, and revenues that were raised were not always used for their intended purpose, instead often being used to subsidize less efficient transportation facilities and services.

The classic books by Meyer et al. (1959) and Meyer, Kain, and Wohl (1965) identified in detail and quantified to some extent the costs of the most inefficient parts of the 1950s and 1960s US transportation system. Generally, the authors took issue with what microeconomists call the engineering approach to improving a transportation system, which can involve increased government spending and investment without considering efficient policies to optimize the system's performance that could reduce public spending and investment.[1]

Improvements in the US Transportation System

Consequently, poor policy became the primary source of the system's inefficiencies. For example, the large investments in the highway system attracted more traffic and led to congestion, increased accidents, and more fatalities, and contributed to premature deterioration of the capital stock. Those significant social costs of highway travel could not be reduced very much by increasing government spending on transportation.

At the same time, increasing government spending could not improve the efficiency of regulated intercity modes that were characterized by inflated costs, due in part to regulatory-induced excess capacity, and by inflated prices for travelers and shippers. Finally, the growth of automobile ownership and suburbanization significantly reduced public transit's market share and required greater government subsidies to cover transit's growing deficits while doing little to reverse transit's loss of market share.

Adam Smith is recognized for stressing the importance of competition to improve an economy, but he did not envision that increasing competition would be necessary to improve a transportation system that had been severely compromised by poor government policy. Yet, beginning in the mid-1970s, deregulation led to significant efficiency improvements in the intercity transportation system by increasing competition between and within the surface freight modes (railroads and trucking) and water carriers, as well as within and between airlines and other passenger modes (cars, buses, and trains). Deregulation also spurred technological and operating innovations that reduced the modes' costs and prices and improved service quality (Morrison and Winston 1999).[2]

Greater competition and innovation fostered by deregulation clearly emerged as the sources of significant improvements in intercity transportation. However, those sources of improvement were prevented from affecting the efficiency of the

1. Winston (1991, 2021b) points out that beginning in the late 1980s, macroeconomists also focused on increasing government spending on transportation infrastructure to spur productivity growth but did not focus on efficient infrastructure pricing and investment.
2. Administrative transportation deregulation began with the 1976 Railroad Revitalization and Regulatory Reform Act, which established the basic outlines of regulatory reform in the railroad industry, and with the Civil Aeronautics Board's liberalization of fares by allowing, for example, "supersaver" fares on some routes before fares were fully deregulated by the 1978 Airline Deregulation Act.

international and urban transportation systems, because those systems remained highly regulated by various levels of government, or in many cases owned and operated by government agencies.

In the past few decades, new sources of competition and innovation have begun to improve the international and urban transportation systems to some extent. For example, beginning in 1992 with the Netherlands, the United States has negotiated open skies agreements with some countries, which have stimulated competition by deregulating airline prices and entry on US international routes, resulting in lower fares and greater service frequency (Winston and Yan 2015). Beginning in 2010 when Uber launched its first on-demand car service in San Francisco, ridesharing companies have used advances in information technology to provide a new form of transportation service in metropolitan areas that has become a popular alternative to the private automobile, taxis, and public transit.

Remaining Transportation Problems

Unfortunately, the improvements in the US transportation system are often overshadowed by the system's formidable problems. The most important ones are that the system:

— does a poor job of enhancing mobility for less affluent, disabled, and elderly people;

— continues to be plagued by externalities, including the nation's largest share of greenhouse gas emissions; highway, airport, and port congestion; and some forty thousand annual fatalities and millions of annual injuries from highway accidents;

— does not maintain or expand the infrastructure capital stock efficiently in response to growing use of the transportation system by travelers and shippers;

— attracts only a small share of travelers on public transit and Amtrak intercity passenger rail service in most markets, which run increasingly large deficits that are financed by taxpayers;

— has failed to integrate efficiently its domestic and international subsystems, which increases prices, lengthens travel and shipping times, and reduces reliability; and

— is characterized by inflexible operations and outdated technology that contribute to supply chain disruptions on domestic and international routes, which cause shortages of products and raise consumer prices.

New sources of competition and innovation can significantly help to address those transportation problems and others that may arise in the future. However, government policymakers must unleash those sources in two ways. First, they must enact constructive policy reforms that give private transportation entities greater freedom to compete and innovate and that also facilitate public adoption of autonomous vehicle technology and transportation services. Second, they must increase the benefits that travelers and shippers obtain from using the transportation system by using cost–benefit analysis to reform current infrastructure policies to improve the system's pricing and physical condition, optimize traffic flows, and enhance safety.

Unfortunately, as noted, policymakers have not prioritized those reforms because they persistently rely on an engineering approach that focuses on spending increasingly large sums of taxpayers' money in unsuccessful efforts to solve transportation problems, but which consistently fall short of producing significant improvements in the system. Passage of the $1.2 trillion Infrastructure Investment and Jobs Act in 2021 takes the same approach and is likely to produce the same disappointing outcome, because it does not seek to ameliorate the system's pervasive inefficiencies.

Transportation inefficiencies persist because policymakers, stakeholders, and the public often fear the prospect of competition and new technologies and generally prefer that government own and operate transportation services and facilities, regulate their behavior, or even prohibit their operation. For example, although automated elevators were introduced in the 1850s as a new transportation technology, they had a human operator for another century until passenger-operated emergency equipment, such as a stop button, alert bell, and telephone, helped to convince the public that they could use the technology safely (Lokshin and Newsom 2020). As another example, gasoline-powered vehicles became a successful alternative to the horse only after steam-powered vehicles were effectively legislated out of business.

Government may have had plausible reasons for owning and operating transportation facilities and for regulating private firms' prices and operations. However, government policy is very slow to react to the dynamic changes in competition and transportation technology that motivate innovation and reform. Indeed, the government should have implemented airline, railroad, and trucking deregulation, which significantly benefited the public, decades earlier than it actually did.

Government also should be much further along with exploring how efficient infrastructure pricing and investment work together to enable transportation users to make the best use of the nation's limited infrastructure capacity and to keep the infrastructure in good repair. Unfortunately, the various government authorities that own much of the US transportation infrastructure generally have paid little attention to the inefficiencies their pricing and investment policies create. It may turn out that new autonomous modes provide the incentive for government to reform its infrastructure policies because the failure to do so will significantly compromise the performance of those new modes. Privatizing more of the US transportation infrastructure may be necessary to realize the substantial benefits from new modes because private owners are more likely than the government to implement efficient pricing and investment policies.

Comprehensive Approach to Analyzing the US Transportation System

A modern transportation system is composed of subsystems that provide urban and intercity passenger and freight service. The subsystems operate on surface, water, and aviation infrastructure. By reducing the out-of-pocket, time-related, and safety-related costs of distance, an efficient transportation system can provide the foundation for the development and growth of the entire economy.

Previous research in transportation has tended to be conducted in silos, where only a subsystem or a single mode of transportation is analyzed without considering the implications of the analysis for other parts of the transportation system. To the best of our knowledge, this book is the first to provide an empirical microeconomic analysis of the major problems facing the entire transportation system and to make comprehensive recommendations drawing on all the subsystems to improve the efficiency of the entire system.

Recent research, mainly conducted in other fields of economics, has taken the efficiency of the transportation system as given and estimated its effects on labor markets (e.g., Monte, Redding, and Rossi-Hansberg 2018), urban and regional economies (e.g., Duranton and Puga 2019), international trade (e.g., Brancaccio, Kalouptsidi, and Papageorgiou 2020), and productivity growth (e.g., Shatz et al. 2011). However, because this research does not consider the inefficiencies of the modes and infrastructure that it studies, it does not provide evidenced-based policy recommendations for improving the system.

Generally, the benefits from improving the transportation system by increasing competition and innovation reflect the direct benefits to transportation users from lower costs, lower prices, and better service. However, the value of those improvements also may reflect transportation's beneficial effects on other economic sectors. For example, commuters' value of improvements in travel time reflects the benefits of greater labor productivity, shippers' value of more reliable freight delivery times reflects the benefits of reductions in logistics costs from lower inventories, business travelers' value of seamless international air travel reflects the benefits from sharing ideas, and so on.

The benefits from increased competition and innovation also include indirect or general equilibrium benefits that affect other economic sectors. Such benefits can result from transportation improvements that, for example, enable households to improve their welfare by changing their residences and employers and that enable firms to improve their productivity and profitability by changing their locations, production technology, and product quality and variety.

We discuss some of the indirect benefits to other sectors from transportation innovations in our chapters on autonomous cars and trucks. However, we leave it to future research to further quantify the system's indirect benefits, to determine the transportation system's total benefits to the US economy, and to identify how policymakers can increase those benefits.

Plan of This Book

We develop our comprehensive analysis of the transportation system by organizing this book around four parts. The first three parts identify the major current economic and social problems and challenges facing the urban, intercity passenger, and freight transportation subsystems that comprise the US transportation system. We analyze various ways that new sources of competition and innovation could positively affect the modes and infrastructure that comprise those subsystems. We then synthesize our findings and conclusions for each subsystem in the final part of the book and we explain how public policy can enable competition and innovation to realize their full potential to enhance today's as well as the future US transportation system.

Some chapters contain new empirical work that provides evidence on the actual and potential welfare improvements from promoting greater competition and facilitating new innovations in each part of the US transportation system. Other chapters identify and discuss future sources of increased competition and innovation and their potential social benefits.

To achieve these benefits, we argue that US policymakers should take several measures to generate more competition in the entire transportation system, which include:

—negotiating open skies airline service and pricing agreements with all countries;

—granting foreign airlines cabotage rights to spur global deregulation that would facilitate seamless global operations;

—privatizing airports and air traffic control so both airports and airlines can operate more effectively and compete more intensely;

—privatizing ports so they can operate more efficiently and compete more intensely;

—conducting highway privatization experiments to explore the potential benefits and feasibility of private highway competition in the United States;

—withdrawing any obstacles that prevent ridesharing companies and private van and minibus services from competing in urban areas; and

—fully deregulating freight railroads and ocean shipping, including repeal of the Jones Act and Foreign Dredge Act and elimination of rate conferences.

We also argue that government should facilitate and expedite the future adoption of transportation innovations that will use private and public infrastructure, including autonomous electric cars, trucks, railroads, ships, air taxis, and airborne drones. Those innovations, which currently are being developed but are still decades away from being fully adopted, will further stimulate intra- and intermodal competition and will provide enormous benefits to travelers, shippers, and the overall economy.

To be sure, the significant improvements in the US transportation system discussed here are not without potential risks and limitations. For example, technological failure could prevent autonomous modes, especially cars, from generating large benefits. However, we think it is extremely unlikely that the global effort to produce autonomous vehicles will lose its entire $100 billion–plus investment because no firm in the world can build a safe autonomous vehicle that is a significant advance over a nonautonomous vehicle. Indeed, an important feature of the autonomous vehicle industry is the extensive collaboration between producers and between producers and potential users. The former is important for improving the technology and for recognizing and overcoming technological challenges. The latter is important for encouraging society to realize the potential benefits of autonomous vehicles and to have a vested interest in their success.

New sources of competition and innovation will undoubtedly disrupt the transportation labor force by reducing earnings in certain jobs and by changing the types of jobs for which employers will seek workers. However, losses in employment for certain jobs are likely to be offset by the growth of workers in new classifications of employment and by increased productivity and expanded output throughout the economy. That said, firms and policymakers may have to seek constructive ways to ease the potentially difficult adjustment that labor must make during the transition to a more competitive and innovative transportation system.

Finally, no group of travelers or shippers will lose transportation services or pay higher prices because the changes in competition and innovation discussed here have limited their travel options and choice of carriers. Instead, those changes are likely to reduce the cost of transportation and expand access to transportation services, especially for those individuals who are least able to travel and least able to afford transportation expenses.

Because transportation plays such a vital role in the development, application, and success of any innovation, policymakers can promote a stronger culture of competition and innovation throughout the US economy by creating a stronger culture of competition and innovation in the US transportation system. By overcoming the system's current weaknesses, policymakers can enable future transportation systems to be efficient, equitable, and innovative and to revitalize the nation.

PART I

Urban Transportation

The US urban transportation system is plagued by large externalities caused by motor vehicle travel, including congestion, fatal and serious accidents, and vehicle emissions. Policymakers' efforts to simultaneously tax and subsidize automobile travel, and to heavily subsidize public transit to reduce automobile travel, have not ameliorated those externalities. Efficient externality taxes on vehicle miles traveled (VMT) for automobiles are being considered in some parts of the country (Langer, Maheshri, and Winston 2017) and successful demonstrations of their use exist, but VMT taxes have yet to be implemented anywhere in the United States.

In this part of the book, we provide new evidence on the difficulty facing policymakers to simultaneously reduce highway congestion and fatalities, and on the inefficiencies of bus and rail transit operations that policymakers have created by not encouraging bus and rail to be effective competitors. We then examine how new sources of competition and innovation could reduce the cost of urban travel, improve service, and reduce automobile externalities by estimating the benefits of ridesharing and by providing an overview of the potential benefits of electric and autonomous vehicles and the appropriate role of the private sector and government.

2

The Effect of Reductions in Vehicle Miles Traveled on Highway Fatalities and Congestion with Heterogeneous Motorists

VIKRAM MAHESHRI AND CLIFFORD WINSTON[1]

1. Introduction

The nation's highway system is the lifeblood of urban and suburban travel. At the same time, the annual costs of highway congestion, injuries, and fatalities to people involved in highway accidents, and vehicle damage from those accidents, run in the trillions of dollars (Winston and Karpilow 2020). In chapter 5, we discuss pollution from vehicle emissions, another important social cost of highway travel, in the context of electric vehicles.

Because congestion and accidents appear to be positively related to vehicle miles traveled (VMT), policies that decrease VMT could simultaneously reduce both.[2] Such policies include congestion pricing, which is generally advocated for by economists to induce modal and intertemporal shifts by motorists to reduce congestion; and significant investments to build new public transit systems or improve existing systems, which is advocated for by urban planners and policy-makers to attract motorists to public transit. However, policies that have the potential to improve both safety and the speed of travel by reducing VMT could be undermined if they lead to adverse changes in driver behavior that offset those potential improvements.

1. We are grateful to Maryam Khan for research assistance.
2. Congestion and accidents interact with each other because accidents create delay and congestion, while congestion reduces motorists' speeds, which reduces the frequency and severity of accidents. Our primary interest in this chapter is to identify policies that by reducing VMT can reduce congestion and accidents, even accounting for their interaction.

We are not aware of previous research that provides empirical evidence of a specific policy in the United States that has simultaneously improved both safety and congestion.[3] But the Great Recession did have that effect. In Maheshri and Winston (2016), we found that the significant decline in VMT during the 2007–09 Great Recession and its aftermath caused both a reduction in congestion and a decline in motorists' fatalities per VMT. We argued that those twin declines could be explained by the change in drivers' behavior as reflected in the mix of drivers who remained on the road, with a greater share of travel conducted by plausibly safer drivers (and hence a smaller share by plausibly riskier drivers).

The COVID-19 global pandemic provides a new opportunity to explore the effects of a significant decline in VMT on vehicle congestion and safety because it led to a sharp increase in the number of people who worked from home to reduce the spread of COVID-19, rising from 6 percent of workers in 2019 to a peak of 35 percent of workers in May 2020, according to the American Community Survey. Congestion also decreased because the initial decline in peak-period travel was not offset by latent travel demand—that is, travelers did not take advantage of reduced congestion during peak periods by driving more, as the pandemic chilled all forms of travel-generating activity, including recreation.

Like our findings from during the Great Recession, we would expect that the decline in VMT during the COVID-19 pandemic would reduce fatalities because motorists were less exposed to other motorists, thereby reducing the opportunities for multivehicle accidents to occur. However, the effect on safety of the concomitant reduction in congestion also depends on how drivers react to the change in highway travel conditions. For example, by enabling motorists to drive faster, the reduction in congestion could increase the likelihood and severity of accidents, other things equal.

Because the decline in driving during the Great Recession was disproportionately shouldered by riskier drivers, the reduction in congestion did not offset the benefits of less exposure to other motorists by allowing motorists to take greater risks while driving, such as drinking, using drugs, or speeding. But descriptive evidence shown in figure 2.1 suggests that in contrast to their behavior during the Great Recession, when the fatality rate declined considerably, the remaining motorists on the road may have engaged in risky driving behavior during the pandemic, as the fatality rate began to spike in 2020 while the pandemic was

---

3. Tang and van Ommeren (2022) find that the London congestion charge zone reduced congestion and accidents but that it led to an increase in serious injuries and fatalities. In March 2020, Transport for London introduced a 20 miles per hour speed limit on all its roads within the central London congestion charge zone as part of its commitment to eliminate death and serious injury on London's roads. In the United States, the J-Tech Lane Blade is marketed as reducing congestion and improving safety by safely removing debris from travel lanes while enabling workers to safely operate from the cab of the service vehicle. See https://jtechusa.com/laneblade.

Figure 2.1. *Deaths per Billion Vehicle Miles Traveled, 2006–21*

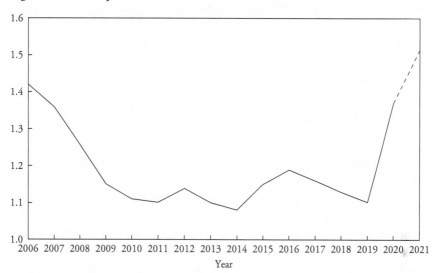

Source: Fatality Analysis Reporting System.
Notes: Data for 2021 are projected using the National Highway Traffic Safety Administration's preliminary estimate of a 10.5 percent increase in deaths per billion VMT from 2020Q1 to 2021Q1.

underway. The problem persisted, as the first quarter of 2022 recorded the highest fatalities on US roads in more than two decades.

In this chapter, we report empirical evidence that suggests the decline in VMT that occurred during the pandemic did not simultaneously improve congestion and automobile safety because it led to a change in the mix of drivers that appears to include a greater share of risky drivers who, among other things, appear to drive at excessive speeds. Although total driving did not change considerably in the aggregate population of drivers, the proliferation of telecommuting and remote schooling shifted highway travel away from conventional peak periods. The intertemporal shift facilitated sharp reductions in congestion, but it also increased the risk to motorists' safety because some took advantage of reductions in congestion to drive at higher speeds that reduced their reaction time to avoid an accident and increased the bodily impact of a collision.[4]

---

4. Gao and Levinson (2021) find that morning traffic flows in Minneapolis–St. Paul developed a pronounced double peak after COVID-19 arrived, which they attribute to a change in the composition of the commuting workforce, with larger reductions in sectors that tend to commute during the middle of the peak. Workers in construction, natural resources, and mining tend to commute early, and cannot switch to telecommuting. Many office workers can telecommute, and they may be safer drivers than workers in construction, natural resources, and mining, who are predominantly male and might, for example, drive pickup trucks to their workplaces in the dark.

We explain why congestion pricing and investments in public transit could reduce VMT but also could lead to more drivers engaging in risky behavior on certain roads at certain times of day. We conclude by pointing out that autonomous vehicles circumvent the travel speed–safety tradeoff, making their eventual widespread adoption an effective way to simultaneously reduce congestion and automobile accidents.

2. Empirical Approach

Our goal is to estimate the effect of congestion on automobile fatalities. Although there is considerable research on the determinants of automobile fatalities in the economics and transportation engineering literature,[5] estimating the effect of congestion on automobile fatalities is challenging because many of the features of the driving environment that affect congestion, including the geography and topography of roads, weather, local economic conditions, and socioeconomic characteristics of drivers, also are potential contributors to auto fatalities. We disentangle the confounding influences on congestion and fatalities by exploiting the unexpected shock to driving that accompanied the COVID-19 pandemic in the United States.

Congestion is a nonlinear phenomenon that increases sharply for a given road capacity after vehicle traffic reaches a certain threshold.[6] Below this threshold, marginal changes in traffic contribute little to nothing to congestion. However, after the threshold is exceeded, small increases (or reductions) in highway traffic may result in dramatic changes in congestion and travel delays. We leverage this feature of congestion in our analysis.

As driving plummeted during the early months of the pandemic, highways that previously were highly congested in large cities, such as Chicago, New York, and Boston, became uncongested overnight. At the same time, highways in other cities that previously were not congested also experienced significant declines in traffic, but they did not become dramatically less congested as a result. We can therefore use a difference-in-differences approach to compare the effect of pandemic-related driving shutdowns on auto fatalities in cities with highways that previously were highly congested with that effect in other cities that previously were not congested to estimate the overall effect of congestion on auto fatalities.

To conduct our analysis, we collect data from four distinct sources. First, we obtain county-level measures of monthly VMT from StreetLight Data, a private company that combines cell phone data, telematic data from vehicles,

---

5. See, for example, Small and Verhoef (2007) and Retallack and Ostendorf (2019).
6. See Lindsey (2012) for a discussion of the technology of highway congestion.

and readings from roadway sensors to estimate VMT at a spatially and temporally fine level. Second, we obtain baseline measures of auto fatalities from the Fatality Analysis Reporting System (FARS) database maintained by the National Highway Traffic Safety Administration (NHTSA). Because those data were available only through the end of 2019, before the pandemic took hold in the United States, we contacted each of the fifty most heavily traveled counties (as measured by 2019 VMT) to obtain monthly measures of auto fatalities from January 2020 through March 2021. Third, we obtained baseline measures of congestion at the metropolitan statistical area (MSA) level from INRIX, a private company that specializes in estimating congestion in cities around the world. Finally, we obtain monthly data on the number of cases and deaths due to COVID-19 in the fifty counties in our sample from reports in the *New York Times*.

We use the monthly data for the fifty most traveled counties in 2019, as measured by VMT, from January 2020 to March 2021 to obtain 750 observations. We also include another 600 observations from monthly data during 2019. Thus, we have a period before the pandemic when there was not any notable change in VMT other than seasonality, a period during the pandemic when VMT declined substantially, and a period toward the end of the sample when VMT had returned to (or even exceeded) its prepandemic level in most counties. Finally, we exclude the fifty observations from January 2019 because we specify month-of-year fixed effects in the model, so January 2019 becomes the reference group.

We use our final sample of 1,300 observations to estimate the effect of congestion on automobile fatality risk as specified in the following two-way fixed effects equation:

$$
\begin{aligned}
\log F_{it} = {} & \beta_1 \times \log VMT_{it} + \beta_2 \times post_t \times congest_i \\
& + \beta_3 \times post_t \times \log VMT_{it} + \lambda_i + \lambda_t + \delta \times \textbf{controls}_{it} + \varepsilon_{it}
\end{aligned}
\tag{1}
$$

where $\log F_{it}$ is the natural log of the number of auto fatalities reported in county i in month t, $\log VMT_{it}$ is the natural log of vehicle miles traveled in county i in month t, $post_t$ is a post-COVID-19 dummy variable that is equal to 1 if the month is after March 2020 and equal to 0 otherwise,[7] and $congest_i$ is a dummy variable equal to 1 if county i experienced very high levels of congestion in 2019

---

7. Because the dramatic reductions in driving due to COVID-19 commenced in the middle of March 2020, March 11 can be considered as the unofficial start of the COVID-19 panic in the United States given it coincided with the date that the National Basketball Association suspended its entire 2020 season and when Tom Hanks revealed his positive test for COVID-19. We also used an alternative definition of *post_t* equal to 1 beginning in April 2020 and equal to 0 otherwise, and we also replicated our analysis omitting data from March 2020 entirely. Those changes did not have any effects on our findings.

Table 2.1. *Summary Statistics: Means and Standard Deviations*

Variable	Prepandemic	Postpandemic
Monthly fatalities	12.94	13.77
	(10.76)	(11.38)
Monthly vehicle miles traveled (billions)	1.76	1.61
	(1.19)	(1.31)
Cumulative COVID-19 cases (millions)		0.36
		(0.30)
Cumulative COVID-19 deaths (thousands)		12.0
		(14.4)
Number of observations	730	620

Notes: Prepandemic includes data from January 2019 until the middle of March 2020, and postpandemic includes data from the middle of March 2020 through March 2021. Sources: StreetLight Data; Fatality Analysis Reporting System; INRIX; *New York Times*.

and equal to 0 otherwise.[8] The λ_i are county fixed effects, which, for example, capture characteristics of the road network; λ_t are month-of-year fixed effects that account for time-varying unobserved determinants of fatalities, including seasonality in driving and weather patterns; and ε_{it} is the error term. Finally, **controls**$_{it}$ is a vector of county- and time-varying controls that includes cumulative reported COVID-19 cases and cumulative reported COVID-19 deaths, and δ is a vector of parameters.

Following the literature on modeling fatality risk, we specify all continuous variables in logarithms. Thus, those factors enter multiplicatively for purposes of interpretation. For instance, VMT enters multiplicatively when describing fatality risk, as in "fatalities per billion VMT"; hence, we can interpret the coefficient β_2 as the differential change in fatality risk in congested counties versus uncongested counties following the introduction of COVID-19 shutdowns.

Table 2.1 reports the means and standard deviations of the variables for the entire sample, divided into pre- and postpandemic. Absolute monthly fatalities have increased, although total VMT has decreased 8.8 percent. The decrease

---

8. It could be argued that we should measure *congest$_i$* continuously and that it should vary over time given declines in VMT decrease congestion. However, we are using *congest$_i$* to capture a threshold that characterizes a metropolitan area that experienced very high levels of congestion before the pandemic. We are not interested in marginal declines in congestion because the metropolitan areas experiencing very high levels of congestion became considerably less congested during the pandemic to the point where marginal changes in congestion would have no effect on fatalities because traffic was generally able to move at free-flow speeds. A city is considered to be very highly congested is one of the four cities where drivers lost, on average, more than 120 hours due to traffic conditions in 2019: Boston, Chicago, New York, and Philadelphia. Measures of congestion come from INRIX. We note later that we use higher and lower levels of hours lost to congestion in 2019 for sensitivity purposes.

Table 2.2. *Maximum Likelihood Estimates of the Effects of Congestion on Auto Fatalities as Mediated through Shutdowns*

Variable	(1)	(2)	(3)
Postshutdown × highly congested		1.12***	1.12**
Log (VMT)	1.48***	1.43***	1.35***
Postshutdown × log (VMT)	0.95*	0.95***	0.99
Month fixed effects	Yes	Yes	Yes
County fixed effects	Yes	Yes	Yes
COVID-19 controls	No	No	Yes
Pseudo R^2	0.53	0.53	0.53
Number of observations	1,300	1,300	1,300

Notes: Maximum likelihood estimates are from a Poisson regression where number of fatalities is the dependent variable. We report incidence rate ratios. An incidence rate ratio > 1 implies a positive marginal effect and an incidence rate ratio < 1 implies a negative marginal effect. Statistical significance is indicated at the ***1 percent, **5 percent, and *10 percent levels.

includes a sizable reduction in peak-period VMT that resulted in zero annual hours lost from congestion after the pandemic began in March 2020 compared with sixty-eight annual hours lost from congestion prepandemic. Finally, we report the monthly COVID-19 cases and deaths during the pandemic.

3. Empirical Findings

Following standard procedures for estimating models with dependent variables that are (small) nonnegative integers, such as automobile fatalities, we estimate the parameters in equation (1) by maximum likelihood using a Poisson regression model.[9] By exponentiating the parameters in equation (1), we obtain incidence risk ratios (IRRs), which we present in table 2.2 along with stars to provide easy interpretation of statistical significance. An IRR greater than 1 corresponds with a positive relationship to vehicle fatalities, and an IRR less than 1 corresponds with a negative relationship to vehicle fatalities. For instance, an IRR of 1.10 indicates that a one-unit increase in the variable corresponds to a 10 percent increase in fatalities, and an IRR of 0.9 indicates that a one-unit increase in the variable corresponds to a 10 percent decrease in fatalities.

9. Although many empirical analyses in the transportation literature estimate fatality equations using a negative binomial model, this is inadvisable because, as pointed out by Wooldridge (1999), the negative binomial estimator is a nonrobust estimator of conditional mean parameters, and this weakness is exacerbated when using fixed effects. Negative binomial regressions may be appropriate if the objective is simply to maximize the fit of the model and there is overdispersion in the dependent variable. However, a Poisson regression is preferable in our case because our dependent variable is underdispersed, with a mean of 13.3 and standard deviation of 11.04. Roback and Legler (2021) provide a textbook discussion of Poisson regression models.

Because our measure of congestion is at the MSA level and some MSAs span multiple counties, we first construct the *congest*$_i$ variable by considering all the counties that are included in an MSA and coding them as congested. For example, Kings County and Queens County are both considered congested because the New York MSA is considered congested. The IRRs capturing the different effects of congestion presented in table 2.2 are based on this approach. Because we may be overstating congestion in certain metropolitan areas, we performed a robustness check where we coded only the largest county in a congested MSA as congested; however, our findings were virtually unchanged.

In column (1), we estimate a baseline regression that does not include information on different congestion levels in the MSAs. We find, unsurprisingly, that VMT is a strong positive predictor of fatalities, and this association declined only slightly postshutdown in March 2020. This finding indicates that driving did not get substantially safer on a per-mile basis after the shutdowns, which is suggestive of our conjecture that although congestion increases exposure to other vehicles in the traffic flow, as it did preshutdown, it can reduce fatalities by causing motorists to drive more slowly and cautiously to avoid a collision. By significantly reducing congestion, COVID-19-related shutdowns and reduced economic activity may have increased auto fatalities under certain driving conditions.

In column (2), we test more directly our conjecture by allowing the effects of the shutdowns to vary by cities' congestion using a flexible specification of congestion: highly congested cities compared with other cities (the omitted category).[10] In column (3), we include the additional control variables noted previously, such as cumulative reported COVID-19 cases and cumulative reported COVID-19 deaths, which are related to the contemporaneous COVID-19 situation. In all specifications, we find that more driving results in more fatalities, all else constant. Quantitatively, a 10 percent increase in VMT corresponds to a 4 to 5 percent increase in fatalities.[11]

Although the first-order effect of the shutdowns was to dramatically reduce VMT and fatalities, that does not imply that all cities experienced a decrease in fatalities. As shown in columns (2) and (3) of table 2.2, the decrease was 12 percent smaller in counties that were highly congested in 2019 relative to those that were not highly congested in 2019, and the estimate is statistically significant. That is, as highly congested counties became less congested, the effect of the shutdowns on fatalities was smaller than in counties that

---

10. We tried lower (100 hours) and higher (125 hours) alternative annual thresholds of our base case for highly congested cities of 120 hours lost due to traffic congestion. We obtained similar results to those presented here.

11. Vickrey (1968) distinguishes between an accident externality elasticity that measures the effect of the quantity of driving on fatalities as opposed to the effect of the quality of driving. We estimate that the elasticity of fatalities with respect to VMT is inelastic, but this estimate is not a pure quantity elasticity because we are not holding the quality of driving constant.

previously were less congested. This finding is consistent with the nonlinear nature of congestion and its effect on driving speed: moderate levels of congestion affect driving speed similarly, but beyond a certain threshold the impact of congestion on driving speed is significantly greater. Accordingly, reductions in congestion would be expected to affect fatalities only when congestion was previously a binding constraint on drivers' ability to engage in risky behavior.[12]

4. Discussion

The different effects of congestion on fatalities for cities that experienced different levels of congestion before the pandemic began suggests that fatalities may have actually increased in previously highly congested cities during the pandemic. We confirm this possibility with the following calculation and then estimate the cost of greater fatalities in those cities.

Based on data from StreetLight, VMT in the highly congested cities of Boston, Chicago, New York, and Philadelphia was observed to decrease 7.4 percent, on average, after the shutdowns in March 2020. Thus, based on the estimated IRRs from our model in column (2) of table 2.2, the decrease in congestion should have resulted in a 2.15 percent *reduction* in fatalities: $100 \times (1.43 - 1.0) \times 0.05$. The four highly congested MSAs in our sample averaged 8.22 fatalities per month in the pre-COVID-19 period and increased to an average of 9.89 fatalities per month in the post-COVID-19 period. However, based solely on the 7.4 percent decrease in VMT in those four MSAs, we would have expected fatalities to have fallen to 8.04 per month in the post-COVID-19 period.

The additional 1.85 fatalities per month $(9.89 - 8.04)$ that we predict in the four highly congested MSAs amounts to roughly 177 more fatalities over a twelve-month period.[13] Assuming the value of a statistical life in 2020 was $11.6 million, based on US Department of Transportation 2020 guidelines, the annual cost attributable to the decline in congestion in those four MSAs alone amounts to roughly $2.05 billion.[14]

This estimate, however, is an extreme lower bound of the annual cost of the decline in congestion because it does not include the large cost of nonfatal but

---

12. Our finding and explanation for it is consistent with Tang and van Ommeren (2022), who find that the London congestion charge led to more accidents resulting in serious injuries and fatalities and argued that by removing traffic along busy roads, the congestion charge reduced bottlenecks and increased traveling speed, resulting in more serious injuries from accidents.

13. In our sample, eight of the counties lie in one of the four highly congested MSAs; thus, we obtain approximately 177 fatalities as the product of $1.85 \times 12 \times 8$.

14. US Department of Transportation, "Departmental Guidance on Valuation of a Statistical Life in Economic Analysis," Office of the Chief Economist, May 2023, https://www.transportation.gov/office-policy/transportation-policy/revised-departmental-guidance-on-valuation-of-a-statistical-life-in-economic-analysis.

Table 2.3. *Sources of Risky Behavior in Fatal Crashes before and after Shutdowns in Select Counties*

	Alcohol		Drugs		Speeding	
	Pre	Post	Pre	Post	Pre	Post
Cook County (Chicago)	67%	59%	89%	86%	36%	56%
Harris County (Houston)	42%	40%	28%	22%	28%	32%
Dallas County	45%	45%	70%	69%	41%	53%
Los Angeles and Riverside Counties	23%	23%	58%	32%	40%	53%

Notes: "Pre" corresponds to January 1, 2019, to December 31, 2019. "Post" corresponds to March 1, 2020, to April 1, 2021.

Sources: Fatality Analysis Reporting System; direct inquiries with county officials.

serious injuries and vehicle damage. In addition, our simple calculation does not account for the fact that MSAs other than those deemed highly congested may also have had increases in fatality risk due to relaxing of the congestion constraint on a limited number of specific roadways, which may pose greater risks than other roadways because of their design, condition, and lack of police traffic enforcement. A more disaggregated analysis would be necessary to explore that possibility.

Recall that in Maheshri and Winston (2016), we found that during the Great Recession, both fatalities per VMT and congestion declined. Why did this relationship change during the pandemic? A natural explanation is that although a change in the mix of safe and risky motorists led to improved safety during the Great Recession, because relatively fewer risky drivers were on the road, the response to the pandemic appears to have led to relatively more risky drivers on the road.

An extreme example is that the Cannonball Run, an illegal cross-country race from the Red Ball Garage in Manhattan to the Portofino Inn in Redondo Beach, California, recorded several record-breaking times in 2020 as drivers took advantage of empty roads that had been created by the COVID-19 lockdowns. Tefft et al. (2022) obtained evidence, based on a national survey where motorists self-reported risky driving behaviors, showing that the relative increase in driving exposure among segments of the driving population with relatively riskier safety profiles contributed to the increase in the rate of traffic fatalities during the COVID-19 pandemic.

Our analysis is at the local level. Given that we cannot identify risky motorists in metropolitan areas during the pandemic based on their specific individual characteristics, we consider whether alternative measures of risky driving behavior that contributed to fatal accidents before and during the pandemic have changed. Table 2.3 presents descriptive evidence that there was little change in alcohol consumption being a factor in fatal crashes for the selected counties where we could obtain recent data—Cook, Illinois; Dallas, Texas; Harris, Texas; and Los Angeles/Riverside, California—and that drug use was even less of a factor.[15] The factors that contribute to fatalities vary in magnitude across counties in ways that we cannot explain, such as, why drugs are much more often a factor in fatalities in Cook County than in Harris County; however, our interest is in the difference in a factor's contribution to a fatal accident for a given county before and during the pandemic. We could not find systematic evidence that other potential factors, such as seat-belt use, drivers' ages, and vehicle safety features, explained much of the change in fatalities during the pandemic.[16]

In contrast, table 2.3 shows that speeding has become a more prevalent factor in fatal accidents for all the selected counties, which is consistent with congestion improving safety before the pandemic by reducing drivers' speeds. Since the pandemic, speeds have increased in cities that were highly congested before the pandemic. Although we do not have data on changes in excessive speeding (exceeding one hundred miles per hour) for those cities during the pandemic, anecdotal evidence for other cities exists, which suggests such changes in speeding also occurred for the cities that were highly congested. For example, Highway Patrol officers in California issued nearly 28,500 traffic tickets for speeds over one hundred miles per hour in 2020, almost double the 2019 total (Baumgaertner and Mitchell 2021); traffic tickets for speeds over one hundred miles per hour have increased 30 percent in Houston, Texas; and along Maryland Route 210, just south of Washington, DC, county speed cameras in 2021 caught thousands of vehicles well above the fifty-five miles per hour speed limit, with the highest recorded speed at 149 miles per hour.[17] Importantly, when a motorist is driving

15. Drug use includes opioids, which have been increasingly used during the pandemic.

16. State laws and public campaigns have increased seat-belt use to 90 percent by 2020. However, some states have reported that the share of people who were involved in a fatal accident during the pandemic and were found to not be wearing a seat belt increased modestly. The age of drivers is generally a factor in the occurrence of driving accidents, with younger and older drivers more likely to be involved in an accident than drivers of other ages. However, the short time span of our analysis and COVID-19's different effects on the vehicle miles traveled of motorists of different ages makes it difficult for us to draw any conclusions about drivers' ages being a factor in fatalities before and after the pandemic started. Finally, the riskiness of drivers may be associated with the safety of the vehicles they use, where, for example, vehicles with Level 1 safety features, such as automatic collision braking systems, are generally safer than vehicles without those features. However, the available evidence from FARS does not indicate that there was a discernible change in the types of vehicles that have been involved in fatal accidents since the pandemic began.

17. ABC Eyewitness News 13 Houston, "100+ MPH Speeding Tickets Up during Quarantine," May 28, 2020, https://abc13.com/houston-speeding-tickets-100-mph-speeders-drivers-fast/6216651/; Gregory Wallace and Pete Muntean, "US Roadway Deaths Rise at a Record Pace," CNN Politics, February 8, 2022, https://www.cnn.com/2022/02/08/politics/record-traffic-fatalities-highway-safety/index.html.

We are not aware of any evidence that police enforcement has changed during the pandemic, which could account for the higher incidence of speeding tickets for speeds over 100 miles per hour.

above fifty miles per hour, even modest increases in speed are sufficient to markedly increase a driver's risk of death in an accident (Malyshkina and Mannering 2008).[18]

As congestion has declined in previously highly congested cities, more motorists have tended to drive at speeds above the speed limit, which appears to have led to greater fatalities in those cities than before the pandemic.[19] Psychologists and other researchers who study risky driving behavior suggest that driving at greater speeds may reflect people releasing their anxieties from being cooped up or locked down during the pandemic or from working in stressful jobs where they deliver goods or provide essential services in workplaces that expose them to greater risks of becoming infected by the coronavirus. Other risky driving that leads to accidents may occur when people are already stretched to the breaking point, and someone else's inconsiderate driving triggers an angry response that leads to a multi- or single-vehicle collision.

As more people return to work, the increase in VMT will have a first-order effect on fatalities. For example, according to our estimates, a 10 to 15 percent increase in VMT would lead to a 7 to 8 percent increase in fatalities, which is broadly consistent with recent aggregate national fatality statistics.[20] It also is possible that some of the bad driving behaviors on uncongested roads that were facilitated by shutdowns will persist, so fatalities are likely to increase further even though road congestion has increased. We also speculate that bad driving behaviors developed more in metropolitan areas that were highly congested prepandemic. The extent of telecommuting and other structural changes in the labor market in the long run also may affect the volume and composition of highway traffic.

5. Implications of the Analysis

We have found that the large reduction in VMT caused by the COVID-19 global pandemic has had the opposite effect on highway fatalities in cities that were highly congested before the pandemic compared with the effect of the large

---

18. More recently, see Insurance Institute for Highway Safety, "New Crash Tests Show Modest Speed Increases Can Have Deadly Consequences," January 28, 2021, https://www.iihs.org/news/detail/new-crash-tests-show-modest-speed-increases-can-have-deadly-consequences.

19. Hughes, Kaffine, and Kaffine (2022) found that during the pandemic, the frequency of severe accidents increased in California even as accidents fell, which suggests that motorists were traveling at higher speeds that increased accident severity. It is possible that drivers' higher speeds above the current speed limits are "appropriate" free-flow speeds based on formulas used in the Highway Capacity Manual. Nonetheless, if a motorist gets into an accident, the higher speed will generally increase the severity of the accident.

20. According to the most recent NHTSA estimates, fatalities in the first quarter of 2022 increased by 7 percent relative to the first quarter of 2021. Meanwhile, VMT almost completely returned to preshutdown levels (national VMT in February 2022 was 99.3 percent of national VMT in February 2020). We estimate that the rebound in VMT of 10 to 15 percent from its low point during shutdowns would increase fatalities by 4.8 to 7.2 percent, which is consistent with NHTSA's estimates. We obtain our estimates by multiplying the increases in VMT by 0.48, which is obtained by subtracting one from the IRR of VMT estimated in column (1) of table 2.2.

reduction in VMT caused by the Great Recession. Because the pandemic has reduced congestion but increased fatalities in those cities, it has raised questions about whether a public policy that reduces VMT would necessarily improve highway safety and congestion. We argue that the key to achieving those improvements is for a public policy not to adversely affect the mix of safe and risky drivers, either because individual drivers change their behavior in response to fewer vehicles on the road or because there is a greater share of risky drivers in the mix.

Unfortunately, it is possible that both congestion pricing and investments in public transit—the policies that are most often advocated to reduce VMT—could increase risky driving behavior on certain roads and at certain times of day. The introduction of congestion pricing could have multiple effects on highway travel conditions and on the mix of drivers, which make its overall effect on automobile fatalities unclear. On one hand, the reduction in congestion during peak travel periods of the day could lead to higher speeds, especially by risky drivers, which could increase the likelihood of a fatal accident on tolled roads. On the other hand, there may be a greater share of safer drivers along with fewer vehicles on the road during peak travel periods because a high congestion toll may cause risky drivers with lower incomes and lower values of time to shift to off-peak travel periods or to use less traveled but longer alternative routes. However, that shift by risky drivers could increase fatalities if those drivers travel at excessive speeds because there are fewer vehicles on the alternative routes, and they may be less patrolled by the police (Lave and Lave 1999). Finally, Winston and Yan (2021) find that congestion pricing reduces automobile fatalities by causing motorists to shift from larger vehicles, which they prefer to drive in congested conditions, to smaller vehicles, which reduces the likelihood of a fatality should a collision occur between those smaller vehicles.

Public transit has experienced a steady decline in its share of travelers to the point where its share was less than the share of telecommuters before the pandemic, and its share has continued to decline during the pandemic.[21] Thus, it would take significant and well-targeted investments in public transit to attract motorists, especially during peak periods. Public transit is thought to be an inferior good; however, suburban rail transit systems have primarily catered to travelers with above-average incomes. The construction of new suburban rail systems or substantial improvements in existing systems may therefore attract commuters with above-average incomes and increase the share of less affluent, risky drivers on the road.[22] Investments in bus transit systems that serve lower-income neighborhoods and that could enable more households to have convenient access to more

21. For example, congestion in New York City outside of Manhattan has recently increased because some commuters became so frustrated by the reduction in transit service, and possibly by fear of a greater likelihood of catching COVID-19, that they bought cars to commute to work.

22. Maheshri and Winston (2016) discuss the relationship between drivers' affluence and their riskiness on the road.

jobs in a metropolitan area could reduce the share of less affluent, risky drivers on the road.[23]

Given these uncertainties about the effects on automobile safety of public policies that could reduce VMT, autonomous vehicles potentially represent the only effective way to achieve both safer and faster travel. As we discuss in greater detail in chapter 6, although it is incautious to commit to when autonomous vehicles will be adopted throughout the United States, their technology continues to evolve and has the potential to eventually eliminate automobile accidents by replacing risky drivers with operations that do not exceed the speed limit, use alcohol or drugs, read and send texts while driving, and the like.[24] Winston and Mannering (2014) discuss other ways that policymakers could use technology to improve highway safety, for example, by setting variable speed limits that are properly aligned with real-time traffic flows and traffic photo enforcement, but policymakers have not pursued those policies.[25]

At the same time, although it has been asserted that autonomous vehicles are likely to increase congestion, it is more likely that they will reduce congestion by eliminating incident delays, which account for roughly one-third of all delays; spreading highway travel more evenly throughout the day by enabling travelers to perform tasks in the vehicle that give them the flexibility to avoid peak travel; and by facilitating the adoption of efficient congestion pricing that sets higher tolls during peak travel periods.

In addition, as we discuss in more detail in chapter 6, autonomous vehicles would effectively increase road capacity in a number of ways, including: (1) enabling vehicles to travel closer together at higher speeds; (2) allowing road authorities to build or redesign roads with more but narrower lanes; and (3) enabling road

---

23. Our assessment of the effect of congestion pricing and investments in public transit on automobile safety and the safety of the overall transportation system is not altered if we consider the relative safety performance of automobiles and public transit, which is typically based on a measure of fatalities per passenger mile (see, for example, National Safety Council, "Deaths by Transportation Mode," 2023, https://injuryfacts.nsc.org/home-and-community/safety-topics/deaths-by-transportation-mode/). That is, congestion prices that cause risky drivers to shift, for example, to public transit will still improve the overall safety of the transportation system when we account for transit's relative safety performance. Similarly, a transit investment that induces safe drivers to shift to public transit and enables risky drivers to drive faster will still decrease the overall safety of the transportation system when we account for transit's relative safety performance.

24. Comparisons of the safety performance of various transportation modes raise the fundamental question of what it is they are measuring. Is it differences in the modes' technology, types of trips, operators, or something else? Automobiles' safety performance is clearly compromised by dangerous operators—that is, risky drivers. Autonomous vehicles have the potential to improve automobiles' absolute and relative safety performance because risky drivers would no longer operate the vehicle.

25. Dynamic speed display devices, which reflect a driver's speed and can provide messages to reinforce adherence to the posted speed limit, and red-light cameras, which photograph a vehicle that has entered an intersection after the traffic signal controlling the intersection has turned red, encourage motorists to drive more safely. However, red-light cameras have met with effective legal and political resistance for violating citizens' privacy.

authorities to expand capacity by eliminating the breakdown lane, given that vehicles would effectively be "inspected" before being able to access the freeway.

Policies in addition to congestion pricing currently exist that could reduce congestion. For example, parking in many urban areas is underpriced and even unpriced (Shoup 2011) while some employers provide free parking as an untaxed benefit to employees. Setting efficient prices for parking and taxing employer-provided parking could help to reduce congestion (Fosgerau and de Palma 2013), but policymakers have not shown much interest in reforming parking policies.

Autonomous vehicles could eliminate parking pricing inefficiencies because travelers would share rather than own their vehicles and they could be dropped off quickly at their destination and the vehicle could either continue to operate and pick up another traveler or could be parked in a garage located in a low-density area. Travelers could be charged a nominal fee for road capacity that is used for dropping them off and picking them up.

In sum, autonomous vehicles are a technological innovation that could free policymakers from setting policies that potentially trade off congestion and safety and could benefit the public by simultaneously reducing the enormous social costs of congestion and accidents.

3

Is Public Bus Transit a Competitor or a Subordinate to Public Rail Transit?

AUSTIN J. DRUKKER AND CLIFFORD WINSTON

1. Introduction

Public ownership and operation of urban transit has been a long-running experiment that followed in the wake of the financial contraction of private transit companies. The growth of household income and automobile ownership in the 1950s caused losses in ridership that in turn led private transit systems to incur large financial losses and confronted city governments with three choices: (1) provide financial assistance and regulatory relief to the private systems and give them a chance to make adjustments that might enable them to once again become financially viable competitors; (2) allow private transit companies to fail if they could not compete against the automobile without assistance; or (3) convert transit companies to subsidized public enterprises, as a few cities had already done.

By 1964, city governments overwhelmingly had chosen the last option, especially because the Urban Mass Transportation Act of 1964 promised them federal grants to do so. Unfortunately, subsidizing public transit service did not improve its competitive position, and its market share of travelers in most urban areas has continued to decline to the point where it was below the share of telecommuters even before the COVID-19 pandemic. Currently, fewer than 5 percent of commuters use public transit. At the same time, transit's subsidies have continued to grow and now exceed $20 billion annually.

Because of its declining ridership and growing subsidies, transit's social desirability was in serious question before the COVID-19 pandemic (Winston

2013).[1] The adverse trends in ridership and subsidies have accelerated since the pandemic, making transit's social desirability even more doubtful. Since the pandemic began in 2020, farebox revenue has dropped to 19 percent of operating expenses compared with 49 percent of operating expenses in 2019. At the same time, transit ridership remains down more than 25 percent nationwide, and more than 50 percent in some large cities, and it is not expected to return to prepandemic levels for at least a decade, because some people who used to commute on public transit will continue to work from home (Quiroz-Gutierrez 2021). Transit also has continued to lose passengers because, as its ridership has declined, it has reduced service frequency and experienced higher crime rates (Bosman et al. 2022) causing some passengers to shift to alternative modes such as automobiles and possibly not returning to transit even when the COVID-19 pandemic is over or transit's service and safety improves.

In response to the sharp drop in ridership and revenue, public transit has received additional taxpayer-funded subsidies in the form of nearly $70 billion of supplemental funding provided during the pandemic. Few limits have been set on the amount of time transit agencies have to spend the supplemental funding or on when they must return any of it.

Generally, public transit's poor performance can be explained by demographic changes and operating disadvantages that have resulted in average load factors (the percentage of seats filled by paying passengers throughout the day) of less than 30 percent for most systems, which is not close to a break-even load factor. Transit cannot keep pace as households' high levels of automobile ownership enable them to move to new suburban communities and the exurbs (Baum-Snow and Kahn 2005).[2] Transit's operations are characterized by the "streetcar problem," when during morning peak periods it commits seat capacity provided by large buses or trains composed of several passenger cars that are filled with passengers who access transit from their residences and board en route to a central destination. Almost the same capacity is offered throughout the day, but it is not filled again until evening peak periods when passengers return from the central business district to outlying residential areas.

Transit's load factor has fallen further when bus systems have expanded their networks and new rail systems have been built where there is low potential demand for public transit. Buses in some cities, such as Los Angeles, were once able to fill

1. Anderson (2014) studies the Los Angeles metropolitan area and argues that the net benefits of public transit systems may be much larger than believed because they reduce congestion. However, considering the findings in chapter 2, it is important to assess whether safety is compromised when congestion is reduced. In addition, transit's benefits from reducing congestion could be achieved at a lower cost by implementing congestion pricing.

2. Expansion of bus and rail are primarily limited by the cost, political difficulties, and the time needed to add new routes to increase service frequency (in the case of bus) or to construct new track to expand coverage (in the case of rail).

nearly 50 percent of their seats over the course of a day, but today, bus transit's average load factor throughout the day in Los Angeles is less than 15 percent and rail transit's load factor is less than 30 percent. We are not aware of a precise estimate of the break-even load factor for public transit, but break-even load factors for airlines are roughly 70 percent.[3]

An important feature of urban transportation is that many metropolitan areas are served by both bus and rail transit systems. When cities took over bus and rail operations, they could have benefited urban travelers by developing those operations such that multimodal transit service generated competition that would improve transit efficiency and would increase its overall market share. Instead, cities have primarily developed their operations in ways that exacerbated transit inefficiencies by raising costs and increasing deficits that must be funded by taxpayers.[4]

We are not aware of any evidence that suggests policymakers have sought to increase urban transit competition. We hypothesize that policymakers in cities with rail systems, which tend to be more heavily subsidized than bus systems, prefer that their rail system does not compete with their bus system—that is, they have designed bus system operations to play a subordinate and occasionally complementary role to the rail system. Such a system would increase the costs of the bus system by reducing its network efficiency and average load factors, without necessarily improving the financial condition of the rail system.

Although it could be argued that rail service quality improves when bus is treated as a subordinate mode, which benefits the overall transit system, we are not aware of any evidence that this improvement in rail has occurred. In fact, from 2012 to 2021, individual boardings on heavy rail and light rail both fell roughly 58 percent, in part because rail is unable to provide service that keeps up with demographic and socioeconomic changes. Rail's current misalignment with travel patterns is that its network and operations are generally designed to transport large volumes of commuters and shoppers to downtown areas. However, the COVID-19 pandemic caused a significant migration out of cities, especially downtown areas, and a shift of workers toward remote workplaces, which in turn caused a sharp decline in rail transit ridership that may be permanent in some cities (Chapple et al. 2023).

In this chapter, we document the effect of rail competition on bus costs by analyzing a sample of bus systems that serve ninety-four US metropolitan areas

3. It could be argued that transit's financial problems, especially rail transit's, are attributable to inefficient road prices that do not account for automobile externalities and reduce their costs to travelers. However, Winston and Shirley (1998) find that transit's share would decline if the urban transportation modes charged efficient marginal-cost prices and if transit provided optimal service frequency.

4. Ley (2022) discusses transit service in Queens where the bus system is used to serve areas that are not served by the rail system. The average travel speed on one of the system's routes is 6.5 miles per hour.

and a sample of light and heavy rail systems that serve twenty-eight of those metropolitan areas. We find that the presence of a rail system significantly increases bus costs, with newer rail systems exacerbating this effect relative to older systems, and that this effect accounts for a notable share of transit's overall deficits. We discuss the possible mechanisms at work and suggest that they strengthen the case for the private sector to play a greater role in urban transportation to improve its efficiency.

2. Conceptual Approach

Multimodal transit systems in US metropolitan areas appear to have a competitive interface because they serve many of the same origins and destinations. For example, when bus and rail provide downtown trips, bus routes often run directly above subway tunnels. Generally, rail fares are higher than bus fares while rail offers faster trip times, especially as the trip distance increases. In theory, transit competition could lead to efficiency and reduce fares, but this does not occur in practice because transit fares are usually established through elaborate political negotiations, including contributions by local jurisdictions based on property or other taxes and are insensitive to competitive forces that reduce costs.

Costs are therefore the relevant performance measure of bus transit that could be affected by the presence of rail service in a metropolitan area. In addition, the same agency operates bus and rail transit service in most cities that are served by both modes, so their cost structures are related and they suffer from the same inflated management overhead.

We hypothesize that transit agencies do not want to attract any unnecessary attention by running excessive deficits, so they avoid having bus and rail compete by giving rail competitive advantages to increase its revenues and decrease its (larger) budget deficits and drain on the public purse. Operationally, transit agencies might reconfigure their bus systems suboptimally to "force feed" their rail systems, inflating bus-operating costs by exacerbating peaking, empty backhauls, deadheading, and the like. We test our hypothesis by estimating how the presence of rail operations affects the cost of bus operations.

We are not aware of previous work that has analyzed the interdependence of bus and rail transit costs; thus, we begin with a model that takes the following generic form:[5]

$$\text{bus cost} = f \text{ (rail, output, capacity, input prices, service quality,} \atop \text{other influences)} \tag{1}$$

5. Viton (1981) and Winston and Shirley (1998) developed equilibrium models of bus and rail transit competing against each other and the automobile.

The presence of rail is captured by a dummy variable, which we assume is exogenous because civic boosters and city officials play a vital role in bringing a rail system to a city through their considerable efforts to generate political support and to obtain outside (usually federal) funding. Such efforts are made because rail systems are thought to enhance a city's reputation and prestige (Winston and Maheshri 2007).[6]

Even with the support of civic boosters and city officials, it can take decades for a city to have a rail transit system; for example, it took some thirty years for Baltimore's Light RailLink system to evolve from a proposal to serving passengers. The gestation period for the Los Angeles rail system took a similar length of time. A rail system's financial performance does not appear to be a factor in the length of time it takes for a rail project to come to fruition because rail's profit motives evaporated when local governments took ownership of those systems and tightly regulated fares, which included subsidies, and did not adjust their service offerings in response to changing demographics. Even the private rail systems that existed previously had been subject to pricing regulations that compromised their profitability (Gómez-Ibáñez and Meyer 1984).

The standard measure of a bus system's output is passenger-miles traveled, defined as the cumulative sum of the distances ridden by each passenger. Capacity is measured by a system's route-miles; input prices include fuel, wages, and capital costs for vehicles; and service quality is typically measured by travel speed and reliability.[7] Regarding other cost influences, bus transit companies are under less pressure to reduce costs if they receive additional revenues from dedicated taxes, and they may incur additional costs by operating in difficult weather conditions or on unfavorable terrain.

Although equation (1) is a plausible specification of transportation costs, the primary goal of our analysis is to estimate the effect that the presence of a rail system has on bus-operating costs, so it is important for us to exclude variables that could capture the effect of the rail system on those costs. For example, it is inappropriate to include passenger-miles in the specification because the presence of an alternative mode of travel, namely, rail, will decrease bus ridership. We therefore cannot hope to identify the true effect of rail presence on bus costs if we include bus passenger-miles as an explanatory variable. In place of passenger-miles, an important omitted variable, we include *current* population, which is highly correlated with passenger-miles but is arguably uncorrelated with the presence of rail, which appears to be explained by political factors

6. Cities do not vary notably in their preferences for or against public rail transit, which supports our assumption that the rail dummy variable is exogenous. Generally, cities are willing to spend more money on rail transit if their subsidies increase. We control for subsidies in our model.

7. Buses use petroleum and diesel fuel, but their prices are highly correlated with the price of gasoline.

and long-standing boosterism. Note that cities with large populations (e.g., Los Angeles) did not have a rail transit system until recently and older cities with smaller populations (e.g., Boston) have had a rail system for more than a century. We explore how our findings are affected by the choice of including current population or passenger-miles in the specification.

We also should not include regional fixed effects because those would be perfectly correlated with the rail dummy, which does not vary for individual transit systems over our period of study.[8] Route-miles and average trip distance also are potentially problematic as explanatory variables because rail could serve destinations that bus might otherwise serve and because systems with rail tend to have shorter average trip distances for bus, especially where buses provide more feeder service and fewer long-distance trips.

Given the preceding considerations, we specify our base-case model of bus costs for transit system i at time t in a log-linear form as a function of the rail dummy and purely exogenous influences:

$$
\begin{aligned}
\ln\left(cost_{it}\right) = {} & \beta \; rail_i + \alpha_1 \ln\left(population_{it}\right) + \alpha_2 \ln\left(fuel \; price_{it}\right) \\
& + \alpha_3 \ln\left(dedicated \; taxes_{it}\right) + \alpha_4 \; days \; freezing_{it} + \gamma_t + \varepsilon_{it}
\end{aligned}
\tag{2}
$$

We measure bus costs as operating expenses because it is not clear why the presence of rail also would affect bus capital costs; we found through sensitivity tests that the results are not changed when we specify total costs, which include operating and capital costs.[9] The explanatory variable of interest is a time-invariant rail dummy indicating the presence of a rail system at location i. We classify a rail system to be either heavy rail (e.g., Washington's Metrorail system) or light rail (e.g., Dallas's DART Light Rail).[10] As noted, population is used as an explanatory variable in place of passenger-miles. Fuel price, specifically, the average price per gallon of gasoline, is an exogenous influence on bus-operating costs. Wages and capital costs do not vary sufficiently to permit their inclusion in the specification and their exclusion did not affect our main findings.[11] Dedicated taxes levied by state or local governments generate revenues that can be used to offset excessive operating costs. We contend that those are largely governed by exogenous political forces. Such revenues reduce the incentive for transit systems to operate efficiently,

8. There are two exceptions: Phoenix's Valley Metro Rail, which began operations in December 2008; and Virginia Beach's Tide light rail, which began operations in August 2011.

9. Capital costs include the annualized value of the bus fleet and structures.

10. We did not find that light rail and heavy rail had notably different effects on bus costs.

11. Our finding is consistent with the lack of a distinct effect of unionization on bus costs. The Amalgamated Transit Union is the largest labor union representing transit and allied workers in the United States. Our main findings did not change when we estimated a specification that included bus operators' median hourly wage.

so we expect dedicated taxes to have a positive effect on operating costs, holding population constant. Days freezing refers to the number of days in the calendar year for which temperatures are below thirty-two degrees Fahrenheit, an influence that increases bus maintenance costs and is clearly exogenous. We also include year fixed effects, γ_t, to control for macroeconomic factors that affect all transit systems in a year, and ε_{it} is the error term. We were unable to obtain data on exogenous measures of service quality.

3. Sample and Data Sources

To construct our estimation sample, we considered the one hundred largest metropolitan areas by population. After making some appropriate adjustments and accounting for limitations of some of the areas because of missing data, we assembled a balanced panel of ninety-four transit systems with annual data from 2002 to 2018 that are included in the US Department of Transportation's (DOT's) National Transit Database.[12]

Table 3.1 summarizes the transit systems in our sample, which include twenty-eight bus-and-rail systems and sixty-six bus-only systems. This sample enables us to identify the effect of a rail system on bus costs in both a geographic dimension (that is, some systems do and some do not have rail service at the same point in time) and a temporal dimension (that is, systems that added rail service did so at different points in time). We classify the systems as old if the bus-and-rail system or bus-only system was operating during or before 1960 and new if the bus-and-rail system or bus-only system began operating after 1960. We conducted sensitivity tests and found that our conclusions do not change much if we use 1965 or 1970 as a cutoff year to distinguish between new and old systems.

We distinguish between old and new systems because we hypothesize that metropolitan areas attempt to increase ridership of their new, expensive rail systems by giving them priority over bus in terms of favorable routes and type of service. Metropolitan areas may be less likely to prioritize old rail systems, so the effect of those systems on bus costs may be less than the effect of new rail systems on bus costs. Rail was introduced to US urban transit beginning with the Boston subway in 1897; thus, it is not surprising that a narrow majority of bus-and-rail systems are old, but a clear majority of bus-only systems are new.[13]

Table 3.2 presents summary statistics for the variables used in our estimations. Most of the data we use come from the DOT's National Transit Database.

12. We dropped Hartford and New Haven, Connecticut; McAllen, Texas; and Poughkeepsie, New York, due to missing data; and we dropped Ogden and Provo, Utah, because they belong to the same transit system as Salt Lake City, Utah.

13. As a point of qualification, some cities that only have buses today once had electric streetcars, which were replaced by buses once buses became less costly to operate. The earliest electric streetcar systems predate subways by a few decades.

Table 3.1. *List of Transit Systems Considered*

Bus-and-rail systems		Bus-only systems			
City	Age	City	Age	City	Age
New York	Old	Riverside	New	Albany	Old
Los Angeles	New	Detroit	Old	Knoxville	Old
Chicago	Old	Tampa	New	Baton Rouge	New
Dallas	New	Orlando	New	Oxnard	New
Houston	New	San Antonio	New	El Paso	New
Washington	New	Las Vegas	New	Allentown	New
Miami	New	Austin	New	Columbia	New
Philadelphia	Old	Cincinnati	Old	Sarasota	New
Atlanta	New	Kansas City	New	Dayton	New
Phoenix	New*	Columbus	Old	Charleston	New
Boston	Old	Indianapolis	Old	Greensboro	New
San Francisco	New	Nashville	Old	Fort Myers	New
Seattle	New	Providence	New	Stockton	New
Minneapolis	New	Milwaukee	Old	Boise	New
San Diego	New	Jacksonville	New	Colorado Springs	New
Denver	New	Oklahoma City	New	Little Rock	New
St. Louis	New	Raleigh	Old	Lakeland	New
Baltimore	New	Memphis	New	Akron	New
Charlotte	New	Richmond	Old	Des Moines	New
Portland	New	Louisville	Old	Springfield, MA	New
Sacramento	New	Birmingham	New	Winston-Salem	New
Pittsburgh	New	Grand Rapids	New	Deltona	New
Cleveland	Old	Rochester	Old	Madison	New
San Jose	New	Tucson	Old	Syracuse	New
Virginia Beach	New*	Fresno	Old	Durham/Chapel Hill**	New
New Orleans	Old	Tulsa	New	Toledo	New
Salt Lake City	New	Honolulu	Old	Wichita	Old
Buffalo	New	Omaha	New	Augusta, GA	New
		Worcester	New	Palm Bay	New
		Bridgeport	New	Jackson, MS	New
		Greenville	New	Harrisburg	New
		Albuquerque	Old	Spokane	New
		Bakersfield	Old	Chattanooga	Old

Notes: Old systems are bus-only systems that were in operation before 1960 or bus-and-rail systems where rail was in operation before 1960. Rail refers to light rail or heavy rail. The New Orleans streetcar system is classified as light rail. * Indicates that operations began mid-sample. ** Indicates that the transit systems were combined to coincide with the metropolitan statistical area definition.

Table 3.2. *Summary Statistics*

Variable	Overall		Old systems		New systems	
	Mean	*SD*	*Mean*	*SD*	*Mean*	*SD*
Operating cost	146,339,535	310,880,544	243,229,816	536,493,923	113,173,560	164,546,022
Passenger-miles	130,261,960	246,240,983	190,040,717	363,314,781	109,799,425	186,155,769
Population	2,113,140	2,676,142	2,637,806	3,960,055	1,933,254	2,030,857
Income	41,623	10,399	41,739	8,731	41,583	10,916
Dedicated taxes	44,889,469	200,676,480	84,490,654	360,536,636	31,333,807	94,463,620
Route-miles	533	425	500	315	544	456
Route density	186	243	281	406	153	136
Fuel price	3.551	0.789	3.581	0.800	3.540	0.785
Days freezing	65	49	74	41	62	52

Notes: Old systems are bus-only systems that were in operation before 1960 or bus-and-rail systems where rail was in operation before 1960. All dollar values are expressed as 2019 dollars. Route density is thousands of people per route per year. Fuel price is dollars per gallon.

Sources: National Transit Database; Census Bureau; National Oceanic and Atmospheric Administration; Energy Information Administration.

Table 3.3. *Estimation Results*

Log operating expenses	(1)	(2)	(3)
Rail	0.555***	0.399***	0.204***
	(0.194)	(0.075)	(0.072)
Log population	1.199***		
	(0.105)		
Log passenger-miles		0.835***	0.936***
		(0.032)	(0.031)
Log gasoline price	3.378***	0.223	–0.146
	(1.246)	(0.289)	(0.400)
Log dedicated taxes for operations	0.014**	0.002	–0.002
	(0.007)	(0.002)	(0.003)
Days below freezing	0.004***	0.001***	0.001***
	(0.001)	(0.000)	(0.000)
Estimator	OLS	OLS	IV
R^2	0.833	0.958	0.952
Number of observations	1,596	1,596	1,596

Notes: All specifications include year fixed effects. The specification in column (3) uses log population as an instrument for log passenger-miles. Robust standard errors clustered at the transit-system level are shown in parentheses. Statistical significance is indicated at the ***1 percent, **5 percent, and *10 percent levels.

Population is at the level of the metropolitan statistical area and is from the US Census Bureau.[14] Weather data are from the National Oceanic and Atmospheric Administration and data on fuel prices are from the Energy Information Administration. All dollar values are deflated using the consumer price index and are expressed in real 2019 dollars.

The old transit systems carry more passengers over a larger network, operate in larger cities, and, as expected, have higher total operating costs than the new systems. However, the systems have comparable operating costs per passenger-mile, suggesting that the old systems are unable to exploit possible economies of size and route density to significantly reduce operating costs.

4. Estimation Results

We present ordinary least squares estimates of our base specification in equation (2) in column (1) of table 3.3. The central finding is that the presence of rail *increases* bus costs, and the effect is large and statistically significant: rail's presence increases bus costs by roughly 71 percent.[15] We discuss below the specific mechanism by

14. We collapse the transit systems of Chapel Hill and Durham, North Carolina, into one system because they belong to the same metropolitan statistical area.

15. Recall that the percentage impact of a dummy variable on the dependent variable in a log-linear regression is equal to $100 \times (\exp(b - SE(b)^2/2) - 1)$, where b is the estimated coefficient on the dummy variable and $SE(b)$ is the estimated standard error of b.

which the presence of rail increases bus costs after we finalize our discussion of the estimates. The remaining variables in the model have their expected signs, as population (a proxy for demand), gasoline prices, dedicated taxes, and days below freezing also bear a positive relationship to bus costs. Overall, the model fits the data well, with an R^2 of 0.83, even though we have not included passenger-miles.

The second column of the table begins our exploration into how the presence of rail affects bus costs—that is, what variables might the rail dummy be capturing? Column (2) of table 3.3 shows that when we replace population with passenger-miles, it has a statistically significant effect on costs and noticeably reduces the effect of the rail dummy, which suggests that rail affects bus costs by causing changes in bus operations in ways that reduce its patronage.

Passenger-miles may be endogenous because it is correlated with unobserved influences on bus costs. Thus, we instrument passenger-miles with population, which is correlated with passenger-miles but is not causally related to costs once we control for passenger-miles in the specification.[16] As we show in column (3) of table 3.3, the coefficient on the rail dummy variable falls even further when we estimate the model in this way.[17] In sum, it appears that the presence of rail increases bus costs primarily by affecting its operations in ways that decrease its traffic.

We checked whether the findings were sensitive to the size of the transit systems by reestimating equation (2) for the top sixty metropolitan statistical areas based on population, composed of twenty-eight bus-and-rail systems and thirty-two bus-only systems. The coefficient estimates for the effect of rail on bus-operating costs with and without passenger-miles are very similar to the estimates obtained from the full sample of ninety-four transit systems. We also estimated equation (2) using a sample of transit systems with system-wide passenger-miles above the median, which resulted in twenty-seven bus-and-rail systems and twenty bus-only systems. Using that sample did not result in any material changes to our findings. Finally, the results did not change much when we excluded New York's transit system from the sample, which accounts for about 40 percent of transit passengers nationwide.

We have assumed that the presence of rail has a homogeneous effect on all bus systems' operating costs, regardless of any important differences between the systems. A key distinguishing feature between transit systems that may influence the effect of rail's presence on bus-operating costs is the age of the system providing bus and rail service. For example, it might be expected that older systems, where bus and rail "grew up together," would be designed in a harmonious way such

16. The first-stage regression using population as an instrument for passenger-miles had an F statistic of 33.73.

17. Note that when we instrument passenger-miles with population, the coefficient for passenger-miles increases and the standard error slightly decreases.

Table 3.4. *Estimation Results for Old Systems versus New Systems*

Log operating expenses	Old systems			New systems		
	(1)	(2)	(3)	(4)	(5)	(6)
Rail	0.585***	0.482***	0.295**	0.651***	0.388***	0.191**
	(0.183)	(0.115)	(0.134)	(0.239)	(0.092)	(0.082)
Log population	1.179***			1.185***		
	(0.104)			(0.133)		
Log passenger-miles		0.852***	0.943***		0.818***	0.916***
		(0.058)	(0.060)		(0.038)	(0.035)
Log gasoline price	5.719***	−0.352	−1.228	2.026*	0.521	0.350
	(1.640)	(0.624)	(0.815)	(1.180)	(0.331)	(0.362)
Log dedicated taxes for operations	−0.001	0.003	0.001	0.025***	0.001	−0.004
	(0.009)	(0.004)	(0.004)	(0.008)	(0.003)	(0.004)
Days below freezing	0.003	0.002**	0.001	0.004***	0.001*	0.001**
	(0.002)	(0.001)	(0.001)	(0.001)	(0.000)	(0.000)
Estimator	OLS	OLS	IV	OLS	OLS	IV
R^2	0.902	0.973	0.970	0.825	0.955	0.949
Number of observations	407	407	407	1,189	1,189	1,189

Notes: Old systems are bus-only systems that were in operation before 1960 or bus-and-rail systems where rail was in operation before 1960. All specifications include year fixed effects. The specifications in columns (3) and (6) use log population as an instrument for log passenger-miles. Robust standard errors clustered at the transit-system level are shown in parentheses. Statistical significance is indicated at the ***1 percent, **5 percent, and *10 percent levels.

that rail has a smaller effect on bus costs compared with newer systems, where rail service was added to an existing system and bus operations had to be adjusted to accommodate rail.

In table 3.4, we present estimation results for the base specification without passenger-miles for old and new systems, and for the specifications with passenger-miles with and without passenger-miles instrumented by population. We set a cutoff year of 1960 to distinguish old from new systems, and we performed some sensitivity tests around this cutoff point. Comparing columns (1) and (4), we find, as hypothesized, that the coefficient for the rail dummy is larger for the new systems than for the old systems when we do not control for passenger-miles.[18] This finding is consistent with the hypothesis that city officials and planners wanted to encourage rail ridership in the new systems even to the detriment of

18. Note the coefficients for the rail dummy variables for the new and old systems are statistically significant and the rail coefficient for the new systems is more than 10 percent larger than the rail coefficient for the old systems, which is nontrivial.

bus, because it was much more expensive to construct those systems in the more recent period than in the past.[19]

However, when we control for passenger-miles, the rail coefficient for the old systems becomes larger than the rail coefficient for the new systems, suggesting much of the effect of rail on new systems' bus-operating costs is captured by passenger-miles. Because new rail systems are those where bus routes were reconfigured to curtail their line-haul service to downtown destinations and feed the rail system by providing more suburban service, higher passenger-miles on rail are partly achieved by using feeder bus service to carry more passengers, which is likely to be more costly than using bus to carry passengers for line-haul service. It is conceivable that the agencies' reduction in bus line-haul service and increase in feeder service could reduce total bus-operating costs. But we did not find that to be the case, perhaps, as we discuss below, because of the relatively higher cost of operating buses to provide feeder service.

Note the small effect of rail in column (6). In contrast, rail's effect on bus-operating costs in old systems, as shown in column (3), is larger and apparently includes additional influences that collectively increase bus-operating costs by roughly 33 percent. We conducted sensitivity tests using alternative cutoffs for new systems as operating during or after 1965 and 1970 and found no substantive change in the results; namely, the presence of rail has a greater effect on bus-operating costs for new systems than for old systems but controlling for passenger-miles explains most of the effect for new systems, although additional influences still affect operating costs for old systems. We discuss those possible influences below.

Based on the parameter estimates in table 3.4, we estimate that the presence of rail in old transit systems raises annual bus-operating costs by about $2.1 billion due to both demand and pure cost effects, and that the presence of rail in new transit systems raises annual bus-operating costs by about $2.7 billion, due primarily to demand effects. The combined $4.8 billion increase in operating costs for new and old systems accounts for a notable share of public transit's total operating and capital subsidies, which exceed $25 billion (Winston and Karpilow 2020).

5. Discussion

What explains the different effects that new and old rail systems have on bus costs? We hypothesize that cities that have built expensive, new rail systems, especially ones that serve suburbs, do not want to be criticized for running excessive rail transit deficits, which might jeopardize additional rail subsidies for system

---

19. Rosenthal (2017) shows that the construction costs of New York's Second Avenue Subway amounted to a record $2.6 billion per mile. The cost of Honolulu's light rail system is likely to significantly exceed $0.5 billion per mile by the time it is completed.

expansion or modernization. Thus, the newer systems attract some riders who may have used bus by removing buses from line-haul service and relegating them to feeding the rail system.

We have been unable to find data that systematically indicate the share of buses that were previously used for line-haul service and then relegated to feeder service after a rail system was built. However, considerable anecdotal evidence supports the hypothesis that certain bus routes have been converted to feeder service when a new rail system is built.[20]

This change in operations increases bus costs because feeder service is more costly to operate than line-haul service. Feeder buses are less intensively utilized because they spend dwell time waiting at rail stations and operate less efficiently by stopping more often, traveling at slower speeds, and so on. Bus system costs also may be higher because fewer resources are allocated to keep buses in good condition. Finally, the change in operations converts for many passengers what was once a direct bus trip into a more time-consuming bus trip plus a rail trip, which reduces bus demand and load factors.[21]

Bus ridership, as measured by passenger-miles, aggravates these cost-increasing effects because much of it is concentrated during peak hours, increasing dwell times at bus stops and rail stations. Thus, when we controlled for passenger-miles in the specification, we found that it captured much of the original effect of the rail dummy variable—that is, the rail dummy was capturing demand-related effects that increase costs.[22]

20. For example, private communications with DOT personnel indicated that bus routes were realigned in the late 1970s and early 1980s to "force feed" Washington's newly constructed Metrorail system, which required riders who previously enjoyed continuous bus service to their destinations to make inconvenient and time-consuming transfers, sometimes at both ends of the rail trip. As another example, the DOT's (1995) report on bus–rail integration in St. Louis in the early 1990s notes that "extensive advertising and promotions" were used to inform bus ridership that "some bus routes would be slightly modified to become a feeder network for the light rail system," and St. Louis employed a "Rail Ambassadors" program to encourage rail ridership. Finally, the completion of the extension of the Silver Line on Washington's Metrorail system was accompanied by an announcement that Northern Virginia bus systems would modify their routes to connect to the new stations (George 2022b). Notably, the Silver Line extension was four years behind schedule, and it is not clear that the new bus routings will attract many riders if the region's travelers are satisfied with the transportation- and nontransportation-related choices that they made during the intervening years.

21. The average number of passengers on board for bus was 5.0 in 2021. Heavy rail and light rail have a higher average number of passengers on board with 11.9 and 9.6 respectively, but the rail modes have much higher vehicle capacities and typically serve higher-density corridors.

22. It could be argued that passenger-miles reflects the equilibrium of demand and supply. Transportation supply is typically measured by seat-miles. Seat-miles multiplied by average load factor yields passenger-miles. As discussed, transit's low load factors exist because its operations do not enable it to keep pace with the nation's demographic and socioeconomic changes. Because rail's operations are even less flexible than bus's operations, a system that favors rail will be more disadvantaged by demographic and socioeconomic changes that affect demand.

However, we also found in old systems that the rail dummy is capturing some additional effects on bus costs even when we controlled for passenger-miles. One explanation is that there may be omitted variables that raise operating costs but do not affect demand, which the rail dummy was capturing. For example, suppose the presence of a rail system forces a bus system to hire additional workers who are used to help coordinate buses with rail operations. This would increase bus-operating costs but would not affect demand, so the rail dummy would be capturing pure cost-related influences on bus costs. The effect also might arise from higher wages for rail operators and mechanics—and perhaps managerial overhead as well—that spills over to bus operations, such that bus drivers and mechanics have higher wages in cities that also have rail systems, especially older ones, than in cities with only bus service.

An alternative explanation is that the inclusion of passenger-miles may introduce endogeneity that biases the estimated coefficient of the rail dummy variable, so it only appears to capture pure cost-related effects. For example, although fares are regulated, costs may affect passenger-miles by reducing service quality. Thus, there may be reverse causality between those variables. Bus passenger-miles are negatively correlated with the rail dummy, so the bias to bus passenger-miles could bias the estimate of the rail dummy. However, when we tested for this possibility by instrumenting passenger-miles with exogenous population to reduce the endogeneity bias, we found that the pure cost-related effect captured by the rail dummy still existed for old systems.

6. Potential Public and Private Sector Improvements in Urban Transportation

Public urban bus and rail transit have accumulated vast inefficiencies and have developed a symbiotic relationship that has increased bus-operating costs and is likely to ensure that transit's financial problems and declining market share persist. In addition, bus service is often relegated to feeding rail service when it could benefit the public in certain situations by substituting for it. For example, both bus and rail transit significantly curtailed service during the COVID-19 pandemic and greatly inconvenienced workers who normally relied on transit to travel to their workplaces (Verma 2020). Those workers would have been less inconvenienced if new bus service had been initiated on line-haul routes served by rail transit. By completely substituting rail for line-haul service and offering greater frequency than rail was offering during the pandemic, the new bus service would have reduced travelers' waiting time (at a possible cost of increasing their overall travel time) and would have reduced taxpayers' overall transit subsidies because rail is more costly to operate than bus transit.

In any case, public transit has continued to decline during the pandemic and is expected to continue to decline after the pandemic. We therefore consider potential public and private sector sources of improvement for urban transportation.

Public Transit's Continuing Decline

The failure to use bus more effectively in metropolitan areas offering both bus and rail transit service harms lower-income travelers because bus riders are generally poorer than rail riders (Winston and Shirley 1998) and are less able to afford an alternative mode, such as auto, and have fewer opportunities to work at home. Bus has recovered much of the ridership that it lost with the onset of COVID-19 in such cities as Washington and Boston, while rail is struggling to recover even half of the ridership that it lost in those cities (Gelinas 2022a). At the same time, rail has cut its service in those cities, while bus routes and frequencies have not been adjusted in response to demographic changes and dislocated rail travelers' dependence on bus service, especially harming essential workers.

In theory, bus systems are more flexible than rail systems and their routes could be more easily reconfigured to adapt to modern traffic patterns, improve the speed and reliability of service, and attract more passengers. However, proposals to redesign a bus network are often shelved because they are met with strong opposition from riders who claim they will be inconvenienced because stops will be eliminated. Thus, current average bus speeds in the densest metropolitan areas in the country are less than ten miles per hour; average bus speeds in the New York metropolitan area, for example, are about eight miles per hour (Ley 2022).

In addition to being hamstrung to improve service quality, bus and rail transit systems seem incapable of taking the most basic actions to reduce their deficits and taxpayer-funded subsidies. For example, the Washington Metropolitan Area Transit Authority (WMATA) has lost millions of dollars in revenue because roughly one in three Metrobus rides goes unpaid, as drivers do not attempt to prevent fare evasion (George 2022a). According to the Metrobus operating training manual, drivers are discouraged from bringing attention to someone who skips a fare and should not stop a fare evader or delay a trip if a passenger avoids paying. In New York City, nearly 30 percent of bus riders and 8 percent of subway users do not pay their fare, costing the city more than $300 million a year, according to data released by the state-operated Metropolitan Transportation Authority (Rosenberg 2022). Fare evasion has contributed to putting the Seattle and Tacoma Sound transit system on a financially unsustainable trajectory and facing insolvency. According to Schulz (2022), the lack of enforcement is to blame for widespread fare evasion, and New York, Seattle, and several other cities with transit systems have reduced or completely withdrawn enforcement efforts.

In response to nearly $25 million in annual losses from fare evasion before the pandemic, the Bay Area Rapid Transit system decided to install a new generation of fare gates to deter fare evasion and has begun to eventually replace 715 fare gates across the system and to raise the height of barriers separating free and paid areas (George 2022c).

The Kansas City Area Transportation Authority decided to avoid the issue of having its users help to finance operations by eliminating fares system-wide in 2020. The program is set to sunset at the end of 2023, but local officials are preparing to make it permanent. The system serves only a small portion of Kansas City's residents and did not cover much of its costs with fares, but policymakers should consider a lower-cost alternative to a multimillion-dollar, fully taxpayer-supported streetcar and bus transit network to serve the system's most dependent transit users.[23]

Can Reforming Automobile Policies and Transit Operations Improve Transit?

The existence of inefficient parking and roadway prices for automobiles is often cited as a justification for subsidizing transit on second-best grounds. The perspective in this book is that policymakers should create an environment where greater competition between the modes and new innovations improve the US transportation system and that they should eliminate inefficient policies toward all modes. We also have argued that, in the long run, the adoption of autonomous vehicles could facilitate the adoption of efficient prices for automobile travel and eliminate its subsidies. In addition, as we discuss in chapter 6, autonomous vehicles also could pose a substantial threat to public transit as a viable mode and could eventually eliminate the need for taxpayer-funded subsidies that have maintained transit operations.

In the short run, subsidies for both automobiles and public transit will continue to exist. Winston and Shirley (1998) found that if policymakers eliminated those subsidies by setting efficient prices and service levels for both modes, then public transit's market share would decline further, and its social desirability would be more questionable. Winston and Shirley (1998) also found that transit's share does not increase much if automobiles are charged congestion prices; instead, highway travel is spread more evenly throughout the day.

Efforts to improve bus service times by instituting exclusive bus lanes also have raised concerns about inefficient policies for both transit and automobiles. For its part, automobiles have slowed bus travel times by violating exclusive bus lanes, but the police have generally not issued traffic citations to discourage such violations.[24] At the same time, exclusive bus lanes reduce welfare by reducing capacity

---

23. WMATA announced that it would be the first large metropolitan area to offer free public bus transit starting on July 1, 2023. Again, policymakers should consider whether they could improve the mobility of the most dependent bus transit users at a lower cost than offering free transit on a costly, inefficient public bus transit system.

24. Camera technology could be used for exclusive bus lane enforcement. See, for example, Skip Descant, "LA Metro Turns to Technology in Bus Lane Enforcement," Industry Insider, April 11, 2022, https://insider.govtech.com/california/news/l-a-metro-turns-to-technology-in-bus-lane-enforcement.

for automobile travel and increasing highway users' congestion costs (Winston and Langer 2006). Again, in the long run, the adoption of autonomous vehicles could resolve the issue because they would not violate exclusive bus lanes if any existed; more likely, those lanes would not exist because public buses would no longer operate.

Electric-Bike and Electric-Scooter Sharing

Electric-bike sharing and electric-scooter sharing could possibly complement transit and increase its ridership by solving the "last mile" problem—that is, enable people who do not live within walking distance of an urban rail station or a bus transit stop to have access to those services (Zhou, Li, and Zhang 2022; Chu et al. 2021). However, it is questionable whether those modes should be subsidized and provided by the public sector, and it is not clear whether they can operate profitably in the private sector. For example, although China has some 300 million bike-share users, its two largest companies discontinued service. In the United States, electric bikes and scooters are unlikely to attract sufficient use to help improve transit's financial picture or to reduce automobile externalities, while even widespread adoption may not be a panacea because it is likely to introduce new safety issues.

Private Urban Transit

An alternative approach to improving the efficiency of public transit is to privatize it and not force bus to be subordinate to rail. Private van and minibus services, which have achieved success throughout the world because of their low costs and responsive service, could improve urban transportation if they were allowed to serve more US urban areas. Currently, such service exists in a handful of major US cities, but the operators tend to keep a low profile because, although some companies are legal, others have not obtained a license to operate. Nonetheless, they exist because they provide a highly valued, low-cost service, with fares that are usually only a few dollars and with a route network made by and for working-class people.

Correal (2018) provides examples of private vans' service areas and fares in the New York City metropolitan area, while Reiss (2014) provides a graphic overview of the service provided by "dollar vans" in New York City, which shows that their routes are generally not served by subways and buses. Said (2019) reports that Via, a private transit operator, will run on-demand vans in Cupertino, California, which are eagerly awaited because the public bus option run by the Santa Clara Valley Transportation Authority is too slow. Indeed, some companies in the San Francisco Bay Area, such as Google, are so dissatisfied with the public transportation system that they provide private transit service to their employees.

The developers of a new app called Dollaride are hoping to generate more business for private vans in New York City (and possibly elsewhere) and to challenge public bus transit in the same way that Uber has taken on the taxi industry (de Freytas-Tamura 2019). The app allows users to see where licensed vans are operating within a one-mile radius, as well as where they are headed, helping commuters decide whether taking a van might be faster than waiting for a bus. The app allows van drivers to spot passengers more easily and to plan for growing demand and possibly future routes. The app may also encourage unlicensed vans to register with the city.

Privatization of all US bus systems could produce large cost savings and eliminate bus subsidies. Jerch, Kahn, and Li (2017) and Winston and Shirley (1998) provide supportive empirical evidence.

Private urban rail systems exist in Hong Kong and Japan, where they take advantage of high traffic density and multiproduct operations that include nontransportation services. It is an open question whether any US urban rail system could be as financially successful as those Asian systems. It is more doubtful that urban transit public–private partnerships would significantly improve US public transit systems.[25]

As we discuss in more detail in chapters 5 and 6, where we discuss electric and autonomous vehicles, greater competition *and* innovation is critical for improving urban transportation. The private sector's role in improving urban transportation will particularly increase when autonomous vehicles are widely adopted. Households will effectively have their own low-cost transit system that provides good service to any destination in a metropolitan area, which will make it difficult for conventional public bus and rail transit to survive financially, even if they are automated (Winston and Karpilow 2020).

Instead of seeking political support to obtain additional subsidies, public bus and rail transit systems should focus on how, if at all, they could possibly complement autonomous vehicles to justify their continued operations. WMATA experienced a false start when it attempted to provide automated urban rail transit service only to suspend it after a deadly train crash in 2009. WMATA is now hoping to restore automated train service on all lines by 2024. On-demand autonomous transit experiments are being explored in some metropolitan areas; for example, the Rideshare, Automation, and Payment Integration Demonstration (RAPID) in Arlington, Texas, hopes to show how autonomous transit could be a viable part of future urban transportation systems.

Unfortunately, transit systems largely dependent on annual government appropriations face a high barrier to investing in automation that would improve service and possibly reduce growing operating subsidies because section 13(c) of the Urban Mass Transportation Act requires that local agencies accepting federal transit grants

---

25. Austen (2022) reports that Canada has had mixed experiences with public–private urban transit partnerships. Rail transit projects in Ottawa, Toronto, and Montreal have been marred by cost overruns and delays, while projects in Vancouver and Kitchener/Waterloo are regarded as successful.

implement protections for existing employees. Thus, automation of an existing transit system may be delayed for several years until the displaced workers can be retrained, transferred, or retire. Alternatively, direct compensation could be paid to affected workers, eliminating the jobs earlier but at an earlier cost.

Privatized bus and rail systems are likely to have greater flexibility and financial incentives than public transit systems to adapt to a world of autonomous urban transportation. Importantly, their financial survival would be subject to the market test of providing services that respond effectively to changes in households' socio-economic and demographic characteristics and that increase social welfare. If private autonomous transit companies cannot compete effectively with autonomous cars, it would be unwise for governments to repeat the mistakes they made with public transit by taking ownership of those companies.

4

Measuring the Benefits of Ridesharing Service to Urban Travelers: The Case of the San Francisco Bay Area

HYEONJUN HWANG, CLIFFORD WINSTON, AND JIA YAN

1. Introduction

Ridesharing consists of drivers who provide private trips with their own cars without intervention from a regulatory authority; passengers who use an app on their smartphone to request transportation from their current locations to various destinations; and transportation network companies (TNCs), such as Uber or Lyft, which have developed a smartphone application that matches passengers' demand for trips with drivers' availability to provide automobile transportation.

Ridesharing services have grown rapidly since 2010 when Uber launched its first on-demand car service, UberCab, in San Francisco. In 2019, Uber completed some 14 million trips per day, serving more than six hundred cities in sixty-five countries around the world, while its main competitor, Lyft, launched in 2012, completed more than 1 million trips per day, serving three hundred US and two Canadian cities. Since 2017, the share of trips by ridesharing has exceeded taxi's share of trips in the United States. By January 2019, daily travel in New York City, for example, included 462,113 trips provided by Uber, 149,142 using Lyft, and 271,135 by taxi, according to the Taxi and Limousine Commission. The growth of platforms such as DiDi in China and Ola Cabs in India indicates that ridesharing services also are widely used in other countries.

Drivers have been attracted to ridesharing because they do not have to purchase medallion permits and meet occupational licensing requirements that apply to taxi drivers (Cramer and Krueger 2016; Angrist, Caldwell, and Hall 2021).

In addition, ridesharing drivers have flexible hours, which enable them to smooth income fluctuations (Hall and Krueger 2018). Finally, capacity utilization, measured by the fraction of business hours or miles that a fare-paying passenger occupies a shared vehicle, is much greater for Uber drivers than for taxi drivers in, for example, New York City and Boston (Cramer and Krueger 2016).[1]

The growth of ridesharing services has not been welcomed by all segments of society. Ridesharing has significantly threatened the financial viability of the taxi industry by causing significant declines in its revenue and in the value of operating medallions; for example, the recent value of a medallion in New York City has dropped 80 percent from its all-time high of $1.3 million. A backlash from taxi drivers has led policymakers in various countries to limit Uber's operations.[2] In the United States, actions include limiting New York City (commercial) drivers' access to the Uber app.

Critics of ridesharing claim that Uber and Lyft take advantage of drivers by treating them as independent contractors, instead of as employees who are eligible for various benefits. In 2020, a California judge ordered Uber and Lyft to treat their drivers as employees. Critics also claim that by creating more automobile travel, ridesharing is increasing congestion, emissions, and traffic accidents, while reducing the use of public transit.

Despite the growing popularity of ridesharing, there has been little empirical assessment of its benefits to travelers. Conceptually, the benefits reflect the value that travelers place on the ridesharing alternative compared with the value that they place on their next best transportation alternative, such as driving their personal vehicle or taking public transit. Cohen et al. (2016) estimate that the benefits generated by UberX in San Francisco, Los Angeles, New York City, and Chicago amounted to nearly $3 billion in 2015; however, their estimated gains do not account for the potential benefits to travelers provided by alternative modes, which causes the estimated benefits from UberX to be biased upward because Uber is not the only mode that provides benefits to travelers. At the same time, the authors do not account for certain nonprice benefits provided by UberX, which causes a downward bias in their estimates.

In this chapter, we estimate a mixed logit model of mode choice to measure the benefits of ridesharing services provided by Uber to travelers in the San Francisco Bay Area. Ordinarily, the benefits of a mode are obtained from a discrete choice

---

1. UberX, the most frequently used Uber service, provides comfortable sedans for up to four people.

2. Al Goodman, Elwyn Lopez, and Laura Smith-Spark, "Spanish Judge Imposes Temporary Ban on Uber Taxi Service," CNN, December 9, 2014, report on efforts to limit Uber operations in Spain; and Hope King, "Uber Suspends UberX Service in South Korea," CNN Business, March 6, 2015, reports on efforts to limit Uber operations in South Korea.

model by deleting the modal alternative from the choice set, including its alternative-specific constant and attributes, and calculating the loss in consumer surplus. However, we cannot use that procedure here because our data set from the 2017 National Household Travel Survey (NHTS) includes a car-hire alternative that combines Uber and Lyft with taxi.[3] Thus, deleting the Uber alternative from the choice set would yield a biased estimate of travelers' value of Uber because taxi's alternative-specific constant would be inflated. Accordingly, we calibrate the alternative-specific constant for car hire such that it equals the value of the alternative-specific constant for taxi based on the 2009 NHTS when Uber was not available. We then compare travelers' total welfare when Uber service was available with travelers' total welfare when Uber service was not available to obtain a welfare difference that is not biased downward by an inflated alternative-specific constant for taxi.

Based on this procedure, we find that Bay Area travelers who have access to Uber gain $0.815 per day in nonfare benefits from higher service quality and personalized pricing, which traditional taxi services have not provided, but those travelers lose $0.005 per day in slightly higher fares. The $0.81 in daily benefits amount to roughly $1 billion annually. Extrapolating this estimate to all US cities with ridesharing services indicates that travelers' annual benefits are at least several billion dollars. The available evidence indicates that ridesharing does not create social costs that offset those benefits and that the social costs of any form of automobile travel could be reduced substantially with efficient policies. We conclude that regulations that limit entry and operations by TNCs reduce travelers' welfare.

2. Transportation Markets and Modes

The geographic transportation market in this study consists of nine counties in the San Francisco Bay Area: Alameda, Contra Costa, Marin, Napa, San Mateo, Santa Clara, Solano, Sonoma, and San Francisco, which are depicted in figure 4.1. We define transportation markets as (exclusive) origin-destination pairs of grids of approximately one mile by one mile within the nine counties, which results in a total of 6,530 grids.[4]

Compared with traditional disaggregate analyses of urban mode choice, our analysis is complicated by the availability of disaggregated data on mode choices

3. As discussed below, we were able to obtain data from Uber to conduct our analysis, but we could not obtain separate data on Lyft's operations. However, Uber and Lyft offer very similar services and fares and, according to several marketing consulting firms, Uber accounts for nearly three-quarters of the ridesharing market in the San Francisco Bay Area. We therefore use data based on Uber's operations and fares to construct attributes of ridesharing services in Bay Area markets.

4. We drew a rectangle covering the nine counties and then formed the grids, but we could not include the northwest part of Sonoma County because the data we obtained from Uber did not include information about that area.

Figure 4.1. *San Francisco Bay Area Counties*

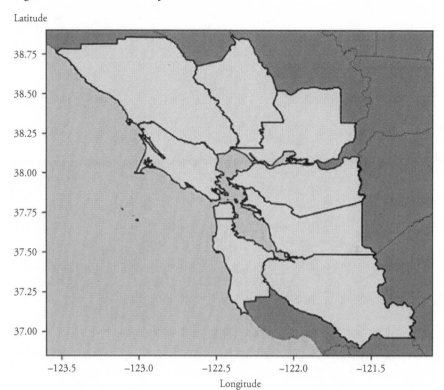

that includes TNCs that do not distinguish between travelers' choice of Uber or Lyft from their choice of taxi service. We therefore employ the following procedure to determine the benefits of Uber.[5]

We use the 2017 NHTS, a national household survey conducted by the Federal Highway Administration, to estimate San Francisco travelers' mode choice in the 2016–17 environments when Uber is an available option. The NHTS contains information on daily trips made by household members, including time of day, the location of the origin and destination based on actual coordinates, trip purpose, mode of transportation, and vehicle occupancy. The five alternative modes that we include are walking, bicycling, driving, public transit (bus and rail), and car-hire services (Uber, Lyft, and taxi). The NHTS does not contain data on the prices that individual respondents pay for the modes that they use and the service times of their trips. Thus, we constructed average values of those variables using data from other sources.

5. As noted, we obtained data for Uber's attributes but not for Lyft's attributes.

Table 4.1. *Mode Shares in the 2009 and 2017 NHTS*

Mode	Number of trips in 2009	Share (%) in 2009	Number of trips in 2017	Share (%) in 2017
Driving	23,477	81.19	18,055	73.44
Car-hire services	20	0.07	221	0.90
Public transit	591	2.04	1,071	4.36
Bicycling	431	1.49	480	1.95
Walking	3,932	13.60	4,448	18.09
Other	465	1.61	310	1.26
Total	28,916	100	24,585	100

Notes: Uber accounts for the vast majority of TNC trips in the Bay Area so we use its attributes for TNC service and fares.

Source: National Household Travel Survey.

The trip data are linked with sociodemographic characteristics of both the household and individual household members who make the trips. Travelers can face different choice sets if they cannot access a mode (for example, respondents that do not use smartphones cannot use Uber or Lyft, so the car-hire services for those respondents include only taxis), and if a mode does not serve an origin-destination pair. We form an origin-destination pair for each trip based on its latitude and longitude provided in the NHTS and we match the trip with the two most appropriate grids that we constructed for the nine Bay Area counties. San Francisco County contains a large share of both work and leisure trips in our sample. We obtain additional data to construct attributes for all the modes that provide trips over the origin-destination pairs in our sample.

Because we cannot distinguish travelers' choices of car-hire services between Uber and taxi, we use the 2009 NHTS to calibrate the estimated choice model to replicate the mode choice outcomes that occurred in the 2008–09 environment, before the existence of Uber services. This is achieved by adjusting the alternative-specific constants that we estimate using the 2017 NHTS. We expect the alternative-specific constant for car-hire services, which no longer includes Uber, to decrease. We then conduct counterfactual simulations that estimate travelers' benefits without Uber service and compare those benefits with the estimated benefits when Uber service was available to determine the benefits generated by Uber.[6]

The 2017 NHTS, conducted between April 2016 and April 2017, contains 3,498 households and 24,585 trips within the geographical market area of analysis, while the 2009 NHTS, conducted between March 2008 and March 2009, contains 3,460 households and 28,916 trips within the geographical market area of analysis. Table 4.1 presents the five modes in our analysis and their total trips

6. This procedure assumes that the decline in car-hire service's alternative-specific constant is attributable to the absence of Uber. We report later that the growth of ridesharing accounts for the entire increase in car-hire trips, including taxi, from the 2009 to the 2017 NHTS.

and mode shares for both samples and previews some possible effects of the introduction of TNCs; namely, the share of driving decreased from 81 percent to 73 percent, while the share of car-hire services increased more than tenfold from 0.07 percent to 0.9 percent.

Although it is not possible to determine directly how many of the 221 trips are by a TNC, we use a travel survey, which we discuss later, conducted by the San Francisco Municipal Transportation Agency in the Bay Area to infer that taxi has not increased its number of trips during the period, thereby indicating that approximately two hundred trips were taken with a TNC. Mode shares in the San Francisco Municipal Transportation Agency study are similar to the ones in the 2017 NHTS, suggesting that the NHTS does not underrepresent ridesharing.

The modes, including Uber and taxi service, differ in their spatial coverage. Figure 4.2 uses the 2017 NHTS data to show, as expected, that travelers drive their own vehicle throughout the nine Bay Area counties. In contrast, travelers use public transit and car-hire services primarily in San Francisco County. We obtained data on Uber trips in August 2016 from Uber engineers, and for comparative purposes we show in figure 4.3 that Uber's service area is more extensive than the service area indicated in the NHTS for car-hire services.[7]

3. Modal Attributes

Travelers obtain utility from the existing modes' price and nonprice attributes and from the price and nonprice attributes of a new mode, such as ridesharing. The data sources we use to measure the attributes of car-hire services (Uber and taxi), public transit, private car, bicycling, and walking are as follows. As is standard in urban mode choice studies, unmeasured modal attributes are captured by the alternative-specific constants.

Uber

Uber engineers provided us with data for two Uber services: UberX, a private car; and Uber Pool, a carpool service where riders share the ride with strangers and split the cost.[8] Data were collected for the morning and evening of each day of the week for the average trip duration (excluding waiting time, which is captured by the alternative-specific constant), distance, and average fare for trips taken during August 2016 in the San Francisco Bay Area. The average fares did not include tips, but Chandar et al. (2019) found that in 2017 only 1 percent of travelers always tip, 60 percent of travelers never tip, and the average tip came out

---

7. Uber's data indicate that Uber serves about 15 percent more markets than are served by car-hire services in the 2017 NHTS data.

8. We are grateful to Jonathan Hall, Andrew Salzberg, and Santosh Rao Danda for providing the data and preparing it for our purposes.

Figure 4.2. *Spatial Distribution of Trips by Mode in the 2017 NHTS*

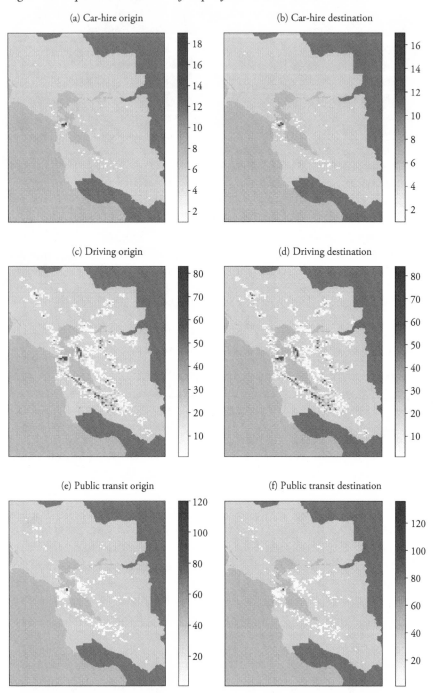

Source: National Household Travel Survey.

Figure 4.3. *Spatial Distribution of Uber Trips*

(a) Origin grids

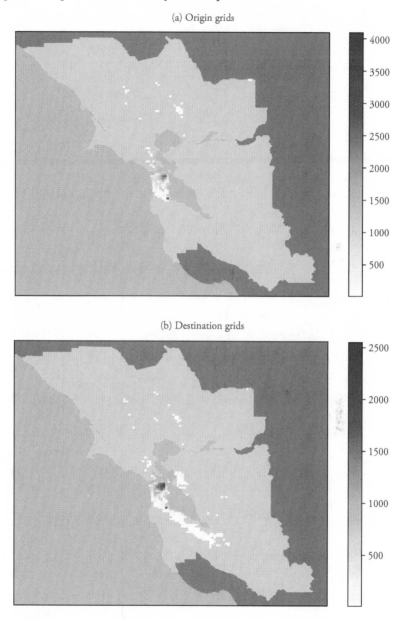

(b) Destination grids

Source: Uber.

Table 4.2. *Summary Statistics for Uber Trips by Type of Service*

Service	Attribute	N	Mean	SD	Min	Max
UberX	Fare ($)	14,342	16.27	10.64	4.75	110.82
	Duration (minutes)	14,342	17.35	10.08	1.67	92.33
	Distance (miles)	14,342	5.33	5.19	0.03	46.81
Uber Pool	Fare ($)	12,868	10.89	5.74	4.27	68.20
	Duration (minutes)	12,868	20.38	10.22	2.00	75.50
	Distance (miles)	12,868	4.99	3.64	0.00	38.18

Source: Uber.

to fifty cents per ride.[9] Because tips represent a voluntary transfer from travelers to drivers, accounting for them would change only the distribution of benefits from Uber but not the total benefits.

The origins and destinations of the trips conformed to the grids that we constructed for our analysis. Note that we were unable to measure the attributes for an Uber trip in an origin-destination market if an Uber trip was never made in that market. Thus, our analysis did not enable Uber to contribute any utility to a traveler's choice set in such a market. As shown in table 4.2, UberX operates in more markets than Uber Pool does. In addition, trips on UberX tend to cover a longer distance, cost more, and take less time than trips on Uber Pool.

Modal Attributes from Google Maps API

The 2017 NHTS provides information on the distance of each trip, which we use to calculate the cost of certain modes, and the duration of the trip for the chosen mode, but it does not provide information on the duration of the trips for the nonchosen modes and on transit fares for both the chosen and nonchosen modes. Given the departure times of the trips in the NHTS and the centroids of the latitudes and longitudes of their origins and destinations, we fill in those gaps by using Google Maps API to identify the available transportation alternatives and their attributes.

Data were collected for 2017 for the distance and travel duration of trips by private auto, bicycling, and walking. We collected the same variables and fares for the public transit options: bus, subway (Bay Area Rapid Transit), and the combination of the two.[10] We assume that people who walk or ride a bicycle to their destinations do not incur out-of-pocket costs.

9. The authors also found that the default tipping suggestions that Uber build into its platform led to only a 2.5 percent increase in tips.

10. The Google Maps API transit fare is the aggregated fare of using bus and/or subway. Our measure of the duration of transit trips does not include the transfer time between buses and subways because it is generally short. Similarly, wait time at the origin tends to be short during peak periods, although it can be long during off-peak periods, such as late in the evening. However, only a small fraction of the trips in our sample occurred during that time.

Travel Decision Survey

The 2017 Travel Decision Survey (TDS) that is conducted by the San Francisco Municipal Transportation Agency summarizes travel behavior in the Bay Area and provides data that we use to help distinguish taxi from TNC operations. According to the TDS, taxis account for roughly 9 percent of all trips using car-hire services based on a modest sample of trips between zip codes and based on a larger sample of trips in the Bay Area.[11] That share is consistent with the increase in the car-hire alternative from the 2009 to the 2017 NHTS that came solely from the growth of ridesharing. The data's spatial patterns also are consistent with patterns that we discussed previously, which indicate that TNCs provide more extensive transportation coverage than taxis do. This is another unmeasured benefit of TNCs that is captured by the alternative-specific constant.

Constructing Monetary Costs for Private and For-Hire Cars

The monetary cost per mile of driving a private car in 2017 is from the American Automobile Association.[12] We assume vehicles accumulate fifteen thousand miles per year and we match the vehicles that a traveler uses to the operating and ownership costs for the vehicle's classification. We do not include parking costs, which fluctuate greatly in the Bay Area depending on the time of day, area, and duration.

Within for-hire services, we distinguish between the monetary cost of TNCs and taxi. Because we have two different Uber services, we use the weighted average fare of UberX and Uber Pool, where the weights are 80 percent and 20 percent, respectively.[13] Note that the average fares include any increase caused by surge pricing adopted by Uber. The taxi fare is calculated based on the common pricing policy adopted by the major taxicab firms in San Francisco as reported by the San Francisco Municipal Transportation Agency.[14] Regulated taxi fares are, in general, based on distance and location, and regulatory authorities have not adjusted them to respond to competition from TNCs. We use the weighted

---

11. See San Francisco County Transportation Authority webpage, "TNCs Today: Overview," https://www.sfcta.org/projects/tncs-today.

12. American Automobile Association, *Your Driving Costs: How Much Are You Paying To Drive?* (2017 edition).

13. The percentage of Uber drivers offering UberX service was nearly 75 percent in 2018; no official statistic for Uber Pool was reported. See Brett Helling, "Ridester's 2018 Independent Driver Earnings Survey," Ridester, https://www.ridester.com/2018-survey.

14. See San Francisco Municipal Transportation Agency, "Taxi Fares," https://www.sfmta.com/getting-around/taxi/taxi-fares. The fares for a trip of a given distance are based on charging travelers $3.50 for the first 0.2 miles and $0.55 for each additional 0.2 miles. We also add $0.55 for each minute of wait time and traffic delay. Out-of-town trips from San Francisco that exceed fifteen miles are charged a fare that is 150 percent of the metered rate. The same fare calculation is applied for trips originating outside of San Francisco because taxis operating in the San Francisco Bay Area generally have the same pricing policy.

Table 4.3. *Means (Standard Deviations) of Modal Attributes*

| Attribute | Car-hire services | | Driving | Public transit | Bicycling | Walking |
	Uber	Taxi				
Fare ($)	24.24	25.32	4.12	4.50	0	0
	(27.14)	(27.15)	(5.98)	(3.02)	(0)	(0)
Duration (minutes)	16.31		13.24	50.04	14.08	8.86
	(10.17)		(11.68)	(33.96)	(13.26)	(29.96)
Distance (miles)	6.18		7.18	12.88	2.35	0.43
	(7.96)		(10.35)	(13.46)	(2.35)	(1.49)

Sources: Uber; Google Maps API; San Francisco Municipal Transportation Agency.

average fare of Uber service and the fare of taxi service as the monetary cost of car-hire services for markets that are served by both taxi and Uber; otherwise, we use the taxi or Uber fare, as appropriate, when only one of those transportation options serves a market.

Summary of Modal Attributes

We summarize the mean and standard deviation of the fare and travel-time duration of each mode in table 4.3. Taxicab and Uber trips are assumed to have the same duration on a given origin-destination pair, which is plausible, although they do have different fares. We also show the average distance of trips that travelers take on each mode. As expected, driving is far less costly on a per-mile basis than are the car-hire services and faster on a per-mile basis than all the other modes, which greatly contributes to its dominant share of urban travel.

4. Empirical Methodology

We quantify the welfare gain to travelers from the introduction of Uber by first using the 2017 NHTS data and the data on modal attributes to estimate travelers' mode choices when ridesharing services were available in San Francisco Bay Area markets. This is the base-case scenario subject to the car-hire option including Uber and taxi. We then construct a counterfactual scenario where ridesharing services do not exist by using the 2009 NHTS data to calibrate the estimated choice model in the base case. We then calculate consumer benefits in the base and counterfactual scenarios and compare the difference to obtain the welfare gain to travelers from Uber services.[15]

---

15. It would be more difficult to execute our analysis if we used the 2009 NHTS to construct the base case because we would have to obtain 2009 data for all the modal attributes, including Uber fares.

Panel Data Mixed Logit Mode Choice Model

Assume households indexed by $h = 1, 2, \ldots, H$ are composed of individuals $i = 1, 2, \ldots, I_h$. The transportation mode for a trip is denoted by $j \in \Omega$, where Ω is the choice set in a market:

$$\Omega = \{\underbrace{\{\text{walking, bicycling}\}}_{\text{nonvehicle nest}}, \text{public transit, driving, car-hire services}\}$$

Define $I(A)$ as an indicator function that equals 1 if A holds and 0 otherwise. We specify the indirect utility function of individual i choosing mode j for trip t as:

$$u_{ijt} = v_{ijt} + \varepsilon_{ijt}$$

$$= \alpha_i p_{jt} + \beta_i d_{jt} + \eta_i I\left(j \in \text{nonvehicle next}\right)$$

$$+ \sum_k \psi_{ik} I\left(k \in \Omega \text{ and } k \neq \text{driving}\right) + \varepsilon_{ijt}$$

$$\psi_{ik} = \mathbf{Z}_i \boldsymbol{\lambda}_k \qquad (1)$$

$$\alpha_i \sim N\left(\mathbf{Z}_i \boldsymbol{\theta}, \sigma_\alpha^2\right)$$

$$\beta_i \sim N\left(\mathbf{Z}_i \boldsymbol{\delta}, \sigma_\beta^2\right)$$

$$\eta_i \sim N\left(0, \sigma_\eta^2\right)$$

where p_{jt} is the fare for alternative j for trip t, d_{jt} is the travel duration, and $\mathbf{Z}_i$ is a vector of ones and sociodemographic variables of the individual and household, such as age, education, household income, and the like. Preference heterogeneity for the fare and travel duration is captured by a vector of random parameters, (α_i, β_i); $(\boldsymbol{\theta}, \boldsymbol{\delta})$ and $(\sigma_\alpha^2, \sigma_\beta^2)$ are the associated vectors of means and standard deviations, respectively, to be estimated; and the random coefficient η_i captures the correlation between the two nonvehicle alternatives.

This mixed logit specification mimics a nested logit specification where a traveler first chooses between nonvehicle and vehicle travel and then an alternative from the chosen nonvehicle or vehicle nest. We choose driving as the base alternative and ψ_{ik} represents the alternative-specific constants that vary across individuals with different sociodemographic characteristics. Finally, ε_{ijt} is assumed to be independent and identically distributed extreme value for trips, individuals, and alternatives.

Let $y_{ijt} \in \Omega$ denote individual i's mode choice for trip t and let T_i denote the number of trips made by individual i; thus, the joint mode choice probability conditional on the random parameters, $\Gamma_i \equiv (\alpha_i, \beta_i, \eta_i)$, is:

$$\Pr\left(y_{ij1},\ldots,y_{ijT_i} \mid \Gamma_i\right) = \prod_{t=1}^{T_i} \frac{\exp\left(v_{ijt}\right)}{\sum_{j' \in \Omega} \exp\left(v_{ij't}\right)} \qquad (2)$$

The unconditional joint choice probability is:

$$L_i\left(\Lambda, \Theta\right) \equiv \Pr\left(y_{ij1},...,y_{ijT_i}\right) = \int_{\Gamma_i} \Pr\left(y_{ij1},...,y_{ijT_i} \middle| \Gamma_i\right)\rho\left(\Gamma_i; \Theta\right)d\Gamma_i \qquad (3)$$

where $\Lambda = \{\lambda_k\}_k$ denotes a vector of nonrandom parameters; $\Theta = (\theta, \delta, \sigma_\alpha^2, \sigma_\beta^2, \sigma_\eta^2)$ denotes the parameters of the random components; and $\rho(\cdot)$ indicates the distribution of the coefficients in the population.

Estimates of the parameters (Λ, Θ) for the mixed logit probabilities of the panel are obtained by maximizing the simulated log likelihood (Train 2009). Note that the random parameters account for the error correlation that arises for travelers who take multiple trips.

Calibrated Model

As noted, the 2017 NHTS combined taxi and Uber in the car-hire alternative; thus, we cannot conduct a counterfactual that simply eliminates Uber from the travelers' choice set because the alternative-specific constant for the taxi alternative that remains is inflated given that its value was determined when Uber services were available. We use the 2009 NHTS data to calibrate a model for the counterfactual scenario in which Uber services do not exist. To do so, we first replace Uber fares, which are the fares of car-hire services, with taxi fares in the 2017 NHTS data. Given those fares, we calibrate the intercepts in $\psi_{ik} = \mathbf{Z}_i\lambda_k$, which are specified in equation (1), to replicate the mode shares in the 2009 NHTS data.[16]

Travelers' Welfare

Travelers' welfare is calculated using the log-sum approach in Choi and Moon (1997):

$$CS = \sum_{i=1}^{I} \int_{\Gamma_i} \frac{1}{\tau_i} \sum_{t=1}^{T_i} \ln \sum_{j\in\Omega} \exp\left(v_{ijt}\left(\Gamma_i\right)\right)\rho\left(\Gamma_i; \Theta\right)d\Gamma_i \qquad (4)$$

where τ_i is the individual's marginal utility of income derived from Roy's identity.[17] We decompose travelers' benefits from Uber services into nonfare and fare benefits. Nonfare benefits come from sources such as higher service quality, more transparent fares, personalized pricing and services, competitive responses to Uber such as expanded taxi service into new markets, and the like.[18] We quantify

16. The share of taxicab (or car-hire services) was only 0.09 in the 2009 NHTS data. As in any counterfactual that relies on different years, the state of the economy in 2009 and 2017 could differ in ways that possibly affect our calibration.

17. Because we have several fare variables, the marginal utility of income is computed using the coefficients of those variables, not just the coefficient for fare when it enters by itself.

18. The benefit of expanded taxi service is reflected in the alternative-specific constant for car-hire services, which includes both Uber and taxi.

those benefits by using the estimated and calibrated model to calculate travelers' welfare using equation (4) on the adjusted data, in which fares of car-hire services in all markets are assumed to be taxicab fares. We measure nonfare benefits as the difference in welfare from the two models on the adjusted data, where the change in nonfare benefits is captured by the change in the alternative-specific constant for car-hire services. We quantify the fare benefits by redoing the calculations on the original 2017 NHTS data in which the fares of car-hire services in markets served by Uber are based only on Uber fares.

5. Empirical Findings

Travelers' utility from their choice of mode for a given trip is influenced by the modal attributes, fare, and trip duration. Those attributes were specified alone; interacted with trip purpose; and interacted with socioeconomic variables, including household size, income, occupation, and dummy variables for whether there is a young child in the household and whether the individual is a frequent smartphone user.

We include random parameters, assumed to be log-normally distributed, for fares and trip duration and for the nonvehicle dummy variable. Bicycling is the base mode in the nonvehicle nest and driving is the base mode in the vehicle nest. Finally, we control for the possible endogeneity of fares by including alternative-specific dummy variables, which capture omitted modal attributes, including attributes that may be correlated with fares.[19]

We present the mixed logit parameter estimates in table 4.4. The coefficients of the mean random parameters have the expected negative sign and along with the standard deviations of the random parameters are statistically significant. All else constant, walking is preferred to bicycling, and nonvehicle modes are less preferred to driving. Transit and car-hire services also are less preferred to driving, although the alternative-specific constant for transit is not statistically significant.

The average value of time (VoT) based on the fare and duration mean coefficients is estimated to be $42.42 per hour, which is broadly consistent with other VoT estimates for travelers in urban areas with high household incomes (Small, Winston, and Yan 2005). The estimated median VoT is slightly lower at $39 per hour, and we measure the implied heterogeneity in VoT by the interquartile difference of the estimated distribution, which is $46 per hour. Note that our sample also has a large share of people who walk to work. As we report below, people with short trips have a very high VoT.

The estimates of the coefficients on the interaction terms indicate that the disutility of a higher fare is increased for shopping trips because it reduces the

---

19. Using alternative-specific dummy variables for this purpose has been common practice in disaggregate choice modeling since the 1970s.

Table 4.4. *Mode Choice Parameter Estimates*

Variable	Coefficient estimate (standard error)
Fare	−0.526 (0.071)
Fare × work trips	−0.005 (0.013)
Fare × shopping trips	−0.109 (0.024)
Fare × household size	−0.055 (0.021)
Fare × high income	−0.104 (0.072)
Fare × household size × high income	0.034 (0.022)
Fare × frequent smartphone	−0.031 (0.052)
SD of fare coefficient	0.370 (0.017)
Duration	−0.372 (0.014)
Duration × professional	0.042 (0.006)
Duration × work trip	0.004 (0.004)
Duration × shopping trip	−0.070 (0.007)
Duration × household size	−0.015 (0.002)
Duration × young child	−0.011 (0.012)
SD of duration coefficient	0.178 (0.007)
Nonvehicle	−3.449 (0.897)
SD of nonvehicle coefficient	2.635 (0.115)
Walking	7.227 (0.742)
Public transit	−0.317 (0.723)
Car-hire services	−9.081 (2.430)
Alternative-specific constants × sociodemographics	Yes
Pseudo R^2	0.43
Number of observations	87,386
Implied median value of time ($ per hour)	39.32 (8.33)
Implied heterogeneity in value of time ($ per hour)	46.18 (12.45)

Notes: Household sociodemographic variables are interacted with the fare, duration, and alternative-specific constants to capture travelers' preference heterogeneity that varies with observed variables. Implied heterogeneity in value of time is measured by the interquartile difference of the estimated distribution.

availability of money that could be spent on goods and services, and it also is increased for larger households because such households have a tighter budget constraint per household member. Similarly, the disutility from a trip with a longer duration that increases time costs is greater for shopping trips and larger households.

Sensitivity by Trip Distance

Travelers' heterogeneity is reflected in sorting across different residential locations. All else constant, travelers with the highest value of travel time live closest to their workplaces, while travelers with the lowest value of travel time live farthest from their workplaces (Calfee and Winston 1998; Winston and Shirley 1998). The nonvehicle modes (bicycling and walking) are unlikely to be chosen by travelers

Table 4.5. *Mode Choice Parameter Estimates for Distances Less than Two Miles*

Variable	Coefficient estimate (standard error)
Fare	−0.143 (0.089)
Fare × work trips	−0.015 (0.015)
Fare × shopping trips	−0.083 (0.029)
Fare × household size	−0.078 (0.024)
Fare × high income	−0.121 (0.076)
Fare × household size × high income	−0.195 (0.082)
Fare × frequent smartphone	0.078 (0.027)
SD of fare coefficient	0.224 (0.019)
Duration	−0.360 (0.030)
Duration × professional	0.055 (0.013)
Duration × work trip	0.011 (0.006)
Duration × shopping trip	−0.058 (0.011)
Duration × household size	−0.003 (0.004)
Duration × young child	0.007 (0.022)
SD of duration coefficient	0.163 (0.013)
Nonvehicle	−11.362 (7.250)
SD of nonvehicle coefficient	21.491 (3.363)
Walking	14.404 (6.813)
Public transit	5.120 (1.454)
Car-hire services	−22.800 (7.383)
Alternative-specific constants × sociodemographics	Yes
Number of observations	39,647
Implied median value of time ($ per hour)	59.04 (11.25)

Notes: Household sociodemographic variables are interacted with the fare, duration, and alternative-specific constants to capture travelers' preference heterogeneity that varies with observed variables.

for long-distance work or shopping trips. Descriptive information in the NHTS indicates that the shares of bicycling and walking declined dramatically for trips greater than two miles, so we reestimated the mode choice model with a sample that included only trips with a distance less than two miles.

The estimation results shown in table 4.5 indicate that travelers' relative valuation of fares is notably different for shorter trips compared with their valuation of those attributes for the full sample of trips. The effect of fares is much smaller, while the effect of duration does not change much.

The estimated average value of time for the restricted sample ($151 per hour) is much higher than the average value of time for the full sample ($42 per hour). However, the distribution of VoT is highly skewed to the right because the estimated median VoT is considerably lower at $59 per hour. Compared with the VoT estimates from the entire sample, the higher VoT estimates for the shorter trips reflect the fact that the most affluent people tend to live closest to their workplaces because they value travel time so highly.[20] Finally, public transit is preferred to driving for short trips, all else constant, which may reflect the unavailability of free parking or some combination of parking price and search time to locate a vacant space.

Estimated Benefits

We measure the benefits that Uber provides to consumers by first removing Uber as an alternative in 2017 Bay Area markets. To do so, we replace Uber fares, which are included in the fares of car-hire services, with taxi fares, and we calibrate the constant for car-hire services so that its market share drops from 0.9 percent to 0.07 percent.[21] We then calculate the total benefits that travelers obtain from the transportation choice set in the counterfactual scenario where Uber is not an available option and we compare it with their total benefits from the transportation choice set in the base-case scenario where Uber is available.

We find that Bay Area travelers (not just Uber passengers) in the NHTS sample gain $4,446 per day, which, given 5,471 travelers, amounts to an average gain per traveler of $0.81. Making the conservative assumption that only half of the Bay Area population has access to Uber,[22] we estimate that the daily benefits to the Bay Area are roughly $2.8 million ($0.81 × 3,484,823), for an annual gain of $1.02 billion.[23] Extrapolating the gain to all US cities suggests the annual benefits from Uber services would amount to several billion dollars.

We offer four checks on the plausibility of the magnitude of the estimated benefits. First, Cohen et al.'s (2016) estimates of the average daily gain per traveler generated by Uber of $1.60 is roughly twice our estimate; however, as noted, their estimate is inflated because they do not account for the benefits provided by alternative transportation modes—that is, they do not estimate the incremental benefits of introducing Uber service in a market where alternative modes are already available.

Second, Gorback's (2021) estimates of the welfare gains from Uber are somewhat higher than our estimates, but they also account for the benefits from improving residents' accessibility and Core Based Statistical Areas' (CBSAs') amenities.

Third, our estimate of the average daily gain per traveler is a modest share (roughly 5 percent) of Bay Area travelers' average daily expenditures on transportation.

20. The high hourly value of time is plausible for people who live in the Bay Area close to their workplace and make, say, $300,000 a year and value travel time greater than the conventionally assumed value of 50 percent of the hourly wage.

21. As expected, the constant for car-hire services, which no longer includes Uber, decreased from –9.08, as reported in table 4.4, to –23.

22. The assumption is conservative because Uber tends to serve the most densely populated areas in an urban metropolis.

23. The figure for the Bay Area population is from the State of California Department of Finance.

Given that our estimate is conservative, as noted previously and discussed further below, and given the high cost of driving in the Bay Area, this relationship is plausible.

Finally, the estimated benefits can be decomposed into nonfare gains of $0.815 and very slight losses from higher fares of –$0.005. Travelers incur a loss from fares because although Uber fares are roughly $2 less than taxi fares for the car-hire trips that were actually taken, Uber fares are higher than taxi fares for the large number of remaining trips that were taken on other modes. Because there is a positive probability, even if small, that Uber could have been chosen for those trips, its relatively higher fares reduce travelers' welfare slightly.

The nonfare benefits reflect Uber's response times and differentiated services, which, as captured by the alternative-specific constant, are more closely aligned with travelers' preferences than are taxi's offerings. Uber also benefits travelers indirectly by causing taxis to increase their geographic coverage to compete more effectively with Uber.[24]

Because our analysis holds the size of the travel market constant, we under-estimate the gains provided by Uber given that Uber's entry has expanded the San Francisco Bay Area travel market by attracting additional travelers who benefit from the service and who would not have taken their trips by other modes, even walking, had Uber not been available. In addition, we do not account for trips by travelers destined outside of the Bay Area, which include new trips gener-ated by Uber to, for example, San Francisco International Airport and possibly San Jose International Airport.[25] Finally, we do not account for any changes in spatial economic activity attributable to Uber. As noted, Gorback (2021) finds that UberX's entry caused house prices to increase by 4 percent for the thirty-four largest CBSAs in the United States by improving residents' accessibility and the area's amenities. Similarly, if Uber has improved travelers' accessibility to Bay Area amenities, then its entry has provided additional social benefits.

Liu, Brynjolfsson, and Dowlatabadi (2021) point out that we may be under-stating the benefits from Uber because taxis have been able to overcharge passen-gers by taking a longer route to their destinations when passengers were unfamiliar with the area or were disinterested in the cost because their employer was paying for the trip. The authors find that taxi drivers take longer routes that are more time consuming than Uber drivers take for matched airport routes by an average of 8 percent, with nonlocal passengers experiencing even longer routes and travel

24. The geographic coverage of car-hire service in the 2017 NHTS data is greater than it is in the 2009 NHTS data, suggesting the competition from TNCs has caused car-hire services to expand their coverage.

25. We possibly overstate the gains because people must choose their next-best alternative mode to Uber when they may get higher utility by choosing not to travel if Uber is not a viable option. But this upward bias is undoubtedly much smaller than the downward bias from holding the size of the travel market constant.

times. Thus, we may be understating the fare benefits from Uber by estimating taxi fares based on standard taxi-fare policies, as summarized previously, instead of using the taxi charges that travelers actually pay. Uber and other ridesharing companies have addressed this information problem with a transparent pricing system, which requires a receipt for the passenger with the name of the driver and a map of the actual journey.

Other Effects of Uber

The available evidence suggests that a full social welfare analysis of Uber, which would go beyond its effect on travelers and account for its effect on automobile-related externalities, including safety, congestion, and emissions, and on other modes and the automobile industry, would not overturn our finding that its effect on society is positive.

Uber is likely to improve safety by providing trips during the evening to travelers who have been drinking or who have been working late and are too tired to drive. Empirical research on the effect of ridesharing on traffic fatalities has yielded inconsistent conclusions. Recently, Anderson and Davis (2021) use proprietary data from Uber to measure rideshare activity more accurately than previous work and find that ridesharing has a robust negative effect on traffic fatalities, which concentrate during nights and weekends, and has decreased US alcohol-related traffic fatalities by 6.1 percent and reduced total US traffic fatalities by 4.0 percent.[26]

Uber's effect on congestion is controversial because although it reduces congestion caused by taxis that cruise for passengers in dense urban areas, it also could cause congestion if it generates more trips during peak travel periods. Li et al. (2022) find that the entry of Uber has mixed effects on traffic congestion, decreasing it in sprawling urban areas and increasing it in compact urban areas.[27]

In any case, the efficient policy is not to limit Uber operations, but for policymakers to set an efficient congestion toll for all motor vehicles that could simultaneously address multiple automobile-related externalities (Langer, Maheshri, and Winston 2017; Winston and Yan 2021). Leard and Xing (2020) conclude that the availability of ridesharing has led to modest increases in total vehicle miles traveled and greenhouse gas emissions; but efficiency calls for setting emission charges on all motor vehicles and fuels to reduce the social costs of pollution.[28]

---

26. Based on conventional estimates of the value of statistical life, the annual lifesaving benefits range from $2.3 billion to $5.4 billion.

27. Uber also might increase congestion when drivers drop off and pick up customers on a curb on the road.

28. Ward, Michalek, and Samaras (2021) simulate replacing private vehicle travel with TNCs in six US cities and find mixed effects of TNCs on emissions.

Ridesharing also has been criticized for plunging the taxi industry into a financial crisis and for displacing a significant portion of public transit trips in some large cities (Leard and Xing 2020).[29] Taxi's financial problems reflect outdated regulations that limit its operations and its inability to cater effectively to travelers' preferences. Indeed, taxis have yet to develop an effective platform using a smartphone application in most major US cities.

As of spring 2022, riders in some cities have been able to open the Uber app and choose a taxi. Uber then refers the request to the two taxi technology companies, Curb and CMT, who notify drivers to pick up the passengers. The fare is based on Uber's pricing and policies, including surge pricing, which can significantly increase the cost at peak times.

As we discussed in the previous chapter, public bus and rail transit are highly inefficient and require large taxpayer-funded subsidies that are likely to exceed their benefits to users (Winston 2013). Thus, ridesharing is increasing, not decreasing, social welfare when it captures some of transit's mode share because transit's ridership consists of highly subsidized passengers.

Uber provides a benefit to transit by licensing its ride-hailing software to public transit agencies. For example, Denver's Regional Transportation District is using Uber's software to manage its fleet of wheelchair-accessible vehicles. The Transportation Authority of Marin County is using Uber's software to facilitate requesting, matching, and tracking its own vehicle fleet.

The introduction of Uber and ridesharing in general has provided benefits to the automobile industry and dealers because it has induced people to purchase cars so they can provide ridesharing services. Ward et al. (2021) estimate that ridesharing has resulted in the ownership of at least 100,000 additional vehicles, although this figure may be partially offset by people who decide to eschew car ownership or to own fewer cars because of the availability of ridesharing.

Ridesharing's financial condition also is a matter of controversy and uncertainty. Uber has yet to be consistently profitable, but its market valuation of $50 billion before COVID-19 suggests that investors believe Uber will be highly profitable in the long run. Accordingly, ridesharing's producer surplus could offset its effect on the financial condition of the taxi industry and public transit.

Finally, ridesharing companies' relationship with labor has created uncertainty about their long-run profitability. The companies have resisted classifying drivers as employees, who would be able to legally obtain certain benefits and protections. In 2018, New York City became the first US city to require Uber and Lyft to pay their drivers a minimum wage. Koustas, Parrott, and Reich (2020) found

---

29. Leard and Xing (2020) show in their figure 4.2 the percentage of each mode, including transit and taxis, that travelers would use if ridesharing were not available. Meredith-Karam et al. (2021) find that transit and ridesharing barely complement each other, while Hall, Palsson, and Price (2018) find, on average, that Uber complements transit.

that the policy led to a modest increase in drivers' earnings and passengers' fares and to a modest decline in Uber's and Lyft's commission rates. And in 2020, a California judge ordered Uber and Lyft to treat their drivers as employees. We await other actions by policymakers and additional research before reaching a conclusion about the long-run distributional effects of labor market policies on ridesharing companies' profits, labor's earnings, and travelers' fares.[30]

6. Conclusion

Utility-maximizing travelers have improved their welfare by shifting to a new mode, ridesharing services, which has grown rapidly by competing effectively against taxi, transit, and private automobile alternatives. We quantified the benefits from the leading rideshare company, Uber, in San Francisco Bay Area markets, accounting for travelers' complete set of transportation options. We find that travelers have gained roughly $1 billion annually from Uber's service, and we argue that a full welfare analysis is more likely to strengthen than to weaken the conclusion that Uber has provided significant positive social benefits.

Nonetheless, ridesharing faces opposition from special interests that is aided and abetted by some policymakers in the United States and in some other countries who have introduced regulatory policies to limit ridesharing operations. Our findings suggest that such actions harm the public interest and that they should be resisted by the public because they unnecessarily interfere with their informed, self-interested transportation mode choices and the evolution toward a more competitive environment.

After decades of inefficiency and technological stagnation in urban transportation, ridesharing is a welcome private sector innovation that many travelers prefer to their private vehicles for certain trips and to government-regulated taxis and public transit. In the coming decades, ridesharing's competitive inroads are likely to expand. As we discuss in chapter 6, ridesharing is likely to operate autonomously in the long run and to further benefit travelers by replacing a large share of privately owned automobiles. Innovative efforts by entrepreneurs should not be discouraged by policymakers because they threaten entrenched financial or political interests, especially if they produce substantial social benefits by displacing less efficient modes of transportation.

---

30. Angrist, Caldwell, and Hall (2021) find that, compared with taxi, rideshare drivers' earnings improve considerably because they do not have to make a fixed payment for their weekly or daily medallion lease. Taxi medallions limit the supply of transportation service because drivers must own or lease a medallion granting them the right to drive. Cook et al. (2021) find that female Uber drivers earn 7 percent less than male drivers, but the difference is not due to discrimination. Instead, the difference can be explained by men driving faster, choosing to drive for more costly trips, and being more experienced, such as knowing when to strategically cancel and accept trips. Uber's pay gap has no implication for social justice because drivers are treated equally.

5

Consumer Adoption of Electric Vehicles: The Appropriate Role of the Private Sector and Government

CLIFFORD WINSTON AND JIA YAN

1. Introduction

The use of petroleum-based fuels, like gasoline, in internal combustion engines (ICEs) is a major source of air pollution that damages lung tissue and can aggravate and lead to repository diseases, such as asthma. In addition, ICEs account for some 10 percent of the world's greenhouse gas emissions and for nearly 25 percent of greenhouse gas emissions generated by the United States, trapping heat and contributing to climate change.[1]

The private sector's innovation of electric vehicles (EVs) powered by an electric motor instead of an ICE can improve human health and the environment by significantly reducing externalities stemming from gasoline and diesel use. At long last, this innovation is gaining measurable public adoption, as indicated by EVs' growing share of new car sales in the United States, which has increased from roughly 2 percent in 2020, 4 percent in 2021, and 5 percent in 2022, and is expected to exceed 10 percent in 2023.[2] Surveys indicate consumers' growing interest in EVs, as 36 percent of Americans are considering purchasing an

---

1. According to the Environmental Protection Agency, transportation is the largest single source of greenhouse gases generated by the United States, representing 29 percent of the nation's total emissions. Within transportation, light-duty vehicles account for 58 percent of the greenhouse gas emissions and medium- and heavy-duty trucks account for 24 percent of the greenhouse gas emissions.

2. Colin Velez, "J. D. Power Believes the EV Market Will Outperform 2023 Predictions," CBT News, December 20, 2022, https://www.cbtnews.com/j-d-power-believes-the-ev-market-will-out-perform-2023-predictions/.

EV with 25 percent saying that their next vehicle purchase will be an EV.[3] EVs also have become a priority for automakers, as indicated by the $0.5 trillion the industry is on track to invest during the next five years to accelerate the transition to EVs (Ewing and Boudette 2022).

Because there are strong elements in society that are rightfully concerned about the damage that cars inflict on the environment, and because those elements generally do not trust the private sector to take steps on their own to improve the environment, federal and state policymakers have intervened to spur the public's adoption of EVs without drawing much criticism. It is reasonable for the government to take actions, such as implementing efficient emissions taxes or command-and-control policies, to curb a significant externality like vehicle emissions. However, federal government policies toward EVs have eschewed those policies and instead subsidized the price for EVs paid by consumers and allocated funds to construct EV charging stations. The California Air Resources Board has gone a step further and banned the sales of new ICE vehicles by 2035, with intermediate requirements that 35 percent of new passenger vehicles sold by 2026 and 68 percent by 2030 produce no carbon emissions during their operation.

In this chapter, we review the history of EVs' development and the sector's competitive environment, and we discuss the factors that influence households' adoption of EVs.[4] We then consider the efficient mix of market forces and government policy that determines the path that households and automakers should take to make the transition from gasoline-powered to electric vehicles, thus enabling society to benefit from an innovation that curbs harmful vehicle emissions.

We conclude that it would be more efficient if government allowed competitive automakers to take the lead in determining the pace that consumers throughout the nation are encouraged to adopt EVs by not only resolving EVs' remaining technological problems but also by investing in the fast EV charging infrastructure to support EV use. For its part, government should set efficient highway user fees for EVs, enable lithium to be mined more quickly in the United States to facilitate critical lithium-ion battery projects, and ensure that the electric power grid is sufficiently reliable to power the growing fleet of EVs and sufficiently clean so that substituting EVs for gasoline-powered vehicles significantly reduces air pollution and greenhouse gas emissions. Subsidizing EV consumers and investing in EV charging stations is likely to be an unnecessarily costly and potentially counterproductive strategy to achieve those goals.

---

3. Keith Naughton, "A Quarter of Americans Say Their Next Car Will Be an EV," Bloomberg, July 13, 2022, https://www.bloomberg.com/news/articles/2022-07-13/a-quarter-of-americans-say-their-next-car-will-be-an-ev.

4. We point out in chapter 12 that the trucking industry will eventually replace diesel fuel to power trucks with either electric batteries or hydrogen fuel cells.

2. A Brief History of Electric Vehicles and the Current Competitive Environment

Like many innovations, a series of breakthroughs—in this case, in batteries and electric motors—led to the development of the electric vehicle in the 1800s.[5] Practical versions first appeared in France and England, while the first successful electric car, with a top speed of fourteen miles per hour, made its debut in the United States around 1890. By 1900, electric cars accounted for roughly one-third of all vehicles on the road, including steam- and gasoline-powered vehicles, and they continued to show strong sales during the next ten years. Urban residents found electric cars suitable for short trips around the city; poor road conditions outside cities meant few cars of any type could venture farther.

Henry Ford's mass-produced Model T emerged as a formidable competitor to the electric car. Introduced in 1908, the Model T made gasoline-powered cars widely available and affordable. By 1912, the gasoline car cost only $650, while an electric roadster sold for $1,750. That same year, Charles Kettering introduced the electric starter, eliminating the need for the hand crank and giving rise to more gasoline-powered vehicle sales.

By the 1920s, the United States had a more expansive system of roads connecting cities, and Americans wanted to explore the country by automobile. With the discovery of crude oil in Texas, gasoline became cheap and readily available for rural Americans, and gas stations began popping up across the country. In comparison, very few Americans outside of cities had electricity at that time. By 1935, electric vehicles had all but disappeared from passenger transportation.

During the early 1970s, soaring oil prices and gasoline shortages—peaking with the 1973 Arab oil embargo—revived interest in electric cars to reduce US dependence on foreign oil. Congress took note and passed the Electric and Hybrid Vehicle Research, Development, and Demonstration Act of 1976, authorizing the US Department of Energy to support research and development in electric and hybrid vehicles.

In hindsight, it is not clear that government intervention was justified to spur the adoption of electric vehicles to reduce the nation's dependence on foreign oil. Markets did, in fact, respond to fuel woes on their own. For example, Honda and Toyota were able to obtain a strong toehold in the US market in the 1970s by offering ICE cars that were far more fuel efficient and reliable than American offerings. By the time US automakers responded, the Japanese automakers had developed brand loyalty among purchasers of smaller vehicles (Mannering and Winston 1991), and they would build on that loyalty to attract consumers of all

---

5. The historical summary that follows draws heavily on Matulka (2014).

vehicle sizes. Today, Japanese automakers' share of new car sales in the United States exceeds that of US automakers.

Congress should have allowed the market to determine whether automakers were able to offer an electric vehicle that would be sufficiently attractive to consumers to enable automakers to make a profit on it in the long run. If Congress wanted to incentivize consumer demand for electric vehicles efficiently, they should have implemented taxes on vehicle miles traveled that included a charge for vehicle emissions, which would have raised the operating costs of gasoline-powered vehicles and made EVs relatively more attractive to car buyers (Langer, Mahesrhi, and Winston 2017).

As it turned out, automakers began to explore options for developing alternative-fuel vehicles during the 1970s, including electric cars. For example, General Motors (GM) developed a prototype for an urban electric car that it displayed at the Environmental Protection Agency's First Symposium on Low Pollution Power Systems Development in 1973, and the American Motors Corporation produced electric delivery Jeeps that the United States Postal Service used in a 1975 test program. However, those and other electric vehicles still did not compare favorably with gasoline-powered cars in terms of performance and range. Their top speeds usually did not exceed forty-five miles per hour, and their typical range was limited to forty miles before needing to be recharged. Given their low scale of production, electric vehicles also suffered from a cost disadvantage, which was masked by subsidies provided in the 1976 electric vehicles act. Since then, subsidies to both consumers and automakers have continued to be a mainstay of the EV market.[6]

Government involvement in EVs and market forces have continued to evolve, but it is far from clear that government policy has played a constructive role in promoting consumer adoption of EVs. For example, Toyota and Honda introduced hybrid gas-and-electric vehicles during the 1990s without government support, which increased the likelihood that electric vehicles would become a viable part of the US vehicle fleet.

A major change in the EV market occurred when Tesla announced in 2006 that it would start producing a luxury electric sports car. In 2010, Tesla received a $465 million loan from the US Department of Energy's Loan Programs Office—a loan that Tesla repaid a full nine years early—to establish a manufacturing facility in California. In light of Tesla's prompt repayment, it is likely that Tesla could have turned to private markets to get a loan instead of getting it from the government.

---

6. Government subsidies to support innovations that lead to significant social benefits can be justified. However, Winston (2021c) points out that many government efforts to spur innovations amounted to funding that would have been undertaken by the private sector if it believed that it would be profitable to do so.

In any event, Tesla's subsequent success spurred many large automakers to accelerate work on their own electric vehicles. In late 2010, the Chevy Volt and the Nissan Leaf were released in the US market. The first commercially available plug-in hybrid, the Volt featured a gasoline-powered engine that supplemented its electric drive once the battery was depleted, allowing consumers to drive on electricity for most trips and gasoline to extend the vehicle's range. In comparison, the Leaf is an all-electric vehicle. Other automakers began rolling out electric vehicles in the United States to the point where dozens of plug-in electric and hybrid models were available from several different automakers in a variety of sizes.

3. The Current Competitive Environment and EV Performance

Although electric vehicles are gaining acceptance in the United States, their market share ranked tenth among the ten countries with the highest penetration rates.[7] Tesla dominates the US market with roughly 75 percent of sales, while GM, for example, has only a 6 percent share. From a global perspective, in the first half of 2022, BYD, based in Shenzhen, China, sold more EVs and plug-in hybrid vehicles than Tesla sold.

In the coming years, Tesla will be challenged, as BYD plans to sell its e6 in US markets in 2023, and as established automakers and startup companies compete as market conditions allow. For example, GM is planning to go all-electric by 2035 and is investing nearly $7 billion in Michigan to build a new battery plant and to overhaul an existing factory to make electric trucks. GM also has announced a partnership with Honda to codevelop electric vehicles to reduce production costs and introduce significant price competition to the EV market, with new EVs priced below $30,000. The partnership centers around using GM's Ultium EV platform and both automakers' robust manufacturing capabilities. The vehicles are expected to be available in North America in 2027.

Ford has already attracted considerable attention by announcing the production of the all-electric F-150 Lightning. The gas-powered Ford F-150 is the best-selling vehicle in the US, so it is not surprising that more than 200,000 people signed up for the waitlist for the electric F-150 shortly after Ford announced plans for its production. Finally, many startups have entered the EV market, including Rivian, Lucid, Fisker, and several others. It is likely that at least a few will survive the shakeout and provide notable competition.

Electric vehicles still face the fundamental challenges of being cost-competitive with gasoline-powered cars, including their purchase price and the costs of

---

7. Norway leads all countries with electric vehicles accounting for roughly 75 percent of all new car sales. Norway promoted EVs by exempting purchasers from the country's vehicle purchase tax and its 25 percent value-added tax. Extensive charging infrastructure began with government funds, followed by private sector investment.

insurance, maintenance, deprecation, battery replacement, and electricity, as well as of providing sufficient driving range to makes them attractive substitutes for gasoline-powered vehicles. EVs have cost advantages in lower fuel and maintenance costs, but to promote efficient adoption their full costs must come down to match the full cost of gasoline-powered cars without consumers receiving subsidies.

It appears, however, that EVs will continue to be subsidized by state and federal governments. Although the $7,500 federal tax credit for the purchase of Tesla and GM electric vehicles was eliminated as of April 2020 and federal subsidies for other EV models depend on their battery capacity and are limited by their manufacturers' cumulative EV sales, the Inflation Reduction Act of 2022 provides new opportunities for savings on buying an EV. The law extends the current $7,500 tax credit for a new EV and provides a $4,000 tax credit for a used EV. It also eliminates the current cap that cuts automakers off tax credits after they have sold 200,000 EVs, and it is written so buyers can get an immediate discount at the dealership, instead of waiting weeks or months for their tax credit to come through.

An important caveat is that automakers and consumers are unlikely to be able to take advantage of this tax credit over the next few years because of the time it will take automakers to transform their operations to satisfy the tax credit's requirements that EVs be built in North America and their batteries not come from China.[8] Finally, states also provide varying subsidies. For example, the California Clean Vehicle Rebate Project offers qualified consumers rebates of up to $7,000 for plug-in hybrid and fully electric vehicles.

Batteries are another important component of the competitive interface between EVs and gasoline-powered cars. Most EV batteries do not provide enough range for trips beyond urban travel, and they take far longer to charge than refilling a conventional car's gas tank.[9] Range anxiety exists because there is sparse provision of chargers in lightly populated areas. For example, the 550 miles between Reno and Salt Lake City has only a few chargers. The private sector is investing large sums in new kinds of vehicle batteries that will reduce the cost and increase the range of an EV. However, no one can predict how soon and how much better the next generation of EV batteries will be, or the stability of raw materials prices.[10]

8. The tax credit also is limited to trucks, vans, and SUVs under $80,000, and other vehicles under $55,000, and has an income threshold for consumers.

9. EVs can be charged at home or at a charging station. Charging may take thirty minutes or several hours, depending on the size of the battery and the speed of the charging point.

10. For example, the Mercedes-Benz Vision EQXX may get as much as six hundred miles on a single charge. However, it is not clear when it will be available with that range or what it will cost. China's Guangzhou Automobile Group has the Aion LX Plus, which it claims can drive more than six hundred miles on a single charge. And Apple is targeting 2024 to produce a passenger vehicle that could include its own breakthrough battery technology, which could significantly reduce the cost of batteries and increase an EV's range.

Technology that enables EVs to be charged while they are stationary or moving on a road would calm EV range anxiety, but such dynamic charging requires a costly investment to put electric coils underneath the pavement and to connect the road system to the electric grid, so its economic viability is questionable.[11] Alternatively, both public and private sectors intend to put more EV charging stations on roads and to increase their speed, which again raises the question of who should bear responsibility for this investment.

4. An Appraisal of Government Interventions in Electric Vehicles

Government efforts to advance automobile performance have incurred considerable waste when the market could have achieved the desired result more efficiently without costing taxpayers. A textbook demonstration of this point occurred in 1993 when the Clinton administration initiated the "Partnership for a New Generation of Vehicles" with domestic automakers in hopes of producing a high-gas-mileage car using a hybrid propulsion system by the decade's end. At a cost to taxpayers of $1.5 billion, the goal was never accomplished (Winston 2006), yet the two automakers—Honda and Toyota—that began offering hybrid vehicles to American consumers in the 1990s received none of the subsidy.

Electric Vehicles' Market Share

A similarly inefficient outcome has developed in the market for electric vehicles. Despite decades of US taxpayer–funded subsidies to jump-start motorists' adoption of electric vehicles, the EV market share is still too small to affect environmental quality. President Biden intends to spur a dramatic change in EVs' market share, as indicated by setting a national goal that 50 percent of all new cars in the United States be electric by 2030. The subsidies contained in the Inflation Reduction Act of 2022 will help to achieve that goal, but only to a modest extent.

President Biden has failed to consider the role of market forces, even though the incentives for automakers to develop electric vehicles that can displace gasoline-powered vehicles without federal subsidies have grown sharply in recent years, as indicated by the growing interest by consumers who plan to purchase an EV and by manufacturers including, Ford, General Motors, Mercedes-Benz, and Volkswagen, which have set out multibillion-dollar plans to sell only zero-emission vehicles within the coming two decades.

Accordingly, government should stop trying to rush the transition from gasoline-powered vehicles to EVs by setting arbitrary targets, which erroneously serve to justify continued subsidization of automakers' production and sale of

11. Michigan has awarded a contract to Electreon to build the first electric vehicle charging road in the United States by 2023. The roadway would be in the Michigan Central district and could charge electric vehicles while they are in motion or stationery.

electric vehicles. Lieberman (2021) points out that government actions have been regressive because nearly 80 percent of federal tax credits for EVs have gone to households with gross incomes of $100,000 or more after adjusting for certain taxes and deductions.

It also is not yet clear that EVs improve the environment on net, because they may generate more emissions than similar fossil fuel–powered vehicles in certain areas, largely due to the production of batteries and emissions from generating the electricity they require. Rapson and Muehlegger (2021) and Holland et al. (2016) find there is considerable heterogeneity by location and among motorists' accumulated travel when attempting to determine whether the environmental benefits of an electric vehicle compared with a gasoline-powered vehicle are positive or negative. This ambiguity is likely to change in favor of the superiority of electric vehicles as their batteries continue to improve and as electricity generation produces less pollution (Holland et al. 2020).[12]

EV Charging Stations

To help achieve his target, President Biden signed into law a $1 trillion infrastructure package that he initiated, which includes $7.5 billion in subsidies to fund a nationwide network of some 500,000 EV charging stations by 2030, up from the fewer than 50,000 such stations across the entire country today. The stations will be built in Alternative Fuel Corridor designations in all fifty states, as well as Washington, DC, and Puerto Rico.[13]

Although well intentioned, such subsidies may be wasteful if they add considerable charging capacity in many areas long before the demand for it exists or if they are installed in areas where few households own and drive EVs. In addition, car and truck drivers taking long-distance trips will be greatly inconvenienced if they do not have access to fast-charging stations, which will require more acreage. Generally, urban and suburban motorists have been able to charge their EVs overnight at home or, in some cases, at workplaces. Policymakers and some economists have argued that government subsidies are justified because a so-called chicken-and-egg problem (Li et al. 2017) exists between EVs and EV charging stations. The implication is that a suboptimal level of electric vehicle adoption could result because consumers will not buy EVs until charging stations are available en route, while companies will not put in charging stations until there is sufficient demand for EVs. To transportation economists, the problem is like the fundamental challenge facing transportation firms of aligning capacity with demand when capacity must be committed in advance

---

12. Nunes, Woodley, and Rossetti (2022) show that household purchase behavior and use of EVs also contribute to their effect on emissions.

13. The California Public Utilities Commission has approved a $1 billion vehicle electrification project with most of the funds used for charging medium- and heavy-duty trucks.

of demand and when demand and capacity influence each other. For example, airlines must commit to providing a level of capacity in advance of passenger demand by purchasing or leasing planes and choosing which routes to serve and how often to serve them. Those choices affect schedule delay (the difference between a traveler's preferred departure time and actual departure time), which is an important aspect of service quality that affects passenger demand for air transportation. At the same time, passenger demand affects airlines' capacity investment decisions.

Airlines have addressed the problem by forecasting macroeconomic performance and passenger demand and expanding (or contracting) their aircraft fleets, adjusting flight frequency, and changing the cities they serve to align their capacity with expected demand. To be sure, airlines make forecasting errors, but they adjust fares and capacity to reduce the financial cost of those errors (Morrison and Winston 1995). However, to the best of our knowledge, no one has justified continual government intervention in the airline industry because carriers may make forecast errors.

Airline fares and entry and exit were regulated because the industry was alleged to have characteristics of a natural monopoly that would lead to destructive competition. Yet the airline industry became *more* competitive after it was deregulated, and the intensified competition spurred the industry to greatly improve its efficiency and to become more profitable (Morrison and Winston 1999).[14]

The deregulation experience revealed that one must use caution when claiming market failures may prevent competition from working efficiently. The alleged market failures in transportation, such as those stemming from economies of density and scale, have reflected a mix of carriers' technology and regulatory restrictions that prevented inefficient operations. When transportation firms were deregulated, they had both the managerial ability and economic incentive to reduce excess capacity and operate more efficiently, thereby reducing costs and prices and increasing social welfare.

While the chicken-and-egg problem as applied to electric vehicles is a plausible theory and network externalities in the provision of EV charging stations may exist (whereby providing additional charging locations makes other locations more valuable to EV owners), those factors are not sufficient to justify government

14. Morrison and Winston (1986) assessed whether airline deregulation led to the social optimum, accounting for fares and service frequency, and found that it came close but that travelers originating at nonhubs and small hubs could benefit from additional service. We are not aware of more recent assessments, which could show that airlines have provided more service to nonhubs and small hubs over time. Chapter 7 reports that low-cost and ultra-low-cost carriers currently serve routes that account for a large fraction of US passengers. Morrison and Winston (1986) also found that government's effort to increase service to small communities by providing subsidies through the Essential Air Service program resulted in less, not more, airline service to small communities because the program masked profit opportunities for carriers and discouraged additional entry to airports serving those communities.

subsidies for EV charging stations for several reasons. These include inherent private sector incentives to correct potential market failures, private provision of EV charging stations, the significant potential for government failure in providing charging infrastructure, and the availability of an efficient approach (vehicle-miles-traveled charges) to spur electric vehicle adoption.[15]

PRIVATE SECTOR INCENTIVES. The electric vehicle industry has a strong incentive to spur EV adoption by increasing the availability of fast-charging stations to help incentivize consumers to prefer EVs over a gasoline-powered car when they conduct a full cost comparison of those vehicles. Accounting for the cost of the gas and electricity and the value of time spent waiting to "fill up" a vehicle, it could cost drivers more to find an electric charger and charge an electric vehicle compared with filling up a gasoline-powered car unless they have access to a charger at home, which would allow them to charge the EV overnight.

Fast-charging stations that significantly reduce wait times when charging an EV could change the outcome of this comparison and possibly alter the full cost comparison.[16] Dorsey, Langer, and McRae (2022) find that motorists place a high value of time on having to refuel their vehicles and that those who purchase electric vehicles and rely on home chargers would receive significant benefits by eliminating the travel and waiting time costs. Importantly, they find that increasing the charging speed of existing EV chargers would yield nearly five times greater time savings than a proportional increase in the number of charging stations.

PRIVATE SECTOR BEHAVIOR. Historically, the major oil companies created and expanded the US network of gasoline stations without government subsidies. During the 1930s, the oil companies began to lease independently operated stations to local dealers. The oil giants are cognizant of the challenge to their business today as households transition from gasoline-powered to electric vehicles and they oppose government efforts to subsidize electric vehicles and charging facilities.

At the same time, oil companies are taking constructive steps to play a role in an EV future. For example, BP claims the use of its pulse EV chargers is "on the cusp" of being more profitable for the company than filling up an internal combustion–powered car with gas, and they plan to grow their fast-charging business (Borrás 2022). Other oil companies are likely to do the same. Shell entered the EV charging industry by purchasing Greenlots in 2019, an American

---

15. Li et al. (2017) find that the same amount of subsidy spent on building charging stations could result in twice as many EV sales as that spent on subsidizing demand. However, it is difficult to separate causality between charging stations and EVs, while the policy issue at hand is whether spending public money to build EV charging stations is justified because it would significantly improve social welfare.

16. Fast charging may decrease battery capacity over time depending on the EV model and the climate where it is operated.

company that operates fast EV chargers, and plans to rebrand it as Shell Recharge Solutions. Shell USA recently purchased the EV charging company Volta. The combination of Greenlots and Volta will total over 57,000 charging stalls under the Shell brand with plans for Shell Recharge Solutions to operate some 500,000 charge points by 2025.[17]

Currently, most of the fast chargers in the United States have been deployed by Tesla via its proprietary Supercharger network. After intense lobbying from the Biden administration, Tesla has committed to opening roughly 20 percent of its Supercharger network to non-Tesla EVs in the United States by the end of 2024 and has already made deals with Ford and General Motors to give their vehicles access to its charger network. General Motors is launching a program with its dealers to add more than forty thousand Level 2 chargers in local US and Canadian rural communities and other areas underserved by charging infrastructure.[18] Other major providers include EVgo, which is partnering with GM and plans to deploy more than 3,250 charging stations across the country by 2025;[19] Pilot, a travel operator, which is partnering with GM and plans to develop a national network of two thousand EV charging stalls at travel centers to make it easier to recharge near highways; and Electrify America, which is investing $2 billion in US EV charging as part of Volkswagen's Dieselgate settlement agreement. Mobility startups, including, for example, Gravity Mobility, Revel, and Beam Global, are trying to make EV charging faster and easier in urban environments. Finally, TeraWatt Infrastructure has raised more than $1 billion to build EV charging stations for commercial fleets of cars, delivery vans, and trucks.

Commercial firms also see an opportunity to provide EV charging facilities to promote their product. For example, Starbucks is partnering with Volvo and ChargePoint, which operates a network of independently owned EV charging stations in 14 countries, to install EV chargers in its parking lots along a 1,350-mile route from Denver to Seattle, with stops available every one hundred miles. Current plans call for a total of sixty fast chargers to be installed at fifteen Starbucks locations along the route. Other retailers are expected to follow the Starbucks experiment closely, and some are likely to replicate it.

Commercial firms also are expanding their provision of charging stations at their locations. For example, Walmart plans to add fast EV charging stations

---

17. Tom Moloughnet, "Greenlots Renamed: Will Soon Become Shell Recharge Solutions," InsideEVs November 3, 2021, https://insideevs.com/news/545338/greenlots-renamed-shell-recharge-solutions/.

18. Level 2 chargers double the charge speed of Level 1 units, and in most cases add around twenty or so miles of range to car batteries for every hour that it is plugged in. Effectively that means the car must be plugged in overnight to travel a significant distance the next day.

19. EVgo also is partnering with Amazon to allow Alexa, Amazon's voice-activated virtual assistant, to navigate EV drivers to public charging spots and pay for the service.

nationwide to more than a thousand Walmart and Sam's Club stores by 2030, which will more than quadruple its current network of roughly 280 locations.

Interstate Highway rest areas would be a promising venue for commercial EV charging stations.[20] However, by federal law they cannot be used because commercialization of rest areas is prohibited to protect off-Interstate truck stop owners, which is prompting some states to close rest areas. Repealing the law could allow states to partner with private concessionaires to build modern travel plazas (as seen on toll roads that were grandfathered into the Interstate Highway System) along with EV charging stations. Finally, EV charging stations also are not listed in the federal network of alternative fueling and charging infrastructure unless they are located less than five miles from an off-ramp.

In any case, the major oil and automobile companies, commercial firms, and startups are helping to expand the nation's network of fast-charging stations, although it is not clear that all those enterprises will continue to do so as the EV industry and charging network matures. As expected, EV chargers are currently concentrated in areas with high rates of EV adoption, which typically means wealthier neighborhoods. However, like gas stations, the disparity in charging access should decline as companies find it profitable to put in new stations to cater to a broader spectrum of drivers, including drivers who work for rideshare companies like Lyft and Uber that have promised to make the shift to all-electric fleets over the coming decades.

Finally, automobile companies, such as the Chevrolet division of General Motors, are offering to obtain the required permits and to install chargers for its Bolt EVs at no cost in an owner's home or other location.[21] And automobile companies are providing apps that indicate the location of the closest charger to a motorist's location.

In sum, the private sector's strong interest and widespread actions to develop a nationwide EV charging network cast strong doubt on the chicken-and-egg justification for government investments in charging infrastructure to promote the purchase and use of EVs as replacements for gasoline-powered vehicles.

GOVERNMENT BEHAVIOR. The claim that the US government can finance the creation and expansion of the EV charging station network efficiently assumes that policymakers have all the information they need to solve this optimal dynamic investment problem, the ability to implement investment decisions quickly and efficiently, and the flexibility to modify those decisions to adapt to changing technology and market conditions. Those assumptions are highly questionable

20. Robert W. Poole Jr., "Rethinking Interstate Rest Areas," Reason Foundation, April 2021, https://reason.org/wp-content/uploads/rethinking-interstate-rest-areas.pdf.

21. Chevrolet, "Living Electric: Home Charging," https://www.chevrolet.com/electric/living-electric/home-charging.

because government has no established track record in making similar dynamic public investment decisions efficiently.

At the same time, government does have an established track record of misallocating large public expenditures to improve the highway network (Winston and Langer 2006) and air traffic control (Morrison and Winston 2008) by spending funds in areas of the country that yield low benefit–cost ratios. Accordingly, it seems likely that government would waste public funds by building charging stations in places where travelers use them infrequently while failing to build them where travelers' demand is strong.[22]

In addition, government spending on EV chargers could generate social costs by providing disincentives for the private sector to invest in the charging network. For example, as part of the Biden administration's subsidies for EV charging stations, private businesses like hotels and attractions can submit bids for grants to help pay for charging stations at their destination. Although it is possible that those charging stations may be limited to their customers, federal grants may discourage private businesses, such as Starbucks, which is already planning to install unsubsidized, public, EV charging stations, from doing so. In addition, Ferris (2023) points out that virtually every automaker has said that it intends to seek help from the federal government to build some of their charging stations.

Responses to federal government actions by certain states and the private sector identify further problems. For example, the Biden administration's plan to make fast EV charging stations available every fifty miles along major highways, including those in the rural western and midwestern states, is likely to result in building charging stations where travelers use them infrequently. For this reason, some states that are receiving federal funds as part of the 2021 Infrastructure Investment and Jobs Act plan to request waivers of the requirement to build chargers every fifty miles. Wyoming projected that the charging stations the administration wants would not be profitable until the 2040s; thus, the federal funding that lasts only five years would saddle the state with a massive bill for over a decade.

Private investors may reduce their investment in charging stations if states enable regulated utilities, which have competitive advantages because they are subsidized by ratepayer funds, to own charging stations.[23]

---

22. Gabe Klein at the new Joint Office of Energy and Transportation is responsible for overseeing the $7.5 billion to support the construction of EV charging stations over five years. However, Klein has no experience working at the federal level where he will have to mediate various competing interests for government funding.

23. One might argue that in rural areas, where average trip distances tend to be long, the lack of charging infrastructure is an impediment to greater EV ownership levels and that government intervention to build chargers every fifty miles is justified. However, if the lack of charging infrastructure is holding back EV ownership levels in rural areas, the private sector can take advantage of this market opportunity by providing "en route" charging services, which would respond to rural drivers' demand for available charging services for their long-distance trips.

OPTIMAL POLICY. The issue of whether the government should spend public funds on electric chargers to spur EV adoption should be considered in the larger context of the welfare-maximizing policy to reduce vehicle emissions externalities. Langer, Maheshri, and Winston (2017) provide evidence that a VMT tax could generate large social welfare gains, including the reduction of vehicle pollution costs.[24]

Yet, proponents of government expenditures on charging stations claim that a VMT tax would produce a suboptimal level of welfare improvement because it would not address the chicken-and-egg problem. However, given the absence of compelling evidence to the contrary, government spending would, at best, produce a small welfare gain in an environment with a VMT tax and investments by the private sector to develop and expand EV charging facilities nationwide, and would more likely produce a welfare loss because of inefficiencies associated with its dynamic investment decisions and implementation of them.[25]

Finally, as discussed in the next chapter, the chicken-and-egg problem will be eliminated when autonomous electric vehicles are fully integrated into the US transportation system as private companies provide mobility as a service (MaaS) and travelers share but do not own autonomous electric vehicles. In such an environment, private MaaS firms will ensure that the fast-charging network caters effectively to their operations, if necessary, by investing in charging stations themselves.

5. The Appropriate Role for the Private Sector and Government in the Electric Vehicle Market

We have argued that consumers can adopt EVs efficiently by responding to the evolving offerings of private auto companies and that government subsidies to purchase EVs are unnecessary to make that occur. Evidence exists that some consumers are willing to pay as much as $7,000 extra for an EV than for a gasoline-

---

24. Full efficiency calls for the electricity that is used to charge electric vehicles to be priced efficiently. Borenstein and Bushnell (2022) find that electricity prices are generally set above marginal cost, especially in California where regulators have mandated large subsidies for low-income households. Specifically, low-income customers that are enrolled in the California Alternative Rates for Energy program receive a 30 to 35 percent discount on their electric bill and a 20 percent discount on their natural gas bill.

25. Advocates of government spending on EV charging stations may still argue that such spending is justified even if funds are wasted because of the existential threat posed by damage to the environment caused in part by using vehicles powered by internal combustion engines. This argument assumes that the public sector is likely to construct an EV charging network faster than the private sector can or that public sector spending can jump-start private sector investment. Given the incentives that the private sector faces to expedite EV adoption, the current pace of the private sector's investment in EVs and in charging facilities, and chronic delays in public sector infrastructure investments, those assumptions are dubious.

powered vehicle because it contributes to reducing emissions (Gore 2021). We also have argued that the private sector can supply an adequate network of fast EV chargers to meet and encourage consumers' demand for EVs and that government expenditures are not justified by the alleged chicken-and-egg problem. As EV technology improves, the naturally growing share of EVs in the US vehicle fleet will enhance social welfare by reducing the costs of automobile emissions.

As noted, government has had the opportunity to and could still spur EV adoption by setting an efficient vehicle emissions charge as part of a tax on vehicle miles traveled, which would increase the per-mile cost of gasoline-powered vehicles relative to the per-mile cost of electric vehicles. In response to concerns that such charges would enable EV users to avoid taxation, an efficient emissions charge also should include EVs' environmental costs. However, the draconian step, as some have proposed, of a government ban on gasoline-powered vehicles after a certain date would be highly inefficient (Holland, Mansur, and Yates 2021) and could disrupt firms' production of and consumers' adoption to EVs and firms' provision of charging infrastructure.

Resources for Electric-Vehicle Production and Transportation

Electric vehicles require significant resources to produce their batteries and considerable electricity to operate on US roads. One of the key minerals for EV battery production is lithium, the chief component of lithium-ion batteries that power electric vehicles. Currently, most of the world's raw lithium is mined outside of the United States, with China controlling roughly three-fourths of the lithium-ion battery megafactories in the world.[26] The United States is among the top five countries in the world in terms of its lithium reserves, but only one lithium mine, Albemarle's Silver Peak in Nevada, is operating in the country.

Recently, the richest known hard rock lithium deposit in the world was discovered just north of Plumbago Mountain in Newry, Maine (Cline 2022). Other large potential domestic sources of lithium include extracting it from groundwater in the Salton Sea and processing it from spodumene ore from the Piedmont region of North Carolina. However, because of the lengthy permitting process to open a lithium mine and to extract lithium from its deposits, the domestic supply chain for EV battery production is slowed by several years. For example, permitting delays have prevented Piedmont Lithium from breaking ground for its lithium mine in North Carolina. Moreover, even after a permit had been granted many years ago to open the lithium mine in Nevada, environmental groups brought a lawsuit in 2021 to prevent it from operating.

---

26. Jeniece Pettitt, "How the US Fell Behind in Lithium, the 'White Gold' of Electric Vehicles," CNBC, January 15, 2022, https://www.cnbc.com/2022/01/15/how-the-us-fell-way-behind-in-lithium-white-gold-for-evs.html.

President Biden invoked the Defense Production Act in 2022 to help accelerate the creation of a domestic supply chain for EV manufacturing. However, President Biden's action will have little effect on getting critical lithium-ion battery projects running unless the permitting process for mining and raw material operations is significantly streamlined. Similarly, the Infrastructure Investment and Jobs Act signed in November 2021 includes more than $7 billion to help grow the battery supply chain, but it is not clear if those funds will be used constructively if regulatory constraints continue to impede lithium-ion battery projects.

Government also has a critical role to ensure that the United States has enough electricity generating capacity to supply EV transportation. For example, if 60 percent of all US cars were electric vehicles by 2050, the nation's electricity capacity would need to double to meet the nation's demand for electricity (Groom and Bellon 2021), which would require either a massive government investment in the electricity grid or a mechanism whereby private quasi-utilities could undertake those investments. At the same time, the government must respond effectively to various environmental groups that are likely to align with local NIMBY ("not in my backyard") groups to block new transmission lines and other technology.[27]

Autonomous Electric Vehicles

Automakers and technology firms will eventually combine electric vehicles with autonomous vehicles and offer those to the public. We have argued here that the government has inappropriately intervened in the adoption of electric vehicles and in the availability of charging stations. We argue in the next chapter that government must take certain actions immediately that will greatly benefit society by expediting the adoption of autonomous vehicles, which in turn will expedite the adoption of autonomous electric vehicles.

27. Governments also must make a careful decision about whether to spend public funds to construct EV charging roads. As noted, such roads could address the problem of range anxiety and eliminate the time costs of charging an EV because the EV could be charged while it uses the road. On the other hand, the cost of constructing EV charging roads may be considerable and the technology could be obsolete if technological improvements in batteries increase the range of an EV and if fast EV chargers are widely available for public use. Michigan plans to conduct the first test in the United States of embedded technology in the pavement that can charge electric vehicles while they are being driven.

6

Consumer Adoption of Autonomous Vehicles: The Appropriate Role of the Private Sector and Government

CLIFFORD WINSTON AND JIA YAN

1. Introduction

Autonomous vehicles (AVs) represent a significant innovation in transportation, which could eventually solve transportation problems that the public sector has failed to solve for many years, including the automobile-generated externalities of nerve-wracking congestion, millions of fatal and nonfatal accidents, and violent police confrontations with drivers. In addition, in a world where COVID-19 may be a persistent concern, AVs can facilitate greater economic activity without increasing the spread of the coronavirus. Yet, despite those and other potentially significant benefits from AVs and the fact that automakers and technology companies are planning to eventually combine electricity-powered vehicles with automated driving and navigation technologies to produce autonomous electric vehicles, the government has shown little interest in expediting their adoption.

In this chapter, we provide an overview of the history of autonomous vehicles and the technology they utilize, the competitive environment of the emerging AV industry, and AVs' potential benefits and costs.[1] We argue that government has a critical role to play in enabling the public to realize the full benefits from autonomous vehicles by establishing testing and public adoption protocols and by upgrading the highway and road infrastructure to facilitate AV operations.[2]

---

1. Parts of this chapter draw heavily on Winston (2021a) and Winston and Karpilow (2020).

2. Clearly, government must draw on engineering to upgrade the infrastructure, but it should do so in the most efficient way possible.

Government's failure to embrace this role will delay the adoption of autonomous vehicles in the United States and put America behind other countries that are prioritizing their adoption.

2. An Overview of Autonomous Vehicles

The Pentagon has long been interested in developing autonomous tanks for the battlefield and autonomous trucks to deliver food, fuel, and other supplies to soldiers engaged in combat. In 2004, through the Defense Advanced Research Projects Agency, the Pentagon sponsored its first autonomous vehicle competition. However, there was little interest among car companies in making a large investment to build and sell autonomous vehicles. Google and subsequently Waymo, its self-driving car project, took the lead in introducing autonomous vehicles to the world in the 2010s. A few years later, US and foreign automakers, technology firms, and various startup ventures were in hot pursuit, either by themselves or in partnerships. Today, the global autonomous vehicle industry is engaged in integrating the technologies necessary to produce autonomous vehicles, while hundreds of new companies are developing various components of those technologies.

An autonomous vehicle drives itself using a combination of onboard technologies to measure the distance of the car from various objects, including pedestrians, bicyclists, and other cars, and processing that information to produce navigation instructions and pilot the vehicle. GPS, supplemented with highly detailed up-to-date digital maps, locates other vehicles and indicates which one has the right of way. Communications among AVs, as well as between AVs and roadway infrastructure, determine the location and intention of other vehicles, the condition of the roadway, and the status of traffic signals. Cooperative automated driving, in which multiple (or even all) vehicles effectively communicate with one another using a local network, has the potential to smooth traffic flows, reduce travel time and increase its reliability, and virtually eliminate accidents along with the loss of life and property damage.

Because the technologies are advancing at such a rapid pace, with important breakthroughs occurring regularly in different parts of the world, it has become very difficult to keep up with the latest technological advances, new players, new partnerships, and new services in the United States and abroad. Although the timeline for widespread adoption of autonomous vehicles is still in decades, the various technological advancements are encouraging. Some of the most important recent developments in the United States and other countries include:

—MonoCon has enhanced AV visual capability by extracting three-dimensional data from two-dimensional camera views to cut an AV's reliance on lidar (light detection and ranging) while maintaining safety and slashing operating costs.

—X-ray-style vision technology enables autonomous vehicles to see pedestrians and cyclists through obstacles, and ground positioning radar that allows AVs to image a road's subsurface for precise positioning regardless of poor weather, bad visibility, or faint road markings. There is growing recognition that AVs will rely on a combination of sensing modalities, including visible light, near-infrared, thermal imaging, radar, and lidar.

—Techniques enable AVs to navigate complex traffic situations, such as merging into heavy traffic when lanes disappear on a highway (Tajalli, Niroumand, and Hajbabaie 2022).

—AV industry participants, including Google's Waymo, General Motors' (GM's) Cruise, Amazon's Zoox, and Aurora, are committed to offering full Level 4 or Level 5 autonomy.[3] GM's Cruise has petitioned the National Highway Traffic Safety Administration (NHTSA) for permission to put the driverless Level 4 (full automation within a restricted operational design domain) Cruise Origin into commercial service, with delivery of the vehicle beginning in 2023.

—In 2023, Mercedes-Benz received approval from Nevada and California for its Level 3 DRIVE PILOT technology, and will include it as an option in several of its model-year 2024 vehicles. BMW is widely expected to roll out Level 3 technology in its new 7 Series vehicles sold in China and Europe, but it is unlikely to try to certify a Level 3 car in the United States until uncertainties about liability are resolved. At Level 3, the driver can allow the car to operate under automation, but the system may prompt the driver to take over driving if it detects conditions outside of its automation capabilities.

—Sony is entering the global industry with an electric vehicle with autonomous features.[4]

—Apple is accelerating work on an electric car project, aiming for a fully autonomous vehicle by 2025.[5]

—Mobileye, an Israeli subsidiary of Intel, and Geely, China's largest automaker, are teaming up to build a self-driving car that will supposedly go on sale in

---

3. The Society of Automotive Engineers has created a widely accepted scale of automation systems, which ranges from Level 0 (no autonomy) to Level 5. Level 4 indicates systems that are self-driving but operate only under well-specified conditions, such as certain road types or geographic areas. The Operational Design Domain, spanning all scenarios that an AV may encounter, determines the difference between Level 4 versus Level 5 systems. Motorists have already grown accustomed to some level of independence from their cars thanks to advanced driver-assistance systems. Many vehicles, for instance, have collision-avoidance systems or parking-assistance features that place them at Level 1 or 2 on the scale. At Levels 3 to 5, the amount of control the system has increases.

4. Sony, Vision-S Concept, https://www.sony.com/en/SonyInfo/vision-s/safety.html.

5. The Apple car chip is the most advanced component that Apple has developed internally and is made up primarily of neural processors that can handle the artificial intelligence needed for autonomous driving.

China in 2024. Waymo is planning to work with Geely on a fleet of electric robotaxis.

—Autonomous delivery services are being provided by Nuro to deliver Domino's Pizza in Houston and elsewhere, while Waymo has launched its self-driving grocery delivery service in California.

—Fully autonomous passenger services also are being offered. In the United States, GM's Cruise received a permit to charge for fully driverless rides at nighttime in San Francisco, while Waymo is operating its cars without any human control in San Francisco and its robotaxis are providing service to travelers at Phoenix Sky Harbor International Airport. In China, Baidu is operating ride-hailing services without a driver or a person overseeing safety in the cities of Wuhan and Chongqing; AutoX, an Alibaba startup, is operating autonomous robotaxis in Shenzhen; and Baidu and Pony.ai, which is backed by Toyota, are starting robotaxi service in Beijing. The Chinese robotaxi companies also are testing their vehicles on California roads to draw the attention of global investors.

—The United Kingdom is working through legal issues to be resolved in advance of the first iterations of self-driving features on its driverless cars that are expected to be on its roads by 2025; a uniform law in Germany is helping German companies test AVs throughout the country; China is adopting 5G technology for car-to-car communication to help AV adoption; and Toyota's Woven City at the foot of Mount Fuji in Japan will have only autonomous cars, where the city's hand-picked residents will use them in a living laboratory (Davis 2021).

—Because there may be instances when humans must take over and drive an autonomous vehicle, for example, when the AV is operating in an environment that it cannot navigate, General Motors has submitted a design for an autonomous vehicle system to measure and train new drivers. It is an open question whether such training will exist after AVs are fully adopted and whether it will be required for drivers who use AVs in certain environments.

—Finally, AV companies are thinking about passengers' experience and exploring ways to prevent motion sickness that some people may experience when they focus on something within the cabin of the car, such as a book, and the senses in their brain cannot tell them whether they are moving or stationary. GM's Cruise has patented a system that can sense a passenger's motion sickness and prevent it from occurring.[6]

The growing number of places where autonomous vehicles are out on the roads and sidewalks carrying members of the public or cargo for them with no safety driver

---

6. Ibrahim, "GM is Developing Anti–Motion Sickness Tech for Autonomous Vehicles," Luxury Minds, June 15, 2022, https://www.luxury-minds.com/gm-is-developing-anti-motion-sickness-tech-for-autonomous-vehicles.

or other employee in the vehicle is summarized in an "AutonoMap," which can be updated.[7] Currently, autonomous services are largely in the United States and China, with some areas in Europe, Canada, Korea, and the Middle East. The Autono-Map will fill out as autonomous services continue to expand throughout the world.

Importantly, during the current period of investment and experimentation, capital markets are allocating capital to its best use. For example, Argo AI, an autonomous vehicle startup, was forced to shut down because it could not attract new investors; thus, its main backers, Ford and Volkswagen, decided to absorb its technology. At roughly the same time, Mobileye went public, and its shares rose nearly 40 percent, giving the company a valuation of roughly $23 billion. Leading mobility companies also are allocating their capital to its best use. For example, General Motors is making investments to develop autonomous vehicle technology, while Ford believes it can be part of the autonomous vehicle industry without helping to create the technology.

Notwithstanding the abundant recent activity in the global autonomous vehicle industry and much more to come, the skeptics are still skeptical. Winston and Winston (2022) report that AVs are described as "one of the most hyped technology experiments of this century," which are incapable of reversing the growing death toll on American roads for many years to come, if ever. The skeptics ignore that aviation in the early 1900s experienced many setbacks en route to its development as a successful commercial industry, with each setback identifying another problem that eventually was fixed.

In any case, the continuing rapid evolution of autonomous vehicles calls for increasing optimism that global competition and cooperation among auto companies and technology firms will succeed in developing a commercial AV industry that eventually will overcome any serious technological challenges. We return to the skeptics later, but we stress here that it is important not to arouse them by making unrealistic or false claims about when the adoption of autonomous vehicles will begin and when the turnover of the US vehicle fleet will be completed such that autonomous vehicles will account for a large share of highway transportation. It is reasonable to suggest that modest AV adoption will begin in a few decades but more precise estimates of the time frames for greater adoption are not available.

3. Benefits and Costs of Autonomous Vehicles

Autonomous vehicles' most important economic impact is likely to derive from their greater travel speed and reliability, compared with nonautonomous vehicles, which results from a smoother traffic flow as vehicles travel faster and closer

7. Brad Templeton, "This 'AutonoMap' Shows the Many Places Autonomous Vehicles Are Serving the Public Today," *Forbes*, January 17, 2023, https://www.forbes.com/sites/bradtempleton/2023/01/17/this-autonomap-shows-the-many-places-autonomous-vehicles-are-serving-the-public-today/.

together without causing accidents that can tie up traffic for hours, especially during rush hours. Note, too, that unlike drivers of nonautonomous vehicles, the software managing AVs would not be tempted to compound traffic slowdowns by rubbernecking past wreckage.

An improvement in average travel time and a reduction in the variation in travel time are likely to generate efficiency gains that extend well beyond the transportation sector by benefiting urban areas that are now facing limits linked to traffic and parking woes. Shorter and more reliable commute times would expand individuals' choices of employers and employers' choices of workers, adding a welcome increase in potential competition in local labor markets. As discussed in chapter 12, the cost of moving goods by truck would fall, raising productivity, increasing the flexibility of businesses to buy from the best or cheapest suppliers, and lowering logistics costs because firms would be able to reduce their inventories. By reducing firms' costs, autonomous trucks would thus reduce consumer prices.

Winston and Karpilow (2020) caution that no one knows with great precision how much the widespread adoption of AVs could raise the nation's annual economic growth rate. However, using conservative assumptions, they estimate that AVs could raise the nation's annual growth rate by at least one percentage point. Given that the construction of the Interstate Highway System greatly increased US welfare (Allen and Arkolokis 2014), it is intuitively plausible that AVs could generate enormous benefits by significantly reducing travel costs, which would greatly enhance the value of the highway network by exponentially increasing access to the nation's human and physical resources and enabling more people to work, shop, trade, and produce goods.

Importantly, by improving accessibility for disadvantaged travelers, the benefits from autonomous vehicles also would have positive distributional features. The improvements in accessibility would reduce the persistent differences in travel times between Black and white commuters that exist in large, segregated, congested, and expensive cities (Bunten et al. 2023) and would reduce the time-consuming commutes endured by carless households (Winston 2013). Shorter and more reliable commutes would reduce racial employment disparities, increase single mothers' employment and number of work hours per week, and reduce poverty and the use of welfare (Scribner 2021a).

Additional Benefits

Autonomous vehicles also could produce a host of other benefits, including improvements in public health, better access to leisure activities, more efficient land use, and even assistance in addressing two leading social problems: the COVID-19 pandemic and violent police confrontations.

PUBLIC HEALTH. AVs have the potential to produce improvements in public health by making highway travel far safer and by relieving drivers from the stress of driving in congested conditions. According to NHTSA, the social costs from motor vehicle crashes approach $1 trillion annually, accounting for the loss of life of some forty thousand people, injuries to roughly 4 million people, and economic losses from damage to 25 million vehicles.[8] Surveys indicate that commuting is the leading daily activity for which individuals' dominant attitude is negative (Kahneman and Krueger 2006). Indeed, automobile commuting in congested conditions can damage emotional health by causing stress that leads to road rage and household violence. AVs also could generate substantial health and productivity gains by converting stressed-out commuters to more relaxed passengers.

GREATER ACCESS TO LEISURE IN AND OUT OF THE VEHICLES. Manufacturers will have incentives to change the interiors of driverless vehicles to enable consumers to enjoy a variety of activities while traveling—among them, dining, watching movies, and sleeping during long intercity trips. Perrine, Kockelman, and Huang (2020) point out that autonomous vehicles could increase competition in intercity passenger transportation by capturing market share from aviation for trips that now require an hour or two by air (we return to this issue in chapter 10). Finally, autonomous vehicles will increase mobility for people who cannot drive without threatening public safety because of age, infirmity, or lack of a driver's license.

LAND USE. Currently, the United States has more parking spaces than cars, with many residential parking spaces going unused and downtown parking garages rarely full. Because it is widely expected by participants in the autonomous vehicle industry that people would generally share, not own, autonomous vehicles, valuable land that was once used for parking cars in central business districts and for home garages would be freed up to, say, build new housing, which could reduce the cost of housing, and expand existing homes.

The reduced parking footprint for suburban malls also could make land available for housing or other beneficial uses because AVs would leave passengers at designated drop-off zones and would then be directed to parking facilities in less-congested parts of metropolitan areas and in rural areas where they could be stacked vertically and easily retrieved when summoned.

Finally, AVs would weaken the justification for restrictive land-use policies such as parking requirements that aim to reduce congestion but which, in practice, have little effect on congestion and raise housing prices by increasing construction costs and reducing the quantity of available housing. For example, requirements in certain cities to build extra parking spaces for apartments reduce the available space for apartment units and significantly increase rents (Harrison 2023).

---

8. US Department of Transportation, "Traffic Safety Facts," May 2022, https://crashstats.nhtsa.dot.gov/Api/Public/ViewPublication/813298.

FEWER DISAMENITIES FROM HIGHWAYS. Brinkman and Lin (2022) discuss the disamenities associated with downtown freeways, which are reflected in population declines in census tracts nearest to freeways. Autonomous vehicles could potentially reduce the disamenities associated with living close to a freeway by reducing the presence of and noise associated with congestion; decreasing emissions as cars move more smoothly instead of idling (autonomous electric vehicles would produce an even greater decrease in emissions); and virtually eliminating accidents, which would further reduce congestion and the noise created by ambulance and police car sirens.

PANDEMICS. The world is increasingly accepting the likelihood that COVID-19 will be with us for the foreseeable future. AVs will prove invaluable by maintaining economic activity while facilitating social distancing for commuters and delivery services. Lower-paid essential service workers would especially gain by having access to sanitized vehicles for their sole use at manageable cost and, as discussed in chapter 2, by traveling in much safer highway conditions.

SAFE AND EFFICIENT POLICING. A large fraction of police work consists of enforcing traffic laws, which may result in violent encounters with drivers. On average, more than one officer per week is killed in a highway accident, accounting for nearly one-third of all police officer deaths in the line of duty. There also have been high-visibility motorist deaths at the hands of the police that resulted from an alleged traffic violation. AVs could virtually eliminate the need to use the police to enforce traffic laws, eliminating violent encounters with vehicle occupants, and either sparing taxpayers the expense or allowing for police redeployment to ameliorate public safety concerns that are not being addressed.

Costs

The potential costs of autonomous vehicles include added congestion and sprawl, job losses, rising highway and transit deficits, safety and liability concerns, and technology failure. Efficient government policy can play an important role by mitigating some of those costs.

CONGESTION AND SPRAWL. Critics claim that AVs are likely to induce more automobile travel and congestion, and to create sprawl by making longer commutes more practical so people can live in less expensive homes on larger lots farther from their workplaces. What are the counterarguments? First, by eliminating vehicle accidents, AVs will eliminate incident delays, which account for one-third of all delays. Second, AVs will enable highways to accommodate a greater number of vehicles because AVs can safely travel closer together at high speeds; highways can be reconfigured with more, but narrower, lanes; and highways can eliminate the breakdown lane and use it for vehicle travel because AVs will undergo a "safety check" before they can enter a highway and travel en masse with other vehicles.

Finally, even if autonomous vehicles increase the volume of traffic, policymakers can significantly reduce congestion and sprawl by implementing congestion pricing, which would affect households' decisions of when to travel and where to live. Efficient road pricing would be more politically palatable in the new autonomous driving environment because, as noted, people would reduce the cost of automobile travel by not owning cars and instead would hire an autonomous vehicle when they need transportation. Hence, travelers would perceive congestion tolls like a fee that they pay when they use a taxi or surge charges that they pay when they use shared transportation, such as Uber or Lyft, and would therefore be likely to accept those tolls as a valid part of the lower full cost of autonomous vehicle travel, including travel time costs.

JOBS. There is no doubt that the widespread adoption of AVs would force hundreds of thousands of people who drive for a living to look for new work. But it is likely that those job losses would be more than offset by additional jobs created by the demand for workers in everything from maintaining AVs to updating the very accurate maps needed for them to operate safely and, more importantly, by creating new job opportunities throughout a more efficient economy.

HIGHWAY AND TRANSIT FISCAL DEFICITS. Autonomous electric vehicles (AEVs) would virtually eliminate gasoline tax revenues, which are the backbone of highway finance. Efficient per-mile road pricing that charges AEVs for emissions created in the production of electricity and for congestion that AEVs create on the road would simultaneously raise highway revenue while reducing congestion and emissions.[9]

By the same token, AVs will probably increase deficits in urban mass transit by contributing to its long-run decline in ridership. However, the efficient response is to automate transit and see whether it can compete effectively for passengers in the autonomous urban transportation environment. If not, transit's operations should be curtailed because it would effectively be replaced by a more flexible and personalized transit system provided by autonomous vehicles.

SAFETY CONCERNS. Instead of focusing on autonomous vehicles' potential safety benefits, some commentators have raised concerns that AVs will reduce safety as exemplified by incidents involving Tesla vehicles and its Autopilot feature where a driver hit another car and killed two people, and where another driver was killed while playing a video game. Both accidents indicate the importance of the federal government setting national testing and safety standards, which, as we discuss below, it has thus far failed to do.

LIABILITY CONCERNS. The legal community has just begun to confront the issue of who pays when AVs have accidents. Liability has yet to be firmly established and, as with other new products and technologies, the law is likely to evolve as AVs are adopted and the various stakeholders—insurance companies, the tort bar, and the public—gain greater experience with them.

9. Adler, Peer, and Sinozic (2019) study the effects of AEVs on public finance.

It will be important to clarify liability, regardless of how it is assigned, because the AV industry will need certainty on this matter to thrive. At the same time, liability should fade markedly as an issue of contention because AVs will be so much safer than conventional vehicles and because, like airlines, manufacturers will continue to solve new safety issues as they arise. Note, too, that the data automatically collected by AVs will be very useful in determining the cause of an accident and for providing guidance on preventing future accidents attributable to that cause or related causes.

TECHNOLOGY FAILURE. Critics of AVs assert they will never achieve Level 5 or even lower automated levels of operation. Economists have stressed the difficulty of explaining technological change and innovation, with Solow (1957) claiming that it is exogenous and Romer (1990) attempting to identify endogenous influences including but not limited to investments in human capital and research and development.

In the specific case of AVs, Bishop (2022) cautions that it is premature to make any strong predictions about what will happen when autonomous vehicles are deployed. The critics have not offered any dispositive arguments for why automakers and technology firms cannot learn from their mistakes and why AV technologies will not improve over time. In the concluding chapter, we assess concerns about the likely success of autonomous transportation technologies in more detail.

4. Government Actions to Expedite the Adoption of Autonomous Vehicles

Because AVs will operate on a publicly owned and managed road system, policymakers and regulators have a critical (and unavoidable) role to play to ensure that society will realize the potential benefits from AVs. Specifically, policymakers must establish a framework for vehicle testing and adoption, modernize the highway infrastructure to facilitate safe vehicle operations, and reform highway policies to encourage efficient operations. However, policymakers have made little progress in fulfilling those responsibilities, which will slow the adoption of autonomous vehicles.

Testing Framework

In 2018, Congress drafted, but failed to pass, important AV legislation that would have clarified and expedited national vehicle testing and adoption. Five years later, Congress has still not passed a version of this legislation, and a recent hearing showed no movement, as members raised concerns about protection from job losses and differentiating between advanced driver assistance systems and AVs. Republicans assert that AV legislation will advance in 2023 given that they are the majority party in the US House of Representatives following the 2022 midterm elections.

In the absence of new laws tailored to autonomous vehicles, NHTSA has put forward voluntary guidelines and in 2021 required companies to report accidents involving automated driving systems (Shepardson, Jin, and White 2022). But the agency has not issued comprehensive standards for robot-driven cars or trucks.

Motor vehicle manufacturers are free to certify for themselves that a vehicle feature is safe and NHTSA steps in if new features turn out to be a safety hazard. For example, NHTSA has pressed Tesla to improve its vehicles so they do not keep moving through stop signs rather than coming to a complete halt. Recently, it opened an investigation into Tesla's Autopilot. Generally, however, NHTSA approaches Elon Musk, Tesla's CEO, using a combination of pressure, flattery, and threats to persuade him to comply with federal safety measures instead of instituting and strongly enforcing unambiguous guidelines for the autonomous vehicle industry to test vehicles safely (Siddiqui 2022).

NHTSA also has amended the occupant protection Federal Motor Vehicle Safety Standards (FMVSS) to account for autonomous vehicles that do not have the traditional manual controls associated with a human driver because they are equipped with an automated driving system (ADS). The rule makes clear that, despite their innovative designs, vehicles with ADS technology must continue to provide the same high levels of occupant protection that current (nonautonomous) passenger vehicles provide. For example, the rule works through the type of airbags and seat belts autonomous vehicles should install.[10]

States and localities have adopted regulations allowing testing within their borders, sometimes with an eye toward attracting new high-tech businesses. However, federal legislation is necessary to jump-start the formal adoption process and to ensure that vehicles do not have to shift from autonomous to manual operations as they cross a state line.

Government Investments

In a fully optimized system, AVs would be connected to other vehicles and their surroundings, including pedestrians, infrastructure, and the road network. Some states are making investments to upgrade their infrastructure to align it in advance with AV technology. For example, Panasonic and the Utah Department of Transportation are jointly developing a system that enables vehicles, roads, and traffic signals to continuously communicate about conditions, location of obstacles, signal timing, and the speed, direction, and position of all cars in the network.

Michigan, for its part, is working with a Google-funded startup to transform a stretch of road between Detroit and Ann Arbor into a connected highway for

---

10. Automobile and technology companies can petition NHTSA to waive requirements for manual controls on their autonomous vehicles. GM's 2021 Cruise has applied for one, and autonomous delivery vehicle developer Nuro received a waver in 2020.

testing purposes. Recently, Governor Gretchen Whitmer signed the first legislation adopted in the United States specific to the deployment and operation of technology-enabled roadways for connected autonomous vehicles. The legislation authorizes the Michigan Department of Transportation to designate AV roadways throughout the state, enter into agreements with technology partners to operate them, and charge users of Level 3 autonomous vehicles for using the roadways.

Several states are installing fiber-optic lines in roads that can send electronic warnings to AVs about hazards ahead and other information to keep them aware of their surroundings. In contrast, other states seem content to wait for the federal government to provide guidance before moving forward. Regardless of who is at fault, states that delay upgrades to their infrastructure could delay the use of autonomous vehicles on their roads.

The adoption of 5G cellular technology is critical to launching the era of autonomous vehicle-to-vehicle connections, with ultrafast speeds, greater capacity, and ultralow latency, which eliminate the requirement for infrastructure embedded in the roadway to enable those communications. Rollouts have begun, but delays have been caused due to battles between Congress, the Federal Communications Commission, and the Federal Aviation Administration; thus, government's inability to coordinate the activities of regulatory agencies has become another potential source of delay for the nation's adoption of autonomous vehicles. Autonomous vehicle companies also are interested in satellites to update information on road conditions and to have more accurate information about vehicle locations, so government regulators will have to balance the AV industry's desire to use satellites with other interests that wish to use them.

Finally, there are more than 30 million lampposts in the United States, which could be used to mount an electronic communications router or a 5G transmitter, to assist autonomous vehicles' communications with the infrastructure and, for example, to warn of impending delays and indicate alternative routes.

Reforming Highway Policies

AVs are not immune to highway inefficiencies. As noted, their operations could be disrupted, for example, by congestion and by damaged or poorly marked pavement that requires vehicles to slow down or change lanes. Thus, it is important for highway policies to complement AV operations by improving traffic flows.

As summarized in Winston (2021b) and Winston and Mannering (2014), highway performance could be significantly improved by adopting efficient policies, including:

—congestion pricing for cars and trucks and, as discussed in chapter 12, pavement and bridge-wear pricing for trucks;

—optimal investment in highway durability and in pavement design to increase pavement life;

—variable speed limits and real-time traffic signaling to reduce delay and improve traffic safety;[11]

—adopting the latest instrumentation and monitoring technologies to improve highway design and to reduce maintenance costs; and

—reducing project costs by expediting the procurement process, reforming environmental and other regulations to reduce the extent that they delay projects, and selecting socially beneficial projects based on cost–benefit analyses.

Unfortunately, the federal government has shown little interest in reforming highway policy along the preceding lines to improve the system's performance and reduce its costs. The 2021 Infrastructure Investment and Jobs Act (IIJA) increased highway spending more than $100 billion above baseline levels, but no acknowledgment is made of the various ways that accumulated policy inefficiencies substantially compromise highway performance and reduce the returns from highway expenditures. Increasing spending does not constructively address those problems and the IIJA does not contain any other useful actions.[12]

To make matters worse, the US Department of Labor is proposing to further increase the cost of federal and federally assisted highway construction projects covered by the Davis–Bacon Act, which mandates the "prevailing wage" be paid on applicable projects. Research indicates that the Davis–Bacon Act has already significantly inflated the labor costs of highway projects (Winston 2013), while the Labor Department's proposed change will make it easier for a union to have its higher collective bargaining agreement rate set as the prevailing wage in the locality. In addition, President Biden has signed executive orders that increase the stringency of National Environmental Policy Act requirements, which will increase the time and cost of project delays to satisfy environmental mandates. Finally, the IIJA includes a "Buy America" initiative that requires US materials to be used for projects that the IIJA is funding. However, the initiative is delaying projects because the United States no longer produces many of the items needed to modernize roads, bridges, and ports.

Some states are making modest progress in exploring efficient pricing policies, as fourteen states have run pilot vehicle miles traveled–based taxation programs. Oregon, Utah, and Virginia have implemented vehicle-miles-traveled taxes, albeit with voluntary participation by drivers. As in the case of testing, states currently cannot implement a nationwide program that would be immune from disruptions

11. The artificially intelligent SURTRAC (Scalable Urban Traffic Control) system is one of the first to gather information on vehicular flow and use it to adjust traffic lights in real time. Such a system could be used for the entire road system.

12. The IIJA includes funding to test a tax on vehicle miles traveled. However, the US Department of Transportation has not made any progress on testing the tax.

when a vehicle crosses a state line. However, the International Fuel Tax Association, authorized by the Intermodal Surface Transportation Efficiency Act of 1991, is examining a way that states potentially could implement a nationwide road usage charge program.

Even when policymakers are interested in instituting an efficient highway policy, they may encounter difficulties in implementing it promptly and efficiently. For example, in 2019 New York City's legislators approved a congestion pricing plan for motorists driving into Manhattan south of 60th Street. Because some of the roads were built with federal funds, city officials needed to receive federal approval, which was expected to be granted after officials responded to the Federal Highway Administration's technical questions about how the plan would be implemented.

Supporters of the plan have become frustrated because the Metropolitan Transportation Authority has delayed naming the six-person review panel to guide the state through the congestion pricing process and the federal government has dragged its feet in approving a New York City congestion pricing plan. The latest projections are that congestion pricing in New York City will be implemented sometime in 2024, or five years after the city's legislators approve the plan. However, as pointed out by Gelinas (2022b), some New Yorkers may still be asking themselves in 2024: Whatever happened to congestion pricing?

The delays are costly because congestion pricing in New York City is likely to improve travel by discouraging motorists from driving on the most congested routes during the busiest times of day. At the same time, the revenues generated by congestion pricing are likely to be wasted because state legislators have pledged $1 billion of annual toll revenues to support $15 billion in loans for its highly inefficient public transit system instead of using those revenues to improve the road system.

5. The Potential for Highway Privatization

If the lack of constructive reform in highway pricing and investment policies compromises the performance of autonomous vehicles, privatization of the road system could be considered as an alternative approach to improve the system's efficiency and technology. Although privatization is in keeping with this book's theme of competition and innovation to improve the transportation system, it would be a radical departure from government provision of highway services that would raise significant challenges we cannot ignore.

Friedman and Boorstin (1996) argue that it would be feasible for private enterprise to provide certain US highways and benefit users.[13] Based on govern-

---

13. The draft of Friedman and Boorstin (1996) was written in the early 1950s but was not published until 1996.

ment provision, highways appear to be potentially highly profitable, although the public is not fully benefiting from its expenditures on them. The public expresses its demand for highway services by paying for them in the form of license fees, gasoline taxes, and tolls.[14] But a significant portion of public expenditures is used to subsidize other services, such as transit, and, as noted, costs are significantly inflated, which reduces the amount of funds that are used to maintain and expand the highways.

By comparing the size of public expenditures on highways with the larger size of other private transportation industries, the provision of highways is clearly not too expensive nor too large-scale an activity to be conducted by private enterprises. And thanks to technical advances in automated tolling and collection, it is possible to set efficient prices for cars and trucks for their use of the roads without disturbing the flow of traffic.

Highways do have elements of a natural monopoly, which pose a challenge for allowing them to be provided by private enterprise and not subjecting users to monopoly charges. For example, city streets and roads should continue to be provided by governmental authorities. However, the evolution of the US transportation system has facilitated competition for long-distance highway travel provided by alternative modes, such as airlines and passenger rail in some corridors, and for the potential of competition created by alternative intercity highway routes.

In Winston and Yan (2011) we explored the possibility of private highway competition empirically by designing a competitive private highway market on California State Route 91 consisting of two routes with equal lane capacities that would be operated by two different private highway companies. A third party would represent motorists, negotiating tolls and capacities with the private companies to obtain a contract equilibrium. We found that motorists could gain from highway privatization when the contract equilibrium consisted of differentiated prices and service—that is, when motorists were given a choice of paying a high toll to use lanes with little congestion or paying a low toll to use lanes that were highly congested.[15]

In practice, the United States has had little experience with highway privatization. Thus, it is uncertain whether policymakers could effectively design a competitive private highway system and whether sufficient managerial talent exists to operate several competing highway companies that would remain profitable and provide highway services capable of improving motorists' welfare.

The public sector has allowed some privatization to occur to raise revenue to fund highway projects as part of long-term leases and to build new capacity. The most encouraging public–private partnerships have led to high-occupancy

---

14. Some tolls have disappeared when the road has been "paid off."

15. In practice, California State Route 91 sets tolls that motorists can pay to use less-congested lanes but sets no tolls for the other lanes.

toll lanes, where the private sector has built, financed, and maintained express lanes that have benefitted travelers. However, highway public–private partnerships have a limited history in the United States and investments and efficiency gains have been small (Engel, Fischer, and Galetovic 2021).

In theory, owners of private US highways would have the financial incentive to recruit workers from all over the world with the technological expertise to upgrade the infrastructure to facilitate AV operations and to improve the condition of the highways through efficient pricing. Foreign experience also may be encouraging. For example, many roads in Sweden and Finland are operated by the private sector but maintained by local communities, and the government works in conjunction with road owners to reduce the costs of repair and maintenance.

The privatization option should be explored with carefully designed experiments, which eventually could give policymakers valuable guidance on whether to privatize the entire or part of the US highway system and under what conditions. Although policymakers have not shown any interest in conducting highway privatization experiments with that goal in mind (most public–private partnerships have been motivated by the desire to raise revenue), the privatization option may gain attention when autonomous vehicles are adopted if public sector management and operation of the road system significantly limit AV operations.

6. Conclusions

Although autonomous and electric vehicle technologies will ultimately be combined to develop autonomous electric vehicles, the private sector and policymakers have separated the development of and policy toward those vehicles. AEVs will become a game changing innovation that is a product of global competition and cooperation and will enable urban transportation systems to significantly reduce the automobile externalities of congestion, pollution, and accidents, increase productivity, and benefit all socioeconomic groups, especially less affluent people who have limited mobility.

However, government must carry out its critical responsibilities if the United States is to realize those improvements; thus far, it has failed to show much interest in doing so. Recently, for example, in response to GM's petition to NHTSA for permission to put its driverless Level 4 Cruise Origin into commercial service, NHTSA officials simply declined to indicate when they might act on the petition.

Because AEVs are a global endeavor, policymakers will be incentivized to take constructive actions if other countries take the lead in adopting this technology. President Biden famously proclaimed that China was "eating our lunch" in electric vehicles as motivation for increasing funding for EV adoption and charging stations. Hopefully, President Biden will have a similar reaction, and take appropriate actions, if it becomes clear that China is eating our lunch in autonomous vehicles.

In sum, Part I of this book has explained how private sector competition and innovation could evolve to transform the US urban transportation system from a highly inefficient network of highways, public transit, and taxis to a much more efficient system characterized by autonomous electric vehicles whose operations are facilitated by a highway system with advanced communication capabilities. Government policymakers are in a critical position to determine how quickly this transformation can occur.

As we shall see in Parts II and III, private sector competition and innovation also have the potential to greatly benefit the public by transforming the intercity and freight transportation systems (and to some extent have already done so), where again autonomous vehicles can improve efficiency and government will play a critical role in determining the speed of the systems' transformation.

II

Intercity Passenger Transportation

Deregulation of the airline industry in 1978 significantly improved the efficiency of the US intercity passenger transportation system, benefiting both airlines and travelers. Airline safety also continued to improve, to the point where no major commercial airline has been involved in an accident resulting in a fatality in the United States since 2009. A recent summary of the post-deregulation intercity passenger transportation environment reported that in 2020:[1]

—the price to fly, including all extra fees, was more than 60 percent cheaper than in 1980;

—87 percent of the US population said they had taken a commercial airline trip, the highest number ever recorded;

—fewer people must make a connection to reach their destinations, as a record 90 percent of the top two thousand largest domestic markets had nonstop service, up from under 70 percent in 1990;

—almost 90 percent of the US population has access to a low-cost carrier;

—satisfaction with airline travel is at its highest point in the last twenty years, at over 75 percent, according to the American Consumer Satisfaction Travel report;[2] and

1. Specific figures for airlines are from *Facts from Airlines for America*, 2021. The series is updated here and called *Data & Statistics*: https://www.airlines.org/dataset/a4a-presentation-industry-review-and-outlook/.

2. Kelly Yamanouchi, "Study: Airline Passenger Satisfaction Hits Record High During Pandemic," *Atlanta Journal Constitution*, December 16, 2020, https://wwwspokesman.com/stories/2020/dec/16/study-airline-passenger-satisfaction-hits-record-h/.

—deregulation of the intercity bus industry in 1982 benefited the industry and travelers as intercity bus experienced much greater passenger growth than Amtrak experienced.

In this part of the book, we discuss additional ways that competition and innovation could significantly improve the intercity passenger transportation system. We provide new evidence on the potential benefits to travelers in the United States from allowing foreign airlines to serve domestic routes—that is, granting cabotage rights. For example, although British Airways can serve the international route connecting John F. Kennedy International Airport in New York and Heathrow Airport in London, it and other foreign airlines are not permitted to serve US domestic routes. If British Airways and other foreign airlines were granted cabotage rights, they would be free to serve any domestic routes they deemed profitable and that had available gates and operating times.

Cabotage is an essential step toward global airline deregulation because it will allow carriers to provide "seamless" travel from many origins in one country to many destinations in another country, thus eliminating transfers to other airlines and reducing transfer wait times. Allowing this form of global airline competition will spur additional competition on both domestic and international routes.

We also empirically analyze public airport competition to illustrate the potential benefits from privatizing US airports to spur greater airport competition among them, which could lead in turn to greater competition among airlines themselves. In addition, we show that private airports would have greater incentives than public airports to adopt socially desirable innovations, such as heated runways. Finally, we discuss how additional sources of competition and innovation could lead to the introduction of new modes and services, such as air taxis, which could enable the intercity transportation system to provide greater benefits to the public.

7

Would US Travelers Benefit from Entry by Foreign Airlines? Simulating the Effect of Cabotage based on Low-Cost Carrier Competition in US and EU Markets

XINLONG TAN, CLIFFORD WINSTON, AND JIA YAN

1. Introduction

Some forty years after Congress deregulated the US airline industry, controversy remains over whether the industry is sufficiently competitive and whether government should intervene to increase competition. The wave of airline mergers since 2005, which enabled the remaining large legacy carriers (American, United, and Delta) to solidify dominance of their hubs in large cities while they reduced service to smaller cities, spurred concerns that fares would increase and service quality would decrease.[1]

At the same time, low-cost carriers (LCCs), such as Southwest and JetBlue and ultra-low-cost carriers (ULCCs), which include Allegiant, Frontier, and Spirit (Bachwich and Wittman 2017), have gained a greater share of the US market and have offered new service in markets abandoned by legacy carriers.[2] For example,

---

1. Since 2005, the following mergers resulted in three major legacy carriers remaining in the industry: US Airways and America West Airlines (2005), Delta Air Lines and Northwest Airlines (2008), United Airlines and Continental Airlines (2010), and American Airlines and US Airways (2014). In addition, Southwest Airlines acquired AirTran Airways in 2011 and Alaska Airlines acquired Virgin America in 2016. Luo (2014), Shen (2017), Carlton et al. (2019), and Zhang and Nozick (2018) have assessed the effects on fares of the mergers between the legacy carriers and have found that they vary significantly, depending on the carriers involved and the type of route.

2. Three new ULCCs have emerged, including Breeze Airways, Avelo Airlines, and Porter Airlines, and Spirit Airlines consummated its plans to merge with JetBlue.

Delta made significant cuts in service at Cincinnati/Northern Kentucky International Airport, but Allegiant, Frontier, and Southwest added new service. Similar changes are occurring at other former hubs, including Pittsburgh, Cleveland, Memphis, and St. Louis.

Although some larger carriers have exited through consolidation and some smaller low-cost carriers have expanded their networks, no evidence suggests that those competitive dynamics are likely to lead to adverse long-run changes, on average, in fares and service quality. However, because many established airlines have failed and because it has been difficult for new entrants to succeed, policymakers are concerned about the decline in the number of large carriers at the national level and about the long-run financial strength of low-cost carriers.[3] Some research has added to those concerns by characterizing strategic behavior by airlines that could increase fares (Aryal, Cilberto, and Leyden 2022; Sweeting, Roberts, and Gedge 2020), and by pointing out that the largest investors in US airlines own stock in multiple airlines and that common airline ownership raises fares (Azar, Schmalz, and Tecu 2018).

Historically, the US transportation industry has shown that the most effective way for policymakers to protect and enhance consumer welfare is to stimulate competition by eliminating entry barriers, but history also has shown that policymakers have applied this lesson only selectively (Winston 2013). Thus, in the airline industry, policymakers benefited travelers within the United States by deregulating domestic markets (Morrison and Winston 1986, 1995) and benefited international travelers by negotiating open skies agreements with some countries (Winston and Yan 2015).[4] Nevertheless, policymakers have allowed public airports to establish exclusive-use gates and have implemented slot controls that restrict entry and raise fares (Morrison and Winston 2000), and, importantly, they have prevented foreign airlines from providing additional competition in domestic markets by not giving them cabotage rights.

Beginning with the growth of Southwest Airlines, competition provided by low-cost carriers has accounted for a large fraction of the fare savings from deregulating entry into US markets (Morrison and Winston 2000). Similarly, the growth of LCCs Ryanair and EasyJet contributed to the benefits of deregulating entry into European Union markets (Alderighi et al. 2012).

The potential benefits to travelers from liberalizing entry into transatlantic markets are well known. Transatlantic markets are simultaneously attractive to LCCs and difficult for airlines to remain profitable because they are highly

3. JetBlue, which started in 2000, is the most recent large airline in the United States that has not disappeared through merger or bankruptcy.

4. Open skies agreements are an international policy concept that calls for liberalizing rules and regulations of international aviation to promote competition. Alliances between international air carriers, which facilitate interline traffic across the networks of the partners, also reduce fares (Brueckner, Lee, and Singer 2011), but not by as much as open skies agreements do.

competitive. Thus, although LCCs Norwegian Air and Wow Air recently entered and exited transatlantic markets, other European carriers have begun to serve or have announced plans to serve transatlantic markets.[5] Given the significant effects of foreign LCCs on fares in EU and transatlantic markets, allowing foreign LCCs into US markets would be expected to increase US domestic travelers' welfare significantly.

Federal law has continued to justify restricting competition in the airline industry by prohibiting foreign airlines from serving US domestic travelers because the US military might need immediate access to all aircraft during times of war, and because domestic airline labor would mount significant political opposition to additional competitive threats that could reduce its earnings. However, given the nation's increasing reliance on unmanned military aircraft and the weakened political position of airline labor in the wake of deregulation, those arguments have lost much of their force. At the same time, US airlines, labor, and the US Department of Defense would likely still oppose changes to current restrictions regarding cabotage, despite foreign carriers indicating a strong desire to expand their networks to serve US domestic markets.

Nonetheless, it is useful to quantify the potential benefits to travelers from allowing cabotage rights to document the effects of a new source of airline competition that policymakers should consider seriously. We are not aware of previous research that has attempted to estimate the economic effects of cabotage, probably because there are no distinct airline markets where policymakers allow and do not allow cabotage. We develop a special case in this chapter to estimate the potential benefits to travelers of allowing a foreign airline to enter US routes. Specifically, we consider the entry of an LCC that currently serves the European Union because the US and EU LCCs have adopted similar business models, shared similar cost characteristics, and been leading competitors in their respective markets despite the efforts of legacy carriers.

We first provide an overview of the operations and entry patterns of Southwest, the leading US LCC, and Ryanair and EasyJet, the leading EU LCCs. We then obtain evidence about the effects of their actual, potential (Morrison and Winston 1987), and adjacent (Morrison and Winston 2000) entry on fares in their respective US and EU markets. Adjacent competition has gained attention

---

5. Norwegian, like many carriers, experienced financial stress caused by the global pandemic. Recently, it announced that it would end its service to the United States and concentrate on service to Nordic countries. Wow Air went bankrupt in 2019. However, Norse Atlantic Airways (a Norwegian startup), Aer Lingus (the Irish flag carrier), and La Compagnie (an all-business French carrier) are planning to offer transatlantic service. Finally, the Iceland-based newcomer Fly Play is picking up where the defunct Iceland discount airline Wow Air left off, offering service to more than twenty European destinations with plans to operate from US cities; and Fly Atlantic, operating out of Belfast, announced it would begin operations in 2024 offering low-cost flights from Belfast to the United States and Canada.

because of the competitive power of Southwest Airlines, which was able to reduce other airlines' fares on, for example, the route connecting Washington Dulles International Airport and San Francisco International Airport by entering and charging low fares on the parallel route connecting Baltimore/Washington International Airport and Oakland International Airport.

Finally, we extrapolate from those findings to simulate the effect that the entry of an EU LCC would have on fares and travelers' welfare in US markets. Of course, it is premature to assert that Ryanair or EasyJet would actually adjust their operations and undertake the necessary investments to serve US domestic markets if they were granted cabotage rights. However, it is likely that some foreign carriers would eventually serve those markets if US policymakers gave them the opportunity to do so; conducting the analysis with an EU LCC is a useful first step to illustrate the relevant empirical issues and potential welfare effects.[6]

Our analysis contributes to the literature on the effects of LCC competition on fares by developing a new methodology, difference-in-differences (DID) matching with a regression adjustment, that addresses the endogeneity of an LCC's entry as either an actual, potential, or adjacent competitor.[7] The standard DID approach used in previous research does not address fully the potential bias from endogenous entry. Our approach also is suitable for investigating the effects of firm entry in other industries, such as banking, petroleum, and chain stores, where markets are geographically isolated and where firms' initial networks drive their expansion.

We find that entry by Southwest Airlines reduces fares in US markets by as much as 30 percent and that Ryanair and EasyJet reduce fares in EU markets by as much as 20 percent. We also find that the conventional DID approach tends to understate Southwest's effect on fares and to overstate the EU LCCs' effect on fares. We simulate a stylized effect of cabotage by assuming that an EU LCC enters only US markets that are not served by a US LCC or ULCC, and that its effect on fares is comparable to its effect on fares in EU markets, although not as large as Southwest's effect on fares in US markets. Given those assumptions and our estimated models, we find that travelers would gain $1.6 billion annually, which may be more modest than expected because some 80 percent of domestic passengers in the United States are already flying on routes that are served by at least one LCC or ULCC.

---

6. The COVID-19 global pandemic dramatically affected the airline industry as carriers had to adjust to large variations in demand and sought financial assistance from the government. It is not clear how the pandemic will affect the industry in the long run. However, during the pandemic, Southwest, Ryanair, and EasyJet were the only investment grade–rated carriers left in the industry. In fact, Southwest expanded into additional airports. Generally, industry observers believe that low-cost and ultra-low-cost carriers will recover from the shock caused by the pandemic more easily than legacy carriers will recover.

7. We are not aware of previous research that has used this methodology.

It is likely, however, that those initial gains to US travelers would expand greatly under a more comprehensive cabotage policy that allows entry of all foreign carriers in all countries, not just the entry by an EU LCC in the United States. Competition in a fully deregulated and integrated global airline market would encourage both foreign and US carriers to restructure their networks, which would result in greater entry on international routes and on domestic routes that feed those routes, leading to lower fares and improved service.[8]

The case for allowing cabotage is strengthened significantly as the framework evolves from the static network we consider here to a network restructured by new foreign entrants and domestic carriers that facilitates and encourages seamless international travel. As discussed in appendix C of this chapter, seamless international travel would significantly improve service that is highly valued by international travelers by reducing the large disutility associated with long transfer wait times in a foreign airport and total travel time for a connecting flight abroad, and by improving the reliability of travel time.

Importantly, competition in a global airline industry that grants cabotage rights also would provide extra protection for travelers against excessive fares on US domestic routes because those fares would induce entry by foreign carriers. In addition, excessive domestic fares may reduce overall airline profits because they could discourage travel on US international routes.

From the carriers' perspective, an expanded global market could reduce the impact of the periodic unanticipated shocks to the airline industry, most recently the COVID-19 global pandemic, by enabling carriers to diversify and expand their "portfolio" of airline routes by increasing operations in some countries and regions and decreasing them in others.

2. An Overview of LCC Expansions and Entry Patterns in the United States and European Union

Before estimating the effects on fares of Southwest in the United States and Ryanair and EasyJet in the European Union we discuss how LCCs developed their operations and networks to become major competitors in their respective markets. We then present descriptive evidence of patterns of LCC entry behavior, which guides our decomposition of their effects on fares as actual, potential, and adjacent entrants.

Southwest's Expansion in the United States

Southwest Airlines began as an intrastate carrier in Texas and became an interstate carrier following deregulation in 1978, which allowed it to serve cities in

---

8. When airlines introduce service on new routes, they can generate other benefits to the public. For example, Wang, Zheng, and Dai (2022) find that the introduction of a new airline route increases the number of shared kidneys by 7.3 percent.

other states. Southwest developed its business model as a low-cost carrier during the 1980s and captured national and international attention for its efficient operations that some foreign carriers tried to emulate. For decades, Southwest has flown only one type of aircraft, the Boeing 737, which reduces its maintenance and pilot-training costs. In addition, it has avoided congested airports, or airports with high passenger facility charges, in favor of secondary, less-crowded airports that have lower passenger facility charges and that enable Southwest to provide quick turnaround service and increase aircraft utilization (Boguslaski, Ito, and Lee 2004).[9] Southwest's operating cost per available seat-mile has consistently been much lower than that for the other large US airlines, with the exception of JetBlue, a more recent low-cost entrant.[10] Southwest's lower costs have enabled it to charge lower fares and put tremendous competitive pressure on other carriers.

In addition to its low fares, Southwest has grown far beyond its Texas roots (and routes) to serve markets throughout the United States. As shown in figure 7.1, Southwest expanded its network from 148 nonstop markets (501 markets with connections) in 1994 to 490 nonstop markets (2,228 markets with connections) in 2011. Most of those markets tend to consist of short- and medium-haul routes. Although Southwest has entered new routes over time, it has generally not exited many routes.

Ryanair's and EasyJet's Expansion in Europe

Ryanair, an Irish airline established in 1984, followed Southwest's low-cost model and expanded its network when the European Union fully deregulated air transportation in 1997. Similarly, EasyJet, a British airline established in 1995, adopted a low-cost business model and expanded its operations following EU deregulation. As in the case of Southwest, Ryanair and EasyJet attempt to avoid congested airports by using Europe's underused, secondary airports, which helps them to achieve fast turnaround times, reduce their operating costs, and compete more effectively against other European carriers (Barrett 2004). Major European hub airports are often congested, which means that slots are rationed at those airports, giving incumbent carriers a competitive advantage. However,

9. In recent years, Southwest has expanded into congested airports, including Miami International Airport, O'Hare International Airport, George Bush Intercontinental Airport, and Newark Liberty International Airport.

10. According to Southwest's 10-K annual reports filled with the US Securities and Exchange Commission, operating costs per available seat-mile have fluctuated in real 2000 dollars around 8 cents from 1993 to 2011, while the operating costs per available seat-mile of the other large US carriers have fluctuated around 10 cents. In contrast with other air carriers, since the early 1990s, Southwest has reduced its operating costs by hedging the cost of jet fuel. Southwest aims to hedge at least 50 percent of its fuel every year. In some years Southwest has reported hedging losses, but overall Southwest's hedging program has saved the carrier billions of dollars.

Figure 7.1. *Southwest's Expansion in the United States*

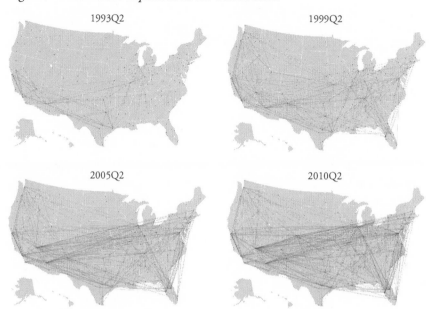

Sources: Airline Origin and Destination Survey; T-100 Domestic Segment Data.
Notes: Dots denote airports and lines denote nonstop routes.

like Southwest, EasyJet has recently expanded to serve major, congested airports as slots became available. Finally, Ryanair and EasyJet serve most of their routes year-round as well as several seasonal routes, primarily to Croatia, Greece, and Turkey.[11]

Within the EU, airlines can serve other member countries from their home country and can operate within other member countries; that is, as part of a protracted process that began in 1990, public authorities fully enacted cabotage rights in 1997. Figure 7.2 shows the number of routes served by Ryanair and EasyJet in the EU from January 2005 to December 2013. Because the two LCCs have expanded rapidly during this period, they have increased competition on many routes. At the same time, their networks do not overlap much because they tend to avoid competing with each other.[12]

11. Ryanair and EasyJet offer charter service. However, we confine our analysis to scheduled commercial service where we can clearly identify entry and exit and estimate the causal effect of a carrier's presence on fares.

12. Wizz Air, a new ultra-low-cost carrier, is expanding rapidly in European markets and is increasingly competing with Ryanair on some routes.

Figure 7.2. *Number of Routes Served by Ryanair and EasyJet, 2005–13*

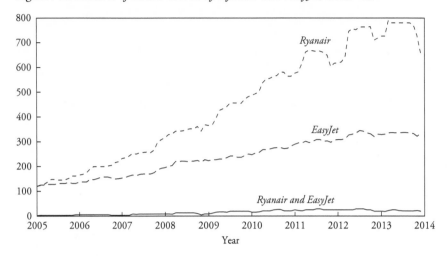

Source: International Air Transport Association.

An Overview of LCCs' Entry Patterns

We investigate the entry patterns of the US and EU LCCs to indicate their ability to affect fares through actual, potential, and adjacent entry. Our empirical overview uses the US Department of Transportation's Airline Origin and Destination Survey (DB1B) and T-100 Domestic Segment Data from 1993 to 2011, and the International Air Transport Association's (IATA's) monthly data on airline operations and fares from 2005 to 2013.[13] The routes in our analysis are nondirectional airport pairs.[14] In our sample, there are 13,590 such routes in the United States and 3,588 in the European Union. Appendix tables 7.A1 and 7.A2 present the means, standard deviations, minimum, and maximum values of the variables used in this and subsequent empirical analyses in the chapter.

ACTUAL ENTRY. Actual entry (exit) occurs when an LCC served (did not serve) a route in a month or quarter but did not serve (served) that route in the previous

---

13. We are grateful to John Byerly and Douglas Lavin for helping us to obtain the IATA data. Because our sample ends in 2011, we do not confound our analysis with the structural effects of Southwest's merger with AirTran Airways, another LCC, in 2011. Our analysis of the European Union market includes the United Kingdom and other European countries, such as Norway and Switzerland, which are not members of the European Union.

14. Morrison (2001) points out that using airport pairs enables one to account for competition from adjacent airports and adjacent airport pairs; for example, the airport pair Baltimore/Washington International Airport to Oakland International Airport provides adjacent competition for the airport pair Washington Dulles International Airport to San Francisco International Airport.

month or quarter.[15] Based on our data and assumptions, the EU LCCs tend to enter and exit routes frequently, as Ryanair made 500 entries on 377 routes and 211 exits on 150 routes, and EasyJet made 438 entries on 323 routes and 231 exits on 134 routes.[16] Some of those entries and exits reflect seasonal operations, but Ryanair and EasyJet do compete with other carriers on their seasonal routes. Figure 7.3 shows that both EU LCCs exhibit strong time patterns of entry and exit by adjusting their networks more in April and November than they do in other months of the year; about 60 percent of Ryanair's entries and exits and about 50 percent of EasyJet's entries and exits are made during those months.

In contrast, Southwest Airlines seldom exits an airport or a city-pair market. In our sample, Southwest ceased operations only at Detroit (1993), San Francisco (2001), and Houston Intercontinental (2005) airports. Because a metropolitan area may be served by multiple airports, an airline's exit from an airport does not necessarily imply that it no longer serves the area. For example, after Southwest exited San Francisco International Airport, it continued to serve Oakland International Airport.

POTENTIAL AND ADJACENT ENTRY. Potential entry occurs when an LCC serves one (Type-1 potential entry) or both (Type-2 potential entry) of the endpoint airports comprising a route but does not serve the airport pair or route itself. Adjacent entry occurs when an LCC enters an adjacent competitive route comprised of two adjacent airports. We define two airports as adjacent airports if the distance between them is less than 100 kilometers or 62.5 miles.[17] To avoid double counting, if an airline enters a given route (actual entry) and then enters an adjacent route, we measure only the effect of actual entry on fares.

LCCs' Patterns of Route Entry

We estimate a probit model to characterize patterns that are associated with LCCs' entry. We express the conditional probability of an LCC entering a route as $\Pr(d_{ijt} = 1 \mid X_{jt}, Z_{it}, Z_{i't})$, where d_{ijt} is a binary indicator equal to 1 if LCC i entered route j in time t for the first time and 0 otherwise; X_{jt} is a vector of market characteristics such as distance and market size; Z_{it} is a vector of variables measuring LCC i's network; and $Z_{i't}$ is a vector of variables measuring the competitors' i' networks at the time of entry.[18]

---

15. More precisely, we assume that an airline entered a route if it provided nonstop or one-stop connecting flights for at least six quarters and offered at least one flight every two days; that is, forty-five flights per quarter.

16. Ryanair's and, to a lesser extent, EasyJet's high route turnover is partially a control on airport costs and airport charges.

17. Our assumption is midway between the seventy-mile radius used by Morrison (2001) and the fifty-mile radius used by Dresner, Lin, and Windle (1996) to construct adjacent competitive routes. When we measured an airport's catchment area based on travel time instead of distance, our primary results did not change.

18. In this exercise, we exclude reentries of an LCC on a route (for example, on seasonal routes) because the reentry decisions could be affected by an LCC's previous entries and exits.

Figure 7.3. *Monthly Entries and Exits by Ryanair and EasyJet, 2005–13*

(a) Ryanair

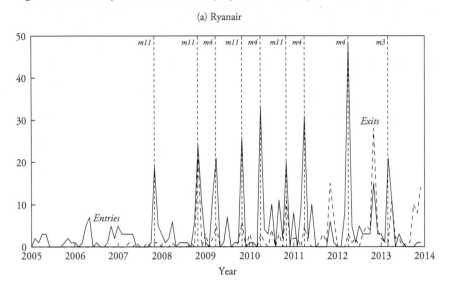

(b) EasyJet

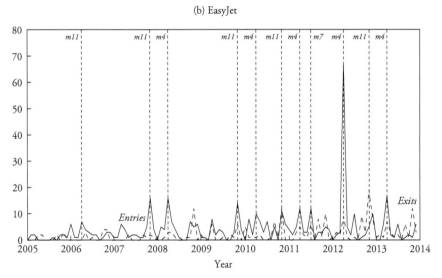

Note: The vertical lines denote months where there is a spike in entries or exits, which typically occur in April or November.

Source: International Air Transport Association.

The estimation results presented in table 7.1 indicate how US and EU LCCs' actual entry behavior is associated with their potential and adjacent entry. The LCCs are more likely to enter a route when they already serve both endpoint airports and, in the case of Ryanair and EasyJet, the likelihood increases as the number of routes connected to the endpoint airports increase.[19] Actual entry also is more likely to occur if the LCCs serve one of the endpoint airports, but in the case of EasyJet that effect is statistically significant only as the number of routes connected to the airport increases. Actual entry by the EU LCCs is less likely if they already provide adjacent competition, which may reflect the difficulty of entering certain routes connected to major EU hub airports. In contrast, actual entry by Southwest is more likely if Southwest already provides adjacent competition. Finally, consistent with our summary of their operations, an EU LCC is less likely to enter a route that the other EU LCC has entered.

3. Difference-in-Differences Estimation of the Effect of LCC Entry on Fares

We begin our exploration of the effect of LCC entry on a route's average fare by using the difference-in-differences approach.[20] The fares in both the DB1B (for Southwest) and IATA (for Ryanair and EasyJet) data sets do not include ancillary charges, which in recent years have become an important source of industry revenues because carriers have unbundled many services, such as checked luggage and ticket reservations by phone, which were included in the ticket price, and have begun to charge additional fees for them. However, this change is unlikely to bias our analysis much, since Southwest charges very few ancillary fees and most European carriers started to unbundle their fares after the end of our IATA sample.[21]

---

19. Our finding on Southwest's actual entry behavior is consistent with work by Zou and Yu (2020).

20. We focus on average fares because our main interest is to obtain an estimate of the potential benefits to travelers on US domestic routes from the entry of an EU LCC. That estimate is obtained by using the estimates of the average effects of Southwest and the EU LCCs on fares on the routes they serve in the US and EU, respectively, to bound the effect of an EU LCC on average fares on US routes.

21. Although fares in the DB1B data do not include ancillary charges, Southwest does not charge travelers for services, such as checked luggage for the first and second bag, changing or cancelling reservations, and so on. In addition, Southwest's charges for oversized and overweight bags are generally lower than legacy carriers' charges. Thus, if anything, our analysis may understate Southwest's effect on the full costs to air travelers because it does not include its effect on the price of other optional services. Ryanair and EasyJet do unbundle services and charge for them. However, our IATA sample ended before the share of revenues that those carriers derived from ancillary services significantly increased. It is unlikely that we are understating the effect of the EU LCCs on the full costs to travelers because most full-service European carriers unbundled their fares and derived significant ancillary revenues after the end of our IATA sample.

Table 7.1. *Spatial Entry Patterns of LCCs from Probit Regressions*

Variables	Note	Ryanair (1)	EasyJet (2)	Southwest (3)
Constant		−3.2791	−3.9192	−4.8442
		(0.2175)	(0.2147)	(0.1435)
Geometric mean of population	Value from	−0.0228	0.0129	−0.0067
of endpoint catchment areas	current period	(0.0150)	(0.0132)	(0.0088)
Geometric mean of income per	Value from	−0.0817	0.0481	0.0095
capita of endpoint catchment areas	current period	(0.0245)	(0.0248)	(0.0030)
Route distance		0.0910	0.0337	−0.0115
		(0.2886)	(0.0346)	(0.0163)
Percentage of first- and business-class passengers in the regional market	Average value from previous year	0.0117 (0.0928)	−0.0599 (0.0187)	—
Presence at one of the endpoint airports	Status from previous period	0.6136 (0.1801)	0.1450 (0.1625)	1.1388 (0.1027)
Presence at one of the endpoint airports × number of served routes connecting the airport	Value from previous period	0.0198 (0.0015)	0.0259 (0.0023)	−0.0015 (0.0009)
Presence at both endpoint airports	Status from previous period	1.6303 (0.1760)	0.7785 (0.1558)	2.1022 (0.1078)
Presence at both endpoint airports × number of served routes connecting the two airports	Value from previous period	0.0032 (0.0013)	0.0149 (0.0019)	−0.0136 (0.0009)
Adjacent route presence	Status from previous period	−0.7568 (0.0596)	−0.8550 (0.0879)	0.3298 (0.0238)
Route presence of the other LCC	Status from previous period	−0.1129 (0.1035)	−0.3585 (0.1738)	—
Adjacent route presence of the other LCC	Status from previous period	−0.0113 (0.0804)	−0.2159 (0.0848)	—
Presence of the other LCC at one of the endpoint airports	Status from previous period	0.2355 (0.0747)	0.1774 (0.0631)	—
Presence of the other LCC at one of the endpoint airports × number of served routes connecting the airport by the other LCC	Value from previous period	−0.0061 (0.0041)	−0.0141 (0.0038)	—
Presence of the other LCC at both endpoint airports	Status from previous period	0.2619 (0.0873)	0.1973 (0.1034)	—
Presence of the other LCC at both endpoint airports × number of served routes connecting the two airports by the other LCC	Value from previous period	−0.0029 (0.0030)	−0.0073 (0.0038)	—

Table 7.1. *Spatial Entry Patterns of LCCs from Probit Regressions (continued)*

Variables	Note	Ryanair (1)	EasyJet (2)	Southwest (3)
Average flights-to-runway ratio at endpoint airports	Average value from previous year	−0.2421 (0.2543)	0.0512 (0.2444)	—
Maximal flights-to-runway ratio at endpoint airports	Average value from previous year	−0.1233 (0.1656)	−0.0680 (0.1682)	—
Number of seats in regional market	Average value from previous year	0.0265 (0.0045)	0.0112 (0.0042)	—
Number of flights in the regional market	Average value from previous year	−0.0043 (0.0007)	−0.0012 (0.0005)	−0.0034 (0.0022)
Number of carriers in the regional market	Average value from previous year	−0.0053 (0.0062)	0.0054 (0.0060)	0.0106 (0.0078)
Herfindahl–Hirschman index of the regional market	Average value from previous year	−0.5900 (0.0967)	−0.2046 (0.1047)	0.0332 (0.0649)
Number of legacy carriers in the regional market	Average value from previous year	—	—	0.1246 (0.0108)
Vacation dummy	1 if an endpoint airport is in Florida or Nevada	—	—	0.0585 (0.0238)
Hub-route dummy	1 if only one endpoint airport is the hub of some major full-service airlines	—	—	−0.0300 (0.0208)
Double hub-route dummy	1 if both of the endpoint airports are hubs of some major full-service airlines	—	—	−0.0431 (0.0386)
Pseudo R^2		0.18	0.16	0.14
Number of routes		3,573	3,573	13,569
Number of observations		258,322	258,322	666,371

Notes: The dependent variable is a dummy for first-time route entry. Period equals month for Ryanair and EasyJet and equals quarter for Southwest. Adjacent routes are the nearby parallel routes to the one under consideration. The endpoint airports of an adjacent route are located within 100 kilometers of the endpoint airports of the route under consideration. The Herfindahl–Hirschman index is calculated based on the seats (Ryanair and EasyJet) or passengers (Southwest) of carriers in a market.

The DID approach is a useful starting point because both the US and EU samples include many instances of LCC entry and many routes that an LCC has never entered. However, we later discuss concerns with the standard DID approach and develop an improved approach.[22]

We define a route's product as the combination of a carrier, itinerary, and ticket class (first, business, economy full, economy discount and others).[23] We implement DID estimation of the average fare on a route for the following specification:

$$\ln(y_{it}) = \alpha_1\ LCC\ route_{it} + \alpha_2\ LCC\ adjacent_{it}$$
$$+ \alpha_3\ LCC\ one\ airpot_{it} \times LCC\ connectivity_{it}$$
$$+ \alpha_4\ LCC\ two\ airpot_{it} \times LCC\ connectivity_{it}$$
$$+ \alpha_5\ LCC\ one\ airpot_{it} \times LCC\ connectivity_{it} \times no\ LCC_i \quad (1)$$
$$+ \alpha_6\ LCC\ two\ airpot_{it} \times LCC\ connectivity_{it} \times no\ LCC_i$$
$$+ \alpha_7 \ln(pax_{it}) \times \alpha_8 \ln(carrier_{it}) + \mu_y + \mu_m + \mu_i + \varepsilon_{it}$$

where,

y_{it}: Average fare on route i at time t;

LCC route$_{it}$: A dummy indicating that route i is served by one of the LCCs at time t;

LCC adjacent$_{it}$: A dummy indicating that one of route i's adjacent routes but not route i is served by an LCC at time t;

LCC one airport$_{it}$: A dummy indicating that one of the endpoint airports of route i but not route i is served by an LCC at time t;

LCC two airport$_{it}$: A dummy indicating that both endpoint airports of route i but not route i are served by an LCC at time t;

LCC connectivity$_{it}$: Number of routes that an LCC serves that are connected to the endpoint airports of route i during period t; in the EU case, if both LCCs operate at the endpoint airports, we use the larger number of routes that they serve;

no LCC$_i$: A dummy indicating that an LCC has never entered route i during the sampling period;

---

22. Previous studies of the effects of Southwest's entry on fares in US markets include Windle and Dresner (1995); Dresner, Lin, and Windle (1996); Morrison and Winston (2000); Morrison (2001); Goolsbee and Syverson (2008); and Brueckner, Lee, and Singer (2013).

23. We use the fare code information in the IATA data to determine the fare classification for the European carriers. However, we cannot use the fare code information in DB1B because each US airline has its own definition of its fare codes. Thus, following common practice, we define the fare class based on the range of fares.

Table 7.2. *DID Parameter Estimates of the Effects of the LCCs on Average Fares*

Variables	Ryanair and EasyJet		Southwest	
	OLS (1)	IV (2)	OLS (3)	IV (4)
LCC route presence	−0.2976	−0.3895	−0.2080	−0.2607
	(0.0035)	(0.0066)	(0.0028)	(0.0033)
LCC adjacent presence	−0.0308	−0.0330	0.0183	0.0199
	(0.0030)	(0.0032)	(0.0035)	(0.0038)
LCC one-airport presence × LCC	0.0052	0.0089	0.0500	−0.0605
connectivity	(0.0126)	(0.0134)	(0.0081)	(0.0093)
LCC two-airport presence × LCC	−0.0435	−0.0491	0.0242	−0.0672
connectivity	(0.0109)	(0.0116)	(0.0047)	(0.0056)
LCC one-airport presence × LCC	0.0011	−0.0018	−0.2159	−0.1549
connectivity × no LCC entry in the	(0.0004)	(0.0004)	(0.0083)	(0.0092)
sample period				
LCC two-airport presence × LCC	−0.0001	−0.0062	−0.1344	−0.0520
connectivity × no LCC entry in the	(0.0003)	(0.0005)	(0.0101)	(0.0111)
sample period				
Log number of passengers	−0.0539	0.1165	−0.0807	0.0641
	(0.0009)	(0.0101)	(0.0004)	(0.0041)
Log number of carriers	0.0078	−0.0445	0.00004	−0.0999
	(0.0016)	(0.0035)	(0.0008)	(0.0029)
Year dummies	Yes	Yes	Yes	Yes
Month or quarter dummies	Yes	Yes	Yes	Yes
Route dummies	Yes	Yes	Yes	Yes
Number of routes	3,573	3,573	13,590	13,590
Number of observations	289,546	289,546	762,534	762,534
R^2 within	0.15	0.03	0.20	0.07
R^2 between	0.47	0.17	0.16	0.02
R^2 overall	0.35	0.13	0.19	0.01

Note: In the IV estimations we use the geometric mean of the population of the endpoint cities as an instrument for log number of passengers.

pax$_{it}$: Number of passengers on route i at time t;

carriers$_{it}$: Number of carriers serving route i at time t;

μ_y, μ_m, and μ_i: year, month or quarter, and route fixed effects;

ε_i: econometric error term.

We present the DID parameter estimates of the effects of LCC entry on average fares in table 7.2. We use the geometric mean of the population of the endpoint cities as an instrumental variable for the number of passengers, which is endogenous.[24] Note that population is correlated with passengers, but holding

24. We address the endogeneity of airline presence on a route later.

passengers constant, it is not correlated with fares. In addition, population varies across routes and over time. The first two columns of the table present ordinary least squares (OLS) and instrumental variables (IV) estimates for the EU LCCs, and the third and fourth columns present OLS and IV estimates for Southwest.[25]

The IV parameter estimates indicate that the LCCs' actual entry has reduced fares, on average, by approximately 39 percent in the EU markets and by 26 percent in the US markets. The estimates also indicate that the EU LCCs reduce fares when they are adjacent competitors, but that Southwest slightly increases fares when it is an adjacent competitor. Finally, the LCCs have similar effects on fares when they are Type-2 potential competitors that serve both airports but not the route, but Southwest has a larger effect on fares than Ryanair and EasyJet have when the LCCs are Type-1 potential competitors that serve one airport comprising the route. In sum, the LCCs have marked impacts on fares in their respective markets, with the EU carriers reducing fares by more than Southwest reduces fares when we account for actual, potential, and adjacent entry.

At first blush, the findings are plausible, and they are broadly consistent with previous estimates of Southwest's effects on fares. We are not aware of previous DID estimates of the effect of the EU LCCs on fares; thus, we cannot assess our findings in the context of previous research. However, we have concerns about the conventional DID regression approach that raise doubts about the accuracy of our initial estimated effects of LCC entry.[26]

Identification of the parameters relies on the assumption that the route and time dummy variables capture the unobserved route-specific factors and time effects that are correlated with the regressors. This assumption is questionable because both samples contain many routes that capture entry at different points in time over several years in different market environments. Unobserved factors affecting market outcomes are unlikely to be captured by the route fixed effects because they are unlikely to remain constant over time. In addition, the timing of an LCC's entry on different routes is affected mainly by the structure of its initial network; thus, we cannot simply compare the outcomes of markets entered by an LCC with the outcomes of markets not entered by an LCC across different years because many other factors also affect market outcomes. Finally, the DID approach does not separate the effects of actual entry, potential entry, and adjacent competition on fares because those actions may occur sequentially on a route. For example, an LCC's actual entry may occur only several months after its potential entry. If we have many routes where that occurs, identification of the coefficients for the actual and potential entry dummy variables would be contaminated.

---

25. Although we present the average effects of Ryanair and EasyJet on fares in table 7.2, their individual effects on fares were similar.

26. Goodman-Bacon (2021) demonstrates formally the potential biases from the DID regression approach using data with differential treatment timings.

4. An Improved Approach: DID Matching with a Regression Adjustment

We take advantage of our large panel data samples to design a new approach to address the identification problems with the standard DID approach. We use a DID matching approach to compare fares on treated routes (entered by an LCC) with fares on control routes (not entered by an LCC) during the same time window. The approach compares the difference in fares on routes entered by an LCC with the difference in fares on matched routes without LCC entry both before and after LCC entry on the treated routes. Importantly, we also separate the effects of LCC actual, potential, and adjacent entry on route fares by first quantifying the effect of actual entry conditional on potential entry and then quantifying the effect of potential entry, excluding the effect of an LCC's adjacent entry. Finally, we quantify the effect of adjacent entry, excluding the effects of both an LCC's actual and potential entry. In appendix B of this chapter, we present the formal framework and less stringent identification assumptions for the DID matching approach we use compared with the standard DID regression method.

We match a treated route to multiple control routes by satisfying a matching criterion that we explain in the next section. For a treated route i, y_i^{pre} and y_i^{post} denote the average fare before and after the LCC's entry, respectively.[27] For a matched route i', $y_{i'}^{pre}$ and $y_{i'}^{post}$ denote the average fare before and after the LCC's entry on the treated route, respectively. The nonparametric DID comparison on a matched pair is given by $\tau_{ii'}$, which measures the net change rate of the route average fare caused by an LCC's entry:

$$
\tau_{ii'} = \underbrace{\left(\frac{y_i^{post} - y_i^{pre}}{y_i^{pre}} \right)}_{\substack{\text{rate of change of the} \\ \text{average fare on a} \\ \text{treated route}}} - \underbrace{\left(\frac{y_{i'}^{post} - y_{i'}^{pre}}{y_{i'}^{pre}} \right)}_{\substack{\text{rate of change of the} \\ \text{average fare on a} \\ \text{treated route}}}.
\tag{2}
$$

The first term on the right-hand side is the rate of change of the average fare on a treated route, and the second term is the rate of change of the average fare on a matched route, which captures the time trend of the fare change in the counterfactual scenario where LCC entry does not occur.

It is possible that a treated route and the matched control routes have different characteristics that are correlated with the average route fare. We therefore construct variables, such as the number of carriers, number of passengers, and population and income at the endpoint airports, to control for differences

---

27. We average the route average fare over the quarters (or months) pre- and postentry.

between the treated and control routes.[28] We remove the effects of the control variables on the computed outcome for our computation of the net change rate of the route average fare caused by an LCC's entry in equation (2).

Formally, we denote $\Delta \mathbf{X}_{ii'} = (\mathbf{X}_i^{post} - \mathbf{X}_i^{pre}) - (\mathbf{X}_{i'}^{post} - \mathbf{X}_{i'}^{pre})$ as the vector of the DID control variables on a treated route i and a control route i' and we run the following regression without a constant term:

$$\tau_{ii'} = \Delta \mathbf{X}_{ii'} \boldsymbol{\beta} + \varepsilon_{ii'} \tag{3}$$

where $\boldsymbol{\beta}$ is a vector of parameters and $\varepsilon_{ii'}$ is the error term. If the DID of the route average fare is completely determined by the DID of the control variables, then $\hat{\varepsilon}_{ii'} \equiv \tau_{ii'} - \hat{\tau}_{ii'}$ would be expected to be close to zero, where $\hat{\tau}_{ii'}$ is the predicted value from the regression equation (3). We therefore interpret a nonzero $\hat{\varepsilon}_{ii'}$ as the net effect of the LCC's entry on the route average fare, after controlling for other differences between the control and treated routes.

In sum, we estimate the average treatment effect of an LCC's entry on a route's average fare, excluding the effects of observed market characteristics, by calculating:

$$\delta = \frac{1}{N} \sum_{i \in \Psi} \frac{1}{M_i} \sum_{i' \in \Gamma_i} \hat{\varepsilon}_{ii'} \tag{4}$$

where Γ_i is the set of matched routes to the treated route, M_i is the number of routes in the set, Ψ is the set of treated routes, and N is the total number of matched pairs. We use the bootstrap technique to construct the confidence interval of the estimator in equation (4) by randomly sampling the matched pairs (i,i') with replacement to obtain a bootstrapped sample with the same size as the original sample of matched pairs. We then compute δ using the bootstrapped sample and we repeat the process one hundred times to obtain the empirical distribution of δ over the bootstrapped samples, from which we construct the confidence interval of the estimator.

A final concern with our methodology is that unobserved market characteristics that are correlated with route fares may influence an LCC to enter a route. We address this concern by restricting the set of matched control routes for a treated route to those that the LCC entered at least two years later.[29] We therefore assume that the timing of an LCC's entry on different routes is driven mainly by the structure of its initial network and not by route characteristics. This assumption

---

28. Intercity rail competition is not an important issue in US markets. In European markets, our matching algorithm accounts for rail competition if the LCC entries followed similar decision rules over time. The Channel Tunnel Rail Link connecting London and Paris has had a modest impact on air passenger volumes.

29. Our basic findings were not affected when we conducted sensitivity analyses of the two-year threshold.

Figure 7.4. *Timeline (in months) of an LCC's Actual Entry on a Treated Route*

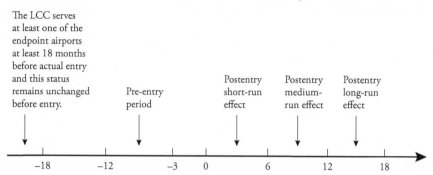

is plausible because the LCCs' networks have primarily evolved from their initial headquarters in Texas (Southwest), England (EasyJet), and Ireland (Ryanair). In addition, as shown in table 1, an LCC tends to enter a route only when it already serves at least one of the endpoint airports, and it is more likely to enter a route when it already serves both endpoint airports.

5. Criteria for Matching Control Routes to Treated Routes

We structure our analysis to characterize the pre-entry and postentry periods and to distinguish between the different types of LCC entry. We define the pre-entry period as four to twelve months before actual route entry and we define the postentry period as eighteen months after actual entry. Within the postentry period, we define zero to six months after entry as the short run, seven to twelve months as the medium run, and thirteen to eighteen months as the long run. We summarize the timeline for a treated route in figure 7.4. Because potential entry occurs at least eighteen months before actual entry, it is likely to be unrelated to the eventual market fare when actual entry occurs. We exclude the three-month period before actual entry because a time lag may exist between an LCC's announcement that it plans to serve a route and when it begins serving the route.[30]

Figure 7.5 shows the timeline for determining the set of control routes that match the treated route. The LCC serves at least one of the endpoint airports on a control route at least eighteen months before actual entry on the treated route. However, its actual entry on a control route occurs at least twenty-four months after its actual entry on the treated route, thereby avoiding any effect its entry on a control route may have on its long-run effect on the treated route.

---

30. We observed that the time gap between an entry announcement and actual entry was, on average, more than one quarter. Thus, in the US case, we excluded two quarters before Southwest's actual entry in a market.

Figure 7.5. *Timeline (in months) for Defining a Control Route and a Treated Route for Routes Entered by a Given LCC*

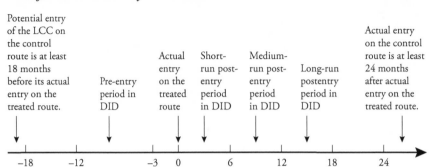

Selection of the Sample of Routes

We now summarize our assumptions to select treated routes and control routes to estimate the distinct effects of LCCs' actual, potential, and adjacent entry on average fares. We construct four modules:

—the effect of Southwest's actual entry without potential entry, excluding the effect of its adjacent entry; this module is specific to Southwest Airlines because it arises in its US domestic route network;

—the effect of an LCC's actual entry conditional on both types of an LCC's potential entry, excluding the effect of an LCC's adjacent entry;

—the effect of both types of an LCC's potential entry, excluding the effects of its actual and adjacent entry; and

—the effect of an LCC's adjacent entry, excluding the effect of its actual and potential entry.

In table 7.3, we list the conditions for a given module that a route must satisfy to be a treated route and that it must satisfy to be a control route. The conditions are aligned with the timelines that we presented in figures 7.4 and 7.5. We also indicate certain robustness checks that we conducted.

Balancing Test

The preceding conditions to define treated and control routes assume that the *timing* of an LCC's entry into different routes is exogenous. We test this assumption formally with a balance test proposed by Rosenbaum and Rubin (1985) by testing whether routes entered by an LCC in earlier years were like those entered by the LCC in later years.

The test statistic, $B(X)$, is based on the standardized difference:

$$B(X) = 100 \cdot \frac{\bar{X}_F - \bar{X}_M}{\sqrt{\dfrac{S_F^2(X) + S_M^2(X)}{2}}} \tag{5}$$

Table 7.3. *Conditions a Treated Route and a Control Route Must Satisfy*

Treated route	Control route
Module 1 (on US markets only): The effect of Southwest's actual entry without potential entry, excluding the effect of its adjacent entry.	
1. Southwest entered a route after 1993 and served the route for at least 8 quarters. 2. Southwest was not a potential competitor on the route before its actual entry. 3. Southwest did not serve an adjacent route before its actual entry.	1. It is not adjacent to the treated route. 2. Southwest did not serve the route and the route's adjacent routes for at least 8 quarters after it actually entered the treated route. 3. Southwest was not a potential competitor on the route before and at least 8 quarters after it actually entered the treated route. 4. Southwest eventually entered the control route in later years without potential entry before the actual entry.
Module 2 (on both US and EU markets): The effect of an LCC's actual entry conditional on both types of an LCC's potential entry, excluding the effect of an LCC's adjacent entry.	
EU markets 1. The LCC entered the route in a month after July 2006 and continued to provide service. 2. The LCC was a potential competitor on the route for at least 18 months before actual entry. 3. The LCC did not serve an adjacent route before the actual entry. 4. After the LCC entered the route, the other LCC did not enter the route and an adjacent route for at least 24 months. 5. Before the LCC entered the route, the other LCC was not a potential competitor on the route. **US markets** 1. Southwest entered the route after the second quarter of 1994 and continued to serve the route for at least 8 quarters. 2. Southwest was a potential competitor on the route for at least 6 quarters before the actual entry. 3. Southwest did not serve an adjacent route before actual entry.	**EU markets** 1. It is not adjacent to the treated route. 2. An LCC did not serve the route and the route's adjacent routes for at least 24 months after the actual entry on the treated route. 3. It was potentially entered by an LCC at least 18 months before the actual entry on the treated route. 4. The same LCC that entered the treated route entered the route in at least 24 months after the actual entry on the treated route. **US markets** 1. It is not adjacent to the treated route. 2. Southwest did not serve the route and the route's adjacent routes for at least 8 quarters after the actual entry on the treated route. 3. It was potentially entered by Southwest at least 6 quarters before the actual entry on the treated route. 4. Southwest eventually entered the route at least 8 quarters after the actual entry on the treated route.

(continued)

Table 7.3. *Conditions a Treated Route and a Control Route Must Satisfy (continued)*

Treated route	Control route
Module 3 (on both US and EU markets): The effect of an LCC's potential entry, excluding the effects of its actual and adjacent entry.	
EU markets	**EU markets**
1. An LCC started to operate continually at one or both endpoint airports but not the route itself after July 2006.	1. It is not adjacent to the treated route.
2. Following the potential entry, an LCC did not actually enter the route for at least 24 months.	2. It was free of actual, potential and adjacent entry before the potential entry on the treated route.
3. Before the potential entry, an LCC did not serve the endpoint airports of an adjacent route.	3. The same LCC potentially entered the treated route at least 24 months after the potential entry on the treated route.
US markets	**US markets**
1. Southwest became a potential competitor after the second quarter of 1994 and continued to serve the endpoint airport or airports.	1. It is not adjacent to the treated route.
2. If Southwest served both endpoint airports, the time between entering them sequentially was not less than 8 quarters.	2. After Southwest became a potential entrant on the treated route, it did not serve the control route and the adjacent routes for at least 8 quarters.
3. After it became a potential competitor, Southwest did not enter the route for at least 8 quarters.	3. After Southwest became a potential entrant on the treated route, it did not become a potential entrant on the control route for at least 8 quarters.
4. Before it became a potential competitor, Southwest did not enter an adjacent route.	4. The distance of the control route was similar to the distance of the treated route. (Because there are so many routes for potential entry, we use distance as an additional criteria to control for the number of control routes and for heterogeneity.)
5. After it became a potential competitor, Southwest did not serve an adjacent route.	

Table 7.3. *Conditions a Treated Route and a Control Route Must Satisfy (continued)*

Treated route	Control route
Module 4 (on both US and EU markets): The effect of an LCC's adjacent entry, excluding the effect of its actual and potential entry.	

EU markets

1. An LCC operated on one of the adjacent routes after July 2006 for at least 24 months.
2. After adjacent entry, the LCC was not a potential competitor for at least 24 months.
3. The other LCC was not an actual or adjacent competitor of the route.

US markets

1. Southwest served at least one of the adjacent routes after the second quarter of 1994 for at least 8 quarters.
2. After Southwest's adjacent entry, it was not a potential competitor for at least 8 quarters.

EU markets

1. It is not adjacent to the treated route.
2. An LCC did not serve the route and its adjacent routes for at least 24 months after actual entry on the treated route.
3. An LCC was a potential competitor on the route at least 18 months before entry on the treated route.

US markets

1. It is not adjacent to the treated route.
2. After Southwest's adjacent entry on the treated route, it did not serve the control route and its adjacent routes for at least 8 quarters.
3. After Southwest's adjacent entry on the treated route, it was not a potential competitor on the control route for at least 8 quarters.
4. The distance of the control route was similar to the distance of the treated route.

where for each covariate, $\bar{X}_F$ and $\bar{X}_M$ are the sample means for the full (F) affected routes (i.e., all the treated routes in our sample) and the matched (M) treated routes (i.e., the routes entered later by an LCC that are compared with each treated route); and $S_F^2(X)$ and $S_M^2(X)$ are the corresponding sample variances. Intuitively, $B(X)$ measures the difference in the means of a conditioning variable, scaled by the square root of the variances in the samples. Rosenbaum and Rubin (1985) define imbalance for a covariate as exceeding twenty in absolute value.

We found that the standardized differences in both the US and EU samples of the routes' average fares, distances, endpoint populations, and endpoint incomes per capita had absolute values less than twenty, which indicates that those route characteristics pass the balancing test. Other route characteristics, namely the number of carriers and Herfindahl–Hirschman index of the city-pair market, had standardized differences that exceeded twenty in some modules. However, we can use our regression adjustment to remove the effect of that imbalance on the results.

Table 7.4. *DID Matching Results on the Effect of Southwest's Actual Entry without Prior Potential Entry on Route Average Fare*

	All routes entered		Only connecting routes entered	
	Excluding the effects of observed market characteristics (1)	*Including the effects of observed market characteristics* (2)	*Excluding the effects of observed market characteristics* (3)	*Including the effects of observed market characteristics* (4)
Short-run effect	−10.2%	−23.8%	−11.3%	−20.4%
	[−10.5%, −9.8%]	[−24.2%, −23.4%]	[−11.6%, −10.9%]	[−20.8%, −20.0%]
Medium-run effect	−13.2%	−24.3%	−13.1%	−21.0%
	[−13.6%, −12.7%]	[−24.8%, −23.8%]	[−13.5%, −12.5%]	[−21.6%, −20.5%]
Long-run effect	−13.7%	−24.6%	−13.4%	−20.8%
	[−14.1%, −13.2%]	[−25.1%, −24.2%]	[−14.0%, −13.0%]	[−21.4%, −20.4%]
Number of treated routes	227	227	161	161
Number of observations	9,093	9,093	5,204	5,204

Notes: Short run is 1–2 quarters after entry, medium run is 3–4 quarters after entry, and long run is 5–6 quarters after entry. We report the median along with the [5%-ile, 95%-ile] for each of the effects. The confidence intervals are calculated using the bootstrap technique.

6. Estimation Results

Our approach identifies the distinct effects of LCCs' actual, potential, and adjacent entry on average fares in the short, medium, and long runs; thus, we report the estimation results for each type of entry in separate tables. As noted, Southwest entered some routes without prior potential entry, but our data indicated that the EU LCCs entered routes only with prior potential entry. Southwest's entry without prior potential entry, shown in table 7.4, reduces fares, on average, roughly 10 percent in the short run and nearly 14 percent in the long run. The second column of the table shows that the regression adjustment is important because we would have significantly overestimated the effect of Southwest's entry on fares without it. Hereafter, we report results only with the regression adjustment. The third and fourth columns of table 7.4 report findings for entry only on connecting routes and show that they are very similar to the findings for entry on all routes.

Both Southwest and the EU LCCs entered routes conditional on potential entry. As shown in table 7.5, their entry has different effects on fares, which suggests that the EU and US incumbent airlines respond differently to an LCC's actual entry. Entry by an EU LCC, conditional on its potential entry at one or both endpoint airports, reduces fares roughly 15 percent in the short and medium run and 10 percent in the long run, possibly because an LCC cuts prices substantially in the

Table 7.5. *DID Matching Results on the Effect of a LCC's Actual Entry with Potential Entry on Route Average Fare*

	EU conditional on both types of potential entry (1)	*US conditional on Type-1 potential entry* (2)	*US conditional on Type-2 potential entry* (3)
Short-run effect	–14%	–17.7%	–4.0%
	[–16%, –12%]	[–18.7%, –16.9%]	[–4.6%, –3.4%]
Medium-run effect	–15%	–17.5%	–5.0%
	[–17%, –12%]	[–18.2%, –16.8%]	[–5.7%, –4.4%]
Long-run effect	–10%	–18.8%	–3.8%
	[–13%, –8%]	[–19.9%, –17.8%]	[–4.5%, –3.0%]
Number of treated routes	120	159	136
Number of observations	477	2,925	1,800

Notes: Southwest did not potentially enter the control route up to 8 quarters after the actual entry on the treated route. Type-1 potential entry indicates presence at only one endpoint airport. Type-2 potential entry indicates presence at both endpoint airports. The effects of observed market characteristics are excluded in all results. Short run is 0–6 months after entry, medium run is 7–12 months after entry, and long run is 13–18 months after entry. We report the median along with the [5%-ile, 95%-ile] for each of the effects. The confidence intervals are calculated using the bootstrap technique.

short and medium runs to capture market share, but gradually adjusts prices after the initial entry shock. In contrast, the last two columns of table 7.5 show that Southwest's entry, conditional on it being a potential competition at one endpoint airport, reduces fares by nearly 18 percent in the short run and nearly 19 percent in the long run.[31] However, its effect on fares is much less (roughly 4 percent) when it is a potential competitor at both endpoint airports and in all likelihood has had a strong effect on fares before it actually enters a market.

As expected, we find in table 7.6 that when an LCC is a potential competitor, it reduces fares more if it serves both endpoint airports (Type 2) than if it serves only one of the endpoint airports (Type 1). Generally, Southwest has a much larger effect for this type of entry than the EU LCCs have. In fact, Southwest's effect as a Type-1 potential competitor, shown in column (3), is somewhat greater than the EU LCC's effect as a Type-2 potential competitor.

We previously speculated that Southwest's effect as an actual competitor is less when it is a Type-2 potential competitor than when it is a Type-1 potential competitor because it already has had a strong effect on fares when it provides Type-2 potential competition. Column (4) of table 7.6 is consistent with this speculation because we find that when Southwest is a Type-2 potential competitor,

31. We found that the fare effect of Southwest's actual entry conditional on being a Type-1 potential competitor was somewhat greater when it entered routes that were more concentrated and when it entered hub routes.

Table 7.6. *DID Matching Results on the Effect of a LCC's Potential Entry on Route Average Fare*

	EU		US	
	Type 1 (1)	Type 2 (2)	Type 1 (3)	Type 2 (4)
Short-run effect	−0.1% [−0.2%, −0.0%]	−1.3% [−2.8%, −0.1%]	−2.3% [−2.9%, −1.9%]	−8.3% [−8.7%, −7.9%]
Medium-run effect	−0.3% [−0.1%, −0.4%]	−2.2% [−3.6%, −0.6%]	−3.3% [−3.9%, −2.9%]	−9.7% [−10.0%, −9.1%]
Long-run effect	0.6% [−0.1%, 1.1%]	−0.3% [−1.3%, 0.8%]	−3.2% [−3.8%, −2.7%]	−7.2% [−7.7%, −6.8%]
Number of treated routes	180	82	2,287	224
Number of observations	4,025	1,198	73,889	7,944

Notes: In column (4), the time interval between carriers entering the two airports is not less than 6 quarters. Type-1 potential entry indicates presence at only one endpoint airport. Type-2 potential entry indicates presence at both endpoint airports. The effects of observed market characteristics are excluded in all results. Short run is 0–6 months after entry, medium run is 7–12 months after entry, and long run is 13–18 months after entry. We report the median along with the [5%-ile, 95%-ile] for each of the effects. The confidence intervals are calculated using the bootstrap technique.

it reduces fares by roughly 8 percent to nearly 10 percent in the short and medium runs but roughly 7 percent in the long run. Finally, we tested whether Southwest's effect as a potential competitor is consistent with its behavior, noted previously, of primarily entering short- and medium-haul markets. We found that Southwest reduced fares as a Type-1 potential competitor by 8 percent on routes less than five hundred miles and that this effect declined with distance, becoming negligible on routes greater than 1,500 miles because incumbent carriers were presumably less concerned that Southwest would eventually enter those routes.

Southwest also has a larger effect on fares as an adjacent competitor than the EU LCCs have, especially in the long run. We show in table 7.7 that adjacent competition provided by all the LCCs reduces fares roughly 3 percent in the short and medium runs; however, in the long run, Southwest reduces fares 5 percent and the EU LCCs reduce fares by slightly more than 1 percent.

In sum, we have developed a methodological approach, DID matching with a regression adjustment, that enables us to provide a more detailed and more accurate empirical assessment of the effect of LCC competition on fares than the conventional DID approach does. Importantly, we can identify distinct effects of actual, potential, and adjacent competition on fares and show variations in those effects for Southwest and the EU LCCs. Our major findings include:

Table 7.7. *DID Matching Results on the Effect of a LCC's Adjacent Entry on Route Average Fare*

	EU (1)	US (2)
Short-run effect	–2.8%	–3.0%
	[–4.4%, –1.2%]	[–3.4%, –2.6%]
Medium-run effect	–3.5%	–3.9%
	[–5.2%, –1.9%]	[–4.3%, –3.5%]
Long-run effect	–1.3%	–5.1%
	[–2.7%, 0.01%]	[–5.5%, –4.6%]
Number of treated routes	77	441
Number of observations	823	7,348

Notes: Short run is 0–6 months after entry, medium run is 7–12 months after entry, and long run is 13–18 months after entry. The effects of observed market characteristics are excluded in all results. We report the median along with the [5%-ile, 95%-ile] for each of the effects. The confidence intervals are calculated using the bootstrap technique.

—Depending on the type of potential entry that an LCC provides, Southwest's actual entry in a market reduces fares more than when an EU LCC enters a market.

—When Southwest is a potential or adjacent competitor, it reduces fares notably more than when an EU LCC is a potential or adjacent competitor.

—Considering the effect of all types of entry, Southwest reduces fares by as much as 30 percent on average, with potential and adjacent entry accounting for a nontrivial amount of the decline in fares.

—Considering the effect of all types of entry, an EU LCC reduces fares, on average, by as much as 20 percent, with actual entry accounting for most of the decline in fares.

—Competition provided by an LCC appears to be more intense in US markets than in EU markets, likely because entry into US airports is less constrained by slot controls and by the limited availability of gates.[32]

—Compared with our main findings, the estimates that we obtained using the traditional DID approach overestimate the full effect of EU LCCs on fares and underestimate the full effect of Southwest on fares, which indicates that the

32. For example, in 2016, according to IATA, of the 180 slot-controlled airports in the world, ninety-three were in the EU and two were in the United States. See Nathalie Lenoir, "Research for TRAN Committee—Airport Slots and Aircraft Size at EU Airports," 2016, http://www.europarl.europa.eu/RegData/etudes/IDAN/2016/585873/IPOL_IDA(2016)585873_EN.pdf.

In the EU, slots are allocated based on the "grandfather rights" rule, which tends to benefit incumbent, mainly national, airlines by restricting the slots available to potential new entrants (Barrett 2004). The difference in constraints imposed by slot controls in the EU and US is unlikely to be affected by possible differences in the criteria for imposing slot controls.

Table 7.8. *DID Matching Results on the Route Average Fare Effect of Southwest's Actual Entry on Routes without Other LCCs' Entry*

	Direct entry without potential entry (1)	Southwest operated at only one endpoint airport before entry (2)	Southwest operated at both endpoint airports before entry (3)
Short-run effect	−10.8%	−20.0%	−4.9%
	[−11.4%, −10.3%]	[−21.4%, −18.8%]	[−5.7%, −3.9%]
Medium-run effect	−13.7%	−20.7%	−6.2%
	[−14.4%, −13.0%]	[−22.5%, −19.1%]	[−7.3%, −4.9%]
Long-run effect	−14.8%	−23.0%	−5.3%
	[−15.4%, −14.1%]	[−24.6%, −21.0%]	[−6.7%, −4.2%]
Number of treated routes	146	133	89
Number of observations	3,617	811	736

Notes: No other LCCs served either the treated or the control routes up to 8 quarters after the actual entry of Southwest on the treated route. The effects of observed market characteristics are excluded in all results. Short run is 1–2 quarters after entry, medium run is 3–4 quarters after entry, and long run is 5–6 quarters after entry. We report the median along with the [5%-ile, 95%-ile] for each of the effects. The confidence intervals are calculated using the bootstrap technique.

methodological improvements provided by our approach are important for accurately assessing the effect on fares of allowing cabotage and for other applications.

7. Additional Robustness Checks

In addition to Southwest, other LCCs and ULCCs serve US markets, including Allegiant Air, Frontier Airlines, JetBlue, Spirit Airlines, Sun Country Airlines, and Virgin America (now part of Alaska Airlines), which could affect fares and potentially bias our estimates of Southwest's effect on fares if they provide service on the control routes. As a robustness check, we performed calculations where we considered only those routes where the preceding airlines did not serve the treated or the control routes for at least eight quarters after Southwest actually entered the treated routes. We present the results in table 7.8.[33] As expected, we find that without the presence of other LCCs and ULCCs as actual competitors, the effect of Southwest's entry on average fares under alternative states of potential entry is greater, but the quantitative effect is not much greater than the effect in the base case, which can be interpreted a lower bound.

Ryanair and EasyJet account for most of the traffic carried by LCCs in the European Union during our sample. Given that Southwest's effect on fares was

---

33. Because it is difficult to exclude all routes where other LCCs and ULCCs were potential competitors, we focused on the effect of Southwest's actual entry.

modestly affected when we controlled for other LCCs and ULCCs in the US, Ryanair's and EasyJet's effect on fares is likely to be even less affected if we controlled for other LCCs on EU routes.

Because LCCs are growing, the number of routes that connect to their endpoint airports varies over time; greater connectivity increases the probability that an LCC will enter a route. In response, incumbent carriers may employ different pricing strategies as the probability of an LCC's entry changes with its connectivity. As a robustness check, we reevaluated the effect of Southwest's potential entry controlling for the number of routes that it served from its endpoint airports; however, we found that Southwest's effect on fares as a potential competitor increased only slightly.

8. Travelers' Potential Gains from Cabotage

We have found that Southwest's actual, potential, and adjacent entry has reduced fares, on average, 30 percent in US markets. Although Southwest does not serve every US route, and it particularly avoids long-haul routes with highly congested endpoint airports, it does serve many short-haul and medium-haul routes. Without Southwest's presence, those routes are more likely than long-haul routes to have elevated fares because they are more likely to be underserved.

Southwest's entry also has generated significant gains in consumer surplus. To quantify those gains, we assume a simple function with a constant elasticity of demand:

$$Q = aP^e \tag{6}$$

where Q is the demand for air travel, a is a positive constant, P is the average fare, and e is the constant elasticity of demand. We assume a route elasticity of demand of -1.4 based on Smyth and Pearce's (2008) analysis of US city-pair routes and we derive a as the mean of Q/P^e for each route.[34] We then calculate the change in consumer surplus, ΔCS, caused by Southwest's entry using the following expression:

$$\Delta CS = -\sum_t \Delta CS_t = -\sum_t \sum_r \int_{p_c}^{p_0} \hat{a}_r p_{rt}^e \, dp \tag{7}$$

where p_c is the counterfactual average fare following Southwest's entry in category c (actual, potential, or adjacent), p_0 is the observed average fare after Southwest's entry, and r is the route affected by Southwest's entry.[35] We appropriately account for the sequential pattern of Southwest's entry as an actual, potential, and adjacent

---

34. We do not distinguish between short-haul and long-haul markets here because Smyth and Pearce (2008) obtained very similar elasticity estimates for both types of markets.

35. Because the demand elasticity has a minus sign, we include a minus sign in equation (7) so consumer surplus is positive if the average fare following Southwest's entry is lower than the average fare before Southwest's entry.

competitor, and we find that travelers gained roughly $5 billion from Southwest's entry in US markets during the last year of our sample and gained $67.6 billion (2000 dollars) from its entry during the entire sample period 1994 to 2014.

The recent motivation for a policy that grants cabotage rights to foreign airlines has arisen from concerns that the reduction in the number of airlines at the national level following several mergers has reduced competition. Given our findings about the large effects of Southwest, an LLC, on fares and travelers' welfare, the entry of another effective LCC might be desirable to address those concerns.

We assume that Ryanair or EasyJet would take advantage of the opportunity to serve US domestic markets and we simulate the effect that such entry could have on fares. This simulation captures to a notable extent the effect that a Southwest-type foreign entrant would have on fares for three reasons. First, the EU LCCs' business plans were modeled after Southwest's; thus, they primarily serve short- and medium-haul markets and tend to avoid highly congested airports. Second, like Southwest, the EU LCCs' costs per seat-mile are notably lower than their competitors'. Third, EU LCCs' entry has reduced fares significantly despite formidable entry barriers that limit competition.

Because the EU LCCs nor any other foreign carrier do not serve US domestic routes, we make some plausible assumptions to execute the simulation. First, we assume that an EU LCC would not enter routes that Southwest or another US LCC or ULCC currently serve. This assumption is consistent with Ryanair and EasyJet's tendency to avoid competing on the same routes. Second, we assume that an EU LCC's entry on US routes would not reduce fares by as much as Southwest's entry has reduced fares, but we assume its entry would reduce fares more than its entry in EU markets has reduced fares because it would be less constrained by airport entry barriers. Thus, we assume that an EU LCC's entry would reduce fares 25 percent, on average, in US markets, midway between our 20 percent and 30 percent estimates of fare reductions resulting from entry by the EU LCCs and Southwest.

Under those assumptions, we find that an EU LCC's entry in US markets would, in the short-run, generate a modest but nontrivial $1.6 billion annual gain to travelers (we discuss long-run effects below). Our qualitative finding would not change if we used the upper and lower bound assumptions of –2.5 and –0.7 for the elasticity of demand or if we assumed that an EU LCC's entry reduced fares by plus or minus 5 percentage points.

The new entrant would address a potential gap in airline competition by entering city-pair markets that in our sample have, on average, 2.58 carriers, compared with the 3.94 carriers on average that serve the city-pair markets that LCC carriers currently serve. At the same time, the welfare gain is modest because competition on US routes is generally very intense, as indicated by the fact that Southwest and the other LCCs and ULCCs serve routes that account for 80 percent of US domestic passengers. Policymakers should be reassured that the state of airline competition is healthy, but they should not be diverted from the possibility that travelers could still benefit significantly if foreign airlines were granted cabotage rights.

Cabotage would usher in a new era of airline competition, which in the long run would affect domestic and international markets, because airlines would focus on providing seamless service in a global market. For example, companies such as Google and airlines such as Emirates are envisioning seamless travel and lifestyle experiences, which rely on one airline to transport passengers from their domestic origins, possibly in low-density markets, to their foreign destinations, also possibly in low-density markets, with customized amenities.

Travelers' value of potential service improvements indicates that seamless travel could generate significant welfare gains to travelers. For example, Yan and Winston (2014) estimate that travelers' willingness to pay for nonstop flights to avoid connecting flights exceeds $200 per hour. The high valuation reflects passengers' disutility associated with transfer wait time in US airports. American travelers would likely have an even greater value of transfer wait time at foreign airports because they may fear that they could miss critical announcements about their connecting flight, and they may be less comfortable waiting for a flight in an unfamiliar environment. Total transfer wait time for international trips also is long, typically more than three hours. So, seamless travel that tightens connections and reduces the disutility associated with transfer wait time at a foreign airport could generate several billion dollars in benefits to airline travelers. A rough calculation that provides supporting evidence for this claim is provided in appendix C to this chapter.

Almost all carriers would have the incentive and ability to restructure their domestic and international networks to compete effectively in a deregulated global airline market. As in the case of domestic deregulation and open skies, travelers would then accrue gains from lower fares and improved service on international routes and on domestic routes of all hub classifications that could help feed international routes. Policymakers' anecdotes about the lack of competition on selected routes also would be addressed because the airlines that comprise the deregulated global air transportation industry would be unlikely to "leave any domestic route behind."[36]

---

36. Azar, Schmalz, and Tecu (2018) argue that the largest investors in US airlines own stock in multiple airlines and that common ownership raises fares. If so, entry by foreign airlines may also reduce fares by diluting the extent of common ownership of competing carriers. Currently, US law prevents foreign companies and individuals from owning more than 25 percent of a US airline, but policymakers have not considered ownership restrictions on companies and individuals investing in a foreign airline operating in the United States. Currently, US carriers hold stock in European airlines; for example, Delta has a 49 percent holding in Virgin Atlantic. If cabotage rights were granted, it is not clear whether the largest investors in US airlines could or would attempt to increase their ownership of foreign airlines.

9. Summary

Given the absence of foreign airlines that serve US domestic routes, we have argued that LCC competition in the United States and European Union is a useful starting point to explore the potential effects of cabotage because the LCCs have adopted a similar business model, shared similar cost characteristics, and been leading competitors in their respective markets. After estimating the fare effects of actual, potential, and adjacent entry by Southwest, the leading US LCC, and by Ryanair and EasyJet, the leading EU LCCs, we have extrapolated from those estimates to simulate the effect of entry by an EU LCC in US markets.

We designed a new methodological approach, DID matching with a regression adjustment, to estimate the fare effects of LCC entry, which addresses the bias from endogenous entry that is not addressed by the conventional DID approach used in previous research, to estimate the fare effects of Southwest's entry. The potential bias is important because we found that the conventional DID approach underestimates the fare effect of Southwest's entry and overestimates the fare effect of the EU LCCs' entry. In general, our methodology could overcome the bias from using the conventional DID approach to analyze the effects of entry in other industries that are characterized by markets that are geographically isolated and firms with an initial network that drives their expansion.

We found that Southwest's entry reduces fares by 30 percent in US markets, with potential and adjacent entry having important effects, and that the EU LCCs reduce fares by 20 percent in EU markets, with actual entry accounting for most of the effect. To the best of our knowledge, the latter is the first estimate of the effect of the EU LCCs' entry on fares. We then found from our simulation that an EU LCC's entry in US markets would generate a modest $1.6 billion annual welfare gain to travelers.

We have acknowledged that we do not know whether an EU LCC or other foreign carriers would enter US markets if the US government granted cabotage rights to foreign airlines. However, we are confident that some US airlines would enter European markets if European governments reciprocated and granted those airlines cabotage rights; thus, it is reasonable to believe that, in practice, cabotage would eventually lead to foreign entry in US markets that would benefit travelers.

We also have qualified our finding because it captures the effect of only one carrier's entry in US markets and does not account for the change in global airline networks, including competition from other carriers on domestic and international routes. We argued that changes in the global network would be the largest source of gains from cabotage because carriers would seek to provide seamless air travel throughout the world. We therefore conclude that the potential gains from allowing cabotage are likely to be substantial and that the influx of new entry should finally assuage policymakers' fears of insufficient airline competition in US markets. At the same time, the arguments against cabotage have greatly weakened.

Finally, we have focused on granting global cabotage rights for passenger traffic, but cabotage rights also should be granted for freight traffic, especially because international air cargo has grown substantially during the past several decades. A multilateral system of cargo cabotage rights would allow air freight carriers to optimize their networks, which tend to be circular instead of point-to-point, by enabling them to transport cargo through domestic points and third countries and to set up regional air cargo hubs. The deregulated global air freight system would benefit shippers by reducing their costs and by increasing intermodal competition with ocean freight transportation.

Hopefully, this chapter is the beginning of a strong case for granting passenger and freight cabotage rights to all air carriers, which policymakers throughout the world will consider and eventually implement to benefit the world's airline travelers and shippers by deregulating the global airline passenger and freight transportation industry.

Appendix A. Supplemental Tables

Table 7.A1. *Summary Statistics of US Data*

Variable	Mean	SD	Min	Max
Presence of Southwest on the route	0.113	0.317	0	1
Presence of Southwest at the origin airport	0.352	0.478	0	1
Presence of Southwest at the destination airport	0.424	0.494	0	1
Number of low-cost carriers on the route	0.172	0.464	0	5
Number of legacy carriers on the route	2.545	1.715	0	8
Number of carriers in the city market	3.941	2.917	1	18
Number of legacy carriers in the city market	3.002	1.923	0	8
Number of passengers on the route (thousands)	0.701	2.25	1	50.54
Average fare on the route (dollars)	215.10	76.89	16.55	1,501
Number of passengers in the city market (thousands)	2.6	10.8	1	243.4
Herfindahl–Hirschman index of the city market of the city market	0.610	0.279	0.111	1
Number of flights in the city market (thousands)	3.21	6.41	45	67.13
Number of routes served by Southwest at the origin airport	10.17	16.22	0	64
Number of routes served by Southwest at the destination airport	12.46	17.44	0	63
Origin hub dummy	0.211	0.408	0	1
Destination hub dummy	0.194	0.395	0	1
Geometric mean of the populations of the endpoint cities (millions)	1.622	1.855	0.068	16
Geometric mean of income per capita of the endpoint cities (thousands of dollars)	30.21	3.87	14.83	54.35
Route distance (thousands of miles)	1.045	0.648	0.025	4.004
Number of observations	762,534			

Notes: We do not include taxes in the fares because the tax does not vary across domestic markets.

Table 7.A2. *Summary Statistics of EU Data*

Variable	Mean	SD	Min	Max
Average fare on the route (euros)	141.8	70.28	26	4,430
Route distance (thousands of kilometers)	1.141	0.796	0.1	4.996
Number of carriers in the regional market	7.002	5.862	1	48
Presence of Ryanair on the route	0.167	0.373	0	1
Presence of EasyJet on the route	0.088	0.283	0	1
Number of passengers in the regional market (thousands)	11.48	20.45	1	227.9
Percentage of first-class passengers in the regional market	0.016	0.051	0	1
Percentage of business-class passengers in the regional market	0.037	0.074	0	1
Number of served routes by Ryanair at the origin airport	7.026	13.790	0	99
Presence of Ryanair at the origin airport	0.406	0.491	0	1
Number of routes served by Ryanair at the destination airport	7.132	16.29	0	99
Presence of Ryanair at the destination airport	0.431	0.495	0	1
Number of routes served by EasyJet at the origin airport	5.084	8.574	0	69
Presence of EasyJet at the origin airport	0.563	0.496	0	1
Number of routes served by EasyJet at the destination airport	4.687	8.750	0	69
Presence of EasyJet at the destination airport	0.506	0.500	0	1
Number of flights in the regional market	146.9	236.4	1	2,832
Number of seats in the regional market (thousands)	19.28	33.33	19	388.3
Herfindahl–Hirschman index of the regional market	0.639	0.308	0.070	1
Geometric mean of the population of the endpoint catchment areas (millions)	2.581	1.926	0	13.95
Geometric mean of income per capita of the endpoint catchment areas (thousands of euros)	35.26	11.39	3.79	97.04
Number of observations	289,546			

Notes: We obtained tax information in the European data but to be consistent with our treatment of the US data we did not include taxes in the fares.

Appendix B. Identification Assumptions of the Difference-in-Differences Matching Approach

This appendix presents formally the identification assumptions of the DID matching approach. They are less stringent than the assumptions in the standard DID regression approach, allowing for a more flexible analysis. The estimand of the treatment effect of an event (actual, potential, or adjacent entry) is:

$$\tau(\Delta t) = E\left[Y_{j,\Delta t}(1) - Y_{j,\Delta t}(0) \mid w_j = 1\right] \tag{B1}$$

where $Y_{j,\Delta t}(1)$ is the observed percentage change of the average route fare on route j after Δt periods of the event; $Y_{j,\Delta t}(0)$ is the counterfactual outcome; w_j is the binary indicator of the event.

Let Ω_1 denote the set of treated routes in the sample period T and the event $j \in \Omega_1$ date on a route is denoted by $E_j = \min\{t : w_{jt} = 1\}$. We define

$$\tau_{jt}(\Delta t) = Y_{j,t+\Delta t}(1) - Y_{j,t+\Delta t}(0), \quad \forall j \in \Omega_1 \text{ and } E_j = t \in T \tag{B2}$$

Assumption 1 (constant treatment effect): $\tau_{jt}(\Delta t) = \tau_{j't}(\Delta t)$, $\forall j, j' \in \Omega_1$ and $\forall t \in T$.

Assumption 1 says that the treatment effect is homogeneous over routes with different treatment timings. Given assumption 1, the estimation target for the average treatment effect treated in equation (B1) is:

$$\hat{\tau}(\Delta t) = |\Omega_1|^{-1} \sum_{j \in \Omega_1} \tau_{jt}(\Delta t) \tag{B3}$$

Assumption 2 (overlap): $\Pr(w_{j't} \mid Z_{j't}) \in (\eta, 1 - \eta)$ for some $\eta \in (0,1)$ and for some $j' \in \Gamma(j) \equiv \{j' \in \Omega_1 : E_{j'} > E_j = t \text{ and } 0 < K(Z_{jt}, Z_{j't}) < k\}$.

In assumption 2, Z_{jt} indicates a LCC's airport presence on route j at time t and $K(\cdot, \cdot)$ is a distance metric. Assumption 2 says there exists comparable "yet-to-be-treated" routes to route j and these routes have a similar airport presence by an LCC. Given assumption 2, the estimation target in equation (B3) can be implemented by the matching estimator defined as follows:

$$\hat{\tau}(\Delta t) = \sum_{j \in \Omega_1} \sum_{j' \in \Gamma(j)} Y_{j,t+\Delta t} - Y_{j',t+\Delta t}, \quad \text{where } E_j = t \tag{B4}$$

In equation (B4), N is the total number of matched route pairs. In the matching estimator, one treated route can be matched to multiple control routes and one control route can be matched to multiple treated routes (matching with replacement). As indicated by assumption 2, control routes for a treated route are those entered by the same LCC in later periods and that have the same LCCs' airport presence status before treatment on the treated route. Thus, the matching procedure of the estimator is based on both observables (LCCs' airport presence) and unobservables that matter for LCCs' entry.

The matching estimator in equation (B4) can be interpreted as a DID matching estimator of the natural log of the outcome as:

$$\hat{\tau}(\Delta t) = \frac{1}{N} \sum_{j \in \Omega_1} \sum_{j' \in \Gamma(j)} Y_{j,t+\Delta t} - Y_{j',t+\Delta t}$$

$$\approx \frac{1}{N} \sum_{j \in \Omega_1} \sum_{j' \in \Gamma(j)} (\ln y_{j,t+\Delta t} - \ln y_{j,t-l}) - (\ln y_{j',t+\Delta t} - \ln y_{j',t-l})$$

(B5)

where l denotes the pretreatment period.

Given the DID interpretation, we have the following assumptions.

Assumption 3 (conditional parallel time trend within the time window of comparison): Let $E_j = t$ and $\forall j' \in \Gamma(j)$, $t' \in [t - l, t + \Delta t]$, we have

$$E[\ln y_{jt'}(0) | \mathbf{X}_{jt'}, \mathbf{Z}_{j,t-1} = \mathbf{z}] = E[\ln y_{j't'}(0) | \mathbf{X}_{j't'}, \mathbf{Z}_{j',t-1} = \mathbf{z}]$$

$$= \alpha_j + \delta \times (t' - t + l) + \mathbf{X}_{jt'}\beta$$

(B6)

Assumption 3 relaxes the traditional parallel trends assumption in DID identification by allowing the parallel time trend to be conditional on both observed and unobserved pretreatment profiles ($\mathbf{z}$), and on time-varying route characteristics ($\mathbf{X}_{jt}$). Given assumption 3, we further assume:

Assumption 4 (time selection on observables): Holding both observed and unobserved pretreatment profiles constant and conditional on the observed time-varying covariates, there are no route-level temporary shocks that influence the timing of entry in the time-window of comparison.

Assumption 4 is plausible because entry decisions of LCCs often follow long-run planning.

Assumption 5 (no anticipation up to periods before treatment): Let $E_j = t$, we have $\ln y_{jt'} = \ln y_{jt'}(0) \ \forall t' \le t - l$ and $\ln y_{j't'} = \ln y_{j't'}(0) \ \forall t' \in [t - l, t + \Delta t]$ and $\forall j' \in \Gamma(j)$.

Assumption 5 is a weaker version of the no-anticipation condition than the one in the DID regression approach.

Assumption 6 (no contamination from other events): Outcomes on both the treated and matched control routes in the designed time window of comparison are not influenced by other entry events.

The research design outlined in figures 7.4 and 7.5 of the text avoids contamination from other events.

Given assumptions 1 through 6, the DID matching estimation approach uncovers the average treatment effects on the treated routes of an entry event.

Appendix C: Potential Benefits of Seamless International Airline Travel

Austin J. Drukker and Clifford Winston

Airline passengers prefer direct flights over connecting flights, especially for international journeys where the flight times and transfer wait times for connecting flights are considerably longer than those for most domestic flights. We provide a rough estimate of the potential benefits from seamless international travel—that is, travel on the same airline for the entire international journey—that could result from globally deregulated and better integrated airline networks, which would reduce transfer wait times for connecting flights. We compare the difference between the total current disutility that US international travelers incur from transfer wait times for their connecting flights and the lower disutility that they would incur from seamless travel.

We perform the comparison based on a sample of US residents departing the United States for an international flight, which we obtain from the Airlines Reporting Corporation (ARC). The ARC data were derived from online credit card transactions for flights booked through travel agencies, including all subsidiaries of Expedia Group and Booking Holdings. We use scheduling data from the Official Airline Guide (OAG) for all flights in 2018 coupled with routing choice data from ARC.

Worldwide scheduling data from OAG were used to construct possible itineraries for the flight routes chosen by individuals in the ARC sample. We considered all individuals in the ARC data who departed the United States on an international flight with at most one layover. Transfer wait times were constructed to be at least as long as a minimum feasible transfer wait time, which we assume to be three hours to account for the time it takes an international traveler to arrive at the gate for the connecting flight and the time the traveler must wait for the connecting flight to depart from the gate.

For example, consider a traveler flying from the United States to Pisa, Italy, and connecting at London Heathrow Airport (LHR). LHR advises travelers to allow ninety minutes to get to the gate for the connecting flight to Pisa. The traveler then must wait for the flight to Pisa to arrive at and depart from the gate. British Airways offers the only nonstop flight to Pisa from LHR, leaving once a day in the late afternoon. So, it is likely that, on average, a traveler must wait at least ninety minutes before the connecting flight to Pisa arrives at and departs from LHR.

Our sample contains 145 destinations and indicates that a significant share of travelers, nearly 40 percent, takes connecting flights. We assume travelers' hourly value of transfer wait time is $200, based on Yan and Winston's (2014) analysis of air travelers' carrier and routing choices for US domestic flights. This figure is a conservative estimate for our purposes because travelers are likely to place a higher value on transfer wait time in a foreign airport than in a US airport given that they may be concerned about missing important announcements about their flight or they may be less comfortable waiting in an unfamiliar environment. The total loss in utility from transfer wait time for passengers traveling on each connecting route is computed as the number of passengers on each route multiplied by the average transfer wait time (in hours) on each route multiplied by $200 per hour.[37]

Table 7.C1 presents the economic loss to transferring passengers, total wait time, average wait time, and the total number of passengers for the top twenty airports in terms of economic losses incurred by connecting international travelers. Based on all the airports in our sample, the total annual economic loss incurred by travelers from transfer wait time amounts to $24.5 billion.

Table 7.C2 shows the underlying source of the loss in terms of the share of travelers transferring at airports with various transfer wait times in thirty-minute increments. About 60 percent of transferring passengers have wait times between 3 and 3.5 hours, 40 percent of transferring passengers have wait times exceeding 3.5 hours, 20 percent of transferring passengers have wait times exceeding 4.5 hours, and 7 percent of transferring passengers have wait times exceeding 8 hours. Thus, travelers' losses are attributable to all travelers experiencing transfer wait times of at least three hours and to many travelers experiencing wait times that are far greater than three hours.

Global airline deregulation would give airlines the incentive and ability to provide seamless travel that significantly reduces transfer wait times at international airports because carriers could better align their connecting flights with their originating flights coming from the United States. No one knows for certain how much airlines could reduce transfer wait time in a globally deregulated environment. A plausible assumption is that airlines could optimize their scheduling and operations such that passengers do not have to spend more than three hours to reach their gate and wait for the connecting flight to depart to its final destination. The assumed layover would not put passengers at much risk of missing their connecting flight because the incoming flight was late. Based on this assumption, we replace all the current average transfer wait times that exceed three hours in

---

37. The data are representative of the universe of US leisure and unmanaged business travel. To expand our sample to the population, we compared our direct and transfer passenger counts for some large airports with publicly available data reported on their websites. The numbers indicated that we have an approximately 3.5 percent sample; thus, we inflated our passengers counts assuming our sample accounts for 3.5 percent of US international travelers. Our assumption is consistent with internal documentation from ARC. Specifically, ARC reports that approximately 35 percent of domestic travel is booked through travel agencies, of which 20 percent is sent to a credit card processing company to extract details about the purchaser, which would imply an approximately 7 percent random sample for domestic travel. ARC also reports that a smaller share of international travel is booked through travel agencies compared with domestic travel. Our tabulations suggest about half as many travelers book through travel agencies for international travel compared with domestic travel.

Table 7.C1. *Top Twenty Airports in Terms of Annual Economic Losses from Transfer Time*

Country	Airport	Annual economic loss ($ billions)	Annual passengers transferring (millions)	Annual wait time (millions of hours)	Average wait time (hours)
United Arab Emirates	Dubai International Airport (DXB)	1.96	2.09	9.81	4.7
South Korea	Incheon International Airport (ICN)	1.53	2.19	7.63	3.5
Turkey	Istanbul Airport (IST)	1.48	1.53	7.41	4.8
Great Britain	Heathrow Airport (LHR)	1.40	2.18	6.98	3.2
United Arab Emirates	Abu Dhabi International Airport (AUH)	1.23	0.85	6.15	7.2
Germany	Frankfurt Airport (FRA)	1.21	1.81	6.06	3.3
China	Hong Kong International Airport (HKG)	1.09	1.57	5.45	3.5
Japan	Narita International Airport (NRT)	0.91	1.47	4.56	3.1
China	Shanghai Pudong Int'l Airport (PVG)	0.87	1.01	4.33	4.3
China	Beijing Capital Int'l Airport (PEK)	0.83	1.03	4.16	4.0
Taiwan	Taiwan Taoyuan Int'l Airport (TPE)	0.82	1.13	4.08	3.6
France	Paris Charles de Gaulle Airport (CDG)	0.81	1.19	4.07	3.4
Netherlands	Amsterdam Airport Schiphol (AMS)	0.79	1.20	3.93	3.3
Qatar	Hamad International Airport (DOH)	0.69	0.44	3.45	7.8
Canada	Pearson International Airport (YYZ)	0.67	0.95	3.33	3.5
Germany	Munich Airport (MUC)	0.65	0.90	3.26	3.6
Singapore	Singapore Changi Airport (SIN)	0.57	0.43	2.85	6.6
Iceland	Keflavík Airport (KEF)	0.51	0.35	2.52	7.2
China	Guangzhou Baiyun Int'l Airport (CAN)	0.49	0.52	2.44	4.7
Switzerland	Zürich Airport (ZRH)	0.48	0.38	2.38	6.2

Sources: Airlines Reporting Corporation; Official Airline Guide; authors' calculations.

Table 7.C2. *Share of Passengers*
with Various Transfer Wait Times

Transfer wait time	Share of passengers
3 to 3.5 hours	0.601
3.5 to 4 hours	0.132
4 to 4.5 hours	0.060
4.5 to 5 hours	0.042
5 to 5.5 hours	0.026
5.5 to 6 hours	0.014
6 to 6.5 hours	0.022
6.5 to 7 hours	0.016
7 to 7.5 hours	0.008
7.5 to 8 hours	0.007
8+ hours	0.072

Sources: Airlines Reporting Corporation;
Official Airline Guide; authors' calculations.

our sample with an assumed value of three hours, calculate the total economic loss, and subtract it from the current loss to obtain an annual gain in travelers' welfare of $6.9 billion.[38]

Table 7.C3 shows the counterfactual economic gain from seamless travel, total extra wait time, average extra wait time, and total passengers for the top twenty airports, based on travelers' potential benefits. Several of those airports currently have average transfer wait times that exceed 4.5 hours, which should not be difficult for carriers to reduce.

The preceding calculation understates the benefits from seamless travel for three reasons. First, it does not include the potential benefits associated with reducing stochastic delay, which could arise if a US traveler misses their connecting flight in a foreign country because the originating domestic flight is delayed or the connecting flight is cancelled. Currently, in such cases, the traveler may have to wait for a connecting flight that departs the next day or possibly in the next few days. A carrier competing in a globally deregulated environment that provides all the flights on an itinerary would have the incentive and ability to adjust its flight schedules and operations to reduce the length and cost of stochastic delay.

Second, as noted, our assumed value of transfer wait time for international travel is conservative. In the case of stochastic delay, the disutility associated with the unanticipated additional transfer wait time that causes travelers to arrive at their destinations at least a day late could be much greater than the value of the disutility we have assumed for transfer wait time, which is based primarily on

---

38. Even if we assume airlines could reduce all transfer wait times to be no more than four hours instead of three hours, the total gain in travelers' welfare would be $5.4 billion.

Table 7.C3. *Top Twenty Airports in Terms of Counterfactual Welfare Gain from Reducing Transfer Times to Three Hours*

Country	Airport	Annual economic gain from reducing wait time ($ billions)	Annual transfer passengers (millions)	Annual wait time above 3 hours (millions of hours)	Average wait time above 3 hours (hours)
United Arab Emirates	Abu Dhabi International Airport (AUH)	0.72	0.85	3.59	4.2
United Arab Emirates	Dubai International Airport (DXB)	0.71	2.09	3.54	1.7
Turkey	Istanbul Airport (IST)	0.56	1.53	2.81	1.8
Qatar	Hamad International Airport (DOH)	0.42	0.44	2.12	4.8
Singapore	Singapore Changi Airport (SIN)	0.31	0.43	1.56	3.6
Iceland	Keflavík Airport (KEF)	0.30	0.35	1.48	4.2
China	Shanghai Pudong Int'l Airport (PVG)	0.26	1.01	1.30	1.3
Russia	Sheremetyevo Int'l Airport (SVO)	0.26	0.33	1.27	3.9
Switzerland	Zürich Airport (ZRH)	0.25	0.38	1.23	3.2
Austria	Vienna International Airport (VIE)	0.25	0.27	1.23	4.6
China	Beijing Capital Int'l Airport (PEK)	0.22	1.03	1.08	1.0
South Korea	Incheon International Airport (ICN)	0.21	2.19	1.04	0.5
Poland	Warsaw Chopin Airport (WAW)	0.19	0.38	0.97	2.6
China	Guangzhou Baiyun Int'l Airport (CAN)	0.17	0.52	0.87	1.7
China	Hong Kong International Airport (HKG)	0.15	1.57	0.74	0.5
Taiwan	Taiwan Taoyuan Int'l Airport (TPE)	0.13	1.13	0.67	0.6
Germany	Frankfurt Airport (FRA)	0.13	1.81	0.62	0.3
Belgium	Brussels Airport (BRU)	0.12	0.22	0.61	2.8
Germany	Munich Airport (MUC)	0.12	0.90	0.58	0.6
France	Paris Charles de Gaulle Airport (CDG)	0.10	1.19	0.51	0.4

frequency delay, because travelers could miss the first day or few days of a long-awaited vacation or an important business meeting.

Finally, seamless travel is likely to reduce the incidence of lost luggage that occurs on connecting flights when luggage transported by the originating airline must be transferred to a different airline, which may depart from a different terminal. Lost luggage and travelers' exasperation from trying to find it and get it delivered to their hotel or residence is less likely to occur when the same carrier is transporting the luggage for the entire itinerary.

8

Public Airport Competition and Some Potential Benefits of Private Airport Competition

AUSTIN J. DRUKKER AND CLIFFORD WINSTON

1. Introduction

Commercial airports in the United States were private enterprises until the Great Depression, when they experienced serious financial problems because of plummeting passenger demand. Governments could have given airports financial assistance so they could remain in the private sector. Instead, they were put under the control of state and local governments, which had the sole authority to issue bonds to pay for airport facilities and operations. Today, almost all commercial airports are owned and operated by public authorities.

When faced with competition, private enterprises are pushed to innovate, improve product quality, and enhance operational efficiency, or be driven out of the market by more efficient firms. But when profit is not a motive, as is the case for subsidized, government-run airports, do competitive forces still improve efficiency that could reduce airline fares?

Competition between multiple airports in a metropolitan area may be limited because new airports rarely enter a market to compete with existing airports and because airports have little financial incentive to attract additional airlines and travelers.[1] In addition to federal subsidies provided by the Airport Improvement

---

1. Some airports have tried to encourage Southwest Airlines to serve them and there are examples of smaller airports trying to increase the number of airlines that provide service.

Program, airports obtain funds in a monopoly environment from automobile parking fees, retail store rents, advertising display charges, rents from terminal facilities such as counters and gates, and weight-based landing fees promulgated by US Department of Transportation policy. Long-term contracts negotiated between airlines and airports before deregulation have deterred new airline entry by containing "majority in interest" clauses, which give airlines that sign long-term lease agreements the right to approve spending to construct new terminals and gates and oppose spending that could facilitate new competition (Winston 2010).[2]

In general, public airports do not fail financially and exit the industry. During major shocks to air travel, including the period after September 11, 2001, the Great Recession, and the COVID-19 pandemic, airports have been in much better financial shape than airlines, several of which have gone into bankruptcy, and a few have been liquidated. In contrast, the Airport and Airway Trust Fund can run (and currently is running) large budget deficits. Financial analysts point out that airports tend to have high bond ratings because they have multiple revenue streams that service their debt, so they are unlikely to default on repayment obligations.

The possibility that public airports engage in competition to some extent is motivated by the hypothesis that air travelers originating from multiairport metropolitan areas pay lower fares, all else constant, than air travelers originating from single-airport metropolitan areas.[3] The reasons are: (1) more airlines—especially low-cost and ultra-low-cost carriers—serve multiairport metropolitan areas than serve single-airport metropolitan areas and they engage in direct competition, and (2) multiple airports facilitate effective adjacent competition (Cho, Windle, and Hofer 2012). Adjacent competition, which was shown in the last chapter to have a measurable effect on airline fares, is possible only in multiairport metropolitan areas.

Additionally, low-cost carriers are attracted to metropolitan areas with multiple airports because they can choose the airport that is best suited to their operations. For example, Southwest Airlines preferred for many years to use less-congested airports and would bypass the most congested airport in a metropolitan area. Cho, Windle, and Dresner (2015) argue that the mere presence of a low-cost carrier at an airport may attract passengers, even to competing carriers, as travelers expand their search activity.

2. As these agreements expire, airports are increasingly replacing them with agreements that lack the "majority in interest" clauses. Airport projects also can facilitate entry. For example, Denver International Airport is building many new gates over a protracted period that will be used by its two largest incumbent carriers, United Airlines and Southwest Airlines. New entrants may possibly use the older gates that United and Southwest abandon. In addition, some airlines reshape their networks by moving their operations to different airports. For example, JetBlue shifted its West Coast service from Long Beach Airport to Los Angeles International Airport.

3. Basso and Zhang (2007) argue that airports and airlines should not be treated separately when analyzing competition in air transportation.

In this chapter, we study the effects of airport competition on airline prices by exploiting exogenous variation in the number of airports serving different metropolitan origins that serve the same metropolitan destination. Airport presence is plausibly exogenous because almost all US airports currently in operation were built when airline fares were still regulated by the Civil Aeronautics Board. In fact, only one new major airport, Denver International Airport, has been built in the United States since 1973.[4]

To the best of our knowledge, ours is the first empirical analysis to examine whether travelers flying out of multiairport metropolitan origins pay lower fares to reach their destinations than do travelers flying to those same destinations from single-airport metropolitan origins. This is an important question because the existence of airport competition suggests that travelers could potentially be made better off if: (1) additional public airports were constructed, (2) public airports were privatized and competed more vigorously for travelers and airlines than public airports currently compete for them, and (3) new private airports entered metropolitan areas that could accommodate additional airports.

We find that travelers flying out of metropolitan origins with at least *three* airports pay lower fares, ceteris paribus, than travelers flying out of metropolitan origins with only one airport; but that fares from metropolitan origins with exactly *two* airports are higher compared with fares out of single-airport metropolitan origins. In other words, our results suggest that the presence of two airports is not sufficient to induce competitive pressures to reduce fares (and may actually be counterproductive), but that three or more airports generate sufficient competition among airlines to reduce fares.

This finding is somewhat surprising a priori, and we investigate possible explanations. Our preferred explanation is that three or more airports competing in a metropolitan origin facilitate more entry by low-cost and ultra-low-cost carriers and facilitate adjacent competition. In other words, the channel by which three or more airports reduces fares is by generating additional *airline* competition. We test for additional channels by which three or more airports could reduce fares, namely *airport* competition—which is affected by eliminating common ownership and by expanding airport capacity, gates, and runways that could reduce delays and airlines' operating costs—but we find no evidence that supports those channels.

In contrast, when two airports serve a metropolitan origin, they tend to differentiate their service by developing distinct business models consisting of network airlines primarily catering to international and domestic markets and

---

4. One small airport, Northwest Florida Beaches International Airport, was built in 2010 to replace Panama City–Bay County International Airport and San Juan International Airport has been operated and managed under a public–private partnership since 2013. In addition, some large general aviation airports, such as Orlando Sanford International Airport, have added passenger service. Finally, Paine Field, north of Seattle, resumed commercial service, currently anchored by Alaska Airlines, at a new privately operated terminal in 2019.

point-to-point airlines primarily catering to domestic markets. The distinct business models do not reduce fares because they do not encourage additional airline competition in the same markets.

We estimate that if metropolitan areas that are currently served by two airports were served by three airports, where such an increase would be feasible based on the metropolitan areas in question having comparable populations to the metropolitan areas served by three airports, travelers would benefit by more than $4 billion in annual fare reductions. A cost–benefit analysis that accounts for the cost of constructing new airports suggests that some large metropolitan areas could benefit from building an additional airport. Because our analysis is based on public airports, we argue that new private airports, which would have greater incentives to compete vigorously to attract and provide facilities for additional airlines, could generate even greater reductions in fares.

2. Characterizing Airport Competition

Airports serve the same originating market if they draw travelers from the same geographic region. Brueckner, Lee, and Singer (2014) attempt to define a multi-airport airline market by using regression analysis to correlate route-level fare changes at a metropolitan area's primary airport with the number of competing airlines at other airports in the area. But anecdotal evidence, as well as work by Shrago (2022) and McWeeny (2019), suggests that Brueckner, Lee, and Singer's (2014) market definition might be too conservative because it neglects some airports in a broad metropolitan area that travelers use.[5]

Hence, we report results based on conservative and liberal market definitions. The conservative definition is aligned with Brueckner, Lee, and Singer's (2014) definition, which includes primary and core airports within seventy-five miles from the city center.[6] The liberal definition includes primary, core, and fringe airports, as defined by Brueckner, Lee, and Singer (2014), as well as some airports that are more than seventy-five miles from the city center, and small airports that primarily serve low- or ultra-low-cost carriers. We also constructed definitions within the preceding extremes (for example, by not including small airports); however, we report results based only on the most conservative and liberal definitions because

---

5. We thank John Heimlich of Airlines for America, Kenneth Strickland of Raleigh–Durham International Airport, Devon Barnett of Tampa International Airport, and Christopher Birch of San Francisco International Airport for helpful conversations regarding airline market definitions from an industry perspective.

6. Shrago (2022) also interprets Brueckner, Lee, and Singer's (2014) definition as a conservative definition. In contrast to Brueckner, Lee, and Singer (2014), we include Richmond International Airport (RIC) and Newport News/Williamsburg Airport (PHF) in the conservative definition. However, our findings do not change if we follow Brueckner, Lee, and Singer (2014) and do not include them in the conservative definition.

the main findings were not affected by small changes to the list of airports that we included in the market definitions.

As shown in the first panel of table 8.1, the airports that comprise multiairport metropolitan areas in the conservative market definition are within an average radius of seventeen miles from the centroid of the metropolitan area, with a maximum radius of fifty-one miles. Under the conservative market definition, the average farthest driving distance between any two airports serving the same metropolitan area is forty-six miles, with a maximum distance of 105 miles (Manchester-Boston Regional Airport (MHT) to Providence Airport (PVD), about one hour and forty-five minutes apart).

As shown in the second panel of table 8.1, airports included in the liberal market definition are within an average radius of twenty-eight miles from the centroid of the metropolitan area, with a maximum radius of sixty-eight miles. The average farthest driving distance between any two airports is sixty-eight miles, with a maximum distance of 140 miles (MHT to Bradley International Airport (BDL), about two hours and fifteen minutes apart).

Some descriptive evidence suggests that the liberal market definition is the more appropriate multiairport airline market definition. For example, according to survey data collected by Ipsos on behalf of Airlines for America, nearly 40 percent of travelers originated their trip during 2018 from an airport that was not the closest airport to their home or office.[7] McWeeny (2019) takes a close look at the behavior of airline travelers in the San Francisco Bay Area and reports that the majority bypass airports that are closer to their homes to take advantage of lower fares out of San Francisco International Airport (SFO), and that, on average, leisure travelers are willing to drive up to two hours to save $100 on fares.[8] A significant share of travelers drives from as far as Sacramento, bypassing Sacramento International Airport (SMF), while Sonoma County Airport (STS) even provides a trip calculator that includes parking fees at and travel costs to SFO to discourage travelers from taking long drives that bypass the flights it offers.[9] Although public airports are not profit-maximizing enterprises, they do have an interest in attracting passengers to generate revenues from the ancillary services they offer and to justify government subsidies.

Figure 8.1 shows the multiairport metropolitan areas in our sample. The light-colored dots correspond to the conservative market definition, and the dark-colored dots plus the light-colored dots correspond to the liberal definition, which are encompassed by circles. The fifteen largest single-airport metropolitan areas are represented by white dots.

7. We thank John Heimlich for providing us access to these data.

8. Generally, the tradeoff is affected by gasoline prices. Higher gasoline prices would reduce the amount of time leisure travelers would be willing to spend driving to save money on lower fares.

9. According to data collected at Tampa International Airport (TPA), a nonnegligible number of international passengers flying out of TPA drive from Orlando, which is roughly ninety miles away. We thank Kenneth Strickland and Devon Barnett for sharing this insight with us.

Table 8.1. *Market Definitions*

	Conservative market definition				Liberal market definition		
Market	Airports	Radius from centroid (miles)	Maximum driving distance (miles)	Market	Airports	Radius from centroid (miles)	Maximum driving distance (miles)
Chicago	ORD:MDW	5	25	Buffalo	BUF:IAG	10	19
Cincinnati	CVG:DAY	34	78	Charlotte	CLT:JQF	7	22
Cleveland	CLE:CAK	14	51	Chicago	ORD:MDW:RFD	68	95
Dallas	DFW:DAL	5	18	Cincinnati	CVG:DAY	34	78
Detroit	DTW:FNT	13	74	Cleveland	CLE:CAK	16	51
Houston	IAH:HOU	25	30	Dallas	DFW:DAL	5	18
Los Angeles	LAX:BUR:LGB	10	41	Detroit	DTW:FNT	13	74
Miami	MIA:FLL	9	29	Fort Myers	RSW:PGD	8	37
New England	BOS:MHT:PVD	51	105	Houston	IAH:HOU	25	30
New York	LGA:JFK:EWR	8	29	Los Angeles	LAX:BUR:LGB:SNA:ONT	21	58
San Francisco	SFO:OAK:SJC	21	35	Miami	MIA:FLL:PBI	48	72
Tampa	TPA:PIE	6	14	New England	BOS:MHT:PVD:BDL	46	140
Virginia Beach	RIC:PHF	12	62	New York	LGA:JKF:EWR:HNP:ISP:SWF	22	108
Washington	DCA:IAD:BWI	31	58	Orlando	MCO:SFB:MLB	23	75
Maximum		51	105	Philadelphia	PHL:TTN:ACY	32	80
Mean		17	46	Phoenix	PHX:TUS:AZA	48	117
				Pittsburgh	PIT:LBE	54	63
				San Francisco	SFO:OAK:SJC:STS:SMF	55	119
				St. Louis	STL:BLV	22	38
				Tampa	TPA:PIE:SRQ	19	53
				Virginia Beach	RIC:PHF:ORF	24	90
				Washington	DCA:IAD:BWI	31	58
				Maximum		68	140
				Mean		28	68

Notes: Radius from centroid measures the distance in miles as the crow flies from the centroid of the metro area. Maximum driving distance measures the distance in miles via road between the farthest two airports in the market.

Sources: Brueckner, Lee, and Singer (2014); Google Maps; authors' calculations.

Figure 8.1. *Airport Locations and Market Definitions*

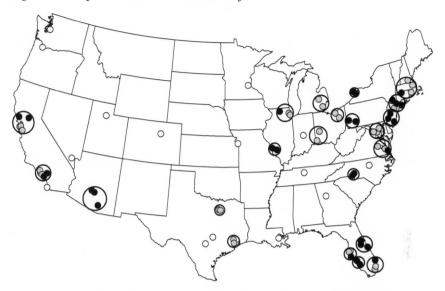

Notes: The white dots are single-airport metropolitan areas. The light-colored dots correspond to the conservative definition of multiairport metropolitan areas. The dark-colored dots plus the light-colored dots correspond to the liberal definition of multiairport metropolitan areas, which are encompassed by circles.

Table 8.2. *Mean Yields in Dollars by Number of Airports in the Market, 1993–2019*

Number of airports in the market	Conservative market definition	Liberal market definition
One	0.187	0.190
Two	0.185	0.209
Three or more	0.156	0.157
All	0.176	0.176

Sources: Bureau of Transportation Statistics; airportcodes.us; authors' calculations.

Table 8.2 presents descriptive evidence of the difference between fares on flights from metropolitan areas served by a different number of airports. Specifically, the table reports average yields (passenger-revenue per passenger-mile) for markets served by one, two, and three or more airports and shows that they are lower for markets served by three or more airports compared with those served by fewer airports, a finding that is robust to the alternative market definitions. In contrast, yields for markets served by two airports are slightly lower than yields

Table 8.3. *Cross-Tabulations of Mean Yields in Dollars by Number of Airports in the Market and Hub Classification, 1993–2019*

Hub classification	Three or more airports	Two airports	One airport
Large	0.144	0.208	0.176
	(18)	(7)	(10)
Medium	0.196	0.205	0.189
	(10)	(5)	(20)
Small and nonhub	0.189	0.198	0.251
	(17)	(8)	(266)

Notes: Statistics are for the liberal market definition. The number of airports in each cross-tabulation is in parentheses.

Sources: Bureau of Transportation Statistics; airportcodes.us; authors' calculations.

for markets served by one airport under the conservative definition, while they are notably higher under the liberal definition. Recall, that the liberal definition includes several more metropolitan areas served by two airports than are included under the conservative definition.

Table 8.3, which disaggregates yields by the number of airports in a metropolitan area and by the hub classification (or size) of the airports, shows that differences in yields are more pronounced.[10] Yields for metropolitan areas with three or more airports are much lower than yields for metropolitan areas with a smaller number of airports when the metropolitan area in question contains a large hub airport. Yields for medium hubs show an interesting pattern where they are lowest for metropolitan areas with one airport and highest for metropolitan areas with two airports. Yields for small hubs and nonhubs are much higher for metropolitan areas with one airport than for metropolitan areas served by multiple airports.

In sum, the lower yields for metropolitan areas with three or more airports may be driven by their lower yields at large hubs that reflect intense competition or lower costs from economies of distance and aircraft size. Metropolitan areas with one airport have lower yields than metropolitan areas with two airports for large and medium hubs, but not for small hubs and nonhubs, likely because those markets may be quite isolated and able to charge high fares or less able to benefit from economies of distance and aircraft size. Because the descriptive comparisons do not hold other important influences on fares constant, we turn to a formal econometric analysis to estimate causal effects.

10. A large hub handles at least 1 percent of national enplanements, a medium hub from 0.25 to 1.0 percent of enplanements, a small hub from 0.05 to 0.25 percent of enplanements, and a nonhub has less than 0.05 percent of enplanements but more than ten thousand annual enplanements.

3. Estimating the Effect of Airport Competition on Fares

We estimate an airline fare regression to determine the causal effect of airport competition on fares. In its basic reduced form, airline fare regressions specify the (log) yield in a market as a function of airline competition, route characteristics such as distance to capture costs and intermodal competition, distance squared to capture economies of length of haul, and population and income to capture exogenous measures of demand (Morrison and Winston 1995).[11] It also is common to include route (airport-pair or city-pair) fixed effects to control for any time-invariant route characteristics (Brueckner, Lee, and Singer 2014).

As we discussed in our analysis in chapter 3 of the effect of bus and rail transit competition on bus costs, it is important to carefully consider which variables should and should not be held constant so that we are able to identify the causal effect of the number of airports on fares. We specify the number of airports serving a metropolitan area as dummy variables for two or three-or-more airports with one airport as the base. Given that this variable is time-invariant and specific to the origin market, we cannot include route fixed effects or origin fixed effects because the origin component of the route fixed effect will be perfectly collinear with the multiairport dummy variables. Thus, instead of specifying route fixed effects, we include destination fixed effects to control for unmeasured time-invariant influences on fares at the destination.

Including multiairport dummy variables in the specification to capture airport competition raises the question of whether *airline* competition should be held constant because it is one of the mechanisms by which *airport* competition— through its ability to attract low-cost competitors and to facilitate adjacent competition—could affect fares. Thus, *airport* competition may be prevented from affecting fares if *airline* competition is held constant. Additionally, airline presence is likely to be endogenous because carriers' entry will be influenced by revenue and average fares on a route, while airport presence is arguably exogenous because, as noted, most US airports were built during the period when fares were regulated.

11. As an additional demand variable, a greater share of business travelers could lead to higher fares, but it would be an endogenous variable in a fare regression. Income at the origin is an exogenous variable that can capture travelers' willingness to pay. As pointed out below, we also restrict the sample to include only destinations that are served by both single- and multiairport metropolitan origins to help control for different characteristics across routes. Additionally, airports that have higher costs per enplanement could have higher fares. However, the relevant issue is how airport costs affect airlines' costs, whose airport operations are subsidized because aircraft are charged only for their takeoff but not landing operations. A representative landing fee per passenger for typical passenger loads is less than three dollars (Morrison and Winston 2007) and any variation would have only a small effect on fares. Importantly, aircraft also are not charged for their contribution to congestion and delays during takeoffs and landings.

Thus, we do not include airline competition variables in the specification and estimate fare regressions of the following form:

$$\ln yield_{ijyq} = \alpha + \beta_1\ two_i + \beta_2\ three_i + \gamma_1 \ln inc_{iyq} + \gamma_2 \ln pop_{iyq}$$

$$+ \delta_1 \ln dist_{ij} + \delta_2 \ln dist_{ij}^2 + \xi_j + \xi_y + \xi_q + \varepsilon_{ijyq}$$

where $\ln yield_{ijyq}$ is the log of the yield from origin airport i to destination airport j in year y and quarter q. The key variables of interest are two_i and $three_i$, dummy variables that equal 1 if origin airport i is part of a two- or three-or-more-airport metropolitan origin, respectively, and equal 0 otherwise. The base metropolitan origin is served by a single airport. The remaining control variables in the specification include log of income at the origin, $\ln inc_{iyq}$; log of population at the origin, $\ln pop_{iyq}$; log of distance and log of distance squared between the origin and destination, $dist_{ij}$ and $dist_{ij}^2$; destination fixed effects, ξ_j; and year and quarter fixed effects, ξ_y and ξ_q.[12] We also specified slot-control dummy variables for JFK, LGA, and DCA airports, but they were statistically insignificant. We discuss the possible effect of airport capacity on fares later.

We estimate the model using data on fares and flight distances from the US Department of Transportation's Airline Origin and Destination Survey (DB1B), a 10 percent quarterly sample of domestic itineraries. Data on population and income are from the US Census Bureau and Bureau of Economic Analysis. Our sample covers the period from 1993 to 2019 and consists of approximately 3,400 routes and 149,000 observations, depending on the market definition used. The year fixed effects control for national-level structural changes in the airline industry that occurred during our sample period, such as the September 11, 2001, terrorist attacks and the Great Recession.[13] Finally, to partly control for different characteristics across routes, we restrict the sample to include only destinations that are served by both single- and multiairport metropolitan origins, and we include only round-trip direct flights.[14]

We present parameter estimates from ordinary least squares regressions in table 8.4. The results for the airport dummy variables based on the conservative

---

12. One could argue that population should be divided by the number of airports at the origin. However, population is a measure here of potential airport demand throughout the metropolitan area. We have made the point that it is reasonable to assume that travelers consider all airports in a metropolitan area because they frequently use airports that are not closest to their residence or place of business. In addition, dividing population by the number of airports would impose a restriction where the effect of the number of airports on fares is affected by metropolitan area population, which has no theoretical justification.

13. We performed tests of whether our parameters of interest—the effect of multiairport presence on yields—were affected by the September 11, 2001, terrorist attacks and the Great Recession, but we could not reject the null hypothesis that the parameters are equal before and after those shocks to the industry, so the pooled estimation is appropriate.

14. We also exclude lightly traveled routes with fewer than three hundred passengers per quarter.

Table 8.4. *The Effect of Multiairport Markets on Yields, 1993–2019*

Log yield (dollars)	Conservative market definition	Liberal market definition
Two airports	−0.004	0.089**
	(0.049)	(0.039)
Three or more airports	−0.062	−0.101***
	(0.049)	(0.038)
Number of observations	149,320	149,600
R^2	0.729	0.741

Notes: Regressions include controls for log population at the origin, log income at the origin, distance and distance squared between the origin and destination, destination fixed effects, year fixed effects, and quarter fixed effects. Robust standard errors clustered at the origin metropolitan statistical area are shown in parentheses. Statistical significance is indicated at the ***1 percent, **5 percent, and *10 percent levels.

Sources: Bureau of Transportation Statistics; Bureau of Economic Analysis; Census Bureau; authors' calculations.

market definition, shown in the first column, lack statistical significance, possibly because there are only fourteen multiairport markets (nine two-airport markets and five three-airport markets, as shown on the left side of table 8.1).

The second column shows results for the airport dummy variables based on the liberal market definition, which results in twenty-two multiairport markets. The parameter estimates are statistically significant, and the signs are consistent with the descriptive differences in yields shown in table 8.2. The estimates indicate that the presence of exactly two airports in a market *increases* yields by 8.9 percent relative to yields in single-airport markets, while the presence of three or more airports in a market *decreases* yields by 10.1 percent relative to single-airport markets. The estimated decrease in yields is plausible given that multiple airports should facilitate both direct and adjacent competitive pressures on fares. As shown in chapter 7, direct competition from Southwest can reduce fares by as much as 30 percent; the presence of other carriers in a market has a smaller but not negligible effect on fares. Chapter 7 also found that Southwest can reduce fares by as much as 5 percent in the long run when it provides adjacent competition.

The finding that two airports do not lower fares, but in fact *increase* fares, relative to single-airport metropolitan areas, is surprising given that we expect that fares should decrease with the number of airports serving a market, or at least not increase with the number of airports serving a market. In the next section, we disaggregate the data further to provide possible explanations for this finding.

4. Explaining the Differential Effects of Airport Competition

The preceding estimates imply that airport competition has differential effects: two airports in a market do not generate sufficient competition to reduce fares and, in fact, their presence increases fares, while three or more airports in a market do generate sufficient competition to reduce fares. We argue that if airport competition affects fares, it does so by affecting competition among airlines serving the metropolitan area. For example, the "Southwest effect"—the observation that originating air travel tends to increase considerably after Southwest's entry into a market—has been well established (Dresner, Lin, and Windle 1996; and Morrison and Winston 2000). We therefore explore the source of airport competition's differential effects on yields and the justification for excluding airline competition from the specification by reestimating our model with measures of airline competition and seeing how they affect our estimates of the airport competition dummy variables.

We measure airline competition as the number of traditional, low-cost, and ultra-low-cost carriers serving the market. Table 8.5 shows the specific airlines in each carrier classification.[15] Data on the airports served by each airline come from the US Department of Transportation's Air Carrier Statistics database (T-100).

Table 8.6 presents ordinary least squares estimation results showing how the previous estimates of airport competition, reproduced in column (1), are affected by including airline competition in the model. Column (2) shows that the number of low-cost carriers reduces yields, and the effect is statistically significant, although the parameter estimate is likely to be biased because the number of low-cost carriers is endogenous. The important finding is that the coefficient for the two-airport dummy increases and it is still statistically significant while the quantitative effect of the three-airport dummy is virtually eliminated, and it becomes statistically insignificant. Thus, the effect of three or more airports on yields appears to be capturing the effect of the number of low-cost carriers on fares, as direct or adjacent competitors, which indicates a specific mechanism by which airport competition reduces fares. At the same time, the effect of two airports is hardly affected by controlling for low-cost carrier competition, which suggests that a different mechanism explains how that form of airport presence affects fares.

Column (3) shows that the preceding findings are not affected when we add the number of traditional and ultra-low-cost carriers to the specification. So, it appears that airport competition in metropolitan areas with three or more airports reduces fares by facilitating additional low-cost carrier competition. However, we need to probe more deeply to understand why the presence of two airports in a metropolitan area increases fares relative to one airport.

---

15. As Southwest and JetBlue expand into international service and into more (congested) US airports, the distinction between their operations and traditional carriers' operations is not as stark as it used to be. We do not consider private aviation as a distinct carrier classification because the difference between its cost and commercial carriers' first- or business-class fares is too great to suggest that private aviation and commercial airline service are plausible substitutes for more than a tiny share of travelers.

Table 8.5. *List of Carriers*

Name	Notes
Traditional carriers	
Alaska Airlines	
America West Airlines	Acquired by US Airways in 2005
American Airlines	
Continental Airlines	Acquired by United in 2010
Delta Air Lines	
Hawaiian Airlines	
Northwest Airlines	Acquired by Delta in 2008
Trans World Airways	Acquired by American in 2001
US Airways	Acquired by American in 2015
United Airlines	
Low-cost carriers	
ATA Airlines	Acquired by Southwest in 2008
AirTran Airways	Acquired by Southwest in 2014
JetBlue Airways	
Southwest Airlines	
Virgin America	Acquired by Alaska in 2018, which remains a traditional carrier
Ultra-low-cost carriers	
Allegiant Air	
Frontier Airlines	
Spirit Airlines	
Sun Country Airlines	

Source: Bureau of Transportation Statistics.

Table 8.6. *Yields, Multiairport Markets, and Number of Carriers by Classification, 1993–2019*

Log yield (dollars)	(1)	(2)	(3)
Two airports	0.089 (0.039)**	0.109 (0.035)***	0.104 (0.034)***
Three or more airports	−0.101 (0.038)***	−0.035 (0.032)	−0.029 (0.031)
Number of traditional carriers			−0.009 (0.006)
Number of low-cost carriers		−0.061 (0.010)***	−0.050 (0.010)***
Number of ultra-low-cost carriers			−0.026 (0.008)***
Number of observations	149,600	149,600	149,600
R^2	0.741	0.746	0.748

Notes: Results are for the liberal market definition. Regressions include controls for log population at the origin, log income at the origin, log of distance and distance squared between the origin and destination, destination fixed effects, year fixed effects, and quarter fixed effects. Robust standard errors clustered at the origin metropolitan statistical area are shown in parentheses. Statistical significance is indicated at the ***1 percent, **5 percent, and *10 percent levels.

Sources: Bureau of Transportation Statistics; Bureau of Economic Analysis; Census Bureau; authors' calculations.

Table 8.7 presents descriptive evidence on yields, airport size (based on hub classification), and the share of international traffic for each airport in markets with two airports (first panel) and with three or more airports (second and third panels) to assess the extent that airports within those markets compete with each other. For example, consider two airports in the same metropolitan area with only one of the airports offering international flights. Those airports may be less likely to be served by airlines with overlapping domestic route networks that compete intensely with each other. The reason is that airlines offering international service tend to be major network carriers that align their domestic and international routes accordingly, while airlines that do not offer international service tend to be smaller point-to-point carriers with route networks that have a small overlap with larger carriers' route networks. In contrast, a third airport in a metropolitan area is likely to increase airline competition because it will be served by major network carriers or point-to-point carriers or both.

Recall that air travelers often bypass airports closest to their homes and use airports farther away to obtain lower fares, better service, or both. We presented McWeeny's (2019) evidence for the San Francisco multiairport market to illustrate that travelers with the option to use three or more airports may drive to a farther airport to obtain lower fares to their metropolitan destination, which may be served by different carriers operating out of different origin airports. In addition, those travelers may drive to a farther airport to fly on their preferred carrier based on frequent flier mileage accumulation. In contrast, travelers in two-airport markets are less likely to have the option to use an alternative airport to obtain lower fares, although they might drive to a farther airport to take international or domestic flights that are not offered at the airport that is closest to their home or workplace.[16]

Evidence from Airlines for America's 2019 "Air Travelers in America" survey is consistent with the conjecture that travelers from metropolitan areas with three or more airports are more likely than travelers from metropolitan areas with two airports to use an airport that is farther from their home or workplace. Specifically, 39.7 percent of travelers flying from metropolitan origins served by three or more airports used an airport that was not the closest airport to their home or office, while 28.7 percent of travelers flying from metropolitan origins served by two airports used an airport that was not the closest airport to their home or office.[17]

---

16. Canadians living close to the US border often drive to US airports because airfares and airport fees are lower in the US. The main instances of substitute airports along the US–Canada border are those near Toronto (Niagara Falls International Airport and Buffalo Niagara International Airport), Montreal (Plattsburgh International Airport), Ottawa (Ogdensburg International Airport), and Vancouver (Bellingham International Airport).

17. It is more likely that the survey results capture the effect of exogenous characteristics of airports, including airlines with low fares, better service, and the like, on travelers' airport choice behavior rather than those airport characteristics being caused by travelers' airport choice behavior.

Table 8.7. Yields in Dollars, Hub Classification, and International Market Penetration, 1993–2019

Market	Hub class	Yield	% Int'l
Buffalo			
BUF	Medium	0.222	0.0
IAG	Nonhub	0.082	0.3
Charlotte			
CLT	Large	0.284	4.5
JQF	Nonhub	0.111	0.0
Cincinnati			
CVG	Large	0.251	3.2
DAY	Small	0.304	0.0
Cleveland			
CLE	Large	0.191	0.6
CAK	Small	0.193	0.0
Dallas			
DFW	Large	0.203	4.3
DAL	Medium	0.228	0.0
Detroit			
DTW	Large	0.190	7.5
FNT	Small	0.163	0.0
Fort Myers			
RSW	Medium	0.141	1.0
PGD	Nonhub	0.086	0.0
Houston			
IAH	Large	0.196	10.7
HOU	Medium	0.216	0.5
Pittsburgh			
PIT	Large	0.223	1.3
LBE	Nonhub	0.075	0.1
St. Louis			
STL	Large	0.201	0.6
BLV	Nonhub	0.091	0.3

Market	Hub class	Yield	% Int'l
Chicago			
ORD	Large	0.181	9.8
MDW	Large	0.151	0.3
RFD	Nonhub	0.100	0.0
Los Angeles			
LAX	Large	0.120	19.2
BUR	Medium	0.260	0.0
LGB	Small	0.153	0.0
SNA	Medium	0.201	0.0
ONT	Nonhub	0.198	0.1
Miami			
MIA	Large	0.146	43.7
FLL	Large	0.117	10.3
PBI	Medium	0.148	0.7
New England			
BOS	Large	0.173	12.5
MHT	Medium	0.237	0.0
PVD	Medium	0.206	0.4
BDL	Medium	0.190	0.5
New York			
LGA	Large	0.219	0.5
JFK	Large	0.110	49.1
EWR	Large	0.162	22.8
HPN	Small	0.303	0.3
ISP	Small	0.145	0.0
SWF	Nonhub	0.193	3.6
Orlando			
MCO	Large	0.139	7.1
SFB	Small	0.093	36.2
MLB	Nonhub	0.242	0.2

Market	Hub class	Yield	% Int'l
Philadelphia			
PHL	Large	0.178	9.0
TTN	Nonhub	0.110	0.0
ACY	Small	0.097	0.1
Phoenix			
PHX	Large	0.155	0.5
TUS	Medium	0.200	0.0
AZA	Nonhub	0.092	1.6
San Francisco			
SFO	Large	0.136	16.8
OAK	Large	0.172	0.7
SJC	Medium	0.177	1.1
STS	Nonhub	0.274	0.0
SMF	Medium	0.197	0.0
Tampa			
TPA	Large	0.159	1.7
PIE	Small	0.095	0.1
SRQ	Small	0.191	0.0
Virginia Beach			
RIC	Small	0.370	0.5
PHF	Small	0.224	0.0
ORF	Medium	0.302	0.0
Washington			
DCA	Large	0.259	0.3
IAD	Large	0.170	25.0
BWI	Large	0.166	2.4

Note: Percent international is the percentage of passengers with destinations outside of North America.
Sources: Bureau of Transportation Statistics; authors' calculations.

The first panel of table 8.7 shows that in two-airport metropolitan areas, one of the airports is often served by airlines that provide international service and is either a large or medium hub airport while the other airport is often a small or nonhub airport that is not served by airlines providing international service. For example, in the Detroit area, Detroit Metropolitan Airport (DTW) is a large hub that provides international flights and is served by almost all the major carriers, while Flint Bishop Airport (FNT) is a small hub that provides few, if any, international flights and its only major carrier is Delta Air Lines. Note that yields at FNT are 15 percent lower than yields at DTW, likely because international flights tend to be more expensive than domestic flights and because more passengers flying out of DTW are likely to be paying more expensive business- and first-class fares on longer flights.[18]

In sum, the airlines providing service in two-airport metropolitan areas appear to segregate and specialize their operations such that they provide different services at each airport in accordance with their different business models and they cater to different types of travelers to a significant extent. It is thus plausible that airlines that serve a single-airport metropolitan origin, which includes both network and point-to-point carriers, could generate more competition that reduces yields than airlines that serve a two-airport metropolitan origin.

Regulatory restrictions on international airline competition also may contribute to different airports pursuing different airline business models because burdensome regulations often make it difficult for carriers to provide international service from certain airports. Such restrictions include entry barriers in international markets that are not governed by open skies agreements and entry barriers such as slot and gate restrictions at domestic and foreign airports that comprise US international routes.

The second and third panels of table 8.7 show that in three-airport markets, at least two of the airports are often served by carriers that provide some international service and are large or medium hubs. For example, the Washington market is served by three large hub airports, all of which provide some international service and one of which, Baltimore/Washington International Airport (BWI), has long been served by Southwest Airlines, which, in addition to providing direct competition, has helped to reduce yields by providing adjacent competition for airlines flying out of Reagan National Airport (DCA) and Dulles International Airport (IAD) (Cho, Windle, and Dresner 2015).[19]

---

18. FNT's lower fares in recent years also could be explained by service provided by low-cost and ultra-low-cost carriers.

19. BWI was a hub for US Airways, but Southwest Airlines essentially drove them out of BWI. Of course, other low-cost and ultra-low-cost carriers operate in the three Washington metropolitan area airports.

Table 8.8. *Share of Markets Served by and Number of Low-Cost Carriers,
1993–2019*

Number of airports in the market	Share of markets served		Number of carriers serving			
	Low-cost carriers	Ultra-low-cost carriers	All carriers	Traditional carriers	Low-cost carriers	Ultra-low-cost carriers
One						
Large hubs	0.870	0.814	10.93	7.00	1.85	2.08
	(0.336)	(0.390)	(2.57)	(1.72)	(1.17)	(1.41)
Medium hubs	0.899	0.643	8.46	5.64	1.45	1.37
	(0.301)	(0.479)	(1.83)	(1.63)	(0.84)	(1.26)
Two	0.920	0.749	9.55	5.78	1.92	1.85
	(0.271)	(0.434)	(1.89)	(1.62)	(0.97)	(1.42)
Three or more	0.973	0.906	12.25	6.87	2.79	2.59
	(0.162)	(0.292)	(2.31)	(1.76)	(1.07)	(1.41)

Notes: Statistics are for the liberal market definition. Standard deviations are shown in parentheses.
Sources: Bureau of Transportation Statistics; authors' calculations.

Table 8.8 presents descriptive evidence that a greater number of low-cost and ultra-low-cost carriers serve markets with three or more airports compared with markets with only one or two airports. Ultra-low-cost carriers serve a greater number of large hub single-airport markets than they serve two-airport markets, and low-cost carriers serve a comparable number of single-airport markets and two-airport markets. Medium hub single-airport markets are served by fewer low-cost and ultra-low-cost carriers than are served at two-airport markets. In contrast, metropolitan origins with three or more airports are more likely than single- and two-airport metropolitan origins to be served by low-cost and ultra-low-cost carriers, and, on average, have more low-cost, ultra-low-cost, and total carriers offering flights than single- and two-airport metropolitan origins have.

5. Considering Additional Channels that Enable Airport Competition to Reduce Fares

We have found evidence that we interpret as indicating airport competition reduces fares by facilitating direct and adjacent airline competition, especially involving low-cost carriers. However, there are additional channels by which the presence of multiple airports in a metropolitan area could reduce fares, including true airport competition and capacity expansion.

In true airport competition, airports would take certain actions that reduce airlines' operating costs to attract additional airlines to serve their airports. Airlines that are induced to serve airports that provide such incentives would have lower costs and possibly lower fares. We have pointed out that most (subsidized) public airports do not aggressively seek to attract additional airlines. However, if such an incentive existed, airports operating in the same metropolitan area would be more likely to take actions to attract additional airlines if they were operated by different airport authorities instead of by a monopoly authority that has little incentive to encourage competition among the airports that it operates.

Metropolitan areas that are served by three or more airports and where at least two of the airports are operated under the same airport authority include the Chicago (ORD, MDW), New York (LGA, JFK, EWR, SWF), and Washington (DCA, IAD) metropolitan areas. Thus, as an empirical test of the possible effect of true airport competition on fares, we added a new variable to our specification where we specified a same-airport-authority dummy variable, interacted it with the three-or-more-airports dummy variable, and reestimated the fare model. We found that its coefficient was statistically insignificant and that its inclusion had little effect on the magnitude and statistical significance of the three-or-more-airports dummy variable, which indicates that pure airport competition is unlikely to be a channel that reduces fares.

The capacity expansion channel suggests that the presence of multiple airports results in more runways and more gate and terminal capacity that could, for example, reduce takeoff and landing delays, and reduce operating costs and fares. We tested for the effect of additional capacity directly by interacting the three-or-more-airports dummy with the total number of airport runways in the metropolitan area.[20] Including this interaction term in our regression did not change the magnitude of the coefficient on the three-or-more-airports dummy, and the coefficient on the interaction term was small and statistically insignificant.

Because capacity expansion also may encompass more gates and terminals, we used hub size as a broader measure of capacity. Generally, larger airports and greater airport capacity are associated with larger hub sizes, which are associated with larger metropolitan areas. We again created a new variable where we interacted the dummy variable for three or more airports with dummy variables that identified metropolitan areas with either two large hub airports or with one large hub airport and two medium hub airports and we reestimated the fare model. We found that the coefficient for the new (capacity expansion) variable was statistically insignificant and that its inclusion had little effect on the magnitude and statistical significance of the three-or-more-airports dummy variable. In sum, the statistically insignificant effects of the number of runways and hub sizes suggest

20. We included only runways that were longer than five thousand feet, which is an adequate length for most commercial aircraft to take off and land. Data on runway length are from the Federal Aviation Administration's National Flight Data Center. We are grateful to Jan Brueckner and Alberto Gaggero for sharing the data with us.

Table 8.9. *Aggregate Consumer Savings from Expanding to Three Airports*

Three-airport markets		Two-airport markets			
Market	Population (million)	Market	Population (million)	Annual savings on fares ($ billion)	Break-even airport construction cost ($ billion)
New York	19.22	Dallas	7.57	1.604	31.43
Los Angeles	13.21	Houston	7.07	0.837	16.41
Chicago	9.46	Detroit	4.32	0.605	11.85
New England	7.70	St. Louis	2.80	0.262	5.13
Washington	6.28	Charlotte	2.64	0.790	15.49
Miami	6.17	Total	24.40	4.098	
Philadelphia	6.10	*One-airport markets*			
Phoenix	6.00	Atlanta	6.02	0.874	8.56
San Francisco	4.73	Seattle	3.98	0.594	5.82
Tampa	3.19	Minneapolis	3.64	0.393	3.86
Virginia Beach	3.06	San Diego	3.34	0.276	2.70
Orlando	2.61	Denver	2.97	0.708	6.94
Total	87.73	Total	19.95	2.844	

Notes: Results are for the liberal market definition. Annual savings on fares measures the total annual reduction in fares for all domestic flights from the market. Break-even airport construction cost is per airport and is found by setting the annualized capital cost of building an airport equal to the annual savings, assuming a thirty-year lifetime and a 3 percent discount rate. Populations are for 2019 metropolitan statistical areas. The New England market includes Boston, Manchester, Providence, and Hartford. The Phoenix market includes Tucson. The Virginia Beach market includes Richmond.

Sources: Bureau of Transportation Statistics; Census Bureau; authors' calculations.

that capacity expansion is unlikely to be a channel that reduces fares in multiairport metropolitan areas.[21]

6. The Potential Gains from Additional Airport Competition

Given that our analysis suggests airport competition in metropolitan areas with three or more airports can help to reduce fares, it is of interest to calculate the potential benefits of increasing the number of airports in metropolitan areas served by fewer than three airports. The left panel of table 8.9 lists the markets, as defined by metropolitan area, served by three or more airports, alongside

21. In theory, there could be a "delay" channel where airports take actions to reduce delays, which increases effective competition and reduces fares, although, conversely, such action may increase airport demand and raise fares. Regardless, fewer delays would increase consumers' surplus and benefit travelers. However, in practice, airports do not set congestion fees to reduce delays and only a few airports limit flights with slot controls, which raise fares. Efforts to reduce delays by building more runways is likely to generate induced demand—as in the case of highway expansions—and may not have very much effect on delays.

their populations. The right panel identifies markets served by one or two airports that could plausibly sustain three airports, given that their populations are comparable to markets currently served by three or more airports. We have simply identified those markets as candidates for a cost–benefit assessment; we do not assert that they could sustain more airports with certainty.

In addition to raw population comparisons, other factors make those markets reasonable candidates for additional airports. For example, Dallas and Houston are large metropolitan areas with millions of passengers flying through their airports annually, and land prices in Texas are relatively low compared with land prices in the rest of the United States. The Detroit metropolitan area *did* at one point have three functioning airports—DTW, FNT, and Coleman A. Young International Airport (DET)—but following Detroit's declaration of bankruptcy in 2013, DET was listed as an asset of the city that could be sold to cover debts and it currently does not serve any commercial passengers. Charlotte is currently served by a hub for American Airlines, Charlotte Douglas International Airport (CLT), and could plausibly sustain a third airport in addition to Concord Regional Airport (JQF). St. Louis, which currently has a larger population than Charlotte, also could possibly sustain a third airport in addition to Lambert International Airport (STL) and MidAmerica Airport (BLV). In addition, several large single-airport metropolitan areas could possibly sustain two additional airports, including Atlanta (home to the busiest airport in the world), Seattle, Minneapolis, San Diego, and Denver.

Benefits of Additional Public Airports

We calculate the annual fare savings from adding additional public airports using our parameter estimates from table 8.4. For the two-airport markets, we calculate the reduction in yields caused by the addition of a third airport, which is the difference between the coefficient estimates for the three-airport dummy and the two-airport dummy: $-0.101 - 0.089 = -0.190$. This figure represents the percentage change in fares per passenger-mile. We then multiply -0.190 by the annual passenger-miles for the markets. This calculation assumes that the total volume of passenger-miles is unchanged with the addition of a third airport, which provides a lower bound on total benefits. We estimate that the annual fare savings from adding an additional airport to the five two-airport metropolitan areas shown in table 8.9 is roughly $4.1 billion.

Considering the benefits from fare reductions alone is not enough to justify building a new airport because the construction and capital costs may exceed the benefits. Setting the annual savings on fares equal to the annualized capital cost of building an airport allows us to solve for the maximum airport construction cost that would still result in net benefits.[22] The results of this cost–benefit

22. The calculation assumes a thirty-year lifetime for the airport and a 3 percent discount rate.

analysis also are reported in table 8.9. We estimate that the addition of a third airport in Dallas, for example, would provide net benefits if the cost to build the airport were less than $31.43 billion. We do not know what the cost of a new airport in Dallas would be, but it would likely be far less than $31.43 billion, given that Denver International Airport (DEN) was completed in 1995 at a cost of about $8.2 billion in 2020 dollars.[23] Taking DEN as the baseline, new airports in Houston, Detroit, and Charlotte would almost certainly provide positive net benefits from fare reductions alone.

Table 8.9 also presents the results of similar calculations for the five largest single-airport markets. The annual savings from adding two additional airports are calculated analogously to the two-airport case, except that we need only the coefficient estimate for the three-airport dummy from table 8.4: −0.101. Multiplying −0.101 by the annual passenger-miles for the one-airport markets yields the annual savings on domestic fares. We report the maximum cost *per airport* that would provide net benefits. Building two new airports in Atlanta, for example, would provide net benefits from fare reductions alone if the construction cost for *each airport* were less than $8.56 billion. Given the construction cost of DEN, it is possible that building two new airports in Atlanta would provide net benefits, while the cost to build two new airports in Seattle, Minneapolis, San Diego, and Denver would have to be much lower than the cost to build DEN to provide net benefits.

As noted, our estimates of the benefits from fare reductions are conservative because we hold annual passenger-miles constant. Importantly, the *total* benefits from building a new airport include much more than the benefits from fare reductions. Additional airports would attract more airline service and more flights and possibly increase a metropolitan area's economic development (Green 2007), which would generate significant benefits to travelers and residents and strengthen the case for building additional airports.

A possible argument against the potential benefits of additional airports, associated with Delta Air Lines' operations in Hartsfield–Jackson Atlanta International Airport (ATL), a monopoly airport, is that Delta's dominant position has enabled it to develop an extensive network that provides a large choice of nonstop destinations and more frequent service. Delta also has been able to consolidate flow-through traffic to achieve economies of density that reduce its operating costs and fares to some extent. However, there is no reason why Delta's alleged benefits to travelers cannot be subjected to a market test. If an additional airport or airports were built in Atlanta and other airlines entered those airports and provided service, then travelers would reveal their preferred combinations of airline fares, service quality, and airlines. In the process, Delta's market share would be affected in

---

23. The costs of building new airports today are likely to be inflated by a modest amount by increasingly higher capital costs and higher costs of environmental review, legal services, and the like.

accordance with travelers' preferences, which would leave travelers at least as well off as before the additional airport or airports were built.[24]

Another consideration when assessing the potential benefits of new airports is whether air traffic control is significantly disrupted by multiple airports in the same region and whether it is appreciably more difficult with multiple airports to create flight paths that would avoid generating noise over heavily populated areas. We are not aware of evidence that travel in metropolitan areas with multiple airports is compromised by air traffic problems that are more common in such areas or that residents in those metropolitan areas experience more noise than residents in single-airport metropolitan areas. In any case, those issues should be addressed efficiently by improving air traffic control services and government airplane noise policies (Morrison, Winston, and Watson 1999).

Potential Benefits When Airports Are Private

It is important to bear in mind that our estimates of the effects of airport competition are based on an analysis of *public* airports, which have vast pricing, investment, and operating inefficiencies (Winston 2013). As we have indicated, public airports do not have strong incentives to compete for airlines and travelers, and we have found that those incentives are not increased in the case of pure airport competition, even when each airport operates under different airport authorities. In practice, public airports may face opposition from incumbent airlines to build additional terminal space and gates that would enable new carriers to provide service (Winston 2010).[25] Morrison and Winston (2000) estimated that the restriction on available gates cost travelers $4 billion in higher fares. In addition, Delta is an example of an airline that has made aggressive efforts through lobbying to protect its strong competitive position at ATL by preventing Atlanta-area general aviation airports from adding commercial airline service.

In contrast to US cities, many cities throughout the world, including London, New Delhi, Rome, Sydney, and Tokyo, have privatized their airports subject to varying degrees of regulation. Winston (2013) reports that case studies find that privatization has improved airport efficiency in some countries, and Oum, Yan,

24. If the additional airport or airports were public, the taxpayers would bear the cost if those airports could not overcome Delta's advantage and attracted few carriers and passengers. Airport investors would bear the cost if the additional airport or airports were private, and they would have the incentive to give careful thought to whether a new airport entrant could compete successfully and to vigorously explore alternative strategies following entry to overcome any advantage for Delta that existed.

25. A few public airports have attempted to overcome that opposition. For example, in 2018, Miami International Airport changed its gate fees policy from per-use to flat monthly fees, which opened the door for Frontier and other low-cost carriers (including Southwest) to enter an airport that had been too costly to use. Passenger facility charges have enabled some airports to more easily finance terminal expansions that would have been much harder to do when most airports were locked into long-term leases with legacy carriers that gave them veto power over terminal expansions.

and Yu (2008) find in a worldwide comparison of airports that airport privatization has promoted competition and reduced costs. Howell et al. (2022) also find in their study of airports in more than two hundred countries that airport competition leads to efficiency improvements, especially for private airports owned by investment funds.

Suggestive evidence that private airport competition could reduce fares and improve service is provided by the experience of the United Kingdom and other European countries. Starkie (2009) concludes that private airport competition in the United Kingdom has been an effective regulator of what an airport can charge an airline. Of particular interest to the United States is that, like contract rate negotiations that have enabled railroad shippers to obtain lower rates by playing one railroad off against another, UK airports have had to compete for airlines by offering beneficial long-term contracts that stipulate the charge and service quality that an airline can expect from an airport.

Another benefit of UK airport privatization is that the local airport at Luton renamed itself as London Luton Airport and allowed the emerging low-cost carrier Ryanair into the Dublin–London route, which was at a vital stage in its development.[26] Chapter 7 contained an estimate that Ryanair has reduced fares 20 percent in the EU markets that it serves. The implication of the United Kingdom's experience for the United States is that some existing general aviation airports could expand their operations to provide commercial service and generate airport competition in a privatized environment without requiring substantial capital investments.

Still another potential benefit that has emerged from airport privatization abroad is that larger airports are likely to try to attract low-cost carriers with low airport charges to generate large volumes of passengers for their facilities with spare capacity. Smaller airports have anticipated this competition and have attracted low-cost carriers by building special facilities and providing fast turnaround times.

Because private commercial airports in the United States would seek to maximize the return on their investments, they would have stronger incentives than public airports to compete for all types of airlines and to increase passengers by accommodating airlines that wish to serve their airport and that are willing to pay the (marginal) cost of the facilities.[27] United Airlines, for example, recently decided to suspend service at New York's JFK airport because it was unable to obtain sufficient takeoff and landing slots, administered by the Federal Aviation Administration, to offer a schedule of flight frequencies and departure times that would be competitive with the larger flight schedules offered by JetBlue Airways

---

26. Luton's local government did not actually sell the assets of the airport, but it granted a long-term operating lease to a private company.

27. In 1997, Congress established the Airport Investment Partnership Program, but only a handful of small airports have taken part.

and American Airlines. If JFK were a private airport, it would have an incentive to increase United's operations and its revenues by requesting that the Federal Aviation Administration increase United's slots so United could expand its operations and compete more effectively with other carriers serving JFK.[28]

Yan and Winston (2014) simulated the effect of airport privatization on the welfare of airports, carriers, and travelers by developing a model where privatized airports in the San Francisco Bay Area with separate owners compete for airline operations by setting profit-maximizing runway charges that reduce delays while airlines compete for passengers. Runway charges are determined through separate negotiations between airlines organized as a bargaining unit and each of the three Bay Area airports, Oakland, San Jose, and San Francisco.

The authors find that by setting different charges for different classifications of airport users (scheduled commercial carriers and general aviation), the Bay Area airports would gain from privatization, as would commercial travelers and carriers. Commercial air travelers would pay higher fares because airport charges to airlines would increase, but the time savings from less-congested air travel would more than offset that additional cost. General aviation would face higher charges, but their losses would be softened if policymakers expanded airport privatization to encourage (smaller) private airports to compete for (smaller) aircraft operations.

It also is possible that some private airports would convert their operations and compete for commercial airline traffic by taking advantage of advances in GPS technology that have improved access to smaller airports, by upgrading runways and gates, and by offering van and rental car service to improve travelers' access to the central city and other parts of the metropolitan area. By having more flight alternatives, travelers in low-density markets could especially benefit if private airports nationwide offered commercial service.

In the context of this analysis, private airport competition could reverse the positive sign of the effect of competition on fares in markets with two airports because private airports are likely to encourage all types of airlines to serve them—that is, carriers that serve domestic short-haul and long-haul markets and international markets—and to compete with other airlines serving the two-airport metropolitan area.

Private airports also could enhance competition by constructing additional terminals for low-cost carriers that were willing to pay for the capacity.[29] This would be a less expensive and more feasible alternative than a new entrant incurring the huge expense of building an entirely new airport. Recall that incumbent

---

28. If airports were private, they would be free to set takeoff and landing charges that vary with traffic volumes, which would possibly eliminate the Federal Aviation Administration's justification for intervening in certain airports' operations by instituting slots to limit flights at those airports.

29. Some airports, such as Austin–Bergstrom International Airport, have opened new terminals or concourses for ultra-low-cost carriers in recent years.

airlines could possibly block investments such as new terminals by public airports, but private airports' financial arrangement with airlines would not allow an incumbent airline to prevent a private airport from expanding its capacity to accommodate new airline entrants that were willing to pay the cost of the expanded capacity.

Finally, as private airports shed the inefficiencies that have accumulated in public airports for decades and introduce new policies and operations, pure private airport competition in metropolitan areas with less than three airports may become a channel that reduces airfares and challenges our conclusion based on public airports that such competition has not benefited air travelers. In sum, private airport competition that results in the construction of new airports is likely to generate greater benefits from lower fares and additional service than the estimated benefits that we report based on public airports.

7. Final Comments

Although US airlines have been deregulated for decades, airports are still largely owned and operated by public authorities. We investigated whether public airports compete in the sense of causing fares to decline in metropolitan areas as the number of airports increase. We found that fares are lower when three or more airports serve a metropolitan origin, because those airports facilitate more direct and adjacent competition from low-cost carriers, and they are not segregated to serve different carriers that have different business models.

We estimate that the construction of additional public airports in metropolitan areas served by two and possibly by one airport would benefit travelers by generating billions of dollars in fare reductions and would produce large benefits from additional service. We argue that those benefits are likely to be even greater if airports were privatized and if international airline markets were fully deregulated because US metropolitan areas would be served by more domestic and international carriers that would face fewer barriers from serving airports in those areas. Airline competition in such an environment could result in efficiency gains, technological innovations, and benefits to travelers that we have yet to envision.

9

Private Airport Competition and Innovation: The Case of Heated Runways

JUKWAN LEE, CLIFFORD WINSTON, AND JIA YAN

1. Introduction

Winter storms that produce snow and ice on runways and taxiways reduce the ability of aircraft to take off and land safely, which can delay travelers for hours or even days if a flight is cancelled because the airport closes a runway—significantly slowing operations—or stops operating. Closing a runway is not an arbitrary decision. Although the limits vary for types of aircraft, most are prohibited from operating on runways that are covered by untreated ice or that have accumulated more than half an inch of snow or slush.

Currently, commercial airports in the United States remove snow manually with plows, brushes, blowers, and shovels, in combination with chemical deicers. An alternative and potentially more effective and efficient method for removing snow and ice is to melt it by heating runway and taxiway pavement before it can accumulate and disrupt aircraft operations. However, this innovation is not used on a large scale by any US airport.[1]

---

1. Some airports use heated surfaces on a small scale. For example, at O'Hare International Airport, two taxiway bridges over roadways have embedded pipes that carry heated oil, keeping the surfaces free of snow and ice for planes without having to plow it onto passing cars below. Boston Logan International Airport places giant snow melters in terminal areas because snow cannot be pushed aside without blocking gates and roads. Homeowners purchase electric systems to melt snow and ice on their driveways and walkways and Green Bay's Lambeau Field was the first in the National Football League to install a heating system to keep the turf from freezing.

This chapter examines whether competition among private airports could spur innovation that leads to the adoption of heated airport runways that reduce air travelers' delays due to snow and ice. Although heated runways could potentially enable only the limited set of airports in metropolitan areas in the United States that receive snow to improve their operations, those improvements could generate large benefits by reverberating throughout the US air transportation system. For example, air travel delays attributable to snow that originate in the New York metropolitan area can significantly contribute to delays at many airports in other parts of the country. Thus, reducing delays at the New York airports could benefit travelers and carriers nationwide. Improvements in the operations of major US airports also could reduce delays of international flights, which, if cancelled, can subject travelers to much longer and more costly delays, as discussed in chapter 7, than cancellation of domestic flights because they operate less frequently.

We first assess the case for public US commercial airports to adopt heated runways to improve airline operations and benefit travelers. We do so by estimating the benefits to travelers and airlines, as reflected in reduced aircraft flight delays and passengers' value of reduced waiting time, and comparing those benefits with the costs of installing and operating heated runways.

Consistent with the observed behavior of public commercial airports, we find that a strong case does not exist on cost–benefit grounds for those airports to adopt heated runways. This finding is intuitive because, given that public airports receive government funding and do not make investments to maximize profits, they have little economic incentive to invest in innovations like heated runways regardless of whether travelers would benefit from less snow-related delay. Installing and operating heated runways would adversely affect airports' budgets by increasing their costs, which they could not recover in higher takeoff and landing fees to airlines, because current weight-based landing fees are regulated following Federal Aviation Administration guidelines. Heated runways may be politically attractive to the extent that they reduce fatalities and injuries caused by aircraft accidents, but commercial air travel—even during winter months—has become extremely safe.

We then extend a model of private airport competition developed by Yan and Winston (2014) to investigate whether a private airport would have the incentives to adopt heated runways that could benefit air travelers. In contrast to public airports, a private airport would have an economic incentive to install and operate heated runways because it could increase its profits, after accounting for the higher runway charges that it would be free to charge airlines to cover installation and operating costs. Travelers would benefit from heated runways that reduce snow-related delays if they value the time savings by at least as much as the higher fares they would have to pay to cover airlines' higher (heated) runway charges.

Based on our simulations, we find that a private airport could simultaneously increase their profits and benefit travelers by installing heated runways.

Generally, public production is justified when a facility or service is socially desirable—that is, would generate social benefits that exceed its full costs to provide—but is privately unprofitable (Winston 2021c). However, in this case, public airports would not adopt an innovation (heated runways) that could significantly benefit domestic and international air travelers, while private airports would be willing in certain situations to do so. The analysis provides another example of how an environment of competition and innovation improves the efficiency of the US transportation system and increases the welfare of its users. In contrast, an environment in which the public sector is responsible for enhancing travelers' welfare may not improve the system's efficiency and travelers' welfare because policymakers have little incentive to take actions to do so.

2. Airports and Data Sources

We conduct our analysis using data on airport operations, weather, and weather-related travel delays for the three commercial airports in the greater Boston area: Boston Logan International Airport (BOS), Rhode Island T. F. Green International Airport (PVD), and Manchester–Boston Regional Airport (MHT).[2] We chose the three greater Boston–area airports because although they are currently publicly owned and operated, they could explicitly compete as private airports with separate owners because they are located within a sixty-mile radius and are used by passengers from the same catchment area.[3]

BOS, PVD, and MHT normally experience winter snowstorms that cause extensive flight delays and cancellations. In addition, because airlines operate over a network, their flights also can be delayed by time-varying network-wide shocks to airport operations that, for example, originate at a flight's origin and cause the flight to arrive late to its destination. As a control group, we chose the four commercial airports in the greater Los Angeles area: Los Angeles International Airport (LAX), Hollywood Burbank Airport (BUR), Long Beach Airport (LGB), and John Wayne Airport (SNA). Delays at both the Boston-area and Los Angeles–area airports can arise from network-wide shocks and are therefore correlated. However, unlike the Boston-area airports, the Los Angeles–area airports do not experience snow that causes delays; thus, by using Los Angeles–area

---

2. We attempted to include Worcester Regional Airport (ORH) in the analysis, but we could not collect the complete set of variables that were necessary to conduct our analysis.

3. Using a conservative definition, as discussed in chapter 8, to identify airports in the same market, Brueckner, Lee, and Singer (2014) argue empirically that BOS, PVD, and MHT belong in the same market.

airports as the control group, we are able to separate the effects of snow on flight delays from the effects of time-varying network-wide shocks on airport operations.

The first part of our empirical analysis consists of estimating the impact of hourly snow precipitation on airline flight delays. We conduct it using data from April 2004 to March 2015, during which time there were several major snowstorms in the northeast of the United States. Data on airlines' on-time performance are from the Bureau of Transportation Statistics (BTS) and contain information on flight cancellations and scheduled and actual arrival times of domestic flights for the major carriers. Departure and arrival flight delays at an airport are defined as the difference between the scheduled and actual departure or arrival time. Each airport's hourly weather information is from the National Oceanic and Atmospheric Administration (NOAA) based on its nearest weather observation station, which is often located at the airport itself.

3. Research Design

Identification of our model of the determinants of hourly flight delays is achieved by using both a parametric difference-in-difference-in-difference (DDD) approach and a nonparametric matching approach.

DDD Identification

Figure 9.1 illustrates the intuition behind DDD identification of the effect of snow on flight delays. Winter in the greater Boston area runs from December through March. We use a binary indicator of snow precipitation in an hour as the treatment status of a Boston airport. However, given that there are unobserved weather-related factors that also affect delays, we must control for those. Finally, we use the Los Angeles airports as a control group to remove the effect of network-wide shocks on airport operations.

Controlling for observed weather factors, such as temperature and wind speed, the DDD approach first employs difference-in-differences (DID) during the winter to identify the effects of unobserved weather factors on flight delays. Conditional on the effects of winter weather on flight delays, the DDD approach employs a further difference between snow and nonsnow periods of the year on observations from the treatment group to identify the pure effect of snow events on flight delays.

We implement DDD identification by estimating the following regression equation by ordinary least squares (OLS):

$$delay_{ita} = \beta_0 + \beta_1 \times winter_t + \beta_2 \times Boston_a + \beta_3 \times Boston_a \times winter_t$$
$$+ \beta_4 \times Boston_a \times winter_t \times snow_{ta} + \beta_5 \times \mathbf{X}_{ita} + \eta_a + \eta_m + \varepsilon_{ita} \tag{1}$$

Figure 9.1. *DDD Identification*

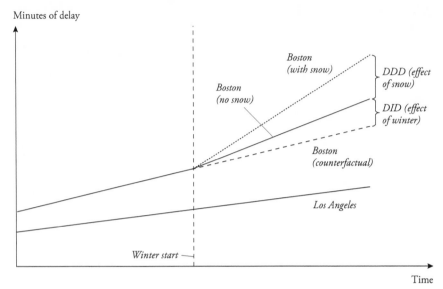

Minutes of delay

Boston
(with snow)

DDD (*effect
of snow*)

Boston
(*no snow*)

DID (*effect
of winter*)

Boston
(*counterfactual*)

Los Angeles

Winter start

Time

where *delay*$_{ita}$ is the delay (in minutes) of flight i in hour t at airport a; *winter*$_t$ is a dummy variable that equals 1 for the period from December to March and 0 otherwise; *Boston*$_a$ is a dummy variable for the Boston-area airports (with the Los Angeles–area airports as the reference group); *snow*$_{ta}$ is a dummy variable indicating the occurrence of snow precipitation in hour t at airport a; $\mathbf{X}_{ita}$ is a vector of observed information about the flight, airport, and weather; η_a are airport fixed effects; and η_m are month (indexed by m) fixed effects. The βs are estimable parameters, where $\delta \equiv \beta_4 - \beta_3$, the main parameter of interest, measures the pure effects of snow on flight delay.

Matching Identification

As an additional identification approach, we take advantage of the large amount of flight data to identify the effect of snow on flight delays nonparametrically based on matching observations with similar weather and traffic conditions. The matching procedure is as follows:

—Step 1: We partition the flight observations into two groups: a treatment group including flights experiencing snow during the hour of their scheduled departure or arrival time, and a control group including flights that do not experience snow during their scheduled departure or arrival time.

—Step 2: We match each flight observation in a treatment or control group to the K most similar ones in the other group, where similarity is based on the Mahalanobis distance between two vectors of observables containing a measure of airport traffic, the total number of scheduled flights at the endpoint airports in an hour, and observed weather information, including temperature, visibility, precipitation, and wind speed.[4]

The matching algorithm generates a set of N one-to-K matched pairs. We then estimate the effect of snow on flight delays for the N matched pairs using the bias-corrected matching estimator (Abadie and Imbens 2011) given by:

$$\tau = \frac{1}{N}\sum_{i=1}^{N}(\hat{Y}_i^1 - \hat{Y}_i^0) \tag{2.1}$$

$$\hat{Y}_i^1 = D_i Y_i + (1 - D_i)\frac{1}{K}\sum_{j \in T_i}(Y_j + \hat{\mu}_1(X_i) - \hat{\mu}_1(X_j)) \tag{2.2}$$

$$\hat{Y}_i^0 = (1 - D_i) Y_i + D_i\frac{1}{K}\sum_{j \in C_i}(Y_j + \hat{\mu}_0(X_i) - \hat{\mu}_0(X_j)) \tag{2.3}$$

In equation (2.1), $\hat{Y}_i^j$, denotes the imputed delay of a flight for observation i under treatment status j (1 if there is snow, 0 otherwise). In equations (2.2) and (2.3), the imputed delay under a treatment status equals the actual observation if it is observed under the treatment status; otherwise, it is computed from the K matched observations from the other group (which have a different treatment status); D_i is an indicator of the treatment status of observation i, taking a value of 1 if the observation is treated and 0 otherwise; and T_i and C_i denote the set of treated and control flights that are matched to observation i and that belong to the control and treated group, respectively. Finally, the conditional mean, $\mu_j(X_i) \equiv E(Y_i^j \mid X_i, D_i = j)$, $j = 0,1$, is estimated by OLS.

4. Descriptive Summary of Delays at Boston and Los Angeles Airports

Figure 9.2 decomposes the components of flight delay from the beginning to the end of a flight ("gate to gate"). Departure delay is the difference between a flight's scheduled and actual departure time from the gate. The flight can incur taxi-out delay after it leaves the gate and must wait until its wheels are off the ground. Once the flight is airborne, it can incur delay that increases the time that its wheels are off and back on the ground if it must reduce its speed or take a circuitous route to its destination. After the flight lands, it can incur taxi-in delay from the time its wheels are on the ground until it arrives at the gate. Finally, arrival delay is the difference between a flight's scheduled and actual arrival time at the gate. Each component of delay is reported separately in our data, so we can measure the effect of snow on departure and arrival delay, as well as its effect on runway-related delays associated with taxiing to and from the gate.

---

4. The Mahalanobis distance is often used to identify outliers in a sample.

Figure 9.2. *Decomposing Flight Delays*

Table 9.1. *Means (Standard Deviations) for the Delay and Weather Data*

	Winter		Nonwinter	
Variables	Boston	Los Angeles	Boston	Los Angeles
Departure delay (minutes)	12.82	9.16	8.438	9.04
	(38.96)	(34.31)	(32.80)	(32.70)
Arrival delay (minutes)	10.13	4.88	3.799	5.75
	(43.32)	(36.71)	(35.68)	(34.65)
Extreme weather delay (minutes)	3.71	1.99	2.031	1.17
	(24.18)	(15.20)	(14.43)	(12.28)
Taxi-out time (minutes)	19.76	15.74	17.462	15.47
	(12.18)	(8.15)	(9.05)	(7.75)
Taxi-in time (minutes)	7.19	8.28	6.878	8.02
	(5.15)	(6.13)	(4.33)	(5.93)
Snow (share of days snowing)	0.12	0	0.007	0
	(0.33)	(0)	(0.09)	(0)
Precipitation (inches per month)	3.8	2.0	3.8	0.3
	(2.3)	(2.1)	(2.2)	(0.6)
Temperature (degrees Fahrenheit)	29.07	63.95	59.87	69.40
	(11.60)	(7.64)	(14.45)	(7.52)
Visibility (miles)	8.76	8.80	9.28	9.52
	(2.79)	(2.32)	(2.10)	(1.36)
Wind speed (miles per hour)	11.08	5.98	10.35	7.89
	(6.00)	(4.41)	(5.13)	(4.86)
Flight distance (miles)	976	1,034	1,015	1,045
	(741)	(816)	(776)	(825)
Flights per day	530	882	558	967
	(242)	(422)	(242)	(456)
Number of observations	60,412	131,475	205,177	426,331

Sources: Bureau of Transportation Statistics; National Oceanic and Atmospheric Administration.
Note: Precipitation refers to the total amount of rain plus melted snow.

Table 9.1 presents the means and standard deviations for delay and weather-related variables for the Boston and Los Angeles airports during the winter and nonwinter seasons for comparative purposes. Two clarifications about the data are in order. First, extreme weather delays are departure or arrival delays caused by extreme weather conditions, but the airlines' on-time performance data do not indicate the specific weather conditions that cause extreme delay, which could help

Table 9.2. *DDD Estimation Results*

Variable	Gate delay (minutes)	Taxi time (minutes)
Boston × winter × snow	5.108 (0.501)	2.414 (0.101)
Boston × winter	3.432 (0.239)	0.504 (0.048)
Boston	–2.782 (0.382)	–1.019 (0.077)
Winter	–2.013 (0.145)	0.958 (0.029)
Temperature (degrees Fahrenheit)	–0.043 (0.005)	0.000 (0.001)
Visibility (miles)	–0.588 (0.022)	–0.176 (0.004)
Flight distance (miles)	–0.001 (0.000)	0.000 (0.000)
Flights per day	0.013 (0.001)	0.005 (0.000)
Departure dummy	3.126 (0.076)	7.957 (0.015)
Constant	8.339 (0.545)	7.455 (0.110)
Month fixed effects	Yes	Yes
Airport fixed effects	Yes	Yes
No. of observations	823,546	823,546

Note: Standard errors are shown in parentheses.

us understand why the mean for extreme delay is much lower than that for other types of delay. Second, the data do not include cancellation delays—that is, the time that travelers must wait for the next available departing flight to their destination. We account for cancellation delays in our analysis of private airports' decisions to invest in heated runways based on an analysis conducted by Yan et al. (2016).

Table 9.1 shows, in general, that the means for the delay variables are considerably less than the standard deviations of those variables, indicating the importance of the effect of variations in weather on delays. Departure delays and (especially) arrival delays at the Boston airports are greater during the winter compared with those delays during nonwinter months. Extreme weather delays also are greater during the winter than during the nonwinter months, as are taxi-out and taxi-in times. In contrast, arrival, departure, and extreme delays and taxi-out and taxi-in times at the Los Angeles airports do not change very much from winter to nonwinter. As expected, the Boston airports operate in colder temperatures, with more snow, less visibility, and greater wind speeds. The Los Angeles airports generally operate in mild weather conditions year-round. Finally, both the Boston and the Los Angeles airports handle fewer flights during the winter than they do during the nonwinter months.

5. Estimation Results for Delays

We present in table 9.2 the DDD estimation results of the determinants of delays at the arrival and departure gates and for taxi-out and taxi-in times. The parameter estimates indicate that a snow event increases flights' arrival and departure delays by roughly five minutes and increases taxi times by two and a half minutes.

Table 9.3. *Matching Estimation Results*

Dependent variable	K = 1	K = 4
Gate delay (minutes)	5.6570 (1.6521)	3.7677 (1.1550)
Taxi time (minutes)	3.1735 (0.6696)	3.8365 (0.5103)
Number of observations	60,412	60,412

Notes: Results shown are for the effect of snow on the dependent variable. Standard errors are shown in parentheses.

Some passengers would incur a much longer delay from a missed connection or a canceled flight because they would be forced to rebook the next available flight to their destination, which may depart much later in the day or even on the following day. Flight delays also are longer in colder temperatures and when there is less visibility. Holding other influences constant, additional airport operations increase flight delays, while flight delays at the Boston airports are less than flight delays at the Lost Angeles airports, and gate delays are less in the winter than in nonwinter months. The positive coefficient for the interaction between the Boston airports and the winter season indicates that flight delays also can be attributed to unobserved weather-related factors.

The findings based on the matching estimator, presented in table 9.3, are robust with respect to the choice of K (the number of the most-similar flights to a given flight) and are broadly consistent with those obtained by DDD estimation. The two matching models' estimates of the effect of snow on gate delay closely bound the DDD estimate of the effect of snow on gate delay, and are only slightly greater than the DDD estimate of the effect of snow on taxi time.

6. Runway Deicing and Heated-Pavement Technologies

Heated runways represent a significant technological improvement over traditional deicing approaches because they have the potential to virtually eliminate snow-related delays by rapidly melting snow and ice before they can accumulate.

Airports use several different pavement deicing and anti-icing agents, including ethylene glycol, propylene glycol, urea, ethylene glycol–based fluid known as UCAR (containing approximately 50 percent ethylene glycol, 25 percent urea, and 25 percent water by weight), potassium acetate, sodium acetate, sodium formate, and calcium magnesium acetate (CMA). Many airports apply these chemical agents after using mechanical equipment to remove heavy accumulations of snow on runways and taxiways, which increases delay times. Airports also apply anti-icing pavement agents based on predicted weather conditions and pavement temperature. Deicing and anti-icing solutions are applied using either truck-mounted spray equipment or manual methods. Table 9.4 shows the approximate unit cost and application rate of the chemical deicers.

Table 9.4. *Unit Costs of Common Deicers*

Deicer	Cost	Source	Application rate
Sodium chloride (NaCl)	$26/ton	Zhang et al. (2009)	170–890 lbs/12-ft lane
	$36/ton	Levelton Consultants (2007)	mile (13–68 g/m²), $0.0003/m²
	$26–$42/ton	Shi et al. (2009)	
	$66–$79/ton	Rubin et al. (2001)	
Magnesium chloride (MgCl₂)	$95/ton	Zhang et al. (2009)	100–150 lbs/12-ft lane
		Levelton Consultants (2007)	mile (8–11 g/m²), $0.0002/m²
Calcium chloride (CaCl₂)	$294/ton	Zhang et al. (2009)	Used along with NaCl
	$120/ton	Levelton Consultants (2007)	in the US, $0.03/m²
	$267/ton	Rubin et al. (2001)	
Calcium magnesium acetate (CMA)	$670/ton	Zhang et al. (2009)	200–500 lbs/12-ft lane
	$1,280/ton	Levelton Consultants (2007)	mile (15–39 g/m²), $0.004/m²
Potassium acetate (KAc)	n/a	Zhang et al. (2009)	0.9–9.1 gal/1,000 ft²
Salt (NaCl) mixed with calcium chloride (CaCl₂)	$98/ton	Zhang et al. (2009)	5–12 gal CaCl₂/ton of NaCl, $0.01/m²

Table 9.5. *Cost Estimates of Heated Pavement Systems*

Heat source	Installation cost	Operation cost	Maintenance cost	Source
Geothermal system	$20/ft²	$3,000	$500	Lund (1999)
Geothermal (bridge)	$48–$70/ft²	$1.48–$1.54/ft²		Minsk (1999)
Electricity (bridge)	$22–$26/ft²	$0.98/ft²		
Geothermal (bridge)	$30/ft²	$18/hr (gas)	$1.74/ft², $500/yr	Hoppe (2001)
Natural gas	$15–$65/ft²	$1.12/ft²		Anand et al. (2017)

Heated pavement technologies include electric systems, which use electricity to heat fluids, and hydronic systems, which rely on heated fluids from a variety of sources. The most efficient system is geothermal waters, but those fluids may be limited only to runways that are sufficiently close to tectonic plate boundaries. Airports in other locations can consider ground-source heat pumps, heat exchangers, or boilers to boost efficiency and reduce operating costs. Alternative heat sources, such as waste heat, may be used if a reliable supply can be guaranteed over the design lifetime of a runway. Table 9.5 summarizes the cost estimates of installing, operating, and maintaining different types of heated pavement systems.

7. Costs and Benefits of Public Boston-Area Airports Installing Heated Runways

Heated runway technologies exist that could benefit travelers by reducing snow-related travel delays that they incur at airports that are not prevented by current deicing technology. However, just because heated runway technology exists does not imply that public airports should adopt that technology or that private airports would find it in their interest to do so.

To shed light on these issues, we conduct a cost–benefit analysis of each Boston-area airport's decision to install a heated runway pavement system to eliminate snow-related delays. We assume that as public airports their observed decision to *not* install such a system was based on a negative present value calculation of heated runways' net benefits. We then assess whether any of the Boston-area airports would install a heated runway pavement system if they were privatized, based on whether the system increased their profits.

We assume public airports take actions independently without accounting for the interactions among them. The net present value of installing a heated-runway pavement system at an airport is given by:

$$NPV = \sum_{t=1}^{T} \frac{R_t}{(1+i)^t} - \text{installation cost} \tag{3}$$

where T is the planning horizon, which is assumed to be twenty years; R_t is the one-period net benefit, which is the difference between the social benefits and operating costs associated with the heated pavement system; and i is the discount factor, which is assumed to be 2.15 percent.[5] The initial installation cost of a heated runway depends on the airport's runway capacity. To account for changes in air traffic over time, we use the Federal Aviation Administration's assumed annual growth rate of 2.8 percent for the next twenty years.

When an airport installs a heated runway, the investment benefits airlines by reducing their operating costs due to snow-related delays and it benefits travelers by reducing their travel-time costs. We calculate the benefits to airlines as:

airlines' benefits (\$) = $\alpha \times$ average delay due to snow (minutes)

$\times$ total flight operation in winter $\qquad$ (4)

$\times$ average flight delay cost (\$ per flight per minute)

---

5. This is roughly the average twenty-year Treasury rate during the past five years. In chapter 8, we assumed a slightly higher discount rate of 3 percent for constructing an airport with a thirty-year lifetime. Of course, interest rates fluctuate, and the findings of our assessment could change if it were conducted in an environment with higher interest rates.

Table 9.6. *Flights and Passengers Affected by Snow at Airports in the Boston Area in 2015*

Airport	Operations during snow	Total operations	Snow-affected cases	Passengers per flight
BOS	7,549	218,605	3.5%	89.7
MHT	289	13,078	2.2%	42.2
PVD	768	23,718	3.2%	54.8

Sources: Bureau of Transportation Statistics; Federal Aviation Administration; authors' calculations.

where α is the share of delay that is reduced by a heated runway, which we assume to be one. We estimated previously that the average gate and taxi delay due to snow is eight minutes per flight. Total flight operations in winter are the aggregated number of arrival and departure flights that are affected by snow precipitation. Table 9.6 reports that in 2015, 7,549 flights at BOS, 389 flights at MHT, and 768 flights at PVD operated during snowy weather.[6] We estimate that the average aircraft cost of one minute of flight delay in 2015 is $62.55, based on cost data from American Airlines.[7]

The last column of table 9.6 shows the number of passengers per flight at each of the airports in the Boston area, which we use to estimate the total number of passengers that experienced flight delay at those airports. The US Department of Transportation (2016) recommends applying a value of travel-time savings for air travelers of $47.10 per hour, which is much lower than the estimate of $104 per hour of air travel delay reported in Yan and Winston (2014) based on data for travelers using the San Francisco Bay Area airports. We use the lower value recommended by the US Department of Transportation (2016) because public airport administrators would be required to use the US Department of Transportation's (2016) values of travel-time savings in cost–benefit analyses, and our purpose is to emulate this decisionmaking process vis-à-vis the decision to install heated runways. We also do not include the higher travel time costs that result from snowy weather that causes flight cancellations and passengers to miss their connections because that information is unlikely to be incorporated by public airports into their decisionmaking.

6. It is possible that airlines would operate more flights if there were fewer delays; thus, the estimated benefits to airlines may be conservative.

7. The cost includes additional operating and maintenance costs, such as crew, pilot salary, extra fuel consumption, and other costs.

Table 9.7. *Annual Benefits of Installing Heated Runways at the Boston-Area Airports*

Airport	Benefits to airlines	Benefits to travelers	Total benefits
BOS	$4,542,467	$5,113,598	$9,656,065
MHT	$173,900	$92,099	$265,999
PVD	$462,129	$317,824	$779,953

Note: Annual benefits are calculated based on data from 2015.

The benefits of a heated runway at an airport to travelers are then calculated as:

$$\text{travelers' benefits (\$)} = \alpha \times \text{average delay due to snow (minutes)}$$
$$\times \text{ total flight operations in winter}$$
$$\times \text{ average number of travelers per flight} \qquad (5)$$
$$\times \text{ average value of time}$$

Table 9.7 presents the benefits of installing heated runways at each of the three Boston-area airports, assuming those runways eliminate snow-related delays. The total annual benefits mainly accrue to airlines and travelers at BOS, and are nearly $10 million, which amounts to a present value of benefits of roughly $165 million. Benefits would be even higher if heated runways also led to more flights during winter.

Table 9.8 shows the construction costs of heated runways at the three airports. Because those costs can vary, we consider low-cost and high-cost scenarios, which correspond to the lower and upper bounds of unit costs of heated runways presented in table 9.5. We include operating costs but, based on the data in table 9.5, those costs are small and would not affect any of the conclusions we reach here.

Table 9.9 combines the benefits and costs in tables 9.7 and 9.8 to present the net present value of installing heated runways at each of the three airports in the Boston area, using a twenty-year time horizon. We find that installing heated runways would not yield a positive net present value of benefits for any of the airports, except for the low-cost scenario at BOS.

It is possible to make alternative assumptions such that installing heated airport runways would yield a positive net value of benefits under any cost scenario. For example, improvements in airline service quality could increase passenger demand and airport concession purchases and revenues, which are not included here.[8] It also is possible that given lower travel demand during the winter, BOS

8. Some of those purchases are likely to be spontaneous and would not have been made outside of the airport.

Table 9.8. *Installation Costs of Heated Runways at the Boston-Area Airports*

Airport (# of runways)	Area of runways (ft²)	Cost of construction	
		$15 per ft²	*$45 per ft²*
BOS (6 runways)	7,861 × 150	$17,687,250	$53,061,750
	10,006 × 150	$22,513,500	$67,540,500
	7,001 × 150	$15,752,250	$47,256,750
	5,000 × 100	$7,500,000	$22,500,000
	2,557 × 100	$3,835,500	$11,506,500
	10,083 × 150	$22,686,750	$68,060,250
	Total	$89,975,250	$269,925,750
MHT (3 runways)	9,250 × 150	$20,812,500	$62,437,500
	7,650 × 150	$17,212,500	$51,637,500
	Total	$38,025,000	$114,075,000
PVD (2 runways)	8,700 × 150	$19,575,000	$58,725,000
	6,081 × 150	$13,682,250	$41,046,750
	Total	$33,257,250	$99,771,750

Source: Authors' calculations.

Table 9.9. *Net Present Value of Installing Heated Runways at the Boston-Area Airports*

Airport	Scenario	Total net benefit
BOS	Low cost	$110,958,239
	High cost	−$68,992,260
MHT	Low cost	−$32,489,815
	High cost	−$108,539,815
PVD	Low cost	−$17,027,173
	High cost	−$83,541,673

Source: Authors' calculations.

could reduce the cost of heated runways by installing fewer of them, such as on only the most highly used runways, and still eliminate snow-related delays that benefit travelers. However, given that BOS has, to the best of our knowledge, not shown any interest in installing heated runways or in conducting a preliminary assessment of their potential benefits, it is likely that any net present value calculation they perform would assume a high-cost scenario and would not include the potential benefits we have noted.

The behavior we ascribe to BOS is consistent with public enterprises conducting assessments, especially for potential urban transportation projects, by making assumptions that fit their preferred decision. Often those assumptions overstate benefits and understate costs, with the outcome that the project is completed and incurs large deficits (Winston 2013). In the case of heated runways, public airports are not making assumptions about benefits and costs with that bias, which fits with their preferred decision to not incur project expenses.

8. Private Airports' Adoption of Heated Runways in a Competitive Environment

Using plausible assumptions, the net present value analysis is consistent with the observed decision of the Boston-area airports not to install heated runways. Although we could make assumptions that would justify BOS installing at least some heated runways, others could make a plausible case against those assumptions. As noted, our finding is intuitively plausible because public commercial airports have little economic incentive to install heated runways.

Privatized airports would have an economic incentive to install one or more heated runways if the investment increased their profits. We assess this possibility and, to account for political considerations, assess whether private airports could find it profitable to install heated runways without reducing airlines' profits and travelers' welfare.

Yan and Winston's (2014) Model of Private Airport Competition

We assess the decision of privatized Boston-area airports to install heated runways by extending Yan and Winston's (2014) model of private airport competition. The model is based on the following three-step sequential-moves game. We apply two versions that make different assumptions about airports' runway charges. In the first version:

—Stage 1: The three Boston-area airports simultaneously make decisions on adopting heated runways, but they do *not* change their landing fees.

—Stage 2: Airlines choose capacity (number of seats) on their spoke routes that are connected to the three airports.

—Stage 3: Airlines set profit-maximizing fares for their flights, which allocates passengers' demands among airlines.

In the second version of the game, the three Boston-area airports simultaneously make decisions on adopting heated runways and set profit-maximizing runway charges.

Airlines take current runway charges as given in the first stage and engage in price and service competition, where flight frequency, which determines schedule delays, is the key service variable.[9] Travelers choose among possible airport–airline

---

9. Schedule delay is the difference between the traveler's desired departure flight time and their actual departure flight time.

routing combinations for domestic trips that originate or terminate in one of the three Boston-area airports. A traveler's choice is a function of a vector of prices, schedule delays, and other exogenous influences. In the second stage, given aircraft size, airlines choose spoke capacities, thereby determining schedule delays. Finally, given spoke capacities, airlines engage in Bertrand competition, as each airline simultaneously chooses prices for the products it offers in the Boston-area markets by maximizing profits subject to the seat capacity it provides to satisfy demand.

New Estimates of Demand and Costs

We update the analysis from Yan and Winston (2014) by using data from the US Department of Transportation's Airline Origin and Destination Survey (DB1B) for the fourth quarter of 2015 and the first quarter of 2016 to estimate an aggregate discrete choice model of travelers' airline choices to and from airports in the Boston area, instead of to and from airports in the San Francisco Bay Area. The parameter estimates are used to solve airlines' profit-maximization problem. We summarize the data for that model in table 9.10. As in Yan and Winston (2014), the data include fares, service attributes for the carriers and airports, and airport and airline dummy variables; we also include various sources of travel delay, including weather delay and flights affected by snow.

The estimates of travelers' demand parameters, presented in table 9.11, have plausible signs and most are estimated with statistical precision. We treat the fare coefficient as a random parameter with a normally distributed standard deviation, to incorporate travelers' preference heterogeneity.[10] Higher fares, more connections, and longer delays reduce the likelihood of a traveler choosing a given alternative, while travelers prefer flights with longer distances but at a decreasing rate. All else constant, travelers prefer the low-cost airlines (with United as the reference group), and prefer PVD (with BOS as the reference group). Based on the coefficients, the implied values of travel delay ($85 per hour) and flight frequency ($11 per hour) are somewhat lower than the values we found for San Francisco Bay Area travelers in Yan and Winston (2014), but they are still plausible. The estimated price elasticity of demand of –1.71 is slightly higher than the elasticity that we estimated for San Francisco Bay Area travelers in Yan and Winston (2014).

Finally, we present the estimates of the airlines' cost coefficients in appendix table 9.A1 and we present the airlines' and airports' marginal costs, which can be derived from the model, in table 9.12. Although several of the coefficients are not

---

10. We estimated the random-coefficient aggregate discrete choice model assuming a normally distributed and a log-normally distributed random parameter for the fare coefficient, but we could not obtain convergence with the log-normal distribution.

Table 9.10. *Summary Statistics for the Dataset*

Variable	Source	Mean	SD
Fare (dollars)	DB1B	521	349
Passengers per quarter	DB1B	89	350
Number of connections	DB1B	3.506	0.751
Flight distance (miles)	DB1B	3,415	1,438
American Airlines	DB1B	0.059	0.236
Alaska Airlines	DB1B	0.007	0.085
JetBlue Airways	DB1B	0.119	0.324
Delta Air Lines	DB1B	0.230	0.421
Spirit Airlines	DB1B	0.006	0.076
Sun Country Airlines	DB1B	0.002	0.047
United Airlines	DB1B	0.099	0.299
US Airways	DB1B	0.100	0.300
Virgin America	DB1B	0.011	0.105
Southwest Airlines	DB1B	0.366	0.482
Departure delay (minutes)	On Time	11.111	2.239
Arrival delay (minutes)	On Time	7.521	3.601
Weather delay (minutes)	On Time	3.265	1.739
Schedule delay (minutes)	On Time	8.422	40.642
Daily departures	On Time	244	166
Snow-affected flights share	On Time	0.105	0.070
Passenger share for BOS	DB1B	0.768	
Passenger share for MHT	DB1B	0.092	
Passenger share for PVD	DB1B	0.140	
Passengers per market (thousands)	DB1B	26.7	31.1
Market size (population in millions)	Census	3.2	2.1
Aircraft size (seats)	T-100	147	18

Sources: Bureau of Transportation Statistics; Census Bureau; authors' calculations.
Note: Flight distance includes all segments of connecting flights.

precisely estimated, the absolute and relative values of the estimated marginal costs are plausible. For example, the legacy carriers American, United, and Delta, have higher marginal costs than Southwest, a low-cost carrier.

Simulation Results

As noted, we assume two different airport privatization scenarios in our simulations. In the first, each airport is privatized but still charges carriers weight-based landing fees, following Federal Aviation Administration guidelines, as well as concession charges. Given the estimated demand and cost functions and airlines' profit-maximizing behavior, we determine whether any of the airports could increase their profits by installing heated runways under each privatization scenario.

Table 9.11. *Random-Coefficient Multinomial Logit Demand Estimates*

Variable	Coefficient estimate	Standard error
Constant	−13.034	0.562
Fare ($100)	−0.413	0.117
Standard deviation of fare coefficient	0.271	0.259
Number of connections	−1.481	0.173
Flight distance	0.715	0.166
Flight distance squared	−0.093	0.002
Airport delay	−0.350	0.014
Schedule delay	−0.011	0.011
American Airlines	−1.712	2.670
Alaska Airlines	−1.839	7.976
JetBlue Airways	0.073	0.391
Delta Air Lines	−0.104	0.485
Spirit Airlines	4.915	4.753
Sun Country Airlines	3.183	3.558
US Airways	−3.563	0.478
Virgin America	9.950	2.645
PVD	10.119	1.874
MHT	−7.664	3.080
Implied mean value of delay	$85 per hour	
Implied mean value of flight frequency	$11 per hour	
Implied mean price elasticity	−1.71	
Number of observations	17,287	

Source: Authors' calculations.

Notes: We assume that the standard deviation for the random fare coefficient is normally distributed. The omitted category is United Airlines at BOS.

Table 9.12. *Marginal Cost Estimates*

Overall	0.15
By airline	
American	0.16
United	0.17
Delta	0.14
Alaska	0.18
US Airways	0.13
Southwest	0.13
JetBlue	0.14
Virgin America	0.15
Other	0.16
By airport	
BOS	0.15
MHT	0.16
PVD	0.14
Number of observations	17,287

Source: Authors' calculations.

Note: The marginal cost estimates are expressed as dollars per passenger-mile.

Table 9.13. *Winter-Season Benefits of Installing Heated Runways at the Boston-Area Airports*

	BOS	MHT	PVD
Annualized installation cost ($ million per year)	7.18	3.17	2.77
Change in airport revenues ($ million)	4.87	1.02	1.08
Change in airline profits ($ million)	22.12	0.08	0.23
Change in demand (seats)	405,223	84,623	89,598
Change in total consumer surplus ($ million)	16.57		

Source: Authors' calculations.

As shown in table 9.13, we find that installing heated runways at the three Boston-area airports would increase demand and reduce airlines' operating costs, which increases airlines' profit and travelers' welfare. Airports increase their revenue because the additional passengers generate additional landing fee revenues of $2 per seat and additional concession revenues of $10 per passenger. Nevertheless, the increase in airport revenue for the winter season cannot cover the annualized cost of installing heated runways at any of the airports, so privatized Boston-area airports would not adopt heated runways.

In the second version of the simulations, we assume private airports make decisions on both the level of runway charges and whether to install heated runways to maximize profits. Because the two smaller airports, MHT and PVD, do not have large enough passenger demand even if they adjust their runway prices to support installing heated runways, we consider a feasible privatization scenario in which only BOS is privatized, and the other two airports do not change their runway charges and runways.

We also include additional benefits from adopting heating runways by including the time savings from flights that otherwise would be cancelled. Based on research by Yan et al. (2016), cancellations and missed connections could cause some passengers to incur delays of more than ten hours, depending on the load factor for their next alternative flights. As a conservative assumption, we assume passengers are delayed five hours and value that airport delay time at $85 per hour, based on the findings of our demand estimation. The assumed value of delay time is conservative because travelers might value the delays caused by cancellations and missed connections higher than they value conventional airport delays given the uncertainty and anxiety associated with the effects of such delay on travelers' trips and activity at the destination.

Airport privatization that has occurred throughout the world has been marked by tension between airports and airlines because airports feel they should be able to pass their costs on to airlines, which can pass those costs on to passengers

Table 9.14. *Equilibrium Outcome of Privatizing Boston Logan International Airport*

	BOS	MHT	PVD
Airport charge ($ per seat)	21	2	2
Heated runway adoption	Yes	No	No
Change in airport profits ($ million per winter season)	16.3	0.00	0.00
Change in airlines' profits ($ million per winter season)	0.8	0.00	0.00
Change in total consumer surplus ($ million per winter season)	0.00		

Source: Authors' calculations.

through higher ticket prices. However, this behavior may spark protests by groups representing travelers and airlines and possibly discourage government transportation authorities from privatizing BOS. Thus, to account for political considerations, we consider profit-maximization behavior by BOS in its choice of runway installation and airport takeoff and landing charges subject to runway price caps that still allow airlines to raise their fares but that prevent air travelers from being worse off.

Table 9.14 shows that under this scenario it is possible for BOS to find it profitable to install heated runways; airlines could increase their profits; and travelers would not be worse off, accounting for the reduction in travel delays and the increase in airport charges that would be passed on in higher ticket prices.

Because we have made conservative assumptions about the benefits to travelers from eliminating delays from cancellations and missed connections, it is conceivable their benefits could be much higher and airports could charge higher runway fees and be more profitable, or that travelers also could gain along with airports and airlines. In addition, we have assumed that BOS would install heated runways for all its runways, which could lead to excessive costs. As noted, it is possible that BOS could install fewer heated runways while still achieving most of the reductions in snow-related travel delays. The lower costs of runway installation could enable all participants to increase their welfare from this innovation. And like all innovations, technological advances that reduce the cost of runway installation are likely to occur as heated runways are increasingly adopted.

Finally, heated runways could provide environmental benefits. Shen et al. (2016) find that heated runways require less energy and produce less greenhouse gas emissions compared with traditional snow and ice removal systems. Heated runways also would reduce the adverse effect that airport deicing operations can have on the aquatic ecosystem and the quality of finished drinking water (Swietlik 2010).[11]

9. Conclusions

Deregulation of intercity transportation enabled the private sector to show how government policy suppressed competition and innovation in transportation. The development of ridesharing showed how innovations can spur competition that had been suppressed in regulated urban transportation markets. Unfortunately, the absence of private sector involvement may enable government intervention in other transportation services and facilities to continue to suppress the potential gains from innovation.

This chapter has shown that public airports may be neglecting the potential benefits to travelers, carriers, and airports from heated runways. Public airports have no incentive to adopt heated runways because they incur a cost that they could not fully recover, and although travelers would benefit, public airports could not make travelers pay for that benefit. In practice, the Federal Aviation Administration, not public airports, would probably have to take the lead if public airports were to install heated runways, which makes it even more likely that the public sector would neglect their benefits because the Federal Aviation Administration has even less incentive than public airports to allocate its funds to cover the expense.

In contrast, private airports would have an incentive to adopt heated runways because they could recover their costs and increase profits by adjusting runway charges. Privatizing airports also could be attractive from a political perspective to the extent that airport authorities could set caps on runway charges that do not disincentivize airports from adopting innovations that make travelers better off. At the same time, because policymakers are frequent air travelers and they along with other travelers in domestic and international markets would benefit from fewer flight delays and cancellations, they might support a policy that benefits them and their constituents.

Typically, government intervention is justified when a service or facility is socially desirable but privately unprofitable. We have revealed an important case in transportation where a government-run airport facility in Boston would not implement a socially desirable innovation (heated runways) but a privatized facility in the Boston metropolitan area would have an incentive to implement the socially desirable innovation. Importantly, in addition to Boston Logan, it is likely that many other major airports in North America and other parts of the world could benefit air travelers and carriers by installing heated runways.

11. The effects of climate change on our analysis are likely to be ambiguous. On one hand, the present discounted value of benefits of heated runways would decrease if snowfall in the Boston metropolitan area occurred less frequently. On the other hand, the present discounted value of benefits would increase if extreme weather events, such as heavy snowfall, occurred more frequently.

Appendix

Table 9.A1. *Estimates of Cost Coefficients*

Variable	Coefficient estimate	Standard error	t	P > t	95% confidence interval	
Number of connections	16.926	10.423	1.624	0.104	−3.505	37.357
Flight distance	75.041	25.138	2.985	0.003	25.768	124.32
Flight distance squared	−9.49	3.474	−2.732	0.006	−16.3	−2.681
American Airlines	−1.944	30.588	−0.064	0.949	−61.9	58.011
Alaska Airlines	22.8	78.893	0.289	0.773	−131.8	177.44
JetBlue Airways	27.965	24.397	1.146	0.252	−19.86	75.785
Delta Air Lines	−6.869	18.375	−0.374	0.709	−42.89	29.148
Spirit Airlines	33.334	86.576	0.385	0.7	−136.4	203.03
Sun Country Airlines	49.024	137.03	0.358	0.721	−219.6	317.61
United Airlines	5.9626	25.763	0.231	0.817	−44.54	56.46
US Airways	−61.53	24.23	−2.539	0.011	−109	−14.04
Virgin America	8.5303	65.392	0.13	0.896	−119.6	136.71
PVD	13.961	20.295	0.688	0.492	−25.82	53.742
MHT	3.0639	24.819	0.123	0.902	−45.58	51.711
Slot control dummy	46.561	32.941	1.413	0.158	−18.01	111.13
Intercept	−192.9	49.843	−3.871	0	−290.6	−95.25

Source: Authors' calculations.

Note: The omitted category is Southwest Airlines at BOS.

10

Competition and Innovation to Further Improve Intercity Passenger Transportation

CLIFFORD WINSTON AND JIA YAN

1. Introduction

If firms continue to compete and innovate, the development of the US transportation system will never end. Potential sources of new competition and innovation currently exist that could enable intercity passenger transportation to continue to improve for the foreseeable future. Of course, the specific providers of transportation are likely to evolve over time, as some fail and others become the leaders of new transportation technology.

As in the past, doubts are likely to be raised about the viability of a new transportation technology and claims will be made that it is overhyped. For example, supersonic air transportation failed during the early 2000s, but investors believe that it may reemerge in the future. As discussed in the final chapter, it is very difficult to predict when innovations occur and their ultimate success. Current signs point to the development of new intercity transportation technologies that could be commercially viable in the long run.

New Modal Sources of Competition and Innovation

In chapter 5, we indicated that electric vehicles are increasing their market share and represent a socially beneficial innovation that can significantly reduce air pollution as they replace cars with internal combustion engines. Their benefits will be most notable in urban areas, but they also will provide environmental benefits as their share of intercity trips increases. In chapter 6, we pointed out that autonomous cars would produce large social benefits when they are adopted both for urban and intercity trips and could provide additional competition for air carriers. Autonomous buses and passenger rail service also could compete for intercity passengers.

The innovations in electrified and autonomous modes in surface intercity passenger transportation also could occur in air transportation, including the introduction of electric planes and even autonomous flying cars. Still another potential improvement in air transportation is commercial supersonic service.

As in the case of efficient adoption of autonomous surface modes, government agencies will play an important role to facilitate the operations of the new air transportation modes as they create additional air traffic, which will add more stress to an already stressed air traffic control system. The Federal Aviation Administration (FAA) will be responsible for enabling the new modes to operate safely and efficiently along with other air traffic.

AUTONOMOUS SURFACE PASSENGER MODES. People who dislike flying or who are traveling with several family members or friends may find autonomous cars and buses attractive for long-distance intercity trips. Autonomous cars could be designed with sleeping compartments and entertainment centers for such trips, while autonomous buses could improve the cost and service of bus transportation.[1] Automation would eliminate a major advantage that the intercity bus has over the automobile because automobile travelers would no longer have to drive. So, intercity bus would be challenged to find a niche in the autonomous intercity passenger transportation market.

Similarly, intercity passenger rail would be severely challenged by automation. The 2021 Infrastructure Investment and Jobs Act includes some $66 billion for Amtrak to repair its aging infrastructure and to expand its routes across the country.[2] However, like bus, automation would cause Amtrak to lose a major advantage it has over the automobile. Commuter rail systems, even if automated, also would face the same problem in retaining passengers.

Private intercity rail passenger transportation competitors may enable rail to compete in an autonomous transportation system. For example, AmeriStarRail is a

1. In 2006, the deregulated intercity bus sector began to expand service nationwide at a fast rate with the emergence and growth of Megabus, a new low-cost operator owned by the successful British company Stagecoach and new East Coast and West Coast operators. Other services emerged including Greyhound's Bolt Bus and the so-called Chinatown buses that connect Washington, DC, and New York City and other origin-destination pairs. Recently, a new startup company, Napaway, began offering premium overnight accommodations between select cities with seats that fold into a flat bed and come with a pillow and plush blanket.

2. Amtrak's efforts to expand its route coverage may conflict with rail freight operations when Amtrak must access track that is owned by private freight railroads. For example, Amtrak sought to provide new service along the Gulf Coast, but negotiations with private railroads stalled for six years over a disagreement about the cost of the capital investment in the rail infrastructure that would be necessary to restore Amtrak's passenger service. Finally, the freight railroads and Amtrak settled their dispute and Amtrak will be able to expand its passenger service in the southern United States.

startup company that wants to take over and run Amtrak's Northeast Corridor service because it believes it can reduce the cost of intercity passenger transportation and improve its travel times. Amtrak has indicated that it has no interest in unbundling any part of its network to allow another rail carrier to serve it. However, AmeriStarRail and other private rail companies could compete for the rights to run parts of Amtrak's system as autonomous transportation evolves and puts greater pressure on Amtrak's troubled finances. Private autonomous rail companies may be more successful than Amtrak at providing a commercially viable service in certain parts of the country that can compete effectively for passengers.

Interest in high-speed rail service has existed in the United States for decades. However, the nation's first experiment with high-speed rail connecting Los Angeles and San Francisco, which was developed and managed by the public sector, turned into a multibillion-dollar fiasco and is unlikely to ever be completed (Vartabedian 2022). Private high-speed rail systems are being developed in Florida and Texas, but they are not complete and have not shown that they can operate without government subsides.

High-speed rail systems operate in countries throughout the world and can complement and compete with air transportation (Zhang, Wan, and Yang 2019). However, strong doubts remain about whether private high-speed rail service—even if it is automated—can be commercially viable in the United States without large government subsidies.

NEW AIR TRANSPORTATION MODES. New air transportation modes include flying cars, electric planes, electric vertical takeoff and landing (eVTOL) craft, electric aircraft, and supersonic air travel.

Flying Cars: Flying cars have evolved into a potentially viable mode as indicated by the FAA now referring to them as advanced air mobility. Recently, Klein Vision's AirCar completed a thirty-five-minute test flight with a fixed-propeller aircraft transforming from aircraft to car in less than three minutes. It was awarded an official Certificate of Airworthiness by the Slovak Transport Authority after completing seventy hours of "rigorous flight testing." Flying cars are attracting investors in various parts of the world to help develop and test the technology.

eVTOL Craft: Several companies are attempting to develop a new generation of eVTOL craft for use as air taxis in highly populated corridors, which could save people considerable travel time compared with surface passenger transportation modes. Joby Aviation, a leading industry participant, recently announced the completion of a 150-mile flight on a single electric charge, new plans to operate an eVTOL in 2024 as an air taxi that is cost competitive with taxis on the street, and an agreement with the Japanese airline All Nippon Airways to establish air taxi service between Japanese cities and Japanese airports. Lilium and Archer also are leading industry participants; other eVTOL companies include AeroMobil, General Motors' Cadillac PersonalSpace, Terrafugia, PAL-V Liberty, Pop.Up Next, and Vertical Aerospace.

US airlines also have shown interest in eVTOLs, as Delta Air Lines made a $60 million investment in Joby Aviation as part of a five-year partnership to operate Joby's eVTOLs exclusively in Delta's network. American Airlines has confirmed delivery slots for the first 50 eVTOL aircraft of an initial preorder of up to 250 aircraft from Vertical Aerospace, with an option for up to one hundred more. United Airlines has put in a deposit on its order with Archer Aviation for a fleet of two hundred eVTOL aircraft to be used in partnership with Mesa Airlines, a regional carrier, and has invested $15 million in Eve Air Mobility, a start-up manufacturer, and signed a conditional agreement to buy two hundred of its aircraft with an option to buy two hundred more. United and Archer are planning to launch a shuttle service in 2025 from a heliport near the southern tip of Manhattan to United's hub at Newark Liberty International Airport.

Finally, the leading commercial aircraft manufacturers are planning to offer autonomous eVTOL aircraft. Airbus is seeking to certify its CityAirbus NextGen four-seat eVTOL by 2025 as a piloted vehicle, eventually moving to autonomy when regulations allow for uncrewed air taxi service. Boeing is partnering with Wisk Aero to develop an autonomous eVTOL.

The private sector's active interest in a new mode and in overcoming the challenges of designing and building air taxis and flying cars that work is encouraging. However, one must not lose sight of the infrastructure—namely, safe and convenient places for takeoff and landing—that are essential for the mode's commercial success. In addition, those operations must be safely and effectively integrated into the current FAA air traffic control systems, which as pointed out below have not been modernized to reduce ongoing air traffic congestion and delays.

The FAA also is responsible for certifying eVTOL aircraft to meet safety and noise standards and to provide the eVTOL industry with a clear certification process. The FAA has provided Joby Aviation with a certification that would allow it to begin its air taxi operations with a conventional airplane. However, Joby still has regulatory hurdles to clear before its five-seat eVTOL aircraft can legally fly passengers.

In May 2022, the FAA announced it would certify eVTOL aircraft that will not need runways to operate under a special "powered-lift" category, rather than as an airplane. The change will require rulemaking and a new set of guidelines for operators to move forward, meaning that pilots will have to obtain certification as a powered-lift operator because they are not flying a traditional plane or helicopter. The FAA has indicated that it does not expect the first eVTOL to begin commercial operations until early 2025. Thus, like other modal innovations, eVTOLs are facing regulatory hurdles that will slow their widespread adoption in the United States.

Electric Planes: Air carriers are planning to use electric aircraft to fly regional routes, which could help to reduce aviation's carbon footprint. United Airlines, for example, has indicated plans to have electric planes flying out of O'Hare

International Airport and Denver International Airports by 2030, and has placed an order for one hundred battery-powered aircraft from the Swedish startup Heart Aerospace. Air Canada, Mesa Airlines, and Icelandair also have placed orders with Heart Aerospace. Initially, electric planes will be used on routes of two hundred miles or less, recharge in less than thirty minutes, and operate at a lower cost than a traditional aircraft serving short-distance routes. Accordingly, smaller cities that have not been served by air carriers may be offered new service and smaller cities that have been served by air carriers may be offered less costly and more frequent service.

Supersonic Air Travel: Supersonic air travel came to a halt in 2003, a few years after the Air France Concorde flight from Paris to New York burst into flames shortly after takeoff. However, the aviation sector is currently attempting to revive commercial supersonic travel using aircraft that does not cause sonic booms when flying over land and can meet environmental and safety standards throughout the world. Such aircraft could enable, for example, travelers flying from the East Coast of the United States to make transatlantic day trips and to fly to Tokyo in six hours.

The Canadian jet manufacturer Bombardier announced that it has successfully tested a smaller private jet at supersonic speeds. Boom Supersonic hopes to have a supersonic jet that can provide business-class service in just over three hours from New York to London by 2029. United Airlines has a firm order for fifteen of Boom's supersonic airliners once the model meets United's safety, operating, and sustainability requirements, and the deal includes options for thirty-five additional aircraft. United plans to configure the aircraft to seat roughly eighty business-class passengers and charge fares that are comparable to current business-class fares. American Airlines and Japan Airlines may each purchase up to twenty supersonic aircraft from Boom. Economically viable and safe supersonic airline service that meets noise and environmental regulatory standards would be a breakthrough for air travel.

The incremental automation of commercial aviation can reduce the cost of air travel by, for example, enabling aircraft operators to relax the minimum crew requirement and to operate with one pilot instead of two (Zakharenko and Luttmann 2023). Additional improvements could occur by modernizing air traffic control.

Modernizing Air Traffic Control

A modernized air traffic control system is essential to enable the current and potentially new users of airspace, from flying cars to supersonic planes, to operate safely.[3] The FAA has long been criticized for its failure to develop and operationalize

---

3. Some of this material synthesizes aviation newsletters on the US aviation system and comments by Robert Poole of the Reason Foundation.

a technologically modern air traffic control system, which could reduce traffic delays and enhance safety.

Nav Canada, Canada's corporatized air traffic control system, is seen as a model for the United States to follow to improve its efficiency, technology, and effectiveness. Nav Canada and NATS, the United Kingdom's air navigation system, are responsible for the operational benefits from faster flying speeds and greater safety facilitated by automatic dependent surveillance–broadcast (ADS-B) in the North Atlantic airspace.

ADS-B was originally designed as an alternative to radar to keep better track of aircraft in flight. It updates the position, altitude, and velocity of aircraft much faster than radar. Given the system's constellation of sixty-six satellites, an aircraft can be under surveillance by as many as seven satellites at one time, providing considerable redundancy to ensure safety. However, because ADS-B relies on GPS (global positioning), FAA and counterparts overseas no longer consider that it will completely replace radar, which, along with some ground beacons, will remain in place for the foreseeable future.

Aireon made a breakthrough by developing ADS-B, which provides global space-based coverage for the 70 percent of global airspace where there is no radar, including over the oceans, polar regions, and many mountainous areas. Nav Canada was the lead investor in Aireon and was subsequently joined by several other air navigation service providers, including the United Kingdom's NATS. Many other air navigation service providers now subscribe to Aireon's services. However, the FAA does not, and it has not implemented ADS-B over the Pacific Ocean airspace, depriving travelers from the United States to Hawaii, Asia, Australia, and other destinations the benefits of a modern air traffic control system.

In another case of the FAA's poor performance, it has been in an interagency battle with the Federal Communications Commission about the rollout of new 5G cell service near airports that could interfere with low-altitude aircraft operations such as takeoffs and landings. Newer radar altimeters (in most large airliners) have adequate shielding against stray signals from the 5G antennas to prevent interference. But older Airbus A320 planes and most of the regional jets produced by Canadair (now Airbus) and Embraer do not have such filters. The FAA is now on an accelerated program to get those planes equipped, which is causing havoc among the regional carriers that serve smaller airports. However, the FAA waited about a year, knowing of the likely problem before raising the issue with the Federal Communications Commission on the eve of its spectrum auction. It is currently estimated that it will take at least five years for all altimeters to be upgraded to allow 5G cell service near airports.

Summary

Thanks to airline and bus deregulation, the intercity passenger transportation system has significantly improved in recent decades and, as we have discussed, new sources of competition and innovation offer additional opportunities for the intercity passenger system to provide faster, more reliable, and less costly service.

Government will again play a critical role to enable the new sources of competition and innovation to move forward. Unfortunately, policymakers continue to impede further competition in air transportation with regulations that fail to grant cabotage rights to foreign airlines and that maintain public ownership of airports. At the same time, policymakers are slowing the adoption of innovations in autonomous surface passenger modes (auto, bus, and rail) that can provide intercity trips, and the FAA's failure to modernize air traffic control facilities could jeopardize the introduction and performance of new aviation services.

It is encouraging that the private sector continues to engage in competition that is leading to new innovations in autonomy and aircraft, some of which may be technologically and commercially successful and may greatly advance intercity passenger transportation. However, governments must provide effective policy guidance and manage transportation infrastructure efficiently to give the innovators a chance to succeed.

PART **III**

Freight Transportation

Deregulation of the railroad and trucking industries in 1980 significantly improved the efficiency of the US intercity freight transportation system and benefited both rail carriers and shippers. Although the trucking industry adjusted to the more competitive environment with the emergence of advanced truckload carriers, more efficient less-than-truckload carriers, and less restricted private trucking operations, it has recently had difficulty attracting drivers and its disrupted operations have contributed to supply chain shipment delays. Following deregulation, railroad mergers left the rail industry with two major carriers in the East (CSX and Norfolk Southern) and two major carriers in the West (Union Pacific and BNSF), raising ongoing concerns that rail freight transportation is insufficiently competitive, especially for so-called captive shippers of bulk commodities, such as coal and grain.

This part of the book provides perspective on competition in the railroad industry as it has evolved since deregulation to achieve a contract equilibrium, where a large fraction of freight traffic, especially coal and grain, move under contract rates. We analyze duopoly competition in coal markets with long-term contract rates and summarize recent evidence on rail competition and policy-makers' efforts to spur more competition by requiring railroads to allow reciprocal switching, where a shipper could potentially receive lower rates from a carrier because another carrier has easier access to its network to offer a competitive alternative. We conclude that government intervention to increase competition in the railroad industry is unlikely to be effective and is not justified.

We then look to the future and argue that freight transportation like other transportation services has the potential to be greatly improved by autonomous operations in all modes that would increase competition and improve service. We discuss autonomous rail freight services and quantify the potential benefits to shippers from autonomous trucking services, which would help address future supply chain disruptions and strengthen trucking as a competitive threat to rail for bulk commodities. We conclude this part of the book by pointing out that more competition and innovation also could improve water transportation and could lead to a new service using unmanned aerial vehicles (drones) that could further improve the speed and reliability of freight delivery services for small shipments.

11

Railroad Competition and Innovation

VIKRAM MAHESHRI, CLIFFORD WINSTON,
JIA YAN, AND SCOTT DENNIS

1. Introduction

F ollowing deregulation in 1980 and various carrier consolidations thereafter,
most shippers in the United States have only two rail carriers competing
for their business, and some have only one. So-called captive shippers and the
various organizations that represent them complain that rail rates are not always
reasonable and that the Surface Transportation Board (STB)—the successor to
the Interstate Commerce Commission, which has the authority to determine
the legality of rates in accordance with maximum-rate regulation—does little to
protect them.[1] In response to such charges, Congress has periodically considered
legislation to increase rail competition and the STB has considered mandating
reciprocal switching to ensure that an alleged captive shipper has access to an
additional railroad.[2]

In this chapter, we assess the evolution of competition in the railroad industry since deregulation. A key feature of such competition is that prices are often

---

1. Under maximum-rate guidelines (49 USC 10707), shippers can challenge a rate if it exceeds
180 percent of variable costs and if the railroad in question has no effective competition. However,
the process is lengthy and costly.

2. In addition, following a public hearing on Urgent Issues in Freight Rail Service held
April 26–27, 2022, the STB announced that freight railroads will be required to provide additional
data and regular progress reports on its service. For their part, the railroads reported that they are
making considerable progress to hire more train crew members to improve service. The Federal
Railroad Administration has concerns with rail safety and is seeking to reimpose a rule that would
require two-person crews to operate freight trains.

determined by long-term contract rates, especially for shipments of coal and grain, which are negotiated between a shipper and a railroad. We determine empirically the competitive equilibrium that develops in the specific case of duo-poly competition between Burlington Northern and Santa Fe (BNSF) Railway and Union Pacific (UP) Railroad for coal shipped from the Powder River Basin (PRB) in the western United States to a power-generating utility, which negoti-ates long-term contract rates with one of the two carriers. We find that a rail carrier's entry into a monopoly market causes the time path of coal transport rates to approach a plausible estimate of the long-run marginal cost of rail service, suggesting that a duopoly in PRB markets provides sufficient competitive pres-sure to substantially eliminate the price markups that one might expect in this competitive setting.

Given that we must restrict the sample in our empirical analysis to 1998, because by 1999 electric utilities began to win a handful of maximum-rate cases before the STB, which could indicate that reductions in coal rates could be attributable to residual regulation, we extend our assessment of rail competition by providing descriptive evidence. Again, we conclude that the evidence suggests that the railroad industry is sufficiently competitive, and that government inter-vention is not justified.

Finally, we provide an overview of autonomous railroad operations, which will reduce rail costs and rates to shippers and improve rail transit time and its reliability. Autonomous rail operations could lead to a seamless North American railroad network, with service to the United States, Canada, and Mexico and will be essential to enable rail to compete effectively with autonomous trucks.

2. An Overview of Rail Competition in Duopoly Coal Markets

Coal from the Powder River Basin in Wyoming and southern Montana burns cleaner than most coal mined in the United States because of its lower sulfur and ash composition. It is extracted by roughly twenty mines from a single, vast, seventy-foot-thick deposit at constant returns to scale, has homogeneous characteristics, and generally at a uniform mine-mouth price. Demand for PRB coal increased substantially between 1988 and 1997 (see figure 11.1) because the 1990 Clean Air Act Amendments required electricity-generating plants to reduce their emissions. By switching to PRB coal, a plant can remove one ton of sulfur dioxide for $113, whereas a plant burning coal from the eastern United States must spend $322 to remove one ton of the pollutant by installing scrubbers.[3]

In our analysis, a rail transportation market is a route consisting of a coal-producing region with multiple mines at the origin and an electric utility plant at

3. Those figures are from *Coal Age*, vol. 104, August 1999.

Figure 11.1. *Share of Coal Used in the United States by Origin*

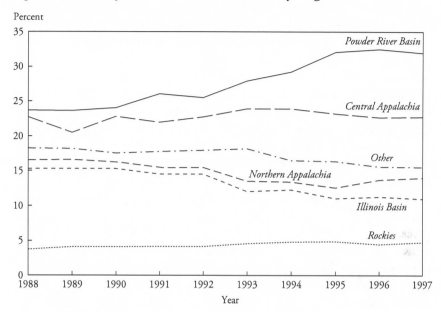

Source: Energy Information Administration, Coal Industry Annual, 1994 to 2000.

the destination. Utilities purchase coal from one or more mines but they do not colocate, so only one generating plant is at each destination. Because virtually all PRB coal shipped to electric utility plants moves by rail for most of or the entire journey, railroads do not compete directly with trucks or barge transportation in those markets.

In the late 1970s, BNSF began transporting substantial amounts of coal from the Powder River Basin and enjoyed a monopoly in many but not all markets. UP had a monopoly in a smaller set of markets, and the remaining markets were solely served by Kansas City Southern Railway or another carrier. Competition between BNSF and UP in particular began to intensify in 1985 and gave a growing number of plants alternative access to PRB coal, as UP and its partner, the Chicago and North Western (CNW) Transportation Company, received authorization from the Interstate Commerce Commission to build into the southern portion of the region. Those carriers also engaged in a joint venture to acquire a share in the main north–south track through the PRB, which had been formerly owned solely by BNSF. UP eventually acquired CNW in 1995 and Southern Pacific (SP) Railroad the following year. BNSF began to enter UP's monopoly markets during the 1980s and was aided in the following decade in a few cases by trackage rights it received as part of the merger between UP and SP. BNSF acquired Atchison, Topeka, and Santa Fe Railroad in 1995.

Given that PRB coal is very similar throughout the basin, with only slight mining cost differences, utility plants that were served by UP and BNSF had two alternative sources of PRB coal. However, because almost all PRB coal is transported under long-term contracts, the full impact of UP's and BNSF's entry on prices was not immediate; instead, it developed as power plants' contracts with both carriers expired and plants renegotiated their contracts in a duopoly market, where UP and BNSF provided direct rail transportation of PRB coal from a mine to the plant.[4] To provide that service, those carriers operated a joint line that enabled them to ship coal from PRB mines to their networks; each carrier then transported coal on one of its mainline routes and delivered it directly to a plant on a section of track known as a buildout, which connected the plant to the carrier's network.

In this study, we define entry into a PRB market as occurring when a carrier can fully provide direct service. Because they operated a joint line from the mines and had extensive networks developed partly through mergers, UP and BNSF generally consummated their entry into specific markets when they completed a buildout that enabled them to provide direct service to a plant.[5] However, as discussed later, the decision to enter a market was determined by the overall profitability of that market.

Railroad technology is often characterized by high fixed costs, but entry into additional markets is not unusual nor particularly costly in the situation we are studying. Electric utilities often provide their own coal cars (but not locomotives), while railroads are able to redeploy or lease their cars and locomotives for use in other markets. Because the incumbent railroad—BNSF or UP in almost all the cases—owned the existing track into an electric utility's plant and could extract most, if not all, monopoly rents, effective entry by another carrier required it to build additional track to connect an electric utility's plant to its rail network. However, the additional track represents a tiny fraction of the distance from mine to plant—in our case, less than 1 percent. Hence, the cost of a buildout is relatively modest and sunk costs are minimal (roughly 2 to 3 percent of the expected revenues over the life of the asset), because small sections of track are often sold to short-line railroads, and rails are frequently reused on other parts of a carrier's system or sold for scrap. Finally, given that mining and rail service in the Powder River Basin are relatively new, UP and BNSF have been able to employ the most

---

4. In 1999, the Dakota, Minnesota & Eastern (DME) Railroad Corporation, indicated an interest in connecting its network to the Powder River Basin. Local landowners, however, have opposed the proposed rail line, and the carrier has been unable to secure private financing and has been turned down by the Federal Railroad Administration for a loan guarantee. DME was acquired by the Canadian Pacific Railway in 2008, but Canadian Pacific announced in 2012 that it would not try to connect its network to the PRB.

5. In a handful of cases, entry was consummated because a carrier secured access to another carrier's track on a mainline route.

efficient operations possible, unencumbered by the older rail infrastructure and outdated technology that railroads have been shedding since deregulation.

In sum, PRB coal transportation markets provide an appropriate setting for determining the quantitative difference in pricing behavior between monopoly and duopoly railroad competition and to assess the competitiveness of duopoly markets for several reasons. First, the physical characteristics of PRB coal distinguish its supply and demand from other domestic coal markets. Second, utilities that receive PRB coal by rail transportation face either a monopoly supplier or a duopoly of suppliers. Third, an entrant into those markets does not incur notable sunk costs. Fourth, the railroads in question provide a homogeneous service. Namely, the primary carriers, BNSF and UP, use the same technology to transport coal from the same source over similar routes; carry ten to fifteen thousand tons of coal in unit trains that do not need to be assembled, disassembled, or switched en route; often use cars that are supplied by the shippers themselves; and offer very similar mean transit times and transit time reliability, while the low value of coal ensures that shippers place little weight on nontransport logistics costs or loss and damage. Fifth, given that coal power plants tend to have the common technological characteristics of operating at constant returns to scale (Sarica and Or 2007) and exhausting their potential for technical efficiency (Olatubi and Dismukes 2000), it seems plausible that shippers' demands for coal are likely to be characterized by the same functional form (up to a scaling factor). Lastly, although rail freight charges are determined through long-term contract negotiations between utilities and rail carriers, this feature does not detract from our analysis of duopoly competition. Utilities negotiate several contracts during any given year, often in response to market fluctuations. Each contract represents a small fraction of the coal transported from the PRB, and the contracts expire at different times.

3. An Econometric Model of Rail Transportation Markets for Coal

We develop a model of supply and demand for coal transportation by rail, where entry affects supply. We then specify a model of carrier entry and jointly estimate the central influences on market prices, tons of coal shipped, and the decision by a second rail carrier to enter a market. Finally, we isolate the effect of a carrier's entry on equilibrium rail transportation price markups by simulating a price path and comparing it with a plausible external estimate of the long-run marginal costs of transporting coal by rail.

Our modeling approach is appropriate because direct estimation of market supply and demand, when possible, remains the surest method to characterize market equilibrium with minimal assumptions on competitive structure. Moreover, we can enrich this framework by incorporating a model of endogenous entry behavior that explicitly accounts for the effect of equilibrium prices and quantities on entry decisions.

Demand

Our empirical analysis is conducted on a panel of electric utility plants. Because rail transportation is derived demand (in this case, it is an input into the final production of electricity), we can follow, say, Friedlaender and Spady (1981), and specify power plant i's cost-minimizing input demand for rail transportation, Q_{it}^D, at time t as:

$$Q_{it}^D = D(p_{it}^D, \mathbf{X}_{it}^D; \varepsilon_{it}^D)$$ (1)

where p_{it}^D is the price of rail transportation (in dollars per ton-mile), $\mathbf{X}_{it}^D$ contains exogenous influences on demand, and ε_{it}^D is an error term.

We include the length of haul from the mine mouth to the plant among the exogenous influences on coal shippers' demand for rail transportation of PRB coal. An electric utility presumably has an inventory policy in which it seeks to maintain a desired stock of coal, and it must receive reliable deliveries by rail to do so. Data on the standard deviation of rail transit time, a common measure of service reliability, are not publicly available at the route level; hence, there is a long tradition in railroad economics of using the length of haul, which is highly correlated with rail service time reliability, to control for this effect (Grimm and Winston 2000). Greater lengths of haul may result in less reliable deliveries of coal and should therefore reduce the demand for rail shipments of PRB coal.

We also include dummy variables that indicate whether the plant can receive non-PRB coal by rail or water transportation to control for alternative coal sources. Those sources can be observed because major coal-fired utility plants report the modes of transportation, including barge and the terminating rail carriers, that they are able to use for their coal deliveries. Effective competition could be provided by rail or water carriers that can ship non-PRB coal to utilities without using carriers operating from the PRB to complete the shipment. We specify separate rail and water dummy variables to measure access to non-PRB coal, thereby allowing for the possibility that the modes have different effects on demand. The availability of an alternative source of coal should reduce the demand for rail shipments of PRB coal.

Because rail transportation of coal is an input into the final production of electricity, we specify the maximum theoretical output (nameplate capacity) of a given plant and the average price of natural gas nationally to capture substitution with an alternative source of energy. We use nameplate capacity because, unlike the actual observed levels of electricity generated, capacity is unaffected by the type of coal that a plant chooses to burn.[6]

---

6. Nameplate capacity is a better measure of derived demand than is the price of coal because in our sample it varies widely between plants each year by up to a factor of ten. In contrast, the price of coal varies very little across mines, so its effect on rail demand was statistically insignificant.

We include an index to capture the sulfur dioxide emission caps imposed in 1995 to implement the standards set by the 1990 Clean Air Act Amendments. Those caps were imposed on some but not every plant in our sample, so our index takes on values between and including zero and one, where a value of zero indicates that the plant is entirely restricted from producing sulfur dioxide (SO_2) (i.e., it must reduce its SO_2 emissions in each year 100 percent from its 1985 level). The index can be entered directly into the specification because it increases smoothly and continuously, with a value of one indicating that the plant has no pollution cap. It is reasonable to treat the caps as exogenous to the extent that most of the plants in our sample did not engage in SO_2 emissions trading, which began in 1994 (Burtraw 1996). We examined the transactions data in the Environmental Protection Agency's Clean Air Markets Division business system to check whether any of the forty-eight electric utility plants in our sample discussed later purchased emissions and we found that only one bought allowances in 1994 and only seven bought allowances in 1998, the last year of our sample. Thus, most plants were effectively bound by their initial allocation of allowances.

Nameplate capacity and natural gas prices should have a positive effect on the demand for PRB coal, thereby increasing the demand for rail transport. The expected sign of the emissions caps is indeterminate because, in response to the caps, plants might reduce their demand for all sources of coal and produce less or substitute cleaner PRB coal for other coal sources and maintain output. The first adjustment would cause their demand for rail transportation to fall while the second would cause their demand for rail transportation to rise. A plant also could install scrubbers to reduce emissions, but this is likely to be a relatively costly option for plants that use low-sulfur coal. Plant-level fixed effects should capture the variation among plants in the use of this option.

The passage of the 1990 Clean Air Act Amendments increased demand for PRB coal by encouraging all electric utilities to seek lower-cost ways to reduce pollution. Our demand specification captures this effect with a dummy variable indicating the years since the act's passage. This dummy should have a positive sign because the demand for electricity grew while the emissions caps were constant. Finally, we specify a time trend, as well as fixed effects at the regional, utility (some utilities own multiple plants), and plant level to capture any unmeasured influences on rail demand in those dimensions.

Supply

Our specification of supply is based on Porter's (1983) model. In a market for a homogeneous good that is produced by firms facing a demand with elasticity η, profit maximization implies that firm k's pricing behavior can be characterized as:

$$p(1 + \theta_k/\eta) = MC_k(q_k) \tag{2}$$

where θ_k is firm k's conduct parameter, MC_k is its marginal cost function (which may be the same as or different from other firms' marginal cost functions), and q_k is its output. This relationship holds under both cooperative and noncooperative assumptions about firms' strategic behavior.

Following Porter (1983), we note that equation (2) can be aggregated across firms so that the relationship between market supply price, output, and entry effectively characterizes an industry supply curve. Because we have plausible estimates of marginal costs, we specify the supply price of rail transportation to power plant i at time t as:

$$p_{it}^S = S(Q_{it}^S, E_{it}, \mathbf{X}_{it}^S; \varepsilon_{it}^S) \tag{3}$$

where p_{it}^S is the price as a function of the quantity of coal transported, Q_{it}^S, the entry of the second carrier, E_{it}, supply characteristics (including marginal cost), $\mathbf{X}_{it}^S$, and an error term, ε_{it}^S. The supply curve is estimated along with the demand curve and a model of entry discussed below, and the resulting parameter estimates are used to simulate the behavior of prices over time to characterize firm conduct as duopoly competition evolves.

We measure the effects of entry with a dummy variable, treated as endogenous, that indicates whether a plant can receive PRB coal from two rail carriers at time t. We can measure this variable because coal-fired utilities identify the rail carriers that provide direct service and that have physical access to their plants.

We recognize that a new entrant's impact on rail prices may intensify over time because a shipper's coal shipments are generally governed by several distinct contracts with the incumbent railroad that may last for several years. Because we do not know precisely how many contracts a shipper had with an incumbent railroad and when each contract expired, we explored alternative ways to capture the dynamic effects of rail competition. We obtained the best statistical fit for our model by interacting the rail entry dummy variable with a variable indicating the number of years the second railroad served the market for those plants experiencing entry. The value of this variable was held constant after three years to capture the fact that most contracts will have expired by that time, thereby making it unlikely that the entry effect continues to intensify. Holding this variable constant after five years produced a slightly worse statistical fit. Specifying time dummies to indicate each year since the entry of a second carrier produced an even worse fit, because more endogenous variables were effectively used to capture the same effect. The entry variable should have a negative effect on rail prices unless carriers engage in some form of collusive behavior.[7]

7. Schmidt (2001) and Grimm, Winston, and Evans (1992) have estimated reduced-form rail-rate equations and found that an increase in the number of rail carriers in a market decreases rail rates.

In contrast to some markets (e.g., airlines), potential rail competition is not likely to be a relevant factor in PRB markets. A common definition of a potential competitor in network industries is a carrier that provides service at the origin and the destination but does not offer service on the route (Morrison and Winston 1987, 1995). Because negotiations over contract rates occur only when actual entry is assured by a carrier's commitment to construct a buildout to connect a utility with its network, a carrier is effectively an actual competitor without ever being a potential competitor.

Supply characteristics consist of other sources of competition and rail costs. We include two dummy variables to indicate whether plants can receive coal from outside the Powder River Basin by an alternative railroad or by water transportation. Both measures of source competition should have a negative effect on rail prices.

Route-specific marginal costs are generally unavailable. Hence, we estimate those costs using Bitzan and Keeler's (2003) translog railroad cost function, which covers virtually the same years as our study and includes ton-miles of unit train traffic at the firm level as a distinct output, factor prices, and operating characteristics. Their cost function results in an expression for marginal cost that yields estimates that vary both across plants through the length-of-haul variable—they find economies of length of haul, meaning that longer hauls reduce the marginal cost of a ton-mile—and over time through an estimated time trend, which captures technological change (productivity improvements) in rail freight transportation.[8] We expect higher marginal costs to increase prices.

Finally, we include a time trend and fixed effects at the regional, utility, and plant level to capture unmeasured influences on prices in those dimensions. Utility-level fixed effects differ from plant-level fixed effects because they account for potentially greater bargaining power that utilities with multiple generating plants may enjoy when negotiating rates.

Entry

Although the primary providers of rail service in the Powder River Basin (UP and BNSF) have expanded their networks to serve more utilities, they have not elected to serve all markets where a utility receives PRB coal, suggesting that their entry decisions are endogenous in our framework because they are undoubtedly based on specific market conditions for coal transportation. Generally, entry represents a strategic decision consistent with profit-maximizing behavior. We first discuss the relevance of dynamic considerations in modeling rail entry and then specify a model of entry based on a firm's profit function.

8. This approach may introduce measurement error because it holds variables other than unit train output and length of haul constant at industry means. But this error is likely to be small because output and length of haul account for most of the variation in marginal costs (Bitzan and Keeler 2003).

A dynamic model of entry may be appropriate in two situations. First, because shippers and railroads negotiate contracts prior to a carrier actually providing service, a dynamic specification of the key determinants of entry (such as prices and quantities) may be necessary unless future values of those variables can be determined from their current values. If current prices and quantities are sufficiently strong predictors of future prices and quantities, then a static model of entry is appropriate, although the effects of entry on prices are likely to be dynamic.

In the case of rail transportation of coal, contracts reflect current and future supply and demand conditions. For example, contracts specifying negotiated rates contain standard cost-escalation provisions based on independent regulatory findings, thereby reducing the uncertainty associated with the supply price. Uncertainty is further reduced for a carrier considering entry because the supply price is bounded from above by the charge that an electric utility is currently paying the incumbent rail carrier for service, and it is bounded from below by the charge that will enable the entrant to earn positive profits on the route. Little uncertainty is associated with transportation demand because the large-baseload plants in this study run at full capacity. Accordingly, exploratory estimations showed that influences at time t are sufficient statistics for predictions of future influences. For example, the quantity of coal that was shipped in each market tended to be stationary throughout the period covered by our sample unless a second railroad entered the market.

Second, a dynamic specification might be appropriate if railroads enter and exit markets and change their prices frequently. However, as noted, contract rates are negotiated for several years and have standard annual provisions that govern rate changes, and no railroads in our sample exit any of the PRB markets; that is, they never relinquish the ability to serve a particular electric utility.

Finally, for exploratory purposes, we attempted to use our data to estimate a dynamic model of entry, supply, and demand, but we concluded that we needed a much larger sample of plants, with a longer time series of market behavior, and more instances of entry to capture possible dynamic influences in a reasonable manner. We specified entry in terms of a Bellman equation as a function of the buildout, and dynamic demand and supply functions assuming an AR(1) process. We found that the entry of a second railroad in a market had a modest effect on reducing rail rates, but that the supply elasticity had the incorrect negative sign, and the demand elasticity was considerably less than 1.0, which raises a red flag because a monopoly rail carrier serves many markets in the sample. In contrast, as we report later, when we used our data to estimate a static model allowing entry to have dynamic effects on rail prices, we did not encounter those empirical problems.

We therefore develop a model of entry behavior based on a static profit function. As pointed out by Jia (2008), a convention in the empirical industrial organization literature on entry is to omit price, quantity, and sales variables from the specification because the relevant data are unavailable for most industries, and to assume that firms' profits decline in the presence of rivals. Because we do have data on prices and quantities, we explicitly include those variables in the specification of profit that determines firm entry.

The profit available to a given firm from entering market i at time t is simply the total revenue less the variable costs of providing service and the fixed costs of entry, and can be specified generically as $\Pi(p_{it}, q_{it}, \mathbf{X}_{it}^{E}; \varepsilon_{it}^{E})$, where $\mathbf{X}_{it}^{E}$ contains observable determinants of service and entry costs and ε_{it}^{E} captures the unobservable determinants of profits.

Assuming entry occurs only in profitable markets (where $\Pi_{it} > 0$) and that the unobservable term ε_{it}^{E} is an additively separable determinant of profit, the probability of observing a second competitor in a market can be written simply in terms of the variables that comprise revenue and cost. Namely,

$$\Pr(E_{it} = 1) = \Pr(\varepsilon_{it}^{E} > -\Pi(p_{it}, q_{it}, \mathbf{X}_{it}^{E})) \tag{4}$$

Equilibrium prices and quantities are endogenously determined by our supply and demand equations, so the error terms in those equations indirectly enter equation (4). Because those error terms are unobservable determinants of prices and quantities, they also will be unobservable determinants of profits; hence, ε_{it}^{E} contains components of both endogenously determined revenues and other unobservable exogenous determinants of entry.

Consistent estimation of the carrier's entry decision and its effect on prices requires that at least one element of $\mathbf{X}_{it}^{E}$ can be excluded from both the vector of supply covariates ($\mathbf{X}_{it}^{S}$) and the vector of demand covariates ($\mathbf{X}_{it}^{D}$). We meet this requirement by using an observed component of carriers' fixed costs of entry that is uncorrelated with the supply and demand error terms. As noted, a carrier must connect an electric utility plant with its physical network to enter a market, which is defined by a coal mine at the origin and the plant at the destination. We capture the fixed cost of this connection by specifying the distance of the buildout from the plant to the closest nonincumbent rail line, which is measured using a publicly available railroad atlas and commercial atlas that depicts rail networks and plant locations. Those costs are a combination of onetime setup costs and ongoing annual fixed costs. We expect that as the required buildout increases, the likelihood of a second entrant decreases; but, crucially, the required buildout does not affect the supply and demand for rail service, all else constant. Moreover, shocks in supply and demand do not causally affect the buildout because it is determined years in advance by utilities' choices of plant locations and nonincumbent rail carriers' choices of mainline track locations.

4. Estimation

Estimation of our model of demand, (inverse) supply, and entry is complicated by the fact that entry must be specified as an endogenous function of quantity (demanded) and (supply) price. Because of the nonlinear relationship between the unobservable determinants of supply and demand that affect entry, we cannot assume a specific distribution for the error term in the entry equation. We must therefore take a semiparametric approach to obtain consistent estimates of the effect of entry on prices (Powell 1994; Rothe 2009). We do so, following Matzkin (1992), using the exogenous measure of the fixed costs of entry (the distance of the buildout) to identify the entry decision of the second carrier. The three equations are then estimated jointly using a generalized method of moments (GMM) approach for systems estimation, which also involves estimating an efficient and heteroskedasticity-robust asymptotic covariance matrix of all the estimated parameters. We present our procedure for obtaining consistent and efficient GMM estimates of our model in the appendix to this chapter.

We assume that supply and demand have a logarithmic functional form, which is plausible (Porter 1983) and fits the data better than a linear functional form does. We make no assumption on the functional form of the entry condition beyond the fact that the error term ε_{it}^E is additively separable. The system of supply, demand, and entry equations to be estimated can therefore be written as:

$$\ln p_{it}^S = \beta_1^S \ln Q_{it}^S + \beta_2^S E_{it} + \beta_3^S \mathbf{X}_{it}^S + \varepsilon_{it}^S \qquad (5)$$

$$\ln Q_{it}^D = \beta_1^D \ln p_{it}^D + \beta_2^D \mathbf{X}_{it}^D + \beta_3^S \mathbf{X}_{it}^S + \varepsilon_{it}^D \qquad (6)$$

$$E_{it} = \mathbf{1}\left(\Pi\left(p_{it}, q_{it}, \mathbf{X}_{it}^E\right) > -\varepsilon_{it}^E\right) \qquad (7)$$

where $\mathbf{1}(\cdot)$ is an indicator function and variables are as defined previously.

Identification of price, quantity, and entry is achieved by instrumental variables. Quantity in the supply equation is identified by exogenous demand variables such as nameplate capacity and SO_2 emissions caps that shift demand but otherwise do not have a direct effect on price or entry. Price in the demand equation is identified by exogenous cost variables, such as route-level marginal cost.

We identify the effect of entry in the supply equation with the entry-specific variable buildout distance, which does not directly affect market equilibrium prices and quantities. Although computational complexities discussed in the appendix prevented us from including other variables that might influence entry, such as measures of variable costs, two points should be stressed. First, our estimators are still consistent. Second, such measures would inevitably involve the quantity of coal traffic shipped (e.g., variable cost per ton-mile multiplied by the number

Table 11.1. *Sample Means and Data Sources for the Variables*

Variable	Units	Mean	SD	Data sources
Freight charge	$/ton-mile	0.017	0.008	EIA, *Cost and Quality of Fuels for Electric Utility Plants, Coal Industry Annual,* and *Annual Coal Report*
Tons of coal shipped	1,000 tons	2,757	2,058	EIA, *Cost and Quality of Fuels for Electric Utility Plants*
Presence of second rail competitor	dummy	0.068	0.256	Fieldston, *Coal Transportation Manual*
Rail source competition	dummy	0.057	0.191	Fieldston, *Coal Transportation Manual*
Water source competition	dummy	0.095	0.246	Fieldston, *Coal Transportation Manual*
Nameplate capacity	million kWh	1.172	0.755	EIA, *Annual Electric Generator Report*
SO_2 emissions caps	1,000 tons	2.110	13.0	1990 Clean Air Act Amendments, Title IV
Natural gas price	$/1,000 ft^3	2.449	0.650	EIA, *Historical Natural Gas Annual*
Route-level marginal cost	$/ton-mile	0.012	0.003	Authors' calculations based on Bitzan and Keeler (2003)
Length of haul from mine to plant	miles	1,024	339	RDI Consulting, *Coal Rate Database* (1997)
Length of buildout for entrant in 1984	miles	9.204	7.34	Rand McNally, *Handy Railroad Atlas of the United States* (1982) and *Commercial Atlas and Marketing Guide* (1991)

Notes: All dollar values are in 1998 dollars. EIA stands for Energy Information Administration.

of ton-miles of coal), which we have controlled for in our analysis.[9] Finally, the entry equation is identified by the exogenous supply and demand shifters that are accounted for by the control variables discussed in the appendix of this chapter.

5. Sample

The data sources for the variables used in our analysis and their sample means and standard deviations are presented in table 11.1. The data are annual observations. Our empirical analysis is based on the shipping activity of the forty-eight electric utility plants in operation from 1984 to 1998 that burned an average of at least one million tons of PRB coal per year. Those plants account for 75 percent of all PRB coal shipped by rail during the period. Plants burning less than one million

9. A measure of variable cost that would account for the difference between the incumbent carrier's and the potential entrant's length of haul does not appear to be useful because the differences are small, roughly thirty miles or 3 percent of the average length of haul.

tons were too small to have received unit train service on a regular basis or were engaged in small "test burns" of PRB coal. In either case, such plants did not receive rates that reflected regular unit train service. Almost all plants in the sample burned more than one million tons of PRB coal in all years. Table 11.1 shows that only 5.7 percent of the plants receive non-PRB coal by rail and 9.5 percent receive non-PRB coal by water; thus, most plants rely on PRB coal for a fuel source. This does not pose a problem here because our interest is in rail competition for PRB coal transportation, the large plants in our sample account for a large fraction of PRB coal shipments, and it is not clear that the smaller plants that are not included in the sample receive a much larger share of non-PRB coal as a fuel source.

We began the sample in 1984 because it was the year before the Interstate Commerce Commission authorized entry into the Powder River Basin. We ended the sample in 1998 because by 1999 electric utilities began to win a handful of maximum-rate cases before the Surface Transportation Board, so recent reductions in coal rates could potentially be attributable to residual regulation. However, no utilities in our sample received a lower rail rate during 1984 to 1998 by winning a maximum-rate proceeding. Of the forty-eight plants, thirty-one were served by a single railroad throughout the sample period and seventeen experienced entry between 1985 and 1998. A few of the single-served plants came online after 1984. Thus, our final sample consists of 711 observations.

It is important to point out that virtually all railroad coal traffic is transported under private contracts that do not reveal the shipper's rate. Thus, we collected publicly available data from the Energy Information Administration (EIA) and estimated rail rates for electric utilities as the difference between the delivered price per ton of PRB coal that is consumed at the plant and the price per ton of coal at the mine mouth. The delivered price of coal reported by the utility includes all the costs incurred by the utility in the purchase and delivery of the fuel to the plant (FERC 1995). The mine-mouth price reported by the mine is the total revenue received using the actual freight on board rail sales price (EIA 1995). The price per ton-mile in each market is obtained by dividing the difference between the delivered price of PRB coal to the utility and the price at the mine mouth by the length of haul. Subsequent discussions that we had with railroad personnel confirmed that our estimates of rail rates in each PRB market were quite close to actual rail rates.

Rail transportation contracts for PRB coal might typically cover three million tons of coal per year for a period of five or more years. However, annual price and quantity data are appropriate to use in our model because rail contract rates have annual variation, minimum annual quantity provisions, and annual quantity discounts. Rail contracts specify a price per ton, which is adjusted annually based on railroad input costs and productivity. Minimum annual quantity provisions limit the impact of a new entrant on rates until the contract expires. Utilities receive annual quantity discounts that are reflected in the annual data on the delivered price of coal. Finally, rail contracts for PRB coal are not two-part tariffs.[10] As noted, utilities may negotiate several contracts with a railroad during a year. Thus, data on the market price for a given year consist of a ton-mile-weighted average of all existing PRB coal transportation contracts, each of which includes the preceding adjustments to reflect current shipping activity.

The presence of a second rail competitor that can deliver PRB coal and the existence of rail and water source competition that can provide non-PRB coal were obtained from the annual Fieldston *Coal Transportation Manual*, which maintains transportation service by specific rail carriers and barge transportation and coal delivery records for major coal-fired utility plants. As noted, entry of a second rail competitor occurred in a market only when that carrier could provide direct service, a condition that in almost every case was met when the carrier constructed a buildout to the plant.

Route-specific marginal costs were derived from Bitzan and Keeler's (2003) translog cost function, specified as a second-degree polynomial in logs of the variables with all variables divided by their sample mean (the base point of approximation). Because Bitzan and Keeler's (2003) coefficients are estimated at the firm level not at the route level, substituting route-specific output would cause the output variable to be very far from the industry mean used in the translog specification and result in poor estimates of marginal costs. We therefore calculated route-specific marginal costs for each market in our sample by evaluating the marginal cost function at Union Pacific's mean unit train output divided by the industry mean, the actual length of haul in each market divided by the industry mean, and the year. The resulting estimates of route-specific marginal costs were consistent with industry operating expenses per ton-mile, cost estimates from other studies, and evidence in railroad coal-rate cases pertaining to the relationship between price and marginal cost.

Figure 11.2 presents a comparison of average annual real rail rates over time for the thirty-one plants in our sample that were served by a single railroad throughout the period and that did not experience entry (*No entry*) and the seventeen plants in our sample that experienced entry sometime between 1985 and 1998 (*Entry*). Because of improvements in rail productivity in growing PRB markets, real rates declined throughout the sample period for both types of plants;[11] but by

10. Two-part tariffs are not considered rates under Section 6 of the Interstate Commerce Act and are therefore illegal in the railroad industry (see *Grain by Rent-a-Train, IFA Territory to Gulf Ports*, 335 ICC 111 (1969); 339 ICC 579 (1971)). Hence ICC's maximum rail-rate guidelines (49 USC 10707) are defined in terms of markups over average variable costs and not as two-part tariffs that require an entry fee to secure transportation.

11. Bitzan and Keeler (2003) find that productivity improvements reduced railroad costs nearly 45 percent during virtually the same period covered by our sample.

Figure 11.2. *Plants' Rail Freight Charges over Time, 1984–98*

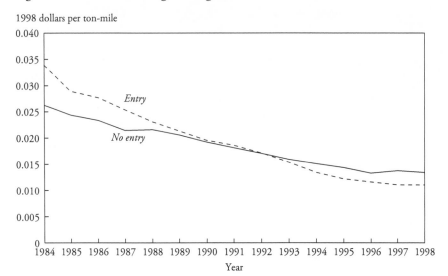

1998 dollars per ton-mile

Notes: No entry refers to the thirty-one plants that were served by a single railroad from 1984 through 1998. Entry refers to the seventeen plants that experienced entry between 1985 and 1998.

Sources: Federal Energy Regulatory Commission; Energy Information Administration; *Coal Transportation Manual*; authors' calculations.

the early 1990s, rates were lower for plants that experienced entry of an additional railroad. Based on our data, in 1984, price markups above marginal cost were 1.3 cents per ton-mile for plants that at some point during our sample experienced entry of another railroad, compared with price markups above marginal cost that were 1.1 cents per ton-mile for plants that were served by a single (monopoly) carrier during our sample. By 1998, those margins decreased to 0.3 cents per ton-mile and 0.5 cents per ton-mile, respectively. Thus, entry tended to occur in the most profitable markets; but by the end of the sample, market power was eroded in those markets such that they were less profitable than the remaining monopoly markets.

Figure 11.3 presents the average annual real rail rate at the time of entry for plants that experience entry of another rail carrier. Plants that experience entry obtain initial reductions of 24 percent in the year that entry occurred (year 0) and obtain much larger reductions of 44 percent by the third year after entry occurred. This finding suggests that rail entry reduces rates, but that its full impact takes time. Importantly, our summary of rail rates in the sample for different market structures and over time does not hold other influences on rates constant, so it cannot isolate the effect of entry. We do so by using our model of rail transportation supply, demand, and entry in PRB markets to simulate the behavior of rates as market structure changes.

Figure 11.3. *Rail Freight Charge Reductions and Years since Entry*

1998 dollars per ton-mile

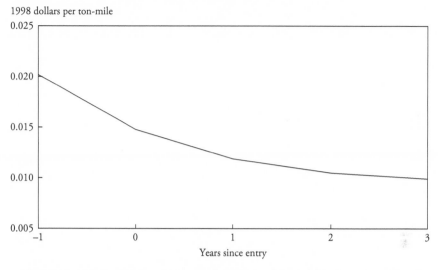

Years since entry

Notes: Entry occurs at time 0 on the horizontal axis; hence, the initial drop from −1 to 0 along the horizontal axis represents the instantaneous effect of entry on prices.

Sources: Federal Energy Regulatory Commission; Energy Information Administration; *Coal Transportation Manual*; authors' calculations.

6. Estimation Results

For purposes of comparison, we present in the first two columns of table 11.2 estimates of the model by a simpler estimation procedure, two-stage least squares (2SLS), which treats entry as exogenous but accounts for the endogeneity of price and quantity as explanatory variables in the demand and supply equations. As noted, we specified a time trend to control for unobserved temporal effects and fixed utility and plant effects, but they were statistically insignificant in the supply and demand equations and their exclusion had little effect on the other parameter estimates so they are not included in the specification presented here.[12]

Generally, the estimated coefficients have their expected signs and are statistically significant. The demand for rail transportation of coal is elastic ($\eta = -1.15$), which is consistent with actual price-cost markups for PRB coal traffic and the high percentage of monopoly routes in our sample. Given that rail freight transportation is derived demand, the elasticity also reflects the utilities' underlying demand elasticity for coal and the (high) share of rail transport costs in the total

12. As discussed, route-level marginal cost includes a time trend to account for technological change.

Table 11.2. *Supply and Demand Parameter Estimates, 1984–98*

	2SLS		GMM	
Variable	Supply	Demand	Supply	Demand
Log freight charge ($/ton mile)	Dep. Var.	−1.147	Dep. Var.	−1.415
		(0.327)		(0.105)
Log tons of coal shipped to plant	0.129	Dep. Var.	0.119	Dep. Var.
(thousands)	(0.020)		(0.007)	
Supply characteristics				
Rail competition dummy × log of	−0.215	—	−0.129	—
1 + years with second PRB rail	(0.042)		(0.013)	
competitor				
Log route-level marginal cost	1.087	—	1.078	—
($/ton mile)	(0.055)		(0.022)	
Demand characteristics				
Log plant nameplate capacity	—	0.136	—	0.134
(millions of kWh)		(0.011)		(0.004)
Log average national price of natural	—	0.309	—	0.414
gas ($/1,000 ft³)		(0.101)		(0.040)
Post–1990 Clean Air Act Amendments	—	0.299	—	0.367
dummy		(0.151)		(0.049)
South regional dummy	—	0.944	—	0.959
		(0.160)		(0.049)
Plant SO$_2$ emissions cap index	—	0.381	—	0.439
		(0.231)		(0.080)
Shipment characteristics				
Log length of haul from mine mouth	—	−0.751	—	−0.959
to plant (miles)		(0.160)		(0.350)
Source competition				
Rail source competition dummy	−0.219	—	−0.280	—
	(0.079)		(0.027)	
Water source competition dummy	0.025	−1.542	0.050	−1.674
	(0.070)	(0.185)	(0.022)	(0.114)
Constant	−5.186	5.658	−5.119	4.394
	(0.157)	(1.123)	(0.057)	(1.059)
Number of observations	711		711	

Notes: The rail competition dummy equals 1 if two carriers serve the root and 0 otherwise, and the inter-action term is unchanged three years after entry. The South region includes Alabama, Arkansas, Louisiana, Mississippi, Oklahoma, and Texas. The plant SO$_2$ emissions cap index is defined as $1 - (\text{emissions cap})^{-1}$ for plants subject to the emissions cap and 1 for plants not subject to the emissions cap. The source competition dummy variables equal 1 if a plant can receive coal from a non-PRB source by a competing railroad or by water transportation, respectively, and equal 0 otherwise. Huber–White robust standard errors are in parentheses.

production costs of coal.[13] The positive elasticity of rail prices with respect to tons shipped in the inverse supply equation, 0.13, indicates a modestly upward-sloping supply curve at the route level that is likely to reflect the effect of congestion or capacity constraints on carrier costs.

The estimates derived from the rail competition variable in the (inverse) supply equation are of central importance for our purposes. We find that the initial entry of a second carrier into a PRB market reduces rail rates 15 percent and that this effect becomes stronger over time, albeit at a diminishing rate.[14] For example, after three or more years of entry, during which time many contracts are likely to have expired, entry of a second carrier will have reduced rail rates 30 percent.[15]

As stressed throughout this chapter, coal shippers negotiate contract rates with railroads that generally last for several years. According to our findings, contract rates dampen the initial impact that a new rail entrant has on observed prices. But as shippers' contracts expire, they can obtain lower rates when they negotiate new contracts, presumably by playing one railroad off against another. Apparently, carriers have not been successful in reaching a tacit understanding to prevent such competition from developing.[16] As discussed previously, we did not expect potential competition to have an influence on rail rates. If it did, its effect would be partly captured in the time trend or year dummies as UP and BNSF entered more markets, but those variables were statistically insignificant.[17]

The remaining parameter estimates reflect the workings of standard economic forces. Rail prices reflect marginal costs of production and other sources of competition.[18] We find that an increase in rail marginal cost is slightly more than fully

13. During our sample period, the average price paid by a utility for a ton of coal was $42 while the cost of shipping one ton of coal one thousand miles, roughly the average length of haul, at an average rate of 1.7 cents per mile amounted to $17 for the movement. Thus, transport costs account for 40 percent of the price and presumably the total production costs of coal.

14. Based on our coefficient, this estimate is obtained by calculating: $\ln(1 + 1 \text{ year}) \times 0.215 = 15$ percent. We expressed the persistent effect of rail entry as $\ln(1 + \text{years of entry})$ for up to three years because $\ln(1) = 0$ and $\ln(0)$ is undefined. This specification captures diminishing marginal reductions in rail prices caused by the entry of a second carrier. We explored other functional forms for this variable, including a Box–Cox transformation, but this functional specification produced the best statistical fit. We also estimated a model that lagged the initial entry variable, but this did not lead to a better statistical fit.

15. This estimate is obtained by calculating $\ln(1 + 3 \text{ years}) \times 0.215 = 30$ percent.

16. Scherer and Ross (1990) provide examples in other industries where large buyers play one seller off against another to elicit price concessions.

17. As noted, UP and BNSF were involved in mergers during the period of our sample; but we did not find that those mergers led to cost savings or rate reductions that were realized in PRB markets because such effects would be captured in time trends or year dummies, which turned out to be statistically insignificant.

18. It has been argued that shippers who provide their own rail cars reduce rail costs and thus receive a lower rate. We specified the percentage of a utility's coal traffic that is shipped in its private cars in the inverse supply equation, but it had a statistically insignificant effect on rail prices and is not included here. We suspect that this finding is because most of the plants in our sample ship large shares of their coal in private cars.

passed on in higher rates, which is consistent with rates that are set as a markup over variable costs. (Recall that rates cannot be challenged unless they exceed 180 percent of variable costs.) Rail source competition lowers rail rates by 24 percent, but the effect of water source competition is statistically insignificant.[19]

Utilities demand more coal shipped by rail from the Powder River Basin as their nameplate capacity increases, as natural gas prices rise, and after the passage of the 1990 Clean Air Act Amendments. We also find that electric utilities located in the South have a greater demand than other utilities in the country have for coal shipped by rail from the Powder River Basin. Southern power plants tend to face more rapidly growing demand than other plants in the country face, so they may prefer large shipments of coal that can be sent by unit coal trains. The Powder River Basin can accommodate this preference more easily than other coal-producing regions in the country are able to because its mines generate more coal than other single-mouth mines. Utilities demand less coal as their distance from a coal mine in the Powder River Basin increases, if they can receive coal from another source by water transportation, and as their sulfur dioxide emission caps become tighter (i.e., the index becomes smaller), leaving them to choose between reducing output or purchasing emissions permits.[20] Apparently, maintaining output and emissions by substituting PRB coal for non-PRB coal is a less efficient option than reducing output.

Before turning to the GMM parameter estimates of our model that treats entry as endogenous, it is useful to provide empirical support for using the build-out distance as an instrument for entry in the supply equation. Although there is no test to satisfactorily determine whether buildout distance affects or is affected by supply and demand, we previously argued that current shocks in supply and demand would not affect a buildout because the buildout would be determined years in advance by a rail carrier's and utility's plant location decisions. We also did not find that buildout had a statistically significant effect on demand or inverse supply. Intuitively, that is not surprising because table 11.1 shows that compared with the length of haul on a route, which influences utilities' demand for coal because it captures the effect of rail reliability, the buildout distance is small and should not affect the reliability of a shipment.

Turning to inverse supply, on routes that do not experience entry, marginal changes in the buildout distance and the associated costs incurred by a potential entrant, especially when annualized, are apparently not large enough to affect the

19. Water competition may have a negligible effect on rail rates because almost all plants with river access also have rail source competition and because rail must be used for part of any shipment of PRB coal by water.

20. Holding rail prices constant, we did not find that the presence of rail source competition had a statistically significant effect on the quantity of coal shipped by rail. The presence of water source competition affects the quantity of coal shipped by rail because it is less expensive to ship coal by water than by rail.

incumbent's price, and on routes that do experience entry, marginal changes in (annualized) buildout costs are apparently not large enough to affect the entrant's price. As noted, entry is influenced by the profitability of the entire route. We provide evidence below that the buildout distance plays a role in that decision, and the entry equation is identified by the exogenous supply and demand shifters that are accounted for by the control variables.

The GMM parameter estimates are presented in the third and fourth columns of table 11.2, many of which are very similar to the 2SLS estimates. We also found that the time trend and the utility and plant fixed effects were statistically insignificant. Robust estimation of the covariance matrix accounts for error correlation across plants. The most important change in the estimates is that we now find that the initial entry by a second rail carrier reduces coal rates 9 percent and after three or more years rates have fallen 18 percent, which are still sizable effects but they are statistically significantly different from the 2SLS estimates and suggest that treating entry as exogenous may cause an upward bias in those estimates.[21] That bias goes in the expected direction because a second railroad is more likely to enter a route with more favorable unobservable characteristics, such as lower costs, which means that an entry dummy that is assumed to be exogenous would be picking up the effect of those unobservables on rates.

In figure 11.4, we indicate how the buildout distance affects the probability that a second railroad enters a route by graphing the findings of a nonparametric regression of the predicted probability of entry (which contains the actual values of the control variables) on the buildout distance. Consistent with our expectations, markets that require a greater buildout for a rail carrier to provide direct service are less likely to experience entry by a second competitor; twenty miles appears to be the threshold distance that virtually eliminates the likelihood of entry.

7. Characterizing Duopoly Railroad Competition

We have argued that rail competition in the Powder River Basin provides an appropriate setting for analyzing duopoly competition because carriers that had monopolies in the region, primarily BNSF and to a lesser extent Union Pacific, gradually experienced new entry from each other to supply a homogeneous service. We use the parameter estimates to simulate the effect of a carrier's entry on rail prices for coal transportation. This exercise is complicated by the fact that several other variables besides a carrier's entry could affect rail rates. For example, rates may fall in PRB markets because of exogenous declines in the marginal cost of rail transportation or productivity growth. To isolate the

21. Using a specification test for nonlinear regressions from Davidson and MacKinnon (1981), we rejected the hypothesis that the coefficients on entry in the 2SLS and GMM specifications are equal at the 99 percent significance level.

Figure 11.4. *Nonparametric Estimate of Entry Probability, 1984–98*

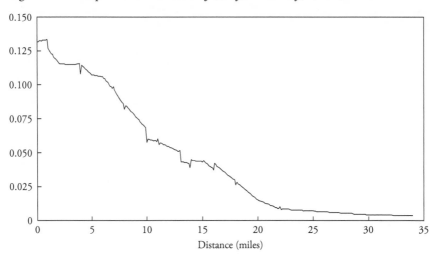

Distance (miles)

Note: The estimates are from a locally weighted least squares regression of the predicted probability of carrier entry on distance.

effect of entry, we hold all variables except the entry variable at their 1984 levels—that is, before carriers began to gradually enter PRB monopoly markets. We then use the inverse supply and demand equations to simulate market equilibrium prices in response to the changes in entry behavior over time.

We provide perspective on the quantitative effect of entry by comparing the simulated price path with a simulated long-run marginal cost of transporting coal by rail. It is reasonable to make this comparison because in PRB markets rail is characterized by constant returns to scale, which allows marginal cost pricing to be financially viable. In addition, shippers and carriers enter rate negotiations with a view toward the long run because contracts typically last for several years. To maintain consistency with the price path, the long-run marginal cost does not reflect changes in rail markets after 1984 that may have affected costs.

The simulated marginal cost is derived from the same Bitzan and Keeler (2003) cost function we used to calculate route-specific marginal costs. However, in the simulation we set the cost function's explanatory variables at their 1984 values, thereby assuming that marginal costs are not affected by entry. This is a reasonable assumption because, as we pointed out, PRB coal transportation markets are relatively new, and the primary rail service providers have been able to employ the same technology and most efficient operations during the sample period.

The price path and long-run marginal cost were converted to 1998 dollars using appropriate indices; the simulated marginal cost of transporting coal in 1984 (in 1998 dollars) is 1.9 cents per ton-mile. Because all variables except entry are held constant in our simulation, marginal cost is not reduced by exogenous

Figure 11.5. *Simulated Rail Freight Charges and Marginal Cost in Markets Experiencing Entry, 1984–98*

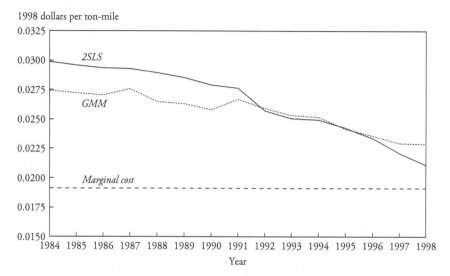

Notes: Rail freight charges are simulated by holding all nonentry variables constant at 1984 values and solving for market equilibrium prices using indicated specifications for supply and demand. We include all markets that experience entry during the period 1984–98.

technological change that may have occurred after 1984. The simulated marginal cost estimate is plausible because it is consistent with previous estimates obtained by Bereskin (2001) and Ivaldi and McCullough (2001) for unit train operations as well as one obtained by Winston et al. (1990) based on data generated before 1984.

To summarize, the price path captures the effect of a second entrant only, the simulated marginal cost is used for purposes of comparison, and all other influences on rates and costs are held constant at their 1984 values. Accordingly, the simulated price path and marginal costs do not represent predictions of actual rail prices and costs, it is appropriate for marginal cost to remain constant during the simulation because no other influences except entry are changing, and one should not expect the simulated rail price path to be aligned with the actual behavior of rail prices in figure 11.2 because the latter reflects changes in all influences on prices.

Figure 11.5 presents price paths based on the 2SLS and GMM parameter estimates and shows that in the markets in which a second carrier has entered at some point between 1984 and 1998, duopoly railroad pricing behavior has evolved slowly, but it appears that rail prices approach marginal cost, and, as indicated, PRB market characteristics lend themselves to this competitive outcome. We have suggested that the 2SLS estimates may overstate the effect of entry by a second carrier on prices and, accordingly, its price path is steeper than the price path based on the GMM estimates, which may depict more accurately the time it has taken to generate intense rail competition. From 1985 to 1994, rail prices declined modestly from their monopoly level. But from 1994 to 1998, they have fallen faster—and by more than in the preceding ten years—as UP in particular has expanded service to a sufficiently large cohort of plants and as BNSF has been forced to compete more extensively with UP for traffic because shippers' contracts with the incumbent carrier have expired.

Although our estimate of long-run marginal cost is consistent with other estimates in the literature, one could argue that if we (and others) have overestimated marginal costs then rail prices may not be declining to the competitive level. However, based on the GMM estimates, 38 percent of the 54 percent decline in actual rail prices from 1984 to 1998 could be attributed to the additional competition supplied by a second entrant and, as shown in figure 11.5, simulated prices were still declining in duopoly markets in the final years of our sample. As time continues to pass following the entry of a second carrier, and as contracts continue to expire after 1998, the GMM-based price path would undoubtedly draw closer to marginal cost before stabilizing, while the 2SLS-based price path may unrealistically fall below marginal cost, even if marginal cost were somewhat lower than we estimated.[22]

Indeed, the pervasive use of contract rates in rail freight transportation is probably the most important reason why the transition from monopoly to duopoly resulted in a significant reduction in rail rates. That is, each carrier faces the prospect of getting none of a utility's business for several years unless it lowers its rate in response to a competitor's bid. Given that a typical contract might call for three million tons of coal to be shipped annually for five or more years, a railroad has a lot to lose if it does not compete fiercely for a utility's business and allows the utility to take its traffic elsewhere. Scherer and Ross (1990) point out that, in general, lumpiness and infrequency of orders limit oligopolistic coordination.

Another factor that facilitates—but does not ensure—intense rail competition is that coal transportation is a homogeneous service. As discussed previously, rail carriers use the same technology to transport coal from the same source over similar routes and offer similar transit time and reliability. A railroad is unlikely to convince shippers that it is providing a different—let alone superior—service. Product differentiation, primarily through advertising, might explain why some oligopolies have been able to maintain high price-cost margins (Baker and

---

22. Both price paths would stabilize shortly after 1998 because the effect of the entry variable was held constant after three years. We also calculated the GMM price path based on a model that specified an entry variable whose effect on price was held constant after five yeargis. The price path based on this model showed a later but steeper drop that nonetheless appeared likely to stabilize close to marginal cost.

Bresnahan 1985). Our findings, however, are not consistent with a successful strategy of product differentiation.

Finally, given that BNSF initially provided rail service for many utilities that demanded PRB coal, UP had less (existing) profits to lose by supplying additional capacity in this market. Moreover, UP could primarily gain revenue from additional traffic by cutting into BNSF's traffic. In such a "market stealing" environment, the two were likely to end up as intense competitors because it is more difficult to compete in quantities in zero-sum situations.

8. A Current Overview of Competition in the Rail Industry

As noted, we are unable to update our analysis of duopoly behavior in the PRB coal markets because rates in those markets may have been affected by STB maximum-rate cases. Thus, we turn to the available descriptive evidence on rail competition to update our discussion of the competitiveness of the railroad industry.

Freight railroads were deregulated in large part because they had failed to earn their cost of capital for several decades and policymakers were concerned that the government might have to take over freight operations like they took over passenger operations by creating Amtrak in 1970. Policymakers hoped that with more freedom to set rates, cut costs, and abandon unprofitable markets that the rail industry would be able to significantly improve its financial health.

Deregulation led to the greater use of contract rates and, as discussed by Grimm and Winston (2000), shippers were able to develop ways to generate competition that helped them negotiate for lower rates, including geographic competition (shipping outputs to different destinations served by different railroads) and product competition (receiving different inputs or products from different origins served by different railroads or modes).

It took many years for rail to shed its regulatory-bequeathed inefficient capital structure, but as shown in figure 11.6, some twenty-five years after deregulation, rail's return on investment has covered its cost of capital for more than a decade. As shown in figure 11.7, rail's return on equity has been broadly comparable in the last decade to the median return on equity of *Fortune* 500 companies.

Rail deregulation accomplished its objective of enabling the railroad industry to increase its earnings, achieve profitability, and attract investment, and little evidence exists that rail is constantly exploiting market power. Although shippers of bulk commodities such as coal and grain have complained that they pay excessive rates in some instances, rail has been subject to product competition in those markets because energy shippers' demand has strongly shifted from coal to natural gas and agricultural shippers' demand has shifted to some extent from grain to other agricultural products. Coal's share of rail traffic originated declined from 30 percent in 1990 to 13 percent in 2021; grain's share declined from 6 percent to roughly 4 percent during the same period.

Figure 11.6. *Rail's Return on Investment Compared with Its Cost of Capital*

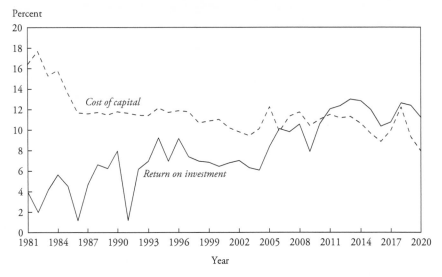

Notes: In 2006, the Surface Transportation Board significantly changed the method by which it calculates the rail industry cost of capital.
Source: Surface Transportation Board.

Figure 11.7. *Rail's Return on Equity Compared with* Fortune *500 Firms' Return on Equity*

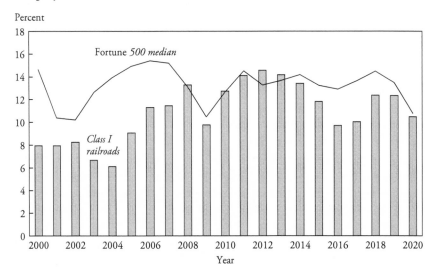

Notes: Return on equity is the ratio of net profit to shareholders' equity.
Sources: Association of American Railroads; *Fortune.*

In addition, the STB Carload Waybill Sample indicates, in general, that a smaller share of traffic is originated or terminated at stations served by a single Class I carrier now than prior to consolidation during the 1990s. Specifically, 59.4 percent of Class I originations and terminations of nonexempt carload traffic occurred at single-served stations between 1992 and 1996, compared with 53.7 percent between 2015 and 2019 (Baranowski and Zebrowski 2022). Although it is difficult to obtain confidential contract-rate information for specific products, as reported by Baranowski and Zebrowski (2022) based on the STB's recent rate study, average rail freight rates measured in terms of real revenues per ton-mile have decreased 7 percent from 1992 to 2019 (from 4.7 cents to 4.4 cents per ton-mile).

In sum, the available evidence indicates that competition is sufficiently vigorous in the rail industry to enable carriers to earn a competitive rate of return but not to earn excessive profits and to significantly exploit market power in particular markets. Accordingly, expanding government intervention with the hope of protecting shippers' welfare is unnecessary and may be counterproductive.

Unfortunately, Congress has been considering, but has not passed, the Freight Rail Shipping Fair Market Act,[23] which, in the alleged interest of promoting competition and reasonable rates, could be used to, for example, institute a policy that would mandate reciprocal switching where a railroad's competitors would have easier access to its network. Like many well-intentioned policies, reciprocal switching could result in unanticipated costs to shippers and railroads, including a railroad abandoning a market if it must provide reciprocal switching, deterioration in regular and intermodal rail service because of the considerable time it may take to provide reciprocal switching, and possible threats to safety while the process of reciprocal switching occurs. Instead of micromanaging railroad operations and competition, policymakers should have a forward-looking vision toward the railroad industry where it is fully deregulated and preparing for competition in an autonomous freight transportation system.

9. Autonomous Railroads

Like other modes, railroads are beginning the process of adopting autonomous operations, which could improve service time and reliability, reduce rail costs because carriers could operate with a smaller crew and move continuously, and enhance safety, which has received congressional interest in the wake of several derailments. In 2019, Rio Tinto, a mining firm, put its AutoHaul fully automated train operations into service in Western Australia. AutoHaul shows how rail can

---

23. H.R.8649—Freight Rail Shipping Fair Market Act, 117th Congress (2021–2022), https://www.congress.gov/bill/117th-congress/house-bill/8649.

exploit its economies of train size even more as it involves the simultaneous operation of up to fifty unmanned trains, each 1.5 miles long and carrying 240 cars of iron ore on a five-hundred-mile journey (Smith 2019). In the United States, an autonomous freight train system built by New York Air Brake was tested in the Colorado desert in 2019.

In 2020, three former SpaceX employees founded Parallel Systems in the United States to provide autonomous electric rail vehicles for shipping freight. Because the railcars are individually powered, they can be joined together to create a larger fleet or split off to multiple destinations with the cargo in hand. It also means that they are more flexible because the "platoons" will not need to have a large amount of cargo before they can start moving and can avoid time-consuming switching yards. In the future, it is conceivable that autonomous trains could lead to integrated North American rail systems with US, Canadian, and Mexican railroads competing and providing service throughout the continent, much like airlines, and eventually like trucking.

Scribner (2021b) points out that autonomous rail operations are not currently prohibited in the United States. However, organized labor has prompted federal and state regulators to pursue minimum-crew-size rules (for example, at least two crewmembers) for railroads operating in their jurisdictions. Those rules would weaken an important cost advantage of autonomous rail operations without being based on any evidence that multiperson crews were safer than a single-person crew.

The Federal Railroad Administration (FRA) has compromised safety by impeding the rail industry's automated track inspection (ATI) technology. ATI uses lasers, cameras, and other sensors to measure the condition of the tracks and provide data on the geometry of the rails, including curvature, alignment, and elevation. Such information can ensure the safe operation of trains and prevent accidents caused by track defects, including broken rails, uneven tracks, and the like, by enabling rail operators to quickly identify and address potential safety hazards, which visual inspections could miss and possibly cause derailments or accidents.

The FRA refused to extend Norfolk Southern's ATI program after its original time period lapsed and refused to extend the geographic scope of BNSF's program (Marsh 2022). Several senators have complained to the FRA, arguing that the data-driven fusion of ATI and visual inspections is producing a superior safety outcome, with track employees' hours being reallocated to verifying and remedying the greater number of defects detected by ATI rather than conducting redundant visual inspections. Like the crew-size issue, labor lobbying appears to be behind slowing progress on the use of ATI.

Like other autonomous transportation networks, autonomous rail operations will have to be coordinated while communications between cars and the infrastructure will have to be effective. In addition, they will have to address concerns about cybersecurity and liability. However, because they own their infrastructure, railroads can begin work on developing a national autonomous rail network without delay.[24]

10. Conclusions

Views about the competitiveness of the railroad industry have changed dramatically over time. In the 1880s, railroads were thought to be monopolies that required strict regulation. Starting in the 1950s, rail lost considerable traffic to trucking and earned low rates of return. By 1980, rail was deregulated so it could regain its financial health. Since deregulation, concerns have been raised periodically that rail is using its market power to charge excessive rates to certain shippers, although the rail industry has not been raising its rates over time and has not been earning excessive profits. Throughout this period, rail's operations and technology have greatly improved, which has enabled the industry to achieve financial health and benefit shippers.

Autonomous operations will fundamentally change all the transportation modes for the better. Because rail owns its infrastructure, it will encounter few constraints by government as it shifts to autonomous operations. Rail must exploit that advantage because, as we discuss in the next chapter, trucking's adoption of autonomous operations is well underway and will enable trucks to be an even more formidable competitor to rail.

Appendix

This appendix describes the procedure to estimate our model of supply, demand, and entry using GMM. It consists of obtaining consistent estimates of the demand (D) and supply (S) parameters, followed by initial consistent estimates of the entry (E) equation, and then estimation of the asymptotic covariance matrix. Finally, we simultaneously compute robust estimates of the parameters of all the equations.

Consistent Estimates of the Demand and Supply Parameters

Because the demand and supply equations contain endogenous independent variables, we require instruments to obtain consistent parameter estimates. Let us represent each endogenous variable by $N \times 1$ column vectors, and the exogenous variables (the X^js) as $N \times q^j$ matrices for $j = D, S, E$, where N is the number of

---

24. Switzerland is moving ahead with underground autonomous cargo delivery, Cargo Sous Terrain, between cities and logistics centers, where automated delivery carts on wheels travel through tunnels and pick up and deliver cargo automatically from designated ramps and lifts. See https://spectrum.ieee.org/cargo-sous-terrain.

observations in the panel data set (that is, N is equal to the number of plants multiplied by the number of time periods T). We construct a matrix of instruments, Z, by concatenating the three matrices of exogenous variables; i.e., $Z \equiv [X^D, X^S, X^E]$. Repeated columns of variables are omitted. Thus, Z is an $N \times q$ matrix, where q is the total number of unique variables in all the X^js. Based on the orthogonality conditions $E[\varepsilon^D{}'Z] = 0$ and $E[\varepsilon^S{}'Z] = 0$, consistent estimators of the demand and supply parameters are defined as

$$\tilde{\beta}^D = \underset{\beta}{\text{argmin}} \left\| \left(\ln Q^D - \left[\ln p^D, X^D \right] \beta \right)' Z \right\| \tag{A1}$$

$$\tilde{\beta}^S = \underset{\beta}{\text{argmin}} \left\| \left(\ln p^S - \left[\ln Q^S, X^S \right] \beta \right)' Z \right\| \tag{A2}$$

where $\| \cdot \|$ is the Euclidean norm.[25] Initial predicted values of supply price and quantity demanded are likewise denoted $\tilde{p}_{it}$ and $\tilde{q}_{it}$, respectively, and predicted values of the first stage supply and demand residuals are denoted $\tilde{\varepsilon}^S_{it}$ and $\tilde{\varepsilon}^D_{it}$.

Initial Consistent Estimator for the Entry Equation

Because the likelihood of entry is a function of revenue, variable costs, and fixed costs—the first two of which are composed of endogenous variables—we take a control function approach in the spirit of Blundell and Powell (2004). Given consistent predictions of price and quantity, we can use the first-stage supply and demand residuals as control variables for endogenous price and quantity. Those variables can control for the endogeneity of price and quantity on entry under the identifying assumption:

$$E(\varepsilon^E \mid Z) = E(\varepsilon^E \mid \tilde{\varepsilon}^S, \tilde{\varepsilon}^D) \tag{A3}$$

The assumption states that deviations of observed entry probabilities from their conditional mean must be the same whether the mean is conditional on the vector of instruments or conditional on the control variables. The assumption is satisfied because the control variables include the full portion of the covariates X^E that is correlated with the instruments Z. Accordingly, entry behavior is identified if we estimate the nonparametric entry equation

$$E_{it} = \mathbf{1} \left(\Pi \left(q_{it}, q_{it}, X^E_{it}, \tilde{\varepsilon}^S_{it}, \tilde{\varepsilon}^D_{it} \right) > \varepsilon^E_{it} \right) \tag{A4}$$

---

25. The estimators $\tilde{\beta}^D$ and $\tilde{\beta}^S$ obtained in this manner are asymptotically equivalent to three-stage least squares estimators. Although we do not have an efficient estimator because we do not introduce a weighting matrix in the minimizations, we require only a consistent estimator at this stage.

Because ε^E is a residual from a fundamentally nonlinear regression, the relationship between the observed determinants of entry and the control variables must be specified nonparametrically.[26] Estimating equation (A4) is difficult because both the functional form of profits and the distribution of the unobserved ε^E are unspecified. In comparison, a standard parametric discrete choice estimation such as probit would require assumptions that enable Π to be fully specified and an assumption that the distribution of the error is normal. Such assumptions are not sufficient to satisfy the identifying condition (A3); informally, under such assumptions the control variables may no longer be able to "control" fully for the endogeneity of price and quantity (Blundell and Powell 2004).

Matzkin (1992) provides a two-step recursive algorithm to estimate the entry equation with minimal parametric and distributional assumptions. To implement Matzkin's (1992) approach, we need only assume that the function Π is continuous, monotone, and weakly concave in the buildout distance and that the error term ε^E is drawn from a density with full support and finite variance. Thus, we identify entry probabilities by mildly restricting the set of profit functions to which Π can belong. In the first step, the relationship between the observable and unobservable determinants of entry choices is taken as given, and a vector of predicted entry probabilities that maximizes the likelihood of entry occurring in markets where entry occurs is computed. This enables us to avoid specifying the distribution of ε^E. In the second step, the relationship between observable and unobservable determinants of entry that maximizes the likelihood function is estimated. This enables us to avoid specifying the functional form of Π. The algorithm is recursive because the first step is embedded in the second step; that is, estimating the relationship between observable and unobservable determinants of entry requires recomputation of the vector of predicted entry probabilities at each step, which significantly increases the computational demands of the estimation process.

Formally, estimating the entry equation is equivalent to maximizing the log likelihood function with respect to a vector of entry probabilities, φ, and a vector of parameters, π, that relates the observable and unobservable determinants of entry through a series of constraints that ensure that profits and the observed entry choices satisfy certain basic conditions and that enable our estimated entry equation to be consistent with a profit function that satisfies the assumptions we made above. The log likelihood function is given by

$$\max_{\pi, \varphi} \sum_{i,t} \left[E_{it} \ln \varphi_{it} + (1 - E_{it}) \ln (1 - \varphi_{it}) \right] \tag{A5}$$

---

26. In contrast, if ε^E were a residual from a linear regression, then the relationship between X^E, $\hat{e}^S$, and $\hat{e}^D$ could be specified linearly, and the estimation procedure would be equivalent to two-stage least squares.

Define the matrix X^{E+}, which is formed by horizontally concatenating p, q, and the two control variables ε^S and ε^D to X^E. The first set of constraints

$$0 \le \varphi_{it} \le 1 \qquad\qquad\qquad \text{for all } i, t$$

$$\varphi_{it} \le \varphi_{js} \quad \text{if } \pi_{it} \cdot X^{E+}_{it} \le \pi_{js} \cdot X^{E+}_{js} \quad \text{for all } i, t, j, s \qquad (A6)$$

$$\varphi_{it} = \varphi_{js} \quad \text{if } \pi_{it} \cdot X^{E+}_{it} = \pi_{js} \cdot X^{E+}_{js} \quad \text{for all } i, t, j, s$$

ensures that entry probabilities fall between 0 and 1 and that the probability of entry must be higher in markets with higher expected profits, conditional on X^{E+}. The second set of constraints

$$\pi_{it} \ge 0 \qquad\qquad\qquad\qquad \text{for all } i, t$$

$$\pi_{it} \cdot X^{E+}_{it} \le \pi_{js} \cdot X^{E+}_{js} \qquad\qquad \text{for all } i, t, j, s \qquad (A7)$$

ensures a consistent relationship between the observable and unobservable determinants of entry assumed in the first stage of the estimation procedure. The two sets of constraints are implied by the assumptions that admit a class of permissible profit functions and they ensure that the entry equation is identified in the solution to equation (A5).

We accomplish the first step of the estimation procedure, maximizing the objective in (A5) over the vector φ taking the vector π as given subject to constraints (A6), using an algorithm described by Cosslett (1983). We express the solution to the maximization as $\varphi^*(\pi)$. We accomplish the second step of the estimation procedure, maximizing the objective in (A5) over the vector π subject to the constraints (A7) and $\varphi = \varphi^*(\pi)$, using an algorithm described by Matzkin (1992). The solution to this step gives us Π_{it}, the scaled predicted profits in a market given the observable variables.[27]

Generally, nonparametric estimation suffers from the "curse of dimensionality"— that is, the inclusion of additional explanatory variables increases the complexity of the estimation process exponentially. Because of the recursive nature of the estimation procedure, the curse strikes twice. Each additional element complicates the optimization with respect to φ in the first step through the constraints (A6), and complicates the optimization with respect to π in the second step through the constraints (A7). Because the first step of the optimization is embedded in the second step of the optimization through construction of the intermediate function $\varphi^*(\pi)$, the computational complexity is scaled

---

27. Predicted profits in a market are scaled according to the empirical distribution of the predicted unobservable determinants of entry. In comparison, the predicted parameter estimates in a probit model are scaled according to the distribution of the normally distributed error term.

exponentially by the *square* of the number of elements of X^{E+}. In exploratory estimations, we found that the twin curses of dimensionality enabled us to estimate the entry equation only with the variables that ensured consistent estimation: price and quantity, with their associated control variables, and the instrument, specifically, the buildout distance, which is excludable from the supply and demand equations.[28]

Asymptotic Covariance Matrix

Given the initial consistent estimates β^D, β^S, and Π, we now turn to robust covariance matrix estimation. Define predicted residuals for the three equations as:

$$\tilde{\varepsilon}_{it}^D = \ln Q_{it}^D - \left[\ln p_{it}^D, X_{it}^D\right]\tilde{\beta}^D \tag{A8}$$

$$\tilde{\varepsilon}_{it}^S = \ln p_{it}^S - \left[\ln Q_{it}^S, X_{it}^S\right]\tilde{\beta}^S \tag{A9}$$

$$\tilde{\varepsilon}_{it}^E = E_{it}\left[\frac{\hat{f}\left(\tilde{\Pi}_{it}\right)}{\hat{F}\left(\tilde{\Pi}_{it}\right)}\right] + \left(1 - E_{it}\right)\left[\frac{1 - \hat{f}\left(\tilde{\Pi}_{it}\right)}{1 - \hat{F}\left(\tilde{\Pi}_{it}\right)}\right] \tag{A10}$$

for all $i = 1, \ldots, N$. The functions $\hat{f}$ and $\hat{F}$ refer to kernel density estimates of the probability distribution function f and cumulative distribution function F of the distribution of predicted residuals in the entry equation.

Given those residuals, we compute, block-by-block, the familiar White heteroskedasticity-consistent systems estimator

$$\Phi = \begin{bmatrix} \Phi^{SS} & \Phi^{SD} & \Phi^{SE} \\ \Phi^{DS} & \Phi^{DD} & \Phi^{DE} \\ \Phi^{ES} & \Phi^{ED} & \Phi^{EE} \end{bmatrix} \tag{A11}$$

Each block of this matrix can be estimated with

$$\hat{\Phi}^{jk} = \frac{1}{N}\sum_{i,t} z_{it}z_{it}'\varepsilon_{it}^j\varepsilon_{it}^k,$$

where the z_{it} refer to the $1 \times q$ rows of the matrix of instruments Z. Denote the corresponding blocks of the inverse matrix as $(\hat{\Phi}^{jk})^{-1}$, and denote $\tilde{X}^E \equiv -\hat{f}(\tilde{\Pi})$.

---

28. Horowitz (2011) describes the computational limitation for nonparametric estimation with endogenous regressors in greater generality.

As with the White estimator for three-stage least squares, the asymptotic covariance matrix of the parameter estimates is given by: [29]

$$
\hat{\Sigma} = \frac{1}{N}
\begin{bmatrix}
X^{S'}Z(\hat{\Phi}^{SS})^{-1}Z'X^{S} & X^{S'}Z(\hat{\Phi}^{SD})^{-1}Z'X^{D} & X^{S'}Z(\hat{\Phi}^{SE})^{-1}Z'\tilde{X}^{E} \\
X^{D'}Z(\hat{\Phi}^{DS})^{-1}Z'X^{S} & X^{D'}Z(\hat{\Phi}^{DD})^{-1}Z'X^{D} & X^{D'}Z\hat{\Phi}^{DE})^{-1}Z'\tilde{X}^{E} \\
\tilde{X}^{E'}Z(\hat{\Phi}^{ES})^{-1}Z'X^{S} & \tilde{X}^{E'}Z(\hat{\Phi}^{ED})^{-1}Z'X^{D} & \tilde{X}^{E'}Z(\hat{\Phi}^{EE})^{-1}Z'\tilde{X}^{E}
\end{bmatrix}
$$

(A12)

Final Estimators

With the asymptotic covariance matrix in hand, we can now compute robust estimators of the supply and demand equation parameters and the predicted probability of entry. The familiar White heteroskedasticity-robust estimator, which accounts for error correlation across plants, for this system of simultaneous equations is given by:

$$
\begin{bmatrix}
\hat{\beta}_{P} \\
\hat{\beta}_{Q} \\
\hat{E}
\end{bmatrix}
= \frac{1}{N}\hat{\Sigma}^{-1}
\begin{bmatrix}
X^{S'}Z(\hat{\Phi}^{SS})^{-1}Z'p^{S} & X^{S'}Z(\hat{\Phi}^{SD})^{-1}Z'Q^{D} & X^{S'}Z(\hat{\Phi}^{SE})^{-1}Z'E \\
X^{D'}Z(\hat{\Phi}^{DS})^{-1}Z'p^{S} & X^{D'}Z(\hat{\Phi}^{DD})^{-1}Z'Q^{D} & X^{D'}Z(\hat{\Phi}^{DE})^{-1}Z'E \\
\tilde{X}^{E'}Z(\hat{\Phi}^{ES})^{-1}Z'p^{S} & \tilde{X}^{E'}Z(\hat{\Phi}^{ED})^{-1}Z'Q^{D} & \tilde{X}^{E'}Z(\hat{\Phi}^{EE})^{-1}Z'E
\end{bmatrix}
$$

(A13)

29. The construction of the asymptotic covariance matrix for a simultaneous system of equations estimated by GMM is explained in more generality in Greene (2003).

12

The Potential Benefits of Autonomous Trucking

CHAD SHIRLEY[1] AND CLIFFORD WINSTON

1. Introduction

Trucking carries roughly two-thirds of the value of freight that is shipped in the United States, and accounts for about 80 percent of freight transportation revenues for primary shipments, according to the American Trucking Association (ATA). Improving the efficiency of trucking operations through automation has the potential to generate large benefits to shippers and the overall economy in several ways.

Characterizing the Benefits

First, autonomous trucks could reduce operating costs by eliminating the driver and significantly improving service times and safety. In recent years, driver wages and benefits have accounted for 44 percent of the average marginal operating costs of for-hire trucking (Leslie and Murray 2022). Autonomous trucks also would allow deliveries to be completed more quickly and reliably and would reduce the frequency of accidents and cost of insurance.

Federal hours-of-service regulations mandate that a driver is allowed to drive a maximum of eleven hours during a fourteen-hour workday after ten consecutive hours of off-duty time. An autonomous truck could move a load of cargo nonstop with little risk of an accident. For example, an autonomous truck could

---

1. The views expressed in this chapter are those of the authors and should not be interpreted as those of the US Congressional Budget Office, where Chad Shirley is employed.

travel from Los Angeles to Dallas in twenty-four hours, compared with the two to three days that it would take a human driver to move the load. Picard (2022) estimates that the cost per mile of the Los Angeles to Dallas trip would drop from $1.76 to $0.96. The reduced operating costs and improved service quality would translate into significant price and nonprice benefits for shippers and into lower prices for final consumers.

Second, nonstop operations and reductions in incident delays caused by accidents also would improve the speed and reliability of freight deliveries, which would enable businesses to improve their supply chains by holding a smaller share of their raw materials and final products in inventory and by facilitating more precise just-in-time inventory operations. Even small service improvements can generate large annual logistics and inventory cost savings for firms because those costs in the aggregate run in the trillions of dollars (Zimmerman et al. 2021).

Third, by reducing service times and increasing service time reliability, autonomous trucks could enable firms to improve efficiency and expand output by reoptimizing their supply and distribution networks. For example, given faster and more reliable deliveries of certain inputs, which they can purchase at lower cost, some firms might receive inputs from longer distances to produce their products more efficiently and at a higher quality standard. Other firms might expand their sales of perishable products whose value would be preserved because those products would reach their destinations much faster.

Fourth, the trucking industry would be less vulnerable to labor shortages. The ATA reports that the trucking industry employed 7 percent fewer truck drivers in 2020 compared with 2019, and in 2021 the industry was eighty thousand drivers short to respond in a timely manner to shippers' demand for trucking services— a number that is expected to double by 2030. The ATA also reports that the trucking industry is responding to the shortage of drivers by raising the annual pay for long-haul truckers to almost $70,000 in 2021, an 18 percent jump from 2019. KLLM Transport has boosted pay 33 percent for over-the-road truckers and for trainees coming out of its academy, while regional company drivers and independent contractors will receive a pay hike of 10 to 16 percent. Recently, Walmart announced that it is paying its drivers up to $110,000 in their first year at the company and more once they work longer for the company. At the same time, higher pay increases shippers' rates and consumer prices. Autonomous trucks could address the fundamental problem that recruiting long-distance drivers is difficult because truck driving is such grueling work.

Fifth, by increasing the speed and reliability of deliveries and by mitigating the shortage of truck drivers, autonomous trucks could help ameliorate the cost of periodic supply chain disruptions that delay shipments at ports arriving from abroad and that delay shipments throughout the supply chain.

Finally, autonomous trucks could contribute to the improvement in highway safety by virtually eliminating accidents involving trucks. According to data from the Insurance Institute for Highway Safety, more than four thousand people die every year in the United States from truck accidents, mostly in passenger cars struck by trucks.

Recent Developments in Autonomous Trucking

Autonomous trucking operations are steadily evolving and expected to become an integral part of the US surface freight transportation system. Several companies have already attracted funds and are testing automated trucks, including TuSimple, Plus, Embark Trucks, Waymo Via, and Aurora. In a step toward full automation, Locomation is developing truck convoying in which a lead vehicle keeps automated follower trucks. Truck convoying is of interest to retailers such as Amazon, Walmart, and Target because they would have more total capacity than traditional human-operated trucks and would be moving all the time.[2]

Several companies are currently focusing on providing automated trucking service between cities. Autonomous trucking companies such as Embark and real estate investors such as Alterra Property Group are forming alliances to create autonomous trucking hubs so that after carrying its cargo on a highway an autonomous truck can park at a hub and enable a human driver to deliver the cargo at destinations in the city. Embark plans to provide service on an autonomous trucking lane between Houston and San Antonio, and Aurora plans to open a new 635-mile route in Texas.

In addition, autonomous trucking companies are collaborating with traditional trucking companies and logistics firms to provide service. Kodiak Robotics, a developer of self-driving trucks, is partnering with U.S. Xpress, a traditional trucking company, to haul goods between Dallas and Atlanta as part of a several-day demonstration to show how self-driving trucks can expedite freight deliveries by being deployed solely on highways, with a driver taking over to navigate city streets. Kodiak Robotics is also working with CEVA Logistics to deliver freight autonomously on routes from Dallas–Fort Worth to Austin and from Dallas–Fort Worth to Oklahoma City. Waymo and C. H. Robinson (a logistics provider) will use Waymo's test fleet of autonomous trucks to make deliveries between Dallas–Fort Worth and Houston.

Another autonomous trucking company, Gatik, is developing short-haul service. Gatik is operating fully driverless trucks to move customer orders between a Walmart dark store in Bentonville, Arkansas (which provides fulfillment for online orders only) and a neighborhood market. In 2023, Gatik began providing self-driving truck deliveries from Kroger's Dallas distribution center to Kroger grocery stores in the Dallas–Fort Worth area.

2. Locomation's initial operating plan combines automated platooning with team driving, so the two-truck convoy has two drivers, one actively driving and one in the sleeper berth complying with Federal Motor Carrier Safety Administration hours-of-service rules.

Chapter Overview

The purpose of this chapter is to explore the potential benefits of autonomous trucking to the US economy. Although most of the potential benefits summarized above are difficult to measure quantitatively, it is possible for us to build on previous work to model firm-level, logistics cost–minimizing behavior. We can then simulate empirically how firms' logistics behavior would be affected by improvements in the cost, speed, and reliability of freight transportation produced by autonomous truck operations and use those simulations to offer a plausible estimate of firms' annual logistics cost savings.

Using representative product and freight data, we find that the widespread adoption of autonomous trucking could reduce firms' annual logistics costs by roughly $140 billion. Those benefits would be in addition to other benefits generated by autonomous trucking, which we discuss qualitatively. In what follows, we describe our approach to modeling a firm's logistics behavior and formulate its cost-minimization problem, indicate the parameters and assumed numerical values that we use for our numerical simulation, report our simulated benefits from autonomous trucking, and discuss qualifications to our analysis and additional benefits that autonomous trucking could provide.

2. Modeling Inventory Logistics Behavior

We develop a model of a representative firm's logistics costs, where transportation attributes affect those costs and can be adjusted to capture the potential service improvements from the introduction of autonomous trucking. It is difficult to develop such a model that can be used for a numerical simulation because of the absence of detailed data for key variables in the model and the limited information about the values of the model's key parameters. We therefore use an approach to modeling logistics behavior developed by Tyworth and Zeng (1998), as discussed by Shirley and Winston (2004), which has been used with data for numerical analysis and can be updated and modified for our purposes here.

The model is based on an economic order quantity (EOQ) transportation-inventory model that incorporates the effects of freight transportation cost, travel time, and the reliability of travel time on annual logistics costs and service levels. We use an EOQ model because transportation characteristics play an important role by affecting the costs of holding inventories, such as warehousing costs and the costs of the capital, and the costs of not having inventories when they are needed, such as backorder costs and the costs of lost sales. The EOQ model applies to inventories, such as raw materials, that are acquired through movement by a transportation mode. Note that transportation characteristics do not play a role in a production smoothing model, which is characterized by increasing marginal costs of production.

The inventory policy used in an EOQ model to minimize logistics costs is called an (S, s) policy because the important values for the firm to decide are the target inventory level (S) and a reorder point (s). When inventories fall below the reorder point, an order is placed. If inventories remain above the reorder point, they continue to be depleted without being replenished. A depiction of inventory levels over time produces a sawtooth shape frequently seen in the literature on money demand (Blinder and Maccini 1991).

Generally, the target inventory level is influenced by a firm's expectations of future sales, the storage costs of inventory, and the interest costs of inventory investment. The reorder point is a buffer stock used to protect against stockouts, which occur when a product is in demand but none is in inventory. Stockouts force a firm to incur extra costs to expedite delivery of the product (backorder costs), or to lose sales, such as for retail and wholesale inventories or when production is delayed if the product is used as an input. Thus, the reorder point is affected by expectations of future sales in conjunction with the stockout or shortage cost and by the expected delivery time.

The target inventory and reorder point values, S and s, are chosen by a firm to minimize the costs associated with placing orders, the costs from suffering a shortage of the good, and the unit costs of transportation, while trading those costs off against the costs of holding larger inventories. In the model, cost-minimizing firms continuously monitor inventory levels, while product demand is independent from one time period to the next. Transit times (the amount of time involved in transporting an order) are assumed to be independent, stationary, random variables to realistically incorporate freight transit time and reliability into the EOQ model.

Logistics costs are comprised of ordering costs, transportation costs, holding costs, and shortage costs. In our analysis:

—Ordering costs consist of employees' time and information technology and communications costs.

—Annual transportation costs equal the number of units demanded each year and the freight rate per unit.

—Holding costs of inventory are complex and depend on a combination of in-transit, cycle, and safety stocks.

• In-transit stocks are those being transported. Their holding costs depend on the holding cost for each expected unit in transit, which include the cost of capital, depreciation, and obsolescence. The expected level of in-transit stocks depends on the mean number of units demanded per day and the mean number of days each shipment is in transit. Transit times, measured in days, are allowed some random variation.

• The remaining holding costs of inventory accrue to units in a warehouse. The units not in transit are either part of the cycle stock or are considered as safety stock. Cycle stock units are those on hand between shipments and are thus influenced by the transit times. Cycle stocks entail the same holding costs incurred by in-transit stocks, plus storage and insurance costs.

• Safety stock units are those still on hand when a new shipment is received. We consider the effects of transportation on safety stock holding costs by letting lead-time demand depend on the lead time and the daily demand. The lead time is directly affected by the time involved in transportation, plus a constant representing a fixed time spent on nontransportation activities in the order cycle, such as order preparation, order processing, manufacturing, or assembly, depending on the context. As with cycle stocks, the holding costs for safety stocks depend on the holding costs for each expected unit stored.

—Shortage costs include the costs of any expedited delivery to satisfy customer demand once inventory is depleted, plus the cost of any lost sales or lost customers that result from a shortage. In a raw materials or work-in-progress inventory, shortage costs may take the form of expedited delivery costs, overtime, or lost production. The shortage cost term depends primarily on the expected level of shortage during the lead time between each order and delivery over the year.

3. Data and Product and Transportation Service Parameters

We use our model of a representative firm's logistics costs to estimate economy-wide logistics cost changes from the adoption of autonomous trucking, which affect transportation costs and the mean and standard deviation of transit time. To do so, we use a set of representative firm data for selected industries on product and shipping attributes and representative data on the characteristics of the transportation system. We then assume plausible changes in those characteristics that could be caused by a firm substituting nonautonomous truck transportation for autonomous trucking.

Detailed representative firm data were obtained from a survey conducted by LaLonde, Cooper, and Noordewier (1988). It should be stressed that obtaining the necessary detail about a firm's logistics costs is very difficult. Indeed, discussions with logistics researchers led us to conclude that LaLonde, Cooper, and Noordewier's (1988) survey was a one-of-a-kind endeavor; we were unable to find any more up-to-date, comparable data that were publicly available. We therefore use LaLonde, Cooper, and Noordewier's (1988) original survey values and other standardized logistics cost assumptions and, as summarized below, adjust them in different ways to characterize current economic conditions.

With help from the Council of Logistics Management, LaLonde, Cooper, and Noordewier (1988) surveyed shippers in various industries about their logistics behavior. Three hundred and eleven responses were sorted according to nine different industry groupings: food and beverage, chemical and plastics, pharmaceutical, automotive, paper, electronics, clothing and textiles, merchandising, and other manufacturing. Respondents included manufacturers, wholesalers, and retailers.

The survey asked for data on several inventory logistics and transportation variables, including average order sizes, order fill rates, unit product values, shipment distances, shipment travel times, and shipment travel time reliability. To increase the accuracy of the survey, respondents were directed to select a representative product and a typical customer for that product and to answer many of the questions with that specific product and customer in mind. The authors reported the mean response for each industry group. In a few instances where large outliers would unduly influence the mean, they reported the median response.

Our base-case adjustments to the survey data to produce plausible 2019 values are as follows (we also conduct sensitivity analysis to explore how our findings are affected by alternative adjustments):

—Changes in quantities demanded are increased to allow for subsequent growth in the US economy. The adjustment uses the increase in real GDP, but because inventories are specific to the sites where they are held, the change also takes into consideration growth in establishments. Establishment numbers for manufacturers' finished goods, materials and supplies, and work-in-process inventories, and retailers' and merchant wholesalers' inventories, are taken from the US Census Bureau's County Business Patterns, which are available to 2018. The standard deviation of mean demand is scaled along with the mean.

—The average values of the items being sold are adjusted according to changes in the producer price index (PPI) for different industries; for years before a separate PPI was calculated for a specific industry, the overall composite PPI was used.

—Trucking costs (described further below) are inflated according to the change in the PPI for trucking, an increase of about 90 percent over the period. Transit times also are assumed to have increased by 10 percent because of greater offshoring of products and an increase in shipping distances.

—Order processing times are assumed to have decreased 20 percent because of the significant improvements in information technology during the past three decades. Ordering costs per order also are assumed to have dropped significantly (40 percent) because of the same improvements in information technology that were assumed to reduce order processing times.

—Warehousing costs are adjusted by comparing the PPI for warehousing with the industry PPIs and applying the relative increase or decrease to the difference between the warehousing holding cost and the in-transit holding cost. Higher values were used when they resulted in an order size that more closely matched the average order size for the industry, with the justification that products that suffer from greater obsolescence and depreciation generally warrant higher holding costs.

—Unit shortage penalties are increased by 20 percent to take account of greater competition in the US economy from globalization and lower information and search costs attributable to the advent of the Internet.

Table 12.1 presents the updated data that we use in the logistics cost model, including average demand, lead time, and product data for a typical product and consumer for each of the nine industry categories. The values of the variables appear to be plausible by inspection, although we acknowledge that we are not aware of any comparable data sets including those variables that we could use for comparison.

Following Tyworth and Zeng (1998), both daily demand and the transit time component of lead time are assumed to be random variables that take a gamma distribution. Daily demand, for instance, ranges from less than ten units on average (for merchandise) to nearly two hundred units (for food), depending on the industry. The important service time variables that we assume will be directly affected by autonomous truck operations are mean transit time, which ranges from 2.75 to 5.5 days, and the standard deviation of transit time, which ranges from 0.55 to 2.42 days. Product values per unit range from $12 to $356 and weights per unit range from less than half a pound to nearly forty pounds.

To execute the numerical simulations of a firm's logistics cost–minimizing behavior, we also need values for the inventory parameters, a specification of the freight rate function, and counterfactual values of the transportation variables that capture improvements from the adoption of autonomous trucking.

Inventory Parameter Values

As shown in table 12.1, inventory costs are expressed as a percentage of the unit value of a good. Holding costs include costs for storage, insurance, taxes, handling, depreciation, interest, and obsolescence, and range from 23 percent to 51 percent across industries. Holding costs for in-transit stock are generally lower than those for warehoused goods, as storage and insurance costs are avoided; for the simulations they are taken to be 20 percent. Unit shortage costs (30 percent) represent the sum of the probabilistically adjusted costs of lost sales and lost customers that result when a product is unavailable.

Freight Rate Function

The freight rate function for an order size Q is based on two alternative power functions presented by Tyworth and O'Neill (1997) and Tyworth and Zeng (1998), which were derived from data originally supplied to them by Yellow Freight Systems. Each specification takes the form: $f(Q) = a \times (z/100) \times (Q \times w)^b$, where a and b are constants, z is the freight class, and w is the weight per unit of the good. Specification (1) takes $a = 306.94$ and $b = -0.3071$, while specification (2) takes $a = 463.80$ and $b = -0.3325$. Both specifications originated with 300-mile shipments at 1995 rates and then considered changes in trucking costs as described above. Preference was given to the freight rate specification that achieved the reorder size that more closely matched LaLonde, Cooper, and Noordewier's (1988)

Table 12.1. Data Used in the Simulations

Variables	Food	Chemical	Pharmaceutical	Auto	Paper	Electronics	Clothing	Other manufacturing	Merchandise
Demand									
Mean of daily demand (units), μ_D	193	41	14	26	21	46	26	33	6
Standard deviation of daily demand (units), σ_D	115.8	24.6	8.4	15.6	12.4	27.6	15.6	19.8	3.6
Lead time									
Constant order processing time (days), v	1.6	1.6	0.8	0.8	3.2	2.4	2.4	0.8	0.8
Mean transit time (days), μ_T	2.75	5.5	3.3	4.4	3.3	4.4	4.4	4.4	4.4
Standard deviation of transit time (days), σ_T	0.55	1.32	1.10	1.76	1.32	2.42	2.42	2.2	2.2
Product									
Unit value, V	$27.06	$356.63	$229.67	$108.80	$52.58	$11.80	$59.61	$52.07	$55.57
Unit weight (lbs.), w	4.4	37.4	0.4	6.0	1.5	0.4	4.3	1.6	3.4
Inventory									
Holding cost (warehouse), W	38%	34%	23%	27%	37%	51%	27%	27%	38%
Holding cost (in-transit), Y	20%	20%	20%	20%	20%	20%	20%	20%	20%
Ordering cost per order, A	$6	$6	$6	$6	$6	$6	$6	$6	$6
Unit shortage penalty fraction, B	30%	30%	30%	30%	30%	30%	30%	30%	30%
Transportation									
Rate discount, d	6%	6%	6%	6%	6%	6%	6%	6%	6%
Freight class, z	70	65	100	100	65	100	100	100	100
Freight-rate specification	1	1	2	2	1	1	1	1	1

average order size for each industry. We indicate the freight rate specification, (1) or (2), that we used for each industry category in table 12.1.

Counterfactual Values of Transportation Variables

As noted, we assume that the widespread adoption of autonomous trucks will affect the transportation time variables, which in turn will affect a firm's logistics costs. Recall the example of large time savings that would accrue to shippers for shipments from Los Angeles to Dallas if they were transported by autonomous instead of nonautonomous trucks. Given their ability to reduce labor, insurance, and accident costs, we also assume that autonomous trucks reduce transportation costs.

The Ryder System and the Socially Aware Mobility Lab (2021) at the Georgia Institute of Technology estimate that autonomous trucking could reduce the cost of transportation 29 to 40 percent. Yang (2021) estimated that self-driving trucks would reduce overall freight prices by 25.6 percent by lowering per-mile freight transportation costs, increasing the daily driving range, and eliminating other human factors related to truck driving. We therefore make conservative assumptions compared with the preceding figures that the widespread adoption of autonomous trucking would yield a 20 percent improvement in transportation cost, time, and reliability. We perform a sensitivity analysis assuming an even lower value of 10 percent improvement of the transportation variables.[3]

The base-case assumption for the improvement in the transportation variables is consistent with previous work on the effects of the development of the Interstate Highway System on costs and service times. Keeler and Ying (1988) estimated that trucking costs were reduced approximately 20 percent over a twenty-three-year period that included the Interstate Highway System construction. Friedlaender (1965) assumed average vehicle speed increases of between five and ten miles per hour after construction of the Interstate Highway System, or roughly 20 percent of the pre-Interstate speed for different types and sizes of vehicles, including trucks. Our simulations assume comparable improvements in

---

3. It is not clear how the full cost of firms' trucking operations will be affected by the adoption of autonomous vehicles. The capital costs of autonomous trucks may be higher than the capital cost of nonautonomous trucks because of additional hardware in the form of additional sensors and powerful computers. Those costs will decline when a sufficient volume of autonomous trucks is produced that exhausts scale economies. At the same time, autonomous trucks are likely to have lower insurance costs than nonautonomous trucks. In addition, the operating costs of autonomous trucks are likely to be lower than the operating costs of nonautonomous trucks because electric autonomous trucks will have lower energy costs than nonautonomous trucks. Gasoline-powered autonomous trucks also will have lower operating costs than nonautonomous trucks because they will get better fuel economy by operating in a smoother traffic flow that is less subject to disruptions, such as stop-and-go driving. Finally, autonomous trucks also will have much lower operating costs than nonautonomous trucks because they will have lower labor costs and because they will be operating most of the time instead of stopping by law for several hours to enable a human driver to rest.

average transit time of roughly a day (given average transit times of as much as five days) and reductions in the standard deviation of transit time of up to half a day.

In this chapter's appendix, we summarize our complete model of a representative firm's total logistics costs, including the updated values of the parameters and variables. Given those values, we assume a firm chooses the reorder quantity (Q) that is expected to reach the desired target inventory level (S) and a reorder point (s) to minimize total logistics costs. We then assume counterfactual values of transportation cost, transit time, and the reliability of transit time, which would exist in an environment where autonomous trucks were adopted, and reoptimize a firm's total logistics costs. We then compare the logistics costs in the two environments to determine the total logistics cost savings for the nation.

4. Gains from Widespread Adoption of Autonomous Trucking

Table 12.2 presents the results of the counterfactual simulation of the effects of autonomous trucking on firms' logistics costs for each of the nine industries under the current conditions of nonautonomous trucking, our base-case counterfactual scenario of a 20 percent reduction in transportation costs, travel time, and travel reliability, and an alternative scenario of a 10 percent reduction in those variables. In the base case, the reductions in logistics costs for the different industries range from 13 to 16 percent, with an overall average of 15 percent. Inventories and their attendant costs decline because of the improvements in transportation. Firms place more frequent orders, reflected in higher ordering costs, of smaller shipment sizes and at lower reorder points.

The results for the electronics industry illustrate the nature of the changes in logistics costs and firm behavior. The effect of the transportation improvements yields a $1,104 decrease in expected annual logistics costs for the included product, representing a reduction of 14.9 percent. Order costs rise from $166 to $191, but order sizes and reorder levels fall, and inventories, backorders, and their associated costs decrease. The transportation charge also drops from $3,551 to $2,968, which accounts for roughly 50 percent of the total savings in logistics costs. Reoptimization of inventory levels, order frequency, and shipment size results in large additional savings that illustrate the indirect benefits from transportation, which enable agents to improve performance in other parts of the economy.

Extrapolating the results from the nine industries to the overall economy, we obtain an estimate of annual savings of $140 billion (2019 dollars) for an average reduction in logistics costs of 15 percent. Assuming the logistics cost savings for the firms in the sample are representative of the savings that could be achieved by other firms in the economy, our national estimate also can be obtained by scaling the estimated cost savings in the sample based on the logistics costs in the rest of the economy, which were $1.62 trillion in 2019 (Zimmerman

Table 12.2. Simulation Results

	Food			Chemical			Pharmaceuticals		
	Pre	10%	20%	Pre	10%	20%	Pre	10%	20%
Transportation variables									
Real transportation cost (% of pre)	100%	90%	80%	100%	90%	80%	100%	90%	80%
Mean transit time (days)	2.75	2.5	2.25	5.5	5	4.5	3.3	3	2.7
Std. dev. of transit time (days)	0.55	0.5	0.45	1.32	1.2	1.08	1.1	1	0.9
Decision variables									
Order size (Q)	2,430	2,253	2,071	373	345	318	77	73	69
Reorder level (s)	1,084	1,026	971	421	394	366	116	109	102
Logistics cost									
Expected annual logistics cost	$55,606	$51,455	$47,225	$115,871	$107,201	$98,363	$11,174	$10,459	$9,739
Change from pre value		7.5%	15.1%		7.5%	15.1%		6.4%	12.8%
Inventory analysis									
Cycle stock	1,215	1,127	1,036	186	173	159	38	36	35
In-transit stock	531	483	434	226	205	185	46	42	38
Safety stock	244	235	228	130	123	116	59	56	53
Expected backorders	6.46	5.73	5.01	1.3	1.13	0.97	0.15	0.14	0.12
Order fill level	99.70%	99.70%	99.80%	99.70%	99.70%	99.70%	99.80%	99.80%	99.80%
Cost analysis									
Ordering	$172	$185	$201	$238	$256	$279	$395	$415	$438
Cycle stock	$12,746	$11,824	$10,875	$22,848	$21,182	$19,485	$2,029	$1,929	$1,830
In-transit stock	$2,931	$2,665	$2,400	$16,264	$14,789	$13,314	$2,128	$1,934	$1,741
Safety stock	$2,509	$2,416	$2,346	$15,759	$14,902	$14,028	$3,112	$2,949	$2,784
Backorders	$1,500	$1,435	$1,365	$5,510	$5,169	$4,832	$695	$654	$614
Transportation cost	$35,750	$32,930	$30,037	$55,253	$50,902	$46,426	$2,816	$2,578	$2,332

	Auto			Paper			Electronics		
	Pre	10%	20%	Pre	10%	20%	Pre	10%	20%
Transportation variables									
Real transportation cost (% of pre)	100%	90%	80%	100%	90%	80%	100%	90%	80%
Mean transit time (days)	4.4	4	3.6	3.3	3	2.7	4.4	4	3.6
Std. dev. of transit time (days)	1.76	1.6	1.44	1.32	1.2	1.08	2.42	2.2	2
Decision variables									
Order size (Q)	473	438	402	189	178	167	600	560	520
Reorder level (s)	238	223	207	161	151	141	446	417	388
Logistics cost									
Expected annual logistics cost	$31,257	$28,953	$26,595	$7,527	$6,947	$6,357	$7,417	$6,863	$6,313
Change from pre value		7.4%	14.9%		7.7%	15.5%		7.5%	14.9%
Inventory analysis									
Cycle stock	236	219	201	95	89	83	300	280	260
In-transit stock	114	104	94	69	63	57	202	184	166
Safety stock	103	98	93	25	21	17	133	122	112
Expected backorders	1.71	1.46	1.24	0.73	0.64	0.56	5.85	5	4.29
Order fill level	99.60%	99.70%	99.70%	99.60%	99.60%	99.70%	99.00%	99.10%	99.20%
Cost analysis									
Ordering	$119	$128	$140	$239	$255	$272	$166	$178	$191
Cycle stock	$7,070	$6,550	$6,018	$1,861	$1,749	$1,637	$1,841	$1,717	$1,597
In-transit stock	$2,535	$2,305	$2,076	$736	$669	$602	$487	$443	$399
Safety stock	$3,017	$2,871	$2,721	$477	$401	$324	$802	$737	$676
Backorders	$1,105	$1,022	$940	$462	$430	$399	$571	$524	$483
Transportation cost	$17,411	$16,076	$14,700	$3,752	$3,441	$3,122	$3,551	$3,265	$2,968

(continued)

Table 12.2. Simulation Results (continued)

	Clothing			Other manufacturing			Merchandise		
	Pre	10%	20%	Pre	10%	20%	Pre	10%	20%
Transportation variables									
Real transportation cost (% of pre)	100%	90%	80%	100%	90%	80%	100%	90%	80%
Mean transit time (days)	4.4	4	3.6	4.4	4	3.6	4.4	4	3.6
Std. dev. of transit time (days)	2.42	2.2	2	2.2	2	1.8	2.2	2	1.8
Decision variables									
Order size (Q)	526	487	447	454	422	389	126	117	109
Reorder level (s)	263	246	230	345	322	299	54	50	47
Logistics cost									
Expected annual logistics cost	$18,899	$17,434	$15,961	$15,446	$14,310	$13,151	$5,786	$5,367	$4,930
Change from pre value		7.8%	15.5%		7.4%	14.9%		7.2%	14.8%
Inventory analysis									
Cycle stock	263	243	224	227	211	194	63	59	54
In-transit stock	114	104	94	145	132	119	26	24	22
Safety stock	86	80	74	174	164	154	23	22	20
Expected backorders	2.69	2.28	1.93	2.04	1.74	1.46	0.83	0.71	0.6
Order fill level	99.50%	99.50%	99.60%	99.60%	99.60%	99.60%	99.3%	99.40%	99.40%
Cost analysis									
Ordering	$107	$115	$126	$157	$169	$183	$103	$111	$119
Cycle stock	$4,323	$3,999	$3,677	$3,233	$3,001	$2,767	$1,367	$1,274	$1,176
In-transit stock	$1,392	$1,266	$1,140	$1,531	$1,392	$1,253	$302	$275	$246
Safety stock	$1,391	$1,284	$1,187	$2,443	$2,305	$2,163	$480	$457	$432
Backorders	$854	$784	$722	$831	$765	$699	$238	$218	$199
Transportation cost	$10,832	$9,986	$9,110	$7,251	$6,677	$6,086	$3,296	$3,033	$2,758

et al. 2021). We make two adjustments to appropriately scale the results. First, we account for the fact that 75 percent of freight transportation expenditures are trucking related (Zimmerman et al. 2021). Second, because all inventories are not influenced by changes in transportation—specifically, final goods inventories and work-in-progress inventories are not necessarily determined by the kind of EOQ model presented here—the model is applicable to the manufacturing raw materials inventories, wholesale inventories, and retail inventories, which account for 77 percent of total inventories.[4]

If we invoke the more conservative assumption of a 10 percent reduction in transportation costs, travel time, and the reliability of travel time, the average reduction in logistics costs would be 7.4 percent instead of 15 percent, resulting in $69 billion (2019 dollars) of annual savings, which is still a sizable gain.

We also conducted another sensitivity analysis where we used the unadjusted (original) values as reported by LaLonde, Cooper, and Noordewier (1988) for the demand, product, inventory, and transportation cost variables to explore the effect of our adjustments. Perhaps surprisingly, we obtained estimates of national savings from the adoption of autonomous trucking that were within $1 billion of the findings for both the 20 percent and the 10 percent reductions in transportation costs and service times that were based on the adjusted values of those variables.

Essentially, our adjusted figures that increased unit demand, shortage costs, and trucking rates lead to larger percentage savings from autonomous trucking, all else equal. However, our adjusted figures that increased unit product values, holding costs, and order costs lead to smaller percentage savings from autonomous trucking. The intuition behind those results is that changes that lead to a higher share of transportation costs within logistics costs, such as higher trucking rates and higher unit demand, provide a greater opportunity for autonomous trucking to reduce those costs. Among those factors, changes in trucking rates and holding costs tend to have the largest impact on national savings because they have the most direct impact on transportation costs and inventory costs, respectively. However, the effect of a change in any single parameter on the estimated national savings is small, and even a doubling of any of those parameters would most likely lead to less than a percentage point increase in the estimated 15 percent logistics costs savings from autonomous trucking under the 20 percent cost and service time reduction scenario. Overall, the changes in those parameters that were realized over the past few decades represented a mix of positive and negative

4. The use of an EOQ model should be qualified by noting it is tailored for industries where shortages are a small fraction of sales (Tyworth and Zeng 1998). The results are less accurate for industries where shortages are a large fraction of sales, but the direction of the bias is not clear. The treatment of shortage costs also may not be straightforward because the cost of shortages may reflect the cost of delayed or forgone use of a product by a consumer, which may be larger or smaller than the cost of shortage to a firm. Again, it is not clear how our findings are affected.

influences on the estimated national savings from the adoption of autonomous trucking.

The gains also might be lower if we assume that autonomous trucking is used only for certain types of trucking operations, such as long-distance trucking. However, in the long run, it is not clear why autonomous trucking, in combination with autonomous vans or other local delivery vehicles, would not be used on all types of roads and for all types of trucking operations.[5]

5. Additional Benefits from Autonomous Trucking

We have found that the adoption of autonomous trucking could produce substantial benefits to the entire US economy by reducing firms' logistics costs. Those benefits do not include reducing the likelihood of a supply chain disruption or shortening its duration should one occur, like the one the United States experienced during 2021 and 2022. Such disruptions can lead to a large increase in trucking costs. Indeed, the US Bureau of Labor Statistics estimated that the annual inflation rate for overall trucking costs during December 2021 was 17 percent and the inflation rate for long-distance trucking was 25 percent (Tett 2021).

The adoption of autonomous trucking also could generate other substantial benefits to the economy. Autonomous trucking will represent a loss of employment to drivers in the seat, but also make the industry less vulnerable to the growing shortage of drivers.[6] Winston and Karpilow (2020) argue that autonomous trucking is likely to increase employment because some drivers will be needed to provide security for a vehicle's cargo and to handle certain logistical matters, while additional jobs will develop at transportation centers that monitor the autonomous road network used by trucks. Jobs also will develop to maintain, repair, and clean autonomous trucks, and to keep maps for optimal routings updated.

---

5. Recent work by the US Department of Transportation (Waschik et al. 2021) analyzes the macroeconomic effects of the introduction of automation in the long-haul trucking sector in the United States by introducing productivity shocks to that form of trucking. Although that work takes a different approach than we take here, the estimated benefits are broadly consistent with what we obtained from our simulations. The US Department of Transportation's calculations of cost savings are based on a computable general equilibrium model of the US economy that includes details on transportation-related industries, including for-hire and in-house trucking. Half of for-hire and 10 percent of in-house trucking are assumed to be long haul in the report, based on employment shares. In the US Department of Transportation's simulation, the estimated benefit is a 2019 GDP equivalent of $68 billion by the end of the thirty-year period, with much of the benefit achieved within fifteen years under a fast adoption scenario. Most of the economic effects come from the labor and capital savings aspects of autonomous trucking, with additional benefits in the form of fuel savings and capital investment.

6. Viscelli (2018) concludes that the current trucking jobs most at risk of displacement are long-distance driving jobs with few specialized tasks, representing fewer than 300,000 drivers. Gittleman and Monaco (2019) reach a similar conclusion.

Finally, by increasing the nation's productivity and output, autonomous trucking could increase economy-wide employment.

Autonomous trucking also would produce gains for firms as they change production operations beyond their logistics operations and realize X-efficiencies from the use of improved inputs shipped longer distances. Firms also would benefit from greater economies of scale (Mohring and Williamson 1969) and scope because their products could be sold at lower cost to more geographically dispersed markets. Firms also may realize savings from changing input mixes, including their use of land and labor, to take advantage of the change in relative factor prices that is attributable to the lower cost of transporting freight by truck. And firms may realize savings by using autonomous freight technology to improve their operations. For example, equipment manufacturers are investing in self-driving tractors that can plow fields by themselves, which can be used by farmers to boost productivity in agriculture. A share of the preceding sources of cost savings to firms will be passed on to consumers in lower product prices. Consumers also will benefit as firms increase the variety of products they offer or create innovative new products in response to changing input prices from lower transportation and logistics costs.

Autonomous trucking also will help reduce the externality costs of highway travel. Drivers and passengers of all vehicles on the road will benefit from reduced congestion as truckers increase off-peak and nighttime driving. Improvements in the safety of trucking operations will reduce the cost of accidents and incident delays. And, as in the case of automobiles, autonomous trucks will eventually operate with emissions-free vehicles, although large truck makers have only begun to mass-produce such vehicles.[7] As discussed in chapter 6, autonomous vehicles will facilitate the adoption of efficient highway pricing policies, including congestion pricing of all vehicles and, in the case of trucking, axle-weight and weight-based charges to reduce the damage that trucks do to road pavement and bridges (Winston 2021b).

Finally, by significantly reducing the costs of shipping freight and providing faster and more reliable service, autonomous trucks will enable truckers to present a stronger competitive challenge to nonautonomous and, as discussed in the previous chapter, autonomous railroads. By providing truck convoys or "road trains," which could carry much larger shipments without stopping until they reach their destination, it is possible that autonomous trucking operations could provide competitive service to so-called captive shippers of bulk commodities, like coal and grain.

---

7. Ewing (2022) describes the dilemma truck makers face of whether to build trucks with batteries (Traton, Volkswagen's truck unit, has made that choice), or to build trucks with fuel cells that convert hydrogen into electricity (Daimler Truck favors that choice although it does not plan to begin mass-producing a hydrogen fuel cell truck until after 2025).

Current government policies are slowing nationwide adoption of autonomous trucking by limiting their operation in some states. Aurora, for example, is testing its autonomous Class 8 trucks in Texas but cannot operate those trucks in California without human drivers. Autonomous intermodal operations could expand in states with autonomous trucking and further increase the efficiency of the nation's surface freight transportation system, but such operations would be prevented in states that do not allow autonomous trucking.

An environment that could particularly benefit from automation—or be harmed by its absence—is the delivery of cargo carried by ocean transportation from abroad, which could facilitate smooth freight flows from ports. Traffic congestion and stranded freight at West Coast ports have been a prominent source of recent disruptions in the supply chain.

Accounting for all the sources of potential benefits from autonomous trucking, the magnitude is likely to be in the hundreds of billions of dollars, or a notable fraction of the magnitude of the potential benefits from autonomous cars. Society is likely to realize the benefits from autonomous trucking sooner than it realizes the benefits of autonomous cars because trucks will operate in autonomous mode primarily on freeways instead of on more complicated city streets.

From a political perspective, autonomous trucking has the support of firms that wish to use autonomous operations and that can improve the overall performance of local and state economies by improving industry productivity and efficiency. Thus, local and state officials recognize the potential benefits of autonomous trucking, and some support its testing and eventual adoption. Accordingly, autonomous trucking may therefore pave the way for faster adoption of autonomous cars by demonstrating to the public that autonomous vehicles are safe and could significantly increase the efficiency of the transportation system and the economy.

Appendix

We assume profit-maximizing firms minimize their expected annual logistics costs, which are decomposed into the sum of ordering costs, transportation costs, holding costs, and shortage costs. In this appendix, we specify those costs mathematically and indicate the firm's logistics cost–minimization problem that we solve numerically.

ORDERING COSTS. The first component of logistics costs is the annual cost of placing orders (c_a). Annual ordering costs are the product of the number of orders per year, which is composed of the annual demand (R) divided by the order size (Q) multiplied by the cost per order (A): $c_a = (R/Q) \times A$.

TRANSPORTATION COSTS. The second component of logistics costs is annual transportation costs (c_t). Annual transportation costs depend on the number of units demanded (R) each year and the rate (F) at which the freight is being carried.

This freight rate may be affected by the quantity (Q) of units being carried per shipment, because a volume discount may be offered when shipping a greater quantity. Thus, the freight rate can be specified as $f(Q)$, where $f(\cdot)$ can be an empirically estimated relationship between the freight rate and the unit lot size. The expression for annual transportation costs is $c_t = f(Q) \times R$.

HOLDING COSTS. The third component of logistics costs is the annual cost of holding inventories (c_h). Holding costs depend on a combination of in-transit, cycle, and safety stocks. In-transit stocks are those in the process of being transported. Product demand (D) is a random variable with a mean value demanded of μ_D units per day and a standard deviation of σ_D. Transit time for a shipment is a random variable with a mean value of μ_T days and a standard deviation of σ_T. The expected level of in-transit stocks can be expressed as the product of the mean number of units demanded per day times the mean number of days each shipment is in transit ($\mu_D \times \mu_T$). The holding costs for these expected in-transit stocks then depend on the holding cost for each expected unit in transit (Y). The rest of the holding costs accrue to units on hand, as in a warehouse. These units can be broken down into cycle stock units and safety stock units. Cycle stock units are those that are on hand between shipments. Because shipment sizes are Q units and the distribution of inventory levels is uniform, the expected level of cycle stock at any point in time is simply half of the shipment size ($Q/2$). Safety stock units are those still on hand when a new shipment is received. New orders are placed when stocks reach the reorder point (s). Expected demand during the lead time before the shipment is received is μ_X. The stock level at the reorder point will be depleted by the expected lead-time demand, so the expected level of safety stock is the difference between the two, $s - \mu_X$.

To consider the effects of transportation on safety stock holding costs, mean lead-time demand can be expressed as the product of the mean lead time and the mean daily demand, $\mu_X = \mu_L \times \mu_D$. Mean lead time can be further broken down into a sum that includes the time involved in transportation, $\mu_L = \mu_T + v$, with μ_T the expected transit time and v a constant representing a fixed time spent on nontransportation activities in the order cycle (such as order preparation, order processing, manufacturing, or assembly, depending on the context). The holding costs for these expected cycle and safety stocks then depend on the holding costs for each expected unit stored in a warehouse (W). The expression for total annual holding costs is:

$$c_h = (\mu_T \times \mu_D) \times Y + (Q/2 + s - (\mu_T + v) \times \mu_D) \times W$$

SHORTAGE COSTS. The fourth and final component of logistics cost is annual shortage costs (c_s). Shortage costs include the costs of any expedited delivery to satisfy demand once inventory is depleted, plus the cost of any lost sales or lost customers that result from a shortage. In a raw materials or work-in-progress inventory, shortage costs may take the form of expedited delivery costs, overtime, or lost production. The shortage cost term depends primarily on the expected level of shortage during the lead time between each order and delivery over the year (ES). These expected shortages can be expressed as a weighted average of conditional expected shortages over the lead-time distribution

$$ES = \int (x - s) f(x)\, dx$$

where $x > s$. Total shortage costs are then derived by multiplying this expectation of the number of units short per order by the annual number of orders (R/Q) and the shortage cost per unit short (B):

$$c_s = ES \times (R/Q) \times B$$

or

$$c_s = \left[\int (x - s) f(x)\, dx \right] \times (R/Q) \times B$$

A firm is assumed to minimize total expected annual logistics costs ($EALC$), which are the sum of the ordering (c_o), transportation (c_t), holding (c_h), and shortage (c_s) cost elements:

$$EALC = c_o + c_t + c_h + c_s$$

Expressed as a function of the decision variables, reorder point (s) and reorder quantity (Q), the expected total annual logistics costs become:

$$EALC(s, Q) = [(R/Q) \times A] + [f(Q) \times R] + [\mu_T \times \mu_D \times Y + (Q/2) + s$$
$$- (\mu_T + v) \times \mu_D \times W] + \left\{ \left[\int (x - s) f(x)\, dx \right] \times (R/Q) \times B \right\}$$

For the simulations, we minimized those logistics costs using the solver function in Excel.

13

Water Transportation and Drones

CLIFFORD WINSTON AND JIA YAN

1. Introduction

Surface freight transportation is complemented by water transportation provided by barges, container and cargo ships, and tankers for domestic shipments transported on major rivers and the Great Lakes and for international shipments transported across the oceans. Drones are an innovation that could improve the freight transportation system by delivering small freight shipments and mail in a timelier fashion than current surface modes.

In this chapter, we briefly discuss how competition and innovation in water transportation and drones could further improve freight transportation performance. We also discuss appropriate government policy to realize this improvement.

2. Water Transportation

Water transportation operations, like highway and airport operations, are not governed by efficient pricing and investment of the natural water environment and the port facilities that they use. Freight transported on container and cargo ships is therefore subject to significant congestion and delays, as indicated by the increasing average number of days that containers were waiting on the docks for handling at major US ports during 2021–22. These so-called dwell times especially delayed shipments that were unloaded at the container port complex at Los Angeles and Long Beach. Shippers have sought less-congested destinations for their international shipments, which has increased dwell times at the Port of

Oakland and at other ports throughout the country, including the Port of Savannah, the Port of Charleston, and, most recently, the Port of New York and New Jersey.

Government policies also have exacerbated supply chain delays by limiting potential efficiency improvements that could be spurred by more competition and innovation in water transportation. In this section, we discuss competition and innovation primarily in ocean freight transportation, but the ideas also apply to freight transportation on rivers and lakes.

Ocean Transportation

Levinson (2006) explains that stacking containers—the basis for containerization—was facilitated by the development of a lock connected to the corners of containers that crane operators could mechanically open and close from their viewing platforms, which caused the shipping container to become the workhorse of globalization.

Recently, ocean shipping has been marked by floating traffic jams that arise because dockworkers are overwhelmed by the volume of freight to unload, dock space is not available to unload all the freight, and truck drivers are sometimes stranded at the entry to a dock and cannot access freight to put it on the truck and transport it to its destinations. Containers that cannot be unloaded also cannot be loaded, adding to delays. The breakdown of the supply chain caused freight rates to skyrocket and contributed to the rise in inflation that began in 2021.

Additional competition and innovation have long had the potential to improve the efficiency of ocean shipping and could help prevent future breakdowns of the supply chain. However, government must reform its policies to facilitate those sources of improvement.

Historically, price competition in ocean transportation had been limited by an antitrust exemption that permitted ocean carriers to fix rates at shipping conferences to prevent destructive competition (Sagers 2006). In addition, ocean carriers have formed shipping alliances, which can limit competition. Entry into ocean shipping is regulated by the 1920 Jones Act, which decrees that ships allowed to call at two consecutive American ports must be built in the United States, owned by American companies, fly the American flag, and be operated by American crews. Inefficiencies created by price and entry regulations have been compounded by inefficient operations of US ports.

The Ocean Shipping Reform Act of 1998 took a first step toward ending rate conferences by allowing shippers to negotiate contracts with carriers, causing rates to decline on certain routes (Reitzes and Sheran 2002). Disbanding all ocean liner rate conferences would effectively end the remaining price-fixing arrangements and could reduce ocean shipping rates by at least 30 percent (Fink, Mattoo, and Neagu 2002). Yet, ocean liner rate conferences still exist.

During the 1990s, ocean shipping carriers ("shipping lines") started to form strategic alliances. Such alliances have a special policy status because many countries, including the United States, China, and countries in the European Union, give alliances antitrust immunity, which enables shipping lines within the same alliance to coordinate capacity and route and network decisions.

Shipping alliances are increasingly dominating the global container shipping market and are raising anticompetitive concerns. For example, although international trade rebounded in 2021, the alliances did not respond by adding capacity that they had significantly reduced at the start of the COVID-19 pandemic. US policymakers, including Congress, the Federal Maritime Commission, and the US Department of Justice, are investigating whether shipping alliances have facilitated collusion that has elevated freight rates and contributed to inflation, and the US government has called on China and the European Union to implement joint action against the shipping alliances. Depending on the evidence, countries, including the United States, could be justified in prohibiting shipping alliances.

The 2010 Open America's Waters Act called for repealing the Jones Act, which, according to Kashian, Pagel, and Brannon (2017), would have generated a $1 billion efficiency gain by reducing the costs of ocean shipping. However, Congress did not pass the act. The Trump administration explored eliminating the Jones Act but decided against doing so without providing a clear explanation for its decision. Thus, the Jones Act continues to prevent competition that could be provided by foreign ocean container ships.

Port Operations

Most US ports are owned by a public authority, where the authority varies in different locations by federal, state, or local government. In 2021, the World Bank and IHS Markit published the Container Port Performance Index, the first effort to offer a systematic ranking of the performance of 351 ports around the world.[1] In general, US ports faired very poorly. As the report notes, the main US West Coast ports are ranked near the bottom of the 351 ports, with Los Angeles (#328), Oakland (#332), Long Beach (#333), and Tacoma (#335). The main US East Coast ports rank higher but even the best performers are not among the top 20 percent, with New York and New Jersey (#89), Savannah (#279), Virginia (#85), and Charleston (#95). The main US Gulf of Mexico port in Houston also is ranked poorly (#266).

The efficiency of US ports is reduced by the 1906 Foreign Dredge Act, which applies the same protectionist requirements to dredging vessels as the Jones Act applies to commercial shipping vessels. Grabow (2022) points out that the Foreign

1. The World Bank and S&P Global Container Port Performance Index 2020 Report, https://ihsmarkit.com/info/0521/container-port-performance-index-2020.html.

Dredge Act forces US ports to rely on dredges that generally are smaller, older, and less efficient than their foreign counterparts. US dredging firms also must pay a 50 percent duty on repairs or maintenance performed in foreign shipyards. The Dutch dredging firm Van Oord estimates that it could perform US dredging projects such as port deepenings for 60 percent of the current cost and three times faster, even if it used US crews and support vessels. Accordingly, the cost savings to government-funded projects from allowing European dredging firms to enter the US market could amount to $1 billion annually.

Although much of the discussion of US ports focuses on international trade, their inefficiencies affect domestic trade as well. Substantial US flows of goods could be shipped up and down the East Coast, the West Coast, or in and out of the Gulf of Mexico. However, much of that ocean-based shipping does not occur because of costly and inefficient ports and entry barriers to less-costly foreign ships created by the Jones Act. Some goods are therefore shipped via surface transportation when it could have been less costly to ship them via water transportation if ports and carriers had the incentive and ability to reduce their costs.

The increase in international trade caused by globalization has caused ocean carriers to use increasingly larger ships to realize economies of vehicle (container ship) size. Because those ships have difficulty fitting into most US ports, a large share of US imports are concentrated at the few ports that can accommodate large ships, such as Long Beach and Los Angeles. By concentrating traffic in a few ports along the West Coast, congestion is increased and a breakdown of the supply chain is more likely, which motivates the importance for the US port system to distribute the volume of ocean freight more evenly by increasing the number of ports that can accommodate large ships.[2]

Deregulation of Ocean Shipping and Privatization of Ports

Ocean transportation has gained attention as an unexpected source of inflation. As reported by Swanson (2022), the spot price to transport a container from China to the West Coast of the United States costs twelve times as much as it did two years ago, while the time it takes a container to make that journey has nearly doubled. The inflated out-of-pocket and delivery-time costs raise consumers' prices by increasing the prices that companies pay for source products and parts from overseas and shrink the scope of their spatial search for more efficient inputs.

The Ocean Shipping Reform Act of 2022 includes regulations that seek to improve shipping opportunities provided by foreign ocean carriers and to prevent them from charging excessive late fees, known as detention and demurrage charges. President Biden characterized the new ocean shipping legislation as an

---

2. Another major source of freight congestion derives from bottlenecks at full warehouses that prevent shippers from unloading their containers and thus quickly picking up containers from ports and rail ramps.

effective way to fight inflation; however, Biden passed on an opportunity to truly fight inflation by deregulating ocean shipping and privatizing US ports.

Deregulation of airlines and trucking occurred during a period of high inflation and could plausibly be characterized as an anti-inflation policy, especially because it succeeded in significantly reducing the price of air and surface freight transportation. Policymakers should learn from the past and pass legislation, in part to reduce inflation, that would eliminate rate conference, the Jones Act, and the Foreign Dredging Act. In addition, deregulation of ocean shipping that allows free entry on all routes would eliminate the alleged justification for ocean shipping alliances and their possible anticompetitive effects. Deregulatory actions in ocean shipping could generate billions of dollars in efficiency gains, reduce shipping rates, and improve service.

The Effects of Privatization

Privatizing ports to stimulate competition could significantly reduce their accumulated cost inefficiencies and encourage ports to improve their operations by adopting the latest technologies to improve the loading and unloading of shippers' freight and the flow-through of traffic.

US shippers that ship and receive international shipments may be located close to or far from a US port. Shippers that are located close to oceanic ports will have a competitive advantage over shippers located farther from such ports because they will incur lower shipping time and out-of-pocket costs for the domestic part of their international shipment. However, many shippers are not located near an oceanic port, and, in theory, the domestic part of their international shipment could be handled by several alternative US ports. For example, shippers in the East and Midwest could have their shipments to Japan routed through ports in San Diego, Los Angeles, Long Beach, Hueneme, Oakland, Portland, or Seattle.

Privatization of the nation's ports could create a more intense competitive environment for international freight and provide the incentive and ability for ports to make investments to increase their market share by reducing costs, using the latest technology, and increasing dredging and expanding their facilities to accommodate larger container ships. Competition among ports for freight from Asia, for example, is limited because the two ports at Los Angeles and Long Beach are among the few that can accommodate the largest ships. Thus, they typically handle more than 40 percent of imports, while their combined share has climbed to more than 50 percent during the global supply chain disruption. Private port competition that increases ports' efficiency and causes a reallocation of freight such that several US West Coast ports increase their market share of traffic from Asia while the market share of the Los Angeles and Long Beach ports declines could significantly reduce the monetary and time-related costs of ocean shipping.

Unions representing port workers have been effective at negotiating high pay and benefits for those workers. For example, union dockworkers represented by the International Longshore and Warehouse Union make an average of $171,000 per year plus free health care (Read 2020). Privatization that increases port competition could put downward pressure on labor costs, which would be passed along the supply chain. Union agreements also limit ports' hours of operations, making it more difficult to reduce ships' dwell times during supply chain disruptions. For example, ports in Asia operate twenty-four hours a day, matching the pace of factories, while the ports of Los Angeles and Long Beach generally operate only sixteen hours a day as part of labor union agreements. Although some docks eventually increased their operating hours as supply chain disruptions intensified, it is likely that the competition spurred by privatization would be necessary to increase all ports' operating hours permanently.

Privatization may overcome unionized dockworkers' resistance to the greater use of autonomous cranes and straddle carriers that can load and unload containers more quickly than manually operated vehicles used by loaders to handle containers. Automation also can reduce maritime accidents and a vessel's berthing and unberthing time at a port. The dockworkers' union has reacted to automation as a threat to high-paying jobs and is seeking in contract negotiations with US West Coast port officials to draw a line against its use (Berger 2022).

US port facilities are generally less automated and less efficient than those in other advanced economies. Their lower total factor and labor productivity results in it taking twice as long on average to move a container from a large ship at the Port of Los Angeles than it does to move a container from a large ship at top ports in China. Compared with US ports, European and Asian ports can clear backlogs more quickly because they have automated cargo-handling equipment that operates around the clock. A minority of those ports, including in China, are private. Tongzon and Heng (2005) provide evidence that privatization of ports throughout the world has led to efficiency gains and would likely generate such gains for privatized US ports.

Finally, privatization may give some smaller ports an incentive to attract more traffic and, if necessary, to expand their dock capacity. For example, smaller ports on the West Coast like Oakland and Seattle can currently handle just a fraction of the shipping containers processed at the ports of Los Angeles and Long Beach. Private owners of those ports, and others in Canada, such as Vancouver and Prince Rupert, which have an advantage of shorter sailing times to and from ports such as Shanghai, would be likely to consider new investments so they could accommodate large ships that seek alternative, less-congested ports to unload their cargo.

Autonomous Ships

The adoption of autonomous ships could help raise the performance of ocean transportation by improving routing efficiency and reducing congestion delays. Autonomous ships operate smoothly in crowded shipping lanes and close to shore and can operate 24/7 at all ports because they require far less labor on land to assist with their operations.

Avikus, a subsidiary of HD Hyundai, the world's largest shipbuilding company, announced that the ultra-large vessel *Prism Courage* completed the world's first transoceanic voyage of a large vessel using autonomous navigation technology on June 2, 2022. *Prism Courage* set off from the Gulf of Mexico and sailed through the Panama Canal before crossing the Pacific Ocean to the Boryeong LNG Terminal in South Korea. According to Avikus, the voyage took thirty-three days to complete, with route optimization increasing fuel efficiency by around 7 percent and reducing greenhouse gas emissions by around 5 percent.[3]

The *Yara Birkeland*, an autonomous container ship, began testing operations between Norwegian ports in 2022, with the expectation that it will gradually transition into autonomous navigation and operations. Policymakers can help expedite the adoption of autonomous ships by setting congestion charges at ports to reduce traffic at peak times, and by using the revenues to fund infrastructure improvements that would enable ships to engage safely in autonomous operations by communicating in real time with each other and port coordination facilities to avoid collisions.

Autonomous trucking operations, discussed in the preceding chapter, would complement autonomous water transportation operations by eliminating delays caused by manual trucking operations at ports and by expediting traffic flows in and out of ports that could reduce ships' dwell times and trucks' delivery times.

3. Drones and Delivery Robots

Drones, a new emerging technology, represent the future of a privatized mail system and the delivery of small packages and shipments. Although they were not initially designed to address the financial problems of the United States Postal Service, commercial drones have significant potential to provide more efficient service than any land-based delivery company because of their automated operations and the vast capacity in low-altitude airspace. The technology also could reduce emissions and vehicle traffic while making extremely fast deliveries in as little as five minutes.[4]

---

3. In January 2022, the ocean container ship *Mikage*, sailing under the flag of Japan, completed a two-day voyage entirely autonomously from Tsuaruga to Sakai.

4. Drones also can be used to improve transportation safety. For example, companies, such as BNSF Railway, use drones instead of employees to inspect parts of their plant that could pose safety hazards, such as underneath a highly elevated railroad bridge. States also are using drones to improve safety. For example, the Alaska and North Carolina Departments of Transportation are using a drone startup company called Skydio to inspect their bridges and highways, New York and West Virginia transportation officials are using drone inspections to lower costs and improve safety, and Connecticut's Senate passed a transportation bill that formalizes the use of drones for infrastructure inspections and traffic monitoring.

Currently, no drone delivery company in the United States is fully certified to fly everywhere without a human controlling or at least monitoring the aircraft. The Federal Aviation Administration (FAA) claims to be developing regulations that would allow it to safely issue such authorization. For the time being, commercial drone delivery services are getting them certified through the same process by which passenger aircraft are certified.

Wing, an offshoot of Google, is the first drone operator to receive US governmental approval to operate as an airline and to drop products to actual customers. It provides service in southwest Virginia and in Finland and Australia. United Parcel Service (UPS) has formed a new drone delivery subsidiary called UPS Flight Forward and has received FAA approval to operate a drone delivery network. UPS is striking agreements with health care groups to use drones to deliver medical supplies—for example, to hospital campuses in Utah and elsewhere—and is making an agreement with CVS to evaluate the use of drones for home delivery of prescriptions and other products. Finally, Amazon launched a trial of its Prime Air drone delivery service for select customers in Cambridge, England, in December 2016, and has recently received approval from the FAA to operate a fleet of delivery drones and to begin testing customer deliveries. Other companies, including Microsoft, Uber, and FedEx, have announced plans for drone delivery service trials as well.[5]

Drones also can be used to move medical supplies quickly and to reduce human contact. However, the FAA requires drones to be certified as Part 135 air carriers, a process that can take months or years to achieve. Zipline, a medical drone delivery business, has been active in Africa for years.[6] At the end of May 2021, Zipline's partner, the hospital system Novant Health in North Carolina, received an FAA waiver to enable Zipline to make its first US delivery of medical supplies from a field in Kannapolis, North Carolina, to a designated spot fifteen miles away, near Novant Health's Huntersville Medical Center. The FAA should allow all drone companies to expand their operations in a faster and more orderly fashion.[7]

Turning to the allocation of airspace capacity, the FAA recently announced that it would allow fully automated commercial drone flights without hands-on piloting or direct observation by human controllers or observers. American Robotics is the first US company to gain this approval for its network.

---

5. Dronamics is using its proprietary cargo drone, the Black Swan, to develop an international air delivery network in Europe. Drone Delivery Canada has begun operating drone flights carrying cargo from Edmonton International Airport.

6. Zipline operates one thousand drones and makes parachute deliveries globally.

7. Draganfly uses its drones to deliver vaccines in rural parts of Texas; Volansi uses its drones to provide similar medical deliveries. Drone Delivery Canada will soon begin flying supplies from a distribution center in Milton, Ontario, to the Oakville Trafalgar Memorial Hospital.

For its part, the US commercial drone industry wants to create a privately funded and operated air traffic control network separate from US air traffic control that would facilitate operations and prevent collisions. The FAA is unlikely to allow private air traffic control for drones, but it is preparing to test technologies at five US airports designed to ensure safe cohabitation of airplanes and drones. However, it is not clear how the FAA will allocate airspace for airplanes and drones efficiently. Alternatives include efficient peak-load pricing and using bidding to lease airspace (Skorup 2022). Failure to allocate airspace efficiently will compromise the potential benefits from drones, especially for shipments needed in an emergency.

Various agencies and public officials are likely to raise security concerns about drones; hence, law enforcement agencies must work constructively with the drone industry to address those concerns and to enable the private sector to develop a technologically advanced mail and small-package delivery industry.

Finally, sidewalk delivery robots are starting to make some so-called last-mile deliveries. Scout, developed by Amazon, is making deliveries in parts of the United States and Helsinki. Other companies using delivery robots include Domino's, FedEx, Walmart, and Grubhub. Delivery robots also might eventually be used to deliver mail.[8]

4. Conclusions

Greater competition and innovation in water transportation of domestic and international freight could enable the US transportation system to become more efficient and the nation to fully realize the benefits of globalization and domestic and international trade.

Deregulating ocean transportation and privatizing ports would provide incentives and opportunities to significantly improve the efficiency of ocean shipping. Autonomous water transportation could provide faster and more reliable service for cargo shipped from abroad and within the United States to ports. Ports could become more efficient by automating more of their operations. And autonomous trucks could deliver and pick up shipments at US ports more easily and with less delay and safely deliver them to receivers or could coordinate with rail to provide intermodal operations. Autonomous railroads also could ship cargo from ports to North American destinations. Finally, drones and delivery robots could increase the speed at which smaller shipments and mail reach their final destinations.

Like other parts of the US transportation system, policymakers must reform their regulatory and infrastructure policies toward freight transportation to spur the vast improvements that would result from greater competition and innovation.

---

8. We are not aware of any issues that have arisen with picking up deliveries by drones and robots.

PART IV

Synthesis and Policy Recommendations

14

Synthesis and Policy Recommendations

CLIFFORD WINSTON AND JIA YAN

1. Introduction

This book has presented detailed empirical analyses of the urban and inter-city passenger and freight transportation subsystems of the entire transportation system that greatly affect the efficiency and equity of the US economy. Unfortunately, despite its importance, the US transportation system is often taken for granted by the public because it draws relatively little attention to itself—until it does.

During 2021, a heavier-than-expected snowfall caused motorists on East Coast highways to be stuck for days; US airline pilots who caught COVID-19 and could not work caused airlines to cancel thousands of flights during the Christmas holidays and created long delays to reschedule flights; and a surge in aggregate demand and logistical problems at ports led to congestion and delays that disrupted supply chains, caused product shortages, and increased producer and consumer prices. In 2022, railroad labor unions threatened a strike that would have brought rail freight service throughout the country to a standstill just before Christmas if Congress had not intervened by passing legislation that prevented the strike.

When transportation modes and infrastructure are disrupted and prevent people and freight from moving, the broader economy is adversely affected by fewer people working and trading, productivity declining, higher inventory and logistics costs and inflation, and fewer personal interactions that could lead to new ideas and innovations.

We have argued that competition and innovation have enabled the urban and intercity passenger and freight transportation subsystems to improve significantly over time and that new sources of competition and innovation could lead to additional improvements, which also could enable the system to rid itself of persistent inefficiencies and to be more resilient and less likely to experience future calamities.

Unlike previous research, our approach has analyzed all the subsystems to draw comprehensive and integrated conclusions that identify certain policies that have increased the efficiency of parts of the transportation system, and to make a series of policy recommendations that could improve the efficiency of the entire system.

Airline, intercity bus, trucking, and rail deregulation; open skies agreements on international airline routes; and the emergence of ridesharing have reduced transportation costs and improved travel time and reliability. As a result, more people and more freight have moved more cheaply, quickly, and reliably and revitalized all sectors of the economy. Importantly, this significant improvement has been accomplished without compromising safety.

We have recommended that policymakers adopt policy reforms that enable new sources of competition and innovation that could further improve the system, including expediting the adoption of autonomous modes, air taxis, and drones; negotiating open skies agreements with all countries and granting cabotage rights to foreign airlines to begin the process of fully deregulating the global air transportation system; eliminating the Jones Act, Foreign Dredging Act, and rate conferences in ocean shipping; and privatizing airports, air traffic control, and ports.

For perspective, consider how some of those improvements could have reduced the effects of the transportation calamities that occurred in 2021. Foreign airlines granted cabotage rights could have helped passengers whose flights were cancelled to obtain alternative flights more quickly to complete their journey. Privatized US ports and ships operating without rate conferences and entry restrictions imposed by the Jones Act and Foreign Dredge Act would have the incentive and ability to improve their operations and significantly reduce the time and cost it takes to complete port improvement projects and to unload and load ships' cargo and get it moving to their final destinations. And the adoption of air taxis and drones could have provided travelers and truckers who were stuck on a highway with emergency transportation services if they were needed.

The existence of autonomous railroad freight operations in 2022 would have greatly reduced rail's dependence on a large labor force to serve the nation's shippers. Rail labor unions would have no choice but to accept the reality that railroads would be using much less labor to move trains while minimizing those costs in an even more competitive environment where they would be competing with autonomous trucks.

Historically, government has regulated prices, entry, and exit of private modes and owned and operated public modes and infrastructure because much of the transportation system appeared to be subject to market failures. However, government regulatory and operating policy inefficiencies gradually became transparent, technological change and new sources of competition indicated that some transportation markets had the potential to correct their alleged failures and the government's actual failures, and those markets proceeded to do so when given the opportunity. This theme has consistently played out in parts of the urban, intercity, and freight transportation subsystems and it could play out more fully in those subsystems.

The theme also may eventually play out as transportation in outer space evolves. Poole (2022) compares the approaches taken by the National Aeronautics and Space Administration (NASA), a federal government agency, and the private sector. NASA has been using obsolete technology, left over from the space shuttle program, to launch its Space Launch System moon rocket. Failure of its obsolete technology forced NASA to cancel its scheduled launch twice. US private sector companies, including SpaceX and Blue Origin, are launching rockets for commercial travel in outer space and, along with startup companies, are planning to go to the Moon and Mars. Private sector companies are competing on innovation and driving down costs, while NASA is stuck in the past and inflating costs to taxpayers. NASA may eventually improve the efficiency and performance of space travel, but if it does so it is likely to be by relying on services provided by a competitive market in space travel.

2. Summarizing New Sources of Competition and Innovation and Their Potential Benefits

The new sources of competition and innovation that we discussed, their potential to address the inefficiencies of the current transportation system, and their potential benefits to travelers, shippers, and the broader economy can be summarized in urban and intercity transportation as follows.

Urban Transportation

Public transit's subsidies continue to grow, and its market share continues to shrink. Automobile externalities of congestion, accidents, and emissions continue to generate large social costs. We provided evidence that ridesharing has benefited travelers by providing a superior service to taxis and transit and, for some trips, the private automobile. We also noted that private van and minibus service, which have achieved success throughout the world because of their low costs and responsive service, could improve US urban transportation if they were allowed to serve more urban areas.

Electric and autonomous vehicles could build on private van and minibus service and ridesharing and eliminate transit subsidies by enabling travelers to effectively have their own transit service and could dramatically reduce congestion, accident, and emissions externalities. The improved mobility from autonomous electric vehicles could generate enormous benefits to the broader economy and help alleviate social issues, such as social distancing during a pandemic and violent altercations arising from police stops. It is possible that the full benefits from autonomous electric vehicles would be more likely to be realized if, following successful experiments, highways were privatized. Thus, competition, if it worked effectively, would encourage highway operators to adopt efficient operations and modern technology, and to manage finances so the highway system does not experience financial crises that result in widespread bankruptcies.

Intercity Transportation

Airline and bus deregulation transformed intercity passenger transportation into an efficient, highly competitive system that generated large benefits to travelers. We provided evidence that negotiating open skies agreements with all countries and instituting global deregulation in air transportation by granting cabotage rights to foreign airlines could provide further benefits to air travelers. We also provided evidence that privatizing airports could potentially lead to more airline competition and innovations, such as heated runways, that benefit travelers, and we argued that privatizing air traffic control could make airlines' operations safer and more efficient.

Deregulation also transformed trucking and railroads into more efficient and innovative services. We provided evidence that autonomous trucking operations could substantially reduce shippers' inventory logistics costs and provide other benefits, and we argued autonomous railroad operations would strengthen rail's competitive position with autonomous trucks while further benefiting shippers.

Creating a more competitive environment by eliminating the Jones Act, the Foreign Dredge Act, and rate conferences and privatizing ports would result in more efficient ocean freight transportation. Autonomous ships and port operations would add to the improvement. Finally, the adoption of new modes (air taxis and drones) would enrich the transportation system by giving travelers and shippers new faster transportation options that would overcome the cost of distance for shorter trips more effectively than current services.

As in the case of the urban transportation system, the greatly improved intercity transportation system would generate enormous benefits to the broader economy by, for example, lowering the cost and expanding the volume of domestic and international trade and increasing agglomeration economies by facilitating more productive engagements among Americans and between Americans and individuals from foreign countries. More seamless airline and ocean travel would reduce the large costs of transferring passengers and freight in international markets.

Table 14.1. *New Sources of Competition and Innovation and Potential Welfare Gains*

Urban transportation	Potential welfare gains
Rideshare companies	Travelers benefit several billion dollars annually
Expanded private van and minibus service	Estimates not yet available
Autonomous electric shared vehicles	GNP could increase at least 1 percentage point annually and the cost of automobile emissions and accident externalities would be substantially reduced
Intercity transportation	Potential welfare gains
Granting cabotage rights	Travelers benefit at least $1.5 billion annually, not including greater benefits from seamless travel
Privatizing airports	Travelers could benefit by several billion dollars annually from private airport competition
Privatizing air traffic control	Estimates not yet available
Freight transportation	Potential welfare gains
Autonomous trucking operations	Shippers would gain at least $140 billion in lower inventory logistics costs
Autonomous rail and ocean operations	Estimates not yet available
Eliminating the Jones Act and rate conferences	Benefits to shippers would be several billion dollars annually
Privatization of ports	Estimates not yet available
Drones and air taxis	Estimates not yet available

Table 14.1 summarizes the sources of new competition and innovation that could improve the US transportation system and their potential welfare gains. Considerable uncertainty is associated with the estimates, but previous experience with deregulation indicates that predicted benefits were significantly underestimated in large part because analysts did not anticipate the full range of innovative responses that led to significant reductions in costs and improvements in service quality. The potential benefits from the new sources we discussed are so large, especially from automation, that even if we have significantly overestimated the benefits, welfare gains for the United States would still amount to hundreds of billions of dollars.

The major obstacles to obtaining those benefits are whether the innovations in autonomy will work in practice and whether policymakers will adopt policies that enable competition and innovation to flourish.

3. Concerns about Autonomous Transportation Innovations

Autonomous transportation modes represent a large part of the innovations that we have argued could greatly benefit the US transportation system and economy. However, we identified in chapter 6 the existence of naysayers who have made harsh comments about autonomous vehicles, such as, they are "one of the most hyped technology experiments of this century" and are "incapable of reversing the growing death toll on American roads for many years to come—if ever." We are not aware of similar comments directed toward autonomous trucks, trains, ocean ships, drones, and air taxis, but it is likely that the naysayers have similar beliefs that all autonomous modes will experience technological failure. An additional concern is that autonomous transportation services will be very disruptive to the transportation labor force, which will be forced to undergo a difficult adjustment during the transition to an autonomous transportation system.

Technological Failure

As noted in chapter 6, we agree with Bishop (2022) that it is premature to make any strong predictions about the effectiveness of autonomous vehicles when they are deployed. At the same time, the history of technological innovations offers some useful perspective. To the best of our knowledge, with the possible exception of the nuclear fusion industry, no US industry—or, in the case of autonomous transportation modes, no global industry—has made a large-scale investment in a new technology that generated zero returns because it failed to produce any product or service that was commercially viable.[1]

Instead, there are many examples where firms within an industry invested in a new technology that failed because it was replaced by a somewhat different technology that led to a similar but better product. In other words, there is considerable learning when firms seek to develop a new technology and there are plenty of failures until commercial success is achieved. However, while some firms fail in their efforts to develop a new technology to produce a new product or service, entire industries have yet to fail when they have made substantial investments in a new technological innovation.

As summarized by Eadicicco et al. (2017), examples of industries where firms failed but other firms subsequently succeeded include but are not limited to: BlackBerry, which was replaced by iPhone; AOL, which was replaced by Gmail and Hotmail; Palm Pilot, which was replaced by iPod and iPhone; Netscape, which was replaced by Microsoft; MySpace, which was replaced by Facebook; Segways, which were replaced by electric scooters and hoverboards; MapQuest, which was replaced by Google Maps; and TiVo, which was replaced by DVR. The process of competition, innovation, and leapfrog technologies that eclipse previous technologies will continue for the foreseeable future.

When we consider the future of autonomous modes, it is possible that some or even several automotive and technology firms will fail, for example, to develop a commercially safe and viable autonomous vehicle. However, we think it is extremely

---

1. Recently, scientists have been able for the first time to produce a fusion reaction that creates a net energy gain, which is a major milestone to develop the technology.

unlikely that the entire global autonomous vehicle industry will lose its entire $100 billion-plus investment because no firm in the world can build a safe autonomous vehicle that is a significant advance over a nonautonomous vehicle. We also doubt that consumer demand for autonomous vehicles will be insufficient to enable producers to make an adequate return on their investment.

An important feature of the autonomous vehicle industry is the extensive collaboration between producers and between producers and users. The former is important for improving the technology and for recognizing and overcoming technological challenges. The latter is important for encouraging society to realize the potential benefits of autonomous vehicles and to have a vested interest in their success.

Users of autonomous cars and shuttle services in experiments in various cities are likely to generate modest interest and excitement in the technology. However, shipping companies that collaborate with autonomous trucking services in experiments in various states can envision the potentially large benefits in reduced inventory and logistics costs from autonomous trucking, which could generate interest and excitement throughout private industry and translate into political support that could expedite testing and adoption before autonomous cars are adopted. Thus, autonomous trucks are likely to be the first autonomous vehicle operations to refute the naysayers' predictions and to eventually lead the way for autonomous cars to do the same.

Other autonomous and nonautonomous transportation technologies that we identified as emerging in intercity passenger and freight transportation are less developed both technologically and financially than autonomous cars and trucks, so considerable uncertainty still exists about their long-run commercial viability. For example, the current valuation of the emerging electric vertical takeoff and landing (eVTOL) vehicle industry is only a fraction of the commercial helicopter business, which it would be expected to displace if eVTOLs become a commercially viable transportation technology. In addition, new eVTOL infrastructure (vertiports) must attract investors and overcome public resistance to noise created by eVTOL operations. As suggested by Robert Poole, eVTOLs may be best suited commercially for regional instead of urban markets to connect cities within a few hundred miles and to use existing airports for their operations.[2]

Like any new technology, eVTOLs have both time and the potential to attract additional investment and human capital to help solve their various challenges to become a viable transportation service. Generally, the greatest threat in our view to the widespread adoption and commercial success of new transportation

---

2. Robert Poole, "Aviation Policy News: Vertiports for Regional Air Mobility, Congress Oblivious to Changing Airline Competition, and More," *Aviation Policy Newsletter*, December 15, 2021, Reason Foundation, https://reason.org/aviation-policy-news/aviation-policy-news-vertiports-for-regional-air-mobility-congress-oblivious-to-changing-airline-competition-and-more/.

technologies is poor government policy that impedes their development and adoption, not the failure of the technology.

Disruptions to Labor

Ideally, the management of firms in an industry develops an entrepreneurial relationship with its labor force to accomplish mutually shared goals of efficiency and financial success. Unfortunately, government interventions in the US transportation system have significantly discouraged that positive relationship from developing. The new sources of competition and transportation innovations that we have discussed here are likely to disrupt the transportation labor force by reducing earnings in certain jobs and by changing the types of jobs for which employers will seek workers.

Economic regulation of the intercity transportation modes created a rent-sharing relationship between firms' management and labor unions, where labor attempted to extract some of the rents that transportation firms received from regulations that limited entry and competition. Deregulation and deunionization ended rent sharing in the intercity transportation industries without ending the tensions between labor and management. As noted, in December 2022, Congress had to intercede to prevent railroad workers from going on a nationwide strike because of a lack of paid sick days.

An important difference between the deregulated railroad industry and, for example, the deregulated airline industry is that the former never experienced new low-cost entry. In contrast, the latter experienced low-cost new entrants, such as Southwest Airlines and other low-cost carriers, which intensified competition and put pressure on labor to accept lower wages and improve productivity to enable legacy carriers to compete more effectively against low-cost carriers.

Global deregulation in airlines and ocean shipping would generate new competition that puts downward pressure on workers' wages in those industries; thus, labor is likely to oppose those policies and attempt to slow their adoption. Policymakers eventually overcame labor's resistance to intercity deregulation without giving labor side payments. Policymakers are likely to respond favorably to credible evidence that international transportation deregulation could produce large social benefits in the United States and overcome labor's resistance, especially because deregulation simply calls for government to get out of the way.

Government ownership and management of transportation infrastructure and its ownership and regulation of transportation services have inflated production costs, including the cost of labor. The lack of new entry and competition has generally increased labor's earnings. However, the entry of Uber and other ridesharing companies into urban transportation markets has shown the effects of a new source of competition by depressing the earnings of drivers of regulated taxi services and the value of taxi medallions. Privatization of transit, airports, air traffic control, and ports also is likely to generate competition that depresses transportation workers' earnings. Like deregulation, privatization calls for government to simply get out of the way, so successful privatization experiments could encourage policymakers to explore various privatizations despite labor's opposition.

The entry of ridesharing companies in urban transportation portends the competitive effects of new autonomous transportation modes on labor. Autonomous vehicles are likely to reduce transit workers' earnings and autonomous trucks and trains are likely to reduce truck drivers' and rail workers' earnings. Autonomy also will reduce, if not eliminate, conventional employment in the driver seat and onboard for all modes. As discussed, the overall losses in employment are likely to be offset by workers in new classifications of employment to maintain and service autonomous vehicles and by increased productivity and greater output throughout the economy.

Nonetheless, firms' adoption of autonomous transportation operations will be very disruptive to the nation's transportation labor force and will require firms and possibly policymakers to find constructive ways to ease the potentially difficult adjustment that labor will have to make during the transition to a more automated transportation system.

Users of the Transportation System

Historically, transportation deregulation has raised concerns that certain travelers in low-density markets and so-called captive shippers of bulk commodities will be disadvantaged because their limited travel and shipping options will force them to pay higher prices. Generally, those concerns turned out to be overstated and government policies were not effective in addressing them. In any case, the changes in competition and innovation discussed here will not disadvantage any group of users and they are likely to provide expanded access to transportation for those who are least able to travel and least able to afford to travel.

4. Government Policy Recommendations and Reality

Given that we have argued that competition and innovation have been the primary sources of improvements in the US transportation system, it naturally follows that government policy that is attuned to improving the performance of the transportation system should stimulate new ways that urban, intercity, and freight transportation can be more competitive and innovative.

Policy Recommendations

We have made specific, immediate recommendations that policymakers increase competition by expanding open skies agreements, granting cabotage rights, privatizing airports and seaports, exploring highway privatization, and eliminating the Jones Act, the Foreign Dredge Act, and rate conferences. We also have recommended that policymakers increase innovation by privatizing air traffic control to modernize the system.

Looking toward the future, we have called for policymakers to increase competition and innovation by establishing testing procedures and modernizing highway, air, and water infrastructure to expedite the adoption and increase the performance of autonomous cars, trucks, air taxis, drones, and ships, and to implement efficient pricing and investment policies to enhance the efficiency of autonomous operations.

Unfortunately, policymakers have generally eschewed our immediate policy recommendations because they prefer to address transportation problems by increasing public spending and intervening to correct alleged market failures. Both policy approaches are often wasteful, and they have not significantly improved the transportation system.

In November 2021, President Biden signed the $1 trillion Infrastructure Investment and Jobs Act, which increased government spending on roads, bridges, electric-vehicle charging stations, airports, seaports, public transit, and passenger rail. However, without efficient pricing and investment guidelines, spending on roads, bridges, airports, and seaports will be excessive and unlikely to reduce congestion and improve travel. Spending public funds on electric-vehicle charging stations is not justified because the private sector should be the sole investor in those stations as motorists increase their adoption of electric vehicles. And greater public expenditures for bus and rail transit are likely to increase those modes' deficits and do little to increase their market shares.

The Surface Transportation Board's concerns about rail competition are misplaced and if they implement a policy that forces a railroad to provide reciprocal switching it is likely the policy would do more harm than good to shippers. Instead of taking steps to spur competition in ocean transportation by deregulating it, Congress is considering legislation that would hand more power to the Federal Maritime Commission by authorizing it to act against alleged anticompetitive behavior, require shipping companies to comply with certain service standards, and regulate how they impose certain fees on their customers. Again, it is unclear how more government oversight and enforcement will bring down shipping rates and costs, which are being driven in large part by soaring consumer demand and persistent bottlenecks in an inefficient transportation environment.

Policymakers have yet to take any of the actions we have recommended that have an eye toward the future to prepare the nation for autonomous transportation. The National Highway Traffic Safety Administration (NHTSA) will have an opportunity to show its interest in expediting autonomous vehicle adoption in its response to General Motors' recent petition for permission to put its Cruise Origin (Level 4 full automation within a restricted operational design domain) into commercial service. If NHTSA grants the petition, it could inform how it will grant future petitions for passenger autonomous vehicles, and how it will proceed in future rulemakings to update its Federal Motor Vehicle Safety Standards to begin the process of fully integrating autonomous vehicles into the nation's vehicle fleet. If NHTSA rejects or delays the petition, it will signal the federal government's disinterest in expediting autonomous vehicle adoption. As noted in chapter 6, NHTSA officials have thus far declined to indicate when they might act on the petition.[3]

Reality

It is important to acknowledge that, in the immediate future, policymakers are highly unlikely to adopt efficient, comprehensive reforms of their transportation policies in ways that are broadly consistent with our recommendations. Because cities compete with other cities by seeking status that is associated with having an urban rail transit system, they go to great lengths to continue to fund their systems even though they operate with large deficits and low ridership.

In chapter 3, we found that cities are willing to raise bus transit costs to support rail transit operations. In addition, the New York and Washington, DC, metropolitan areas, for example, plan to use an influx of toll revenues from new automobile pricing programs to further subsidize rail transit deficits and to fund system expansion. Thus, it is unrealistic to envision that policymakers will take any actions to reduce public transit subsidies by setting efficient fares and curtailing service where little demand for such actions exist. Similarly, policymakers pay little attention to the inefficiencies associated with publicly owned and operated airports, highways, and ports, and instead appear to perceive that they will benefit politically from continuing to spend more money on them.

So, what realistic possibilities exist for competition and innovation to further improve the US transportation system? On one hand, the US government and some foreign governments have occasionally been inclined to improve transportation by simply getting out of the way, as in the case of intercity transportation deregulation, which suggests that it is possible that policymakers would be willing to further deregulate transportation by expanding open skies agreements and eliminating the Jones Act, the Foreign Dredge Act, and rate conferences.

On the other hand, the US government is likely to move slowly to grant foreign carriers cabotage rights because it is uncertain if other countries would reciprocate. Global cabotage rights may be achieved sooner for the cargo market

---

3. NHTSA's delays in responding to petitions can amount to nearly a decade. For example, in 2013, Toyota first petitioned NHTSA to allow for adaptive beam lights. Finally, in 2022, NHTSA issued a final rule to allow adaptive beam lights, which had been used for two decades in Europe and Japan, to update the Federal Motor Vehicle Safety Standards that had allowed only high- and low-beam lights.

than for the passenger market because cargo tends to move in unbalanced flows from manufacturing to distribution centers, or from production to consumption centers, whereas passenger flows are more balanced on round trips. Countries may therefore be less likely to insist on reciprocity for cargo traffic to grant cabotage rights in their country.

Generally, it is important to realize that even if deregulatory policies are eventually implemented, they take decades to be approved because policymakers are not eager to seek market solutions to problems that they have created and have not solved, and because policymakers need to be reassured by experimental evidence in anticipation of criticisms from many ideological opponents of free markets.[4]

The federal government appeared to seriously consider corporatizing air traffic control, in part because Nav Canada served as a credible alternative model. Reforming air traffic control is still a possibility in the future. Privatization of airports, highways, and ports also may become a possibility if government authorities at state and local levels conduct privatization experiments that show that privately run transportation infrastructure facilities perform significantly better than publicly run facilities. Alternatively, a state or city government that experiences a major budgetary shortfall may decide to address it by selling a major infrastructure facility to a private operator. If the private operator improves the facility's performance, then other states or cities might consider privatizing their major infrastructure facilities.

Markets have sometimes shown that if government is unable or unwilling to reduce transportation inefficiencies, then the private sector may attempt to do so. Ridesharing was an innovation from the private sector that improved urban transportation, which, except for private cars, had generally been provided or regulated solely by the government. Autonomous modes have the potential to greatly improve the entire system and private market participants are proceeding without any government assistance. Hopefully, successful demonstrations of the technology will encourage policymakers to do their part to facilitate widespread adoption.

A plausible path therefore exists where new competition produced by additional deregulation and privatization and new innovations derived from artificial intelligence and telecommunications technology could revitalize the US transportation system. It also is possible that policymakers could make that path easier; however, they are more likely to do so if they are persuaded that the political benefits from improved transportation services for their constituents and

4. Winston (2022) provides examples of the *New York Times* publishing highly visible essays that provide a biased discussion against deregulated transportation markets and reports that the *New York Times* was unwilling to publish a response to point out and correct the biases because they have a policy of generally avoiding pieces that criticize the media.

greater international and domestic prestige would be large and that the political risks would be small.

Historically, a select group of visionary political and transportation industry leaders have been able to successfully make the political case for instituting transportation policies that improved the system's performance and raised public welfare. A new generation of leaders must come forward to do the same.

References

Abadie, Alberto, and Guido Imbens. 2011. "Bias-Corrected Matching Estimators for Average Treatment Effects." *Journal of Business and Economic Statistics* 29 (1): 1–11.

Adler, Martin W., Stefanie Peer, and Tanja Sinozic. 2019. "Autonomous, Connected, Electric Shared Vehicles (ACES) and Public Finance: An Explorative Analysis." *Transportation Research Interdisciplinary Perspectives* 2: article 10038.

Alderighi, Marco, Alessandro Cento, Peter Nijkamp, and Piet Rietveld. 2012. "Competition in the European Aviation Market: The Entry of Low-Cost Airlines." *Journal of Transport Geography* 24: 223–33.

Allen, Treb, and Costas Arkolakis. 2014. "Trade and the Topography of the Spatial Economy." *Quarterly Journal of Economics* 129 (3): 1085–140.

Anand, Pritha, Ali Nahvi, Halil Ceylan, Vasiliki Dimitra Pyrialakou, Konstantina Gkritza, Kasthurirangan Gopalakrishnan, Sunghwan Kim, and Peter C. Taylor. 2017. "Energy and Financial Viability of Hydronic Heated Pavement Systems." Report DOT/FAA/TC-17/47. US Department of Transportation.

Anderson, Michael L. 2014. "Subways, Strikes, and Slowdowns: The Impacts of Public Transit on Traffic Congestion." *American Economic Review* 104 (9): 2763–96.

Anderson, Michael L., and Lucas W. Davis. 2021. "Uber and Alcohol-Related Traffic Fatalities." Working Paper 29071. National Bureau of Economic Research.

Angrist, Joshua D., Sydnee Caldwell, and Jonathan V. Hall. 2021. "Uber versus Taxi: A Driver's Eye View." *American Economic Journal: Applied Economics* 13 (3): 272–308.

Aryal, Gaurab, Federico Cilberto, and Benjamin T. Leyden. 2022. "Coordinated Capacity Reductions and Public Communication in the Airline Industry." *Review of Economic Studies* 89 (6): 3055–84.

Austen, Ian. 2022. "Canada's Slow and Troubled Path to Rapid Transit." *New York Times*, July 9.

Azar, José, Martin C. Schmalz, and Isabel Tecu. 2018. "Anticompetitive Effects of Common Ownership." *Journal of Finance* 73 (4): 1513–65.

Bachwich, Alexander R., and Michael D. Wittman. 2017. "The Emergence and Effects of the Ultra-Low-Cost Carrier (ULCC) Business Model in the US Airline Industry." *Journal of Air Transport Management* 62: 155–64.

Baker, Jonathan B., and Timothy F. Bresnahan. 1985. "The Gains from Merger or Collusion in Product-Differentiated Industries." *Journal of Industrial Economics* 33 (4): 427–44.

Baranowski, Michael R., and Nathaniel S. Zebrowski. 2022. "Reciprocal Switching." Verified Statement and Written Testimony before the Surface Transportation Board, STB Ex Parte no. 711 (Sub–no. 1), February 14.

Barrett, Sean D. 2004. "The Sustainability of the Ryanair Model." *International Journal of Transport Management* 2 (2): 89–98.

Basso, Leonardo J., and Anming Zhang. 2007. "An Interpretative Survey of Analytical Models of Airport Pricing." In *Advances in Airline Economics*, vol. 2, edited by Darin Lee. Elsevier.

Baumgaertner, Emily, and Russ Mitchell. 2021. "Car Crash Deaths have Surged during Covid-19 Pandemic. Here's Why." *Los Angeles Times*, December 8.

Baum-Snow, Nathaniel, and Matthew E. Kahn. 2005. "Effects of Urban Rail Transit Expansions: Evidence from Sixteen Cities, 1970–2000." *Brookings–Wharton Papers on Urban Affairs*: 147–206.

Bereskin, C. Gregory. 2001. "Sequential Estimation of Railroad Costs for Specific Traffic." *Transportation Journal* 40 (3): 33–45.

Berger, Paul. 2022. "A Deep Divide on Automation Hangs over West Coast Port Labor Talks." *Wall Street Journal*, June 9.

Bishop, Richard. 2022. "Self-Driving Cars: An Epidemic of Questionable Assertions." *Forbes*, February 21.

Bitzan, John D., and Theodore E. Keeler. 2003. "Productivity Growth and Some of Its Determinants in the Deregulated U.S. Railroad Industry." *Southern Economic Journal* 70 (2): 232–53.

Blinder, Alan S., and Louis J. Maccini. 1991. "Taking Stock: A Critical Assessment of Recent Research on Inventories." *Journal of Economic Perspectives* 5 (1): 73–96.

Blundell, Richard W., and James L. Powell. 2004. "Endogeneity in Semiparametric Binary Response Models." *Review of Economic Studies* 71 (3): 655–79.

Boguslaski, Charles, Harumi Ito, and Darin Lee. 2004. "Entry Patterns in the Southwest Airlines Route System." *Review of Industrial Organization* 25 (3): 317–50.

Borenstein, Severin, and James B. Bushnell. 2022. "Do Two Electricity Pricing Wrongs Make a Right? Cost Recovery, Externalities, and Efficiency." *American Economic Journal: Economic Policy* 14 (4): 80–110.

Borrás, Jo. 2022. "BP Claims EV Charging Stations 'On the Cusp' of Being More Profitable than Gas Pumps." *Electrek*, January 16.

Bosman, Julie, Sophie Kasakove, Jill Cowan, and Richard Fausset. 2022. "Cities Want to Return to Prepandemic Life. One Obstacle: Transit Crime." *New York Times*, April 25.

Brancaccio, Giulia, Myrto Kalouptsidi, and Theodore Papageorgiou. 2020. "Geography, Transportation, and Endogenous Trade Costs." *Econometrica* 88 (2): 657–91.

Brinkman, Jeffrey, and Jeffrey Lin. 2022. "The Costs and Benefits of Fixing Downtown Freeways." *Economic Insights* (Federal Reserve Bank of Philadelphia), quarter 1: 17–22.

Brueckner, Jan K., Darin N. Lee, and Ethan S. Singer. 2011. "Alliances, Codesharing, Antitrust Immunity, and International Airfares: Do Previous Patterns Persist?" *Journal of Competition Law and Economics* 7 (3): 573–602.

———. 2013. "Airline Competition and Domestic US Airfares: A Comprehensive Reappraisal." *Economics of Transportation* 2 (1): 1–17.

———. 2014. "City-Pairs versus Airport-Pairs: A Market-Definition Methodology for the Airline Industry." *Review of Industrial Organization* 44 (1): 1–25.

Bunten, Devin Michelle, Ellen Fu, Lyndsey Rolheiser, and Christopher Severen. 2023. "The Problem Has Existed over Endless Years: Racialized Difference in Commuting, 1980–2019." *Journal of Urban Economics*, forthcoming.

Burtraw, Dallas. 1996. "The SO_2 Emissions Trading Program: Cost Savings without Allowance Trades." *Contemporary Economic Policy* 14 (2): 79–94.

Calfee, John, and Clifford Winston. 1998. "The Value of Automobile Travel Time: Implications for Congestion Policy." *Journal of Public Economics* 69 (1): 83–102.

Carlton, Dennis, Mark Israel, Ian MacSwain, and Eugene Orlov. 2019. "Are Legacy Airline Mergers Pro- or Anti-Competitive? Evidence from Recent U.S. Airline Mergers." *International Journal of Industrial Organization* 62: 58–95.

Chandar, Bharat, Uri Gneezy, John A. List, and Ian Muir. 2019. "The Drivers of Social Preferences: Evidence from a Nationwide Tipping Field Experiment." Working Paper 26380. National Bureau of Economic Research.

Chapple, Karen, Hannah Moore, Michael Leong, Daniel Huang, Amir Forouhar, Laura Schmahmann, Joy Wang, and Jeff Allen. 2023. "The Death of Downtown? Pandemic Recovery Trajectories across 62 North American Cities." Research brief. Downtown Recovery.

Cho, Woohyun, Robert J. Windle, and Martin E. Dresner. 2015. "The Impact of Low-Cost Carriers on Airport Choice in the US: A Case Study of the Washington–Baltimore Region." *Transportation Research Part E: Logistics and Transportation Review* 81: 141–57.

Cho, Woohyun, Robert J. Windle, and Christian Hofer. 2012. "Route Competition in Multi-Airport Cities: An Analysis of US Air Fares." *Transportation Journal* 51 (3): 265–88.

Choi, Ki-Hong, and Choon-Geol Moon. 1997. "Generalized Extreme Value Model and Additively Separable Generator Function." *Journal of Econometrics* 76 (1): 129–40.

Chu, Junhong, Yige Duan, Xianling Yang, and Li Wang. 2021. "The Last Mile Matters: Impact of Dockless Bike Sharing on Subway Housing Price Premium." *Management Science* 67 (1): 297–316.

Cline, Andrew. 2022. "Biden's EV Push May Hit Mining Regs Pothole." *Inside Sources*, April 8.

Cohen, Peter, Robert Hahn, Jonathan Hall, Steven Levitt, and Robert Metcalfe. 2016. "Using Big Data to Estimate Consumer Surplus: The Case of Uber." Working Paper 22627. National Bureau of Economic Research.

Cook, Cody, Rebecca Diamond, Jonathan V. Hall, John A. List, and Paul Oyer. 2021. "The Gender Earnings Gap in the Gig Economy: Evidence from over a Million Rideshare Drivers." *Review of Economic Studies* 88 (5): 2210–38.

Correal, Annie. 2018. "Inside the Dollar Van Wars." *New York Times*, June 8.

Cosslett, Stephen R. 1983. "Distribution-Free Maximum Likelihood Estimation of the Binary Response Model." *Econometrica* 51 (3): 765–82.

Cramer, Judd, and Alan B. Krueger. 2016. "Disruptive Change in the Taxi Business: The Case of Uber." *American Economic Review* 106 (5): 177–82.

Davidson, Russell, and James G. MacKinnon. 1981. "Several Tests for Model Specification in the Presence of Alternative Hypotheses." *Econometrica* 49 (3): 781–93.

Davis, River. 2021. "A City Tailor-Made for Self-Driving Cars? Toyota Is Building One." *Bloomberg*, April 26.

de Freytas-Tamura, Kimiko. 2019. "Can 'Scooby Doo' and the Rest of the Dollar Vans Go High-Tech?" *New York Times*, December 11.

Dorsey, Jackson, Ashley Langer, and Shaun McRae. 2022. "Fueling Alternatives: Gas Station Choice and the Implications for Electric Charging." Working Paper 29831. National Bureau of Economic Research.

Dresner, Martin, Jiun-Sheng Chris Lin, and Robert Windle. 1996. "The Impact of Low-Cost Carriers on Airport and Route Competition." *Journal of Transport Economics and Policy* 30 (3): 309–28.

Duranton, Giles, and Diego Puga. 2019. "Urban Growth and Its Aggregate Implications." Working Paper 26591. National Bureau of Economic Research.

Eadicicco, Lisa, Matt Peckham, John Patrick Pullen, and Alex Fitzpatrick. 2017. "The 20 Most Successful Technology Failures of All Time." *Time*, April 3.

Energy Information Administration (EIA). 1995. "Coal Production Report." Form EIA-7A. US Department of Energy.

Engel, Eduardo, Ronald D. Fischer, and Alexander Galetovic. 2021. "When and How to Use Public–Private Partnerships in Infrastructure: Lessons from the International Experience." In *Economic Analysis and Infrastructure Investment*, edited by Edward L. Glaeser and James M. Poterba. University of Chicago Press.

Ewing, Jack. 2022. "Truck Makers Face a Tech Dilemma: Batteries or Hydrogen?" *New York Times*, April 11.

Ewing, Jack, and Neal E. Boudette. 2022. "Why This Could Be a Critical Year for Electric Cars." *New York Times*, February 8.

Federal Energy Regulatory Commission (FERC). 1995. "Monthly Report of Cost and Quality of Fuels for Electric Plants." Form 423. US Department of Energy.

Ferris, David. 2023. "How Carmakers are Crafting the EV-Charging Experience." *Energywire*, January 9.

Fink, Carsten, Aaditya Mattoo, and Ileana Cristina Neagu. 2002. "Trade in International Maritime Services: How Much Does Policy Matter?" *World Bank Economic Review* 16 (1): 81–108.

Fosgerau, Mogens, and André de Palma. 2013. "The Dynamics of Urban Traffic Congestion and the Price of Parking." *Journal of Public Economics* 105: 106–15.

Friedlaender, Ann F. 1965. *The Interstate Highway System: A Study in Public Investment*. North-Holland.

Friedlaender, Ann F., and Richard Spady. 1981. *Freight Transport Regulation: Equity, Efficiency, and Competition in the Rail and Trucking Industries*. MIT Press.

Friedman, Milton, and Daniel J. Boorstin. 1996. "How to Plan and Pay for the Safe and Adequate Highways We Need." In *Roads in a Market Economy*, edited by Gabriel Roth. Avebury Technical.

Gao, Yang, and David Levinson. 2021. "COVID-19, Travel Time Reliability, and the Emergence of a Double-Humped Peak Period." *Findings* (August).

Gelinas, Nicole. 2022a. "Train Wrecks." *Washington Examiner*, June 2.

———. 2022b. "Whatever Happened to Congestion Pricing?" *City Journal*, June 23.

George, Justin. 2022a. "1 in 3 Metrobus Rides Goes Unpaid amid Rise in Fare Evasions during Pandemic." *Washington Post*, February 8.

———. 2022b. "As Train Shortage Eases, Metro and Bus Systems Prepare for Silver Line." *Washington Post*, October 26.

———. 2022c. "Fare Evasion in DC Is Rising. Money Troubles Are Pushing Metro to Confront It." *Washington Post*, October 1.

Gittleman, Maury, and Kristen Monaco. 2019. "Automation Isn't About to Make Truckers Obsolete." *Harvard Business Review*, September 18.

Gómez-Ibáñez, José A., and John R. Meyer. 1984. *Autos, Transit, and Cities*. Harvard University Press.

Goodman-Bacon, Andrew. 2021. "Difference-in-Differences with Variation in Treatment Timing." *Journal of Econometrics* 225 (2): 254–77.

Goolsbee, Austan, and Chad Syverson. 2008. "How Do Incumbents Respond to the Threat of Entry? Evidence from the Major Airlines." *Quarterly Journal of Economics* 123 (4): 1611–33.

Gorback, Caitlin. 2021. "Ridesharing and the Redistribution of Economic Activity." Working paper.

Gore, Christina. 2021. "What Drives Battery Electric Vehicle Adoption? Willingness to Pay to Reduce Emissions through Vehicle Choice." Job Market Paper. Ohio State University.

Grabow, Colin. 2022. "Dredging Protectionism." *Regulation* 45 (2): 6–7.

Green, Richard K. 2007. "Airports and Economic Development." *Real Estate Economics* 35 (1): 91–112.

Greene, William H. 2003. *Econometric Analysis* (5th ed.). Prentice Hall.

Grimm, Curtis, and Clifford Winston. 2000. "Competition in the Deregulated Railroad Industry: Sources, Effects, and Policy Issues." In *Deregulation of Network Industries: What's Next?* edited by Sam Peltzman and Clifford Winston. Brookings Institution Press.

Grimm, Curtis, Clifford Winston, and Carol Evans. 1992. "Foreclosure of Railroad Markets: A Test of Chicago Leverage Theory." *Journal of Law and Economics* 35 (2): 295–310.

Groom, Nichola, and Tina Bellon. 2021. "EV Rollout Will Require Huge Investments in Strained U.S. Power Grids." Reuters, March 5.

Hall, Jonathan D., Craig Palsson, and Joseph Price. 2018. "Is Uber a Substitute or Complement for Public Transit?" *Journal of Urban Economics* 108 (6): 36–50.

Hall, Jonathan V., and Alan B. Krueger. 2018. "An Analysis of the Labor Market for Uber's Driver-Partners in the United States." *Industrial and Labor Relations Review* 71 (3): 705–32.

Harrison, David. 2023. "America Has Too Much Parking. Really." *Wall Street Journal,* April 2.

Holland, Stephen P., Erin T. Mansur, Nicholas Z. Muller, and Andrew J. Yates. 2016. "Are There Environmental Benefits from Driving Electric Vehicles? The Importance of Local Factors." *American Economic Review* 106 (12): 3700–29.

———. 2020. "Decompositions and Policy Consequences of an Extraordinary Decline in Air Pollution from Electricity Generation." *American Economic Journal: Economic Policy* 12 (4): 244–74.

Holland, Stephen P., Erin T. Mansur, and Andrew J. Yates. 2021. "The Electric Vehicle Transition and the Economics of Banning Gasoline Vehicles." *American Economic Journal: Economic Policy* 13 (3): 316–44.

Hoppe, Edward J. 2001. "Evaluation of Virginia's First Heated Bridge." *Transportation Research Record* 1741 (1): 199–206.

Horowitz, Joel L. 2011. "Applied Nonparametric Instrumental Variables Estimation." *Econometrica* 79 (2): 347–94.

Howell, Sabrina T., Yeejin Jang, Hyeik Kim, and Michael S. Weisbach. 2022. "All Clear for Takeoff: Evidence from Airports on the Effects of Infrastructure Privatization." Working Paper 30544. National Bureau of Economic Research.

Hughes, Jonathan E., Daniel Kaffine, and Leah Kaffine. 2022. "Decline in Traffic Congestion Increased Accident Severity in the Wake of COVID-19." *Transportation Research Record* 2677 (4): 892–903.

Ivaldi, Marc, and Gerard J. McCullough. 2001. "Density and Integration Effects on Class I U.S. Freight Railroads." *Journal of Regulatory Economics* 19 (2): 161–82.

Jerch, Rhiannon, Matthew E. Kahn, and Shanjun Li. 2017. "The Efficiency of Local Government: The Role of Privatization and Public Sector Unions." *Journal of Public Economics* 154: 95–121.

Jia, Panle. 2008. "What Happens When Wal-Mart Comes to Town: An Empirical Analysis of the Discount Retail Industry." *Econometrica* 76 (6): 1263–316.

Kahneman, Daniel, and Alan B. Krueger. 2006. "Developments in the Measurement of Subjective Well-Being." *Journal of Economic Perspecitves* 20 (1): 3–24.

Kashian, Russ, Jeff Pagel, and Ike Brannon. 2017. "The Jones Act in Perspective: A Survey of Costs and Effects of the 1920 Merchant Marine Act." Grassroot Institute of Hawaii.

Keeler, Theodore E., and John S. Ying. 1988. "Measuring the Benefits of a Large Public Investment: The Case of the U.S. Federal-Aid Highway System." *Journal of Public Economics* 36 (1): 69–85.

Koustas, Dmitri, James Parrott, and Michael Reich. 2020. "New York City's Gig Driver Pay Standard: Effects on Drivers, Passengers, and the Companies." New School, Center for New York City Affairs.

LaLonde, Bernard J., Martha C. Cooper, and Thomas G. Noordewier. 1988. *Customer Service: A Management Perspective.* Council of Logistics Management.

Langer, Ashley, Vikram Maheshri, and Clifford Winston. 2017. "From Gallons to Miles: A Disaggregate Analysis of Automobile Travel and Externality Taxes." *Journal of Public Economics* 152: 34–46.

Lave, Charles, and Lester Lave. 1999. "Fuel Economy and Auto Safety Regulation: Is the Cure Worse than the Disease?" In *Essays in Transportation Economics and Policy: A Handbook in Honor of John R. Meyer*, edited by José A. Gómez-Ibáñez, William B. Tye, and Clifford Winston. Brookings Institution Press.

Leard, Benjamin, and Jianwei Xing. 2020. "What Does Ridesharing Replace?" Working Paper 20-03. Resources for the Future.

Leslie, Alex, and Dan Murray. 2022. "An Analysis of the Operational Costs of Trucking: 2022 Update." American Transportation Research Institute.

Levelton Consultants. 2007. "Guidelines for the Selection of Snow and Ice Control Materials to Mitigate Environmental Impacts." Report 577. National Cooperative Highway Research Program.

Levinson, Marc. 2006. *The Box: How the Shipping Container Made the World Smaller and the World Economy Bigger.* Princeton University Press.

Ley, Ana. 2022. "When the Only Way to Get to Work Is This Slow Bus." *New York Times*, May 31.

Li, Shanjun, Lang Tong, Jianwei Xing, and Yiyi Zhou. 2017. "The Market for Electric Vehicles: Indirect Network Effects and Policy Design." *Journal of the Association of Environmental and Resource Economists* 4 (1): 89–133.

Li, Ziru, Chen Liang, Yili Hong, and Zhongju Zhang. 2022. "How Do On-Demand Ridesharing Services Affect Traffic Congestion? The Moderating Role of Urban Compactness." *Production and Operations Management* 31 (1): 239–58.

Lieberman, Ben. 2021. "Why So Many Subsidies for Electric Vehicles?" *InsideSources*, February 23.

Lindsey, Robin. 2012. "Road Pricing and Investment." *Economics of Transportation* 1 (1): 49–63.

Liu, Meng, Erik Brynjolfsson, and Jason Dowlatabadi. 2021. "Do Digital Platforms Reduce Moral Hazard? The Case of Uber and Taxis." *Management Science* 67 (8): 4665–85.

Lokshin, Michael M., and David Newsom. 2020. "Automated Transport Could Propel Development Forward. Can We Turn the Vision into Reality?" *World Bank Blogs*, August 11.

Lund, John W. 1999. "Reconstruction of a Pavement Geothermal Deicing System." *Geo-Heat Center Quarterly Bulletin* 20 (1): 14–17.

Luo, Dan. 2014. "The Price Effects of the Delta/Northwest Airline Merger." *Review of Industrial Organization* 44 (1): 27–48.

Maheshri, Vikram, and Clifford Winston. 2016. "Did the Great Recession Keep Bad Drivers Off the Road?" *Journal of Risk and Uncertainty* 52 (3): 255–80.

Malyshkina, Nataliya V., and Fred Mannering. 2008. "Effect of Increases in Speed Limits on Severities of Injuries in Accidents." *Transportation Research Record* 2083 (1): 122–27.

Mannering, Fred, and Clifford Winston. 1991. "Brand Loyalty and the Decline of American Automakers." *Brookings Papers on Economic Activity: Microeconomics*: 67–114.

Marsh, Joanna. 2022. "Railroads, Union Clash over Use of Track Inspection Technology." *FreightWaves*, May 27.

Matulka, Rebecca. 2014. "The History of the Electric Car." US Department of Energy.

Matzkin, Rosa L. 1992. "Nonparametric Identification and Distribution-Free Estimation of the Binary Threshold Crossing and the Binary Choice Models." *Econometrica* 60 (2): 239–70.

McWeeny, Dennis B. 2019. "Spatial Competition in the Airline Industry." Job Market Paper. University of Wisconsin.

Meredith-Karam, Patrick, Hui Kong, Shenhao Wang, and Jinhua Zhao. 2021. "The Relationship between Ridehailing and Public Transit in Chicago: A Comparison before and after COVID-19." *Journal of Transport Geography* 97: article 103219.

Meyer, John R., John F. Kain, and Martin Wohl. 1965. *The Urban Transportation Problem*. Harvard University Press.

Meyer, John R., Merton J. Peck, John Stenason, and Charles Zwick. 1959. *Economics of Competition in the Transportation Industries*. Harvard University Press.

Minsk, L. David. 1999. "Heated Bridge Technology." Report FHWA-RD-99-158. US Department of Transportation.

Mohring, Herbert, and Harold F. Williamson Jr. 1969. "Scale and 'Industrial Reorganisation' Economies of Transport Improvements." *Journal of Transport Economics and Policy* 3 (3): 251–71.

Monte, Fernando, Stephen J. Redding, and Esteban Rossi-Hansberg. 2018. "Commuting, Migration, and Local Employment Elasticities." *American Economic Review* 108 (12): 3855–90.

Morrison, Steven A. 2001. "Actual, Adjacent, and Potential Competition: Estimating the Full Effect of Southwest Airlines." *Journal of Transport Economics and Policy* 35 (2): 239–56.

Morrison, Steven A., and Clifford Winston. 1985. "An Econometric Analysis of the Demand for Intercity Passenger Transportation." *Research in Transportation Economics* 2: 213–35.

———. 1986. *The Economic Effects of Airline Deregulation*. Brookings Institution Press.

———. 1987. "Empirical Implications and Tests of the Contestability Hypothesis." *Journal of Law and Economics* 30 (1): 53–66.

———. 1995. *The Evolution of the Airline Industry*. Brookings Institution Press.

———. 1999. "Regulatory Reform of U.S. Intercity Transportation." In *Essays in Transportation Economics and Policy: A Handbook in Honor of John R. Meyer*, edited by José A. Gómez-Ibáñez, William B. Tye, and Clifford Winston. Brookings Institution Press.

———. 2000. "The Remaining Role for Government Policy in the Deregulated Airline Industry." In *Deregulation of Network Industries: What's Next?* edited by Sam Peltzman and Clifford Winston. Brookings Institution Press.

———. 2007. "Another Look at Airport Congestion Pricing." *American Economic Review* 97 (5): 1970–77.

———. 2008. "The Effect of FAA Expenditures on Air Travel Delays." *Journal of Urban Economics* 63 (2): 669–78.

Morrison, Steven A., Clifford Winston, and Tara Watson. 1999. "Fundamental Flaws of Social Regulation: The Case of Airplane Noise." *Journal of Law and Economics* 42 (2): 723–44.

Nunes, Ashley, Lucas Woodley, and Philip Rossetti. 2022. "Re-Thinking Procurement Incentives for Electric Vehicles to Achieve Net-Zero Emissions." *Nature Sustainability* 5: 527–32.

Olatubi, Williams O., and David E. Dismukes. 2000. "A Data Envelopment Analysis of the Levels and Determinants of Coal-Fired Electric Power Generation Performance." *Utilities Policy* 9 (2): 47–59.

Oum, Tae H., Jia Yan, and Chunyan Yu. 2008. "Ownership Forms Matter for Airport Efficiency: A Stochastic Frontier Investigation of Worldwide Airports." *Journal of Urban Economics* 64 (2): 422–35.

Perrine, Kenneth, Kara Kockelman, and Yantao Huang. 2020. "Anticipating Long-Distance Travel Shifts Due to Self-Driving Vehicles." *Journal of Transport Geography* 82: article 102547.

Picard, Francois. 2022. "Driverless Trucks Set to Take Over Roads in Texas." RTE News, January 21.

Poole, Robert. 2022. "The Last Gasp of Twentieth-Century NASA." *Wall Street Journal*, September 1.

Porter, Robert H. 1983. "A Study of Cartel Stability: The Joint Executive Committee, 1880–1886." *Bell Journal of Economics* 14 (2): 301–14.

Powell, James L. 1994. "Estimation of Semiparametric Models." In *Handbook of Econometrics*, vol. 4, edited by Robert F. Engle and Daniel L. McFadden. North-Holland.

Quiroz-Gutierrez, Marco. 2021. "It Could Take Nearly a Decade for Public Transit to Return to Pre-Pandemic Levels." *Fortune*, November 7.

Rapson, David S., and Erich Muehlegger. 2021. "The Economics of Electric Vehicles." Working Paper 29093. National Bureau of Economic Research.

Read, Richard. 2020. "A West Coast Union Faces Bankruptcy. Here's Why Unions Nationwide Are Unnerved." *Los Angeles Times*, January 28.

Reiss, Aaron. 2014. "New York's Shadow Transit." *New Yorker*, June 27.

Reitzes, James D., and Kelli L. Sheran. 2002. "Rolling Seas in Liner Shipping." *Review of Industrial Organization* 20 (1): 51–59.

Retallack, Angus Eugene, and Bertram Ostendorf. 2019. "Current Understanding of the Effects of Congestion on Traffic Accidents." *International Journal of Environmental Research and Public Health* 16 (19): 1–13.

Roback, Paul, and Julie Legler. 2021. *Beyond Multiple Linear Regression: Applied Generalized Linear Models and Multilevel Models in R.* CRC Press.

Romer, Paul M. 1990. "Endogenous Technological Change." *Journal of Political Economy* 98 (5): S71–S102.

Rosenbaum, Paul R., and Donald B. Rubin. 1985. "Constructing a Control Group Using Multivariate Matched Sampling Methods that Incorporate the Propensity Score." *American Statistician* 39 (1): 33–38.

Rosenberg, Rebecca. 2022. "NYC Fare Beaters on Bus, Subway Lines Costing Taxpayers Millions." Fox News, February 23.

Rosenthal, Brian. 2017. "The Most Expensive Mile of Subway Track on Earth." *New York Times*, December 28.

Rothe, Christophe. 2009. "Semiparametric Estimation of Binary Response Models with Endogenous Regressors." *Journal of Econometrics* 153 (1): 51–64.

Rubin, Jonathan, Per E. Gårder, Charles E. Morris, Kenneth L. Nichols, John M. Peckenham, Peggy McKee, Adam Stern, and T. Olaf Johnson. 2010. "Maine Winter Roads: Salt, Safety, Environment and Cost." Margaret Chase Smith Policy Center, University of Maine.

Ryder System and the Socially Aware Mobility Lab. 2021. "The Impact of Autonomous Trucking: A Case-Study of Ryder's Dedicated Transportation Network."

Sagers, Chris. 2006. "The Demise of Regulation in Ocean Shipping: A Study in the Evolution of Competition Policy and the Predictive Power of Microeconomics." *Vanderbilt Journal of Transnational Law* 39 (3): 779–818.

Said, Carolyn. 2019. "On-Transit Shuttles to Serve Apple Hometown's Transit Desert." *San Francisco Chronicle*, October 7.

Sarika, Kemal, and Ilhan Or. 2007. "Efficiency Assessment of Turkish Power Plants Using Data Envelopment Analysis." *Energy* 32 (8): 1484–99.

Scherer, Frederic M., and David Ross. 1990. *Industrial Market Structure and Economic Performance* (3rd ed.). Houghton Mifflin.

Schmidt, Stephen. 2001. "Market Structure and Market Outcomes in Deregulated Rail Freight Markets." *International Journal of Industrial Organization* 19 (1–2): 99–131.

Schulz, Dorothy Moses. 2022. "The Gentrification of Fare Evasion." *City Journal*, May 3.

Scribner, Marc. 2021a. "Increasing Access to Cars Advances More Equitable Outcomes." Reason Foundation, June 21.

———. 2021b. "Pathways and Policy for Twenty-First Century Freight Rail." Reason Foundation, September 8.

Shatz, Howard J., Karin E. Kitchens, Sandra Rosenbloom, and Martin Wachs. 2011. *Highway Infrastructure and the Economy: Implications for Federal Policy.* RAND Corporation.

Shen, Weibin, Halil Ceylan, Kasthurirangan Gopalakrishnan, Sunghwan Kim, Peter C. Taylor, and Chris R. Rehmann. 2016. "Life Cycle Assessment of Heated Apron Pavement System Operations." *Transportation Research Part D: Transport and Environment* 48: 316–31.

Shen, Ying. 2017. "Market Competition and Market Price: Evidence from United/Continental Airline Merger." *Economics of Transportation* 10: 1–7.

Shepardson, David, Hyunyoo Jin, and Joseph White. 2022. "Self-Driving Car Companies Zoom Ahead, Leaving U.S. Regulators Behind." Reuters, February 2.

Shirley, Chad, and Clifford Winston. 2004. "Firm Inventory Behavior and the Returns from Highway Infrastructure Investments." *Journal of Urban Economics* 55 (2): 398–415.

Shi, Xianming, Laura Fay, Chase Gallaway, Kevin Volkening, Marijean M. Peterson, Tongyan Pan, Andrew Creighton, Collins Lawlor, Stephanie Mumma, Yajun Liu, and Tuan Anh Nguyen. 2009. "Evaluation of Alternative Anti-Icing and Deicing Compounds Using Sodium Chloride and Magnesium Chloride as Baseline Deicers—Phase I." Report CDOT-2009-1. Colorado Department of Transportation.

Shoup, Donald. 2011. *The High Cost of Free Parking.* Planners Press.

Shrago, Brad. 2022. "The Spatial Effects of Entry on Airfares in the U.S. Airline Industry." *Economics of Transportation* 30: 1–18.

Siddiqui, Faiz. 2022. "How Auto Regulators Played Mind Games with Elon Musk." *Washington Post*, March 28.

Skorup, Brent. 2022. "Drone Airspace: A New Global Asset Class." Center for the Study of Partisanship and Ideology.

Small, Kenneth A., and Erik T. Verhoef. 2007. *The Economics of Urban Transportation.* Routledge.

Small, Kenneth A., Clifford Winston, and Jia Yan. 2005. "Uncovering the Distribution of Motorists' Preferences for Travel Time and Reliability." *Econometrica* 73 (4): 1367–82.

Smith, Adam. 1776. *An Inquiry into the Nature and Causes of the Wealth of Nations.* W. Strahan and T. Cadell.

Smith, Kevin. 2019. "Rise of the Machines: Rio Tinto Breaks New Ground with AutoHaul." *International Railway Journal*, August 9.

Smyth, Mark, and Brian Pearce. 2008. "Air Travel Demand." *Economics Briefing* 9. International Air Transport Association.

Solow, Robert M. 1957. "Technological Change and the Aggregate Production Function." *Review of Economics and Statistics* 39 (3): 312–20.

Starkie, David. 2009. "The Airport Industry in a Competitive Environment: A United Kingdom Perspective." In *Competitive Interaction between Airports, Airlines, and High-Speed Rail.* Organization for Economic Cooperation and Development.

Swanson, Ana. 2022. "With Inflation Surging, Biden Targets Ocean Shipping." *New York Times*, March 21.

Sweeting, Andrew, James W. Roberts, and Chris Gedge. 2020. "A Model of Dynamic Limit Pricing with an Application to the Airline Industry." *Journal of Political Economy* 128 (3): 1148–93.

Swietlik, William. 2010. "The Environmental Impacts of Airport Deicing—Water Quality." US Environmental Protection Agency.

Tajalli, Mehrdad, Ramin Niroumand, and Ali Hajbabaie. 2022. "Distributed Cooperative Trajectory and Lane Changing Optimization of Connected Automated Vehicles: Freeway Segments with Lane Drop." *Transportation Research Part C: Emerging Technologies* 143: article 103761.

Tang, Cheng Keat, and Jos van Ommeren. 2022. "Accident Externality of Driving: Evidence from the London Congestion Charge." *Journal of Economic Geography* 22 (3): 547–80.

Tefft, Brian C., Leon Villavicencio, Aaron Benson, Lindsay Arnold, Woon Kim, Victoria Añorve, and William J. Horrey. 2022. "Self-Reported Risky Driving in Relation to Changes in Amount of Driving during the COVID-19 Pandemic." Research brief. AAA Foundation for Traffic Safety.

Tett, Gillian. 2021. "Why America Has to Keep on Trucking." *Financial Times*, January 21.

Tongzon, Jose, and Wu Heng. 2005. "Port Privatization, Efficiency and Competitiveness: Some Empirical Evidence from Container Ports (Terminals)." *Transportation Research Part A: Policy and Practice* 39 (5): 405–24.

Train, Kenneth E. 2009. *Discrete Choice Methods with Simulation* (2nd ed.). Cambridge University Press.

Tyworth, John E., and Amy Zhaohui Zeng. 1998. "Estimating the Effects of Carrier Transit-Time Performance on Logistics Cost and Service." *Transportation Research Part A: Policy and Practice* 32 (2): 89–97.

Tyworth, John E., and Liam O'Neill. 1997. "Robustness of the Normal Approximation of Lead-Time Demand in a Distribution Setting." *Naval Research Logistics* 44 (2): 165–86.

US Department of Transportation (DOT). 1995. "Bus–Rail Integration." Departmental Guidance, January 17.

———. 2016. "The Value of Travel Time Savings: Departmental Guidance for Conducting Economic Evaluations—Revision 2 (2016 Update)."

Vartabedian, Ralph. 2022. "How California's Bullet Train Went Off the Rails." *New York Times*, October 9.

Verma, Pranshu. 2020. "We're Desperate: Transit Cuts Felt Deepest in Low-Income Areas." *New York Times*, August 15.

Vickrey, William. 1968. "Automobile Accidents, Tort Law, Externalities, and Insurance: An Economist's Critique." *Law and Contemporary Problems* 33 (3): 464–87.

Viscelli, Steve. 2018. "Driverless? Autonomous Trucks and the Future of the American Trucker." Center for Labor Research and Education, University of California, Berkeley.

Viton, Philip A. 1981. "On Competition and Product Differentiation in Urban Transportation: The San Francisco Bay Area." *Bell Journal of Economics* 12 (2): 362–79.

Wang, Guihua, Ronghuo Zheng, and Tinglong Dai. 2022. "Does Transportation Mean Transplantation? Impact of New Airline Routes on Sharing of Cadaveric Kidneys." *Management Science* 68 (5): 3660–79.

Ward, Jacob W., Jeremy J. Michalek, and Constantine Samaras. 2021. "Air Pollution, Greenhouse Gas, and Traffic Externality Benefits and Costs of Shifting Private Vehicle Travel to Ridesourcing Services." *Environmental Science and Technology* 55 (19): 13174–85.

Ward, Jacob W., Jeremy J. Michalek, Constantine Samaras, Inês L. Azevedo, Alejandro Hanao, Clement Rames, and Tom Wenzel. 2021. "The Impact of Uber and Lyft on Vehicle Ownership, Fuel Economy, and Transit Across U.S. Cities." *iScience* 24 (1): article 101933.

Waschik, Robert, Catherine L. Taylor, Daniel Friedman, and Jasmine Boatner. 2021. "Macroeconomic Impacts of Automated Driving Systems in Long-Haul Trucking." Report FHWA-JPO-21-847. US Department of Transportation.

Windle, Robert J., and Martin E. Dresner. 1995. "The Short and Long Run Effects of Entry on US Domestic Air Routes." *Transportation Journal* 35 (2): 14–25.

Winston, Clifford. 1991. "Efficient Transportation Infrastructure Policy." *Journal of Economic Perspectives* 5 (1): 113–27.

———. 2006. *Government Failure versus Market Failure: Microeconomics Policy Research and Government Performance.* Brookings Institution Press.

———. 2010. *Last Exit: Privatization and Deregulation of the US Transportation System.* Brookings Institution Press.

———. 2013. "On the Performance of the U.S. Transportation System: Caution Ahead." *Journal of Economic Literature* 51 (3): 773–824.

———. 2021a. "Autonomous Vehicles." *Milken Institute Review* 23 (1): 56–65.

———. 2021b. "Comment on 'Can America Reduce Highway Construction Costs? Evidence from the States.'" In *Economic Analysis and Infrastructure Investment*, edited by Edward L. Glaeser and James M. Poterba. University of Chicago Press.

———. 2021c. *Gaining Ground: Markets Helping Government.* Brookings Institution Press.

———. 2022. "Debunking the Mainstream Liberal Media's Bias against Free Markets." RealClear Markets, March 28.

Winston, Clifford, Thomas M. Corsi, Curtis M. Grimm, and Carol A. Evans. 1990. *The Economic Effects of Surface Freight Deregulation.* Brookings Institution Press.

Winston, Clifford, and Quentin Karpilow. 2020. *Autonomous Vehicles: The Road to Economic Growth?* Brookings Institution Press.

Winston, Clifford, and Ashley Langer. 2006. "The Effect of Government Highway Spending on Road Users' Congestion Costs." *Journal of Urban Economics* 60 (3): 463–83.

Winston, Clifford, and Vikram Maheshri. 2007. "On the Social Desirability of Urban Rail Transit Systems." *Journal of Urban Economics* 62 (2): 362–82.

Winston, Clifford, and Fred Mannering. 2014. "Implementing Technology to Improve Public Highway Performance: A Leapfrog Technology from the Private Sector Is Going to Be Necessary." *Economics of Transportation* 3 (2): 158–65.

Winston, Clifford, and Chad Shirley. 1998. *Alternate Route: Toward Efficient Urban Transportation.* Brookings Institution Press.

Winston, Clifford, and Joan Winston. 2022. "The Same Old Technophobia Is Holding Back Autonomous Vehicles." *Barron's*, January 7.

Winston, Clifford, and Jia Yan. 2011. "Can Privatization of U.S. Highways Improve Motorists' Welfare?" *Journal of Public Economics* 95 (7–8): 993–1005.

———. 2015. "Open Skies: Estimating Travelers' Benefits from Free Trade in Airline Services." *American Economic Journal: Economic Policy* 7 (2): 370–414.

———. 2021. "Vehicle Size Choice and Automobile Externalities: A Dynamic Analysis." *Journal of Econometrics* 222 (1): 196–218.

Wooldridge, Jeffrey M. 1999. "Distribution-Free Estimation of Some Nonlinear Panel Data Models." *Journal of Econometrics* 90 (1): 77–97.

Yan, Chiwei, Vikrant Vaze, Allison Vanderboll, and Cynthia Barnhart. 2016. "Tarmac Delay Policies: A Passenger-Centric Analysis." *Transportation Research Part A: Policy and Practice* 83: 42–62.

Yan, Jia, and Clifford Winston. 2014. "Can Private Airport Competition Improve Runway Pricing? The Case of San Francisco Bay Area Airports." *Journal of Public Economics* 115: 146–57.

Yang, Ron. 2021. "(Don't) Take Me Home: Home Bias and the Effect of Self-Driving Trucks on Interstate Trade." Job Market Paper. Harvard Business School.

Zakharenko, Roman, and Alexander Luttmann. 2023. "Downsizing the Jet: A Forecast of Economic Effects of Increased Automation in Aviation." *Transportation Research Part B: Methodological* 170: 25–47.

Zhang, Anming, Yulai Wan, and Hangjun Yang. 2019. "Impacts of High-Speed Rail on Airlines, Airports and Regional Economies: A Survey of Recent Research." *Transport Policy* 81: A1–A19.

Zhang, Jing, Debendra K. Das, and Rorik Peterson. 2009. "Selection of Effective and Efficient Snow Removal and Ice Control Technologies for Cold-Region Bridges." *Journal of Civil, Environmental, and Architectural Engineering* 3 (1): 1–14.

Zhang, Yunzhou, and Linda Nozick. 2018. "Investigating the Pricing Impacts of the American Airlines and US Airways Merger." *Transportation Research Record* 2672 (23): 15–19.

Zhou, Zhengyi, Hongchang Li, and Anming Zhang. 2022. "Does Bike Sharing Increase House Prices? Evidence from Micro-level Data and the Impact of COVID-19." *Journal of Real Estate Finance and Economics*, forthcoming.

Zimmerman, Michael, Balika Sonthalia, Alberto Oca, Arsenio Martinez-Simon, Korhan Acar, and Yan Sun. 2021. "Change of Plans." Annual State of Logistics Report. Council of Supply Chain Management Professionals.

Zou, Li, and Chanyan Yu. 2020. "The Evolving Market Entry Strategy: A Comparative Study of Southwest and JetBlue." *Transportation Research Part A: Policy and Practice* 132: 682–95.

Index

absolute value, 125

actual competition, 127, 156

adjacent competition, 105–6, 111n17, 113, 118, 128–29, 146–47, 156

Adler, Martin W., 91n9

Aer Lingus, 105n5

age, of transit system, 32–33, 36–39, 40

aggregate discrete choice modeling, 185, 208

Airbus: A320 planes, 197; CityAirbus NextGen, 195

Air Canada, 196

Aireon, 197

Air France Concorde, 196

airline industry, 28, 75, 87, 89, 101; Air Carrier Statistics database (T-100), 109, 110, 156; Airline Deregulation Act (1978), 3n2; Airline Origin and Destination Survey (DB1B), 109, 110, 113, 116n23, 154, 185–86; Airlines for America, 149, 158; Airlines Reporting Corporation (ARC), 139, 140n37, 141, 142; Airport and Airway Trust Fund, 146; airportcodes.us, 151, 152; Airport Improvement Program, 145–46; Airport

Investment Partnership Program, 167n27; airport pairs, 110n14, 120, 125, 132, 153–55; airspace capacity, 262–63; air traffic control, 79, 166, 196–97, 263, 276, 278; "Air Travelers in America" (Airlines for America), 158; freight traffic, 135; gate control, 104, 129, 160, 166; hub classification, 152, 158–61, 162–63; new air transportation modes, 194–96; open skies agreements, 4, 7, 104, 133, 160, 275, 277; slot controls, 104, 129, 154, 160, 163n21, 167–68; supersonic air transportation, 192, 193, 196. *See also* cabotage rights, foreign airlines in US market; deregulation; Federal Aviation Administration; legacy carriers; low-cost carriers (LCCs); private airport competition; public airport competition; ultra-low-cost carriers (ULCCs)

AirTran Airways, 110n13

Alaska Airlines, 130, 147n4

Alaska Department of Transportation, 261n4

Albemarle's Silver Peak in Nevada, 81

About the Authors

Clifford Winston is a senior fellow in the Economic Studies Program at the Brookings Institution and **Jia Yan** is a professor of economics at Washington State University. Their associates are **Scott Dennis**, Congressional Budget Office; **Austin J. Drukker**, Federal Trade Commission; **Hyeonjun Hwang**, Kyungpook National University; **Jukwan Lee**, Korea Institute for International Economic Policy; **Vikram Maheshri**, University of Houston; **Chad Shirley**, Congressional Budget Office; and **Xinlong Tan**, Langchao Innovation.

Acknowledgments

The authors wish to thank David Brownstone, Robin Lindsey, Fred Mannering, Patrick McCarthy, Don Pickrell, Marc Scribner, David Starkie, and Anming Zhang for carefully reading and commenting on the entire manuscript. They also thank Kenneth Button, Achim Czerny, Martin Dresner, Darius Gaskins, Richard Golaszewski, Caitlin Gorback, Ted Greener, Joshua Hassol, John Heimlich, Ashley Nunes, Robert Poole, David Rapson, Melanie Rose, Kenneth Small, and Joan Winston for their helpful comments on specific chapters. Funding was generously provided by the Smith Richardson Foundation.

Jacqueline Plante and Austin J. Drukker edited the manuscript, Anna Keyser managed the editorial production process, and Stephan Przybylowicz created the index.